CHRIS ALDEN, DANIEL LARGE
AND RICARDO SOARES DE OLIVEIRA

editors

China Returns to Africa

A Rising Power and a Continent Embrace

HURST & COMPANY, LONDON

First published in the United Kingdom by
HURST Publishers Ltd,
41 Great Russell Street, London, WC1B 3PL
© Chris Alden, Daniel Large, Ricardo Soares de
Oliveira and the Contributors, 2008
All rights reserved.
Printed in India

The right of Chris Alden, Daniel Large,
Ricardo Soares de Oliveira and the
Contributors to be identified as the authors
of this volume has been asserted by them
in accordance with the Copyright,
Designs and Patents Act, 1988.

A catalogue data record for this volume is available
from the British Library.

ISBNs
978-1-85065-885-6 *casebound*
978-1-85065-886-3 *paperback*

www.hurstpub.co.uk

CONTENTS

v

TABLES AND FIGURES

ACKNOWLEDGEMENTS

We would like to thank the sponsors of the original July 2006 Cambridge conference for their financial assistance: the FCO Research Analysts Department (Margaret Hall and Peter Clarke in particular), the Rift Valley Institute (John Ryle especially) and Mills and Reeve (and Robert Weatherly in particular). In addition to those already mentioned, our thanks to those who chaired sessions at the conference: Lindsey Hilsum, Nicholas Shaxson, Patrick Smith, Devon Curtis, Stephen Chan. Finally, all speakers also deserve thanks, including those that made special efforts to attend, as does Monique Chu who provided invaluable assistance in running the conference. Other individuals who have provided important assistance include Thorsten Benner, Kato Lambrechts, Rocco Blume, Egbert Wessellink, Gill Lusk, Deborah Bräutigan, Christopher Prior, Jago Salmon, Tom Pattinson, Sarah Keenlyside, Alex Vines, James Mayall, Jonathan Derrick, Michael Dwyer, Maria Petalidou and an anonymous book reviewer.

THE CONTRIBUTORS

Chris Alden is Reader in International Relations at the London School of Economics and Political Science, having taught at the University of the Witwatersrand, Johannesburg, from 1990 to 2000. His books include *China in Africa* (Zed 2007), *Mozambique and the Construction of the New African State* (Palgrave 2002) and, with Garth le Pere, *South Africa's Post-Apartheid Foreign Policy* (Oxford/IISS 2003).

Ana Cristina Alves is a doctoral research student at the London School of Economics. She is a lecturer at the ISCSP/Technical University of Lisbon and has been a researcher at the Instituto do Oriente since 1998.

Deborah Bräutigam has been Associate Professor in American University's School of International Service in Washington, DC since 1994. She is the author of *Chinese Aid and African Development* (St. Martin's Press, 1998), co-editor of *Taxation and State-Building in Developing Countries: Capacity and Consent* (Cambridge University Press, 2008), and is currently working on a new book on China's African aid.

Jørgen Carling is Senior Researcher at the International Peace Research Institute, Oslo (PRIO) with a background in Human Geography. He has done research on various migration issues in Cape Verde and West Africa over the past decade.

Stephen Chan is Professor of International Relations at the School of Oriental and African Studies, where he was the foundation Dean of Law and Social Sciences. He is the 2007 Hood Fellow and Chapman Lecturer at the University of Auckland. His publications include *Robert Mugabe: a Life of Power and Violence* (I.B. Tauris, 2002).

Christopher Clapham (Centre of African Studies, Cambridge University) is editor of the Journal of Modern African Studies.

Gregor Dobler is Lecturer in Social Anthropology at Basel University, Switzerland, and previously worked at Bayreuth University, Germany. He has conducted research in Northern Namibia since 2004.

Manuel Ennes Ferreira is Professor at the Instituto Superior de Economia e Gestão/Universidade Técnica de Lisboa (Department of Economics) and was formerly the Academic Director of the Centre of Research at the Catholic University of Angola.

Adama Gaye is group corporate affairs manager of ECOBANK. A journalist from Senegal, he was Information Director at Ecowas from 1992 to 1996. A former Fellow at St Anthony's College, Oxford University, he is the author of *Chine-Afrique: Le dragon et l'autruche* (Paris: Editions L'Harmattan, 2006).

Bates Gill is the Director of the Stockholm International Peace Research Institute and was previously the Freeman Chair in China Studies at the Center for Strategic and International Studies, Washington, DC. His most recent book is *Rising Star: China's New Security Diplomacy* (Brookings Press, 2007).

Andrea Goldstein is a Senior Economist at the OECD Directorate for Financial and Enterprise Affairs. Involved in various research projects on multinationals from emerging, transition and developing countries, his research interests include the impact of the emergence of China and India on other developing countries, in particular in sub-Saharan Africa.

Heidi Østbø Haugen holds an MA in Human Geography from the University of Oslo, and studied Chinese at Princeton University and Beijing Normal University. She is currently working as a vulnerability analyst at the UN World Food Programme's West Africa Bureau in Dakar.

Wenping He is Professor, Director of African Studies Section of Institute of West Asian and African Studies, Chinese Academy of Social Sciences. Her authored works include *Feizhou Guojia Minzu Hua Jincheng*

Yanjiu [The Study of the Democratisation Process in African Countries] (*Shi Shi Cubanshi [Press]*, 2005).

Chin-Hao Huang is a Research Associate with the Stockholm International Peace Research Institute. He was previously a research assistant with the Freeman Chair in China Studies at the Center for Strategic and International Studies, Washington, D.C. where he assisted on the coordination of its China-Africa project.

Elisabeth Hsu is Reader in Social Anthropology at the Institute of Social and Cultural Anthropology, University of Oxford. She has conducted ethnographic fieldwork on Chinese medicine in East Africa since 2001.

Daniel Large is research director of the Africa Asia Centre, Royal African Society at the School of Oriental and African Studies, London, and director of the Sudan Open Archive (www.sudanarchive.net).

Roland Marchal is Senior Research Fellow at the Centre National de Recherche Scientifique (CNRS), based at the Centre d'Etudes et de Recherches Internationales (CERI), Paris. His publications include *Afrique Asie, une autre mondialisation* (Paris: Presses de Sciences-Po, 2007).

Jamie Monson is Professor of History at Carleton College. In 2004-5 she was a research fellow with the Wissenschaftskolleg zu Berlin (Berlin Institute for Advanced Study). Her current book project is *Africa's Freedom Railway: How a Chinese Development Project Changed Lives and Livelihoods in Tanzania* (Indiana University Press, 2009).

J. Stephen Morrison is the director of the Africa Program at the Center for Strategic and International Studies, Washington, DC. In 2005-6, he was codirector of the Council on Foreign Relations Independent Task Force on Africa. From 1996 through early 2000, Morrison served on the Secretary of State's policy planning staff, responsible for African affairs and global foreign assistance issues.

Nicolas Pinaud has worked at the OECD Development Centre since June 2002 and previously as an emerging markets economist within the Risk Division of Société Générale (Paris) and at the French Trade Commission in Johannesburg. He graduated from the University of Paris-I

Sorbonne from which he holds a DEA in Development Economics and a masters in Political Science.

Helmut Reisen has co-ordinated the OECD Global Forum on Development for the OECD Development Centre since July 2006 and is currently investigating China's and India's economic impact on poor countries. Mr Reisen holds a PhD from Cologne University and is a Professor of International Economics at the University of Basel.

Garth Shelton is Associate Professor of International Relations at the School of Social Sciences, University of the Witwatersrand, Johannesburg. He is Director of the East Asia Project at Wits University, which focuses on Africa-Asia issues, especially China's growing involvement in Africa.

Philip Snow is an Honorary Research Associate of the Department of History at the University of Hong Kong. He is the author of *The Star Raft: China's Encounter with Africa* (Weidenfeld and Nicolson, 1988). Other publications include *The Fall of Hong Kong: Britain, China and the Japanese Occupation* (Yale University Press, 2003).

Ricardo Soares de Oliveira is University Lecturer in Comparative Politics (African Politics) at the Department of Politics and International Relations, Oxford University, Fellow of St Peter's College, Oxford, and a Fellow with the Global Public Policy Institute, Berlin. He was previously the Austin Robinson Research Fellow at Sidney Sussex College, Cambridge and an Associate of the Centre of International Studies, University of Cambridge. He is the author of *Oil and Politics in the Gulf of Guinea* (London: Hurst, 2007).

Denis M. Tull is a researcher at the German Institute for International and Security Affairs in Berlin. He received his PhD for the thesis 'The Reconfiguration of Political Order in Postcolonial Africa: A Case Study of North Kivu (DR Congo)' from the University of Hamburg in 2004. His areas of research include Africa's international relations, state transformation and state-building in Africa, violent conflicts, peacekeeping and insurgency governance.

FOREWORD

Philip Snow

Ever since observers have been on hand to report it the arrival of a Chinese presence in Africa has been greeted with extremes of approval and dismay. One hundred years ago, for example, many European empire-builders applauded the import of Chinese contract labourers, who they believed would open up the continent by shouldering work on the new roads and railways and in the Rand goldfields of South Africa which their African counterparts were unable or unwilling to perform. Others saw the Chinese as a lethal threat. Chinese labourers, they protested, would slip out of their compounds, subvert the morality of the unspoilt 'natives', steal European jobs and businesses; and Johannesburg would become 'practically a Chinese town'.[1] African feelings are less well documented, but there are reports of anxiety among some local people that the effect of importing Chinese would be to force down their wages and drive them off the land. Two generations later, in the 1960s and 1970s, when the first representatives of modern China began to appear in independent Africa in pursuit of their strategic rivalries with the United States, Taiwan and the Soviet Union, the pattern of reactions repeated itself. As Beijing's guerrilla instructors gave training to rebels from the white-ruled territories at remote camps in Ghana and Tanzania, as its civilian aid teams built the TAZARA railway and other spectacular projects and set

---

1 Prediction of Sir William Butler quoted in Brian Gardner, *The African Dream* (London: Cassell, 1970), p. 235.

up medical clinics in the depths of the bush, radical African leaders such as Julius Nyerere acclaimed Maoist altruism and embraced
China as the champion of a new, just world order—while Western
analysts fretted about the 'Red Guard line chugging into Africa',[2]
and a Western-influenced president of Upper Volta (Burkina Faso)
warned that if he allowed Chinese into his country they would settle
there and 'we would disappear within a few years'.[3]

Now the Chinese are once again making their mark on the continent, and on a larger scale than ever before. After a lull in the
1980s, when their strategic interests in Africa faded and their focus
switched to the drive for domestic modernization, they have moved
back impelled by their appetite for export markets, for the foreign
exchange to be earned from contract engineering, and above all for
African oil and other mineral resources—an appetite which has in
the space of just half a decade approximately quintupled their trade
with the continent. Over $55 billion worth of two-way trade by the
end of 2006;[4] almost $12 billion worth of Chinese cumulative invest-
ment in Africa;[5] some 800 Chinese companies and 80,000 Chinese
workers employed on African schemes.[6] This surge of business has
been accompanied by a dramatic enlargement of Chinese influence
in many spheres. With President Hu Jintao playing host in Beijing
to forty-eight African leaders assembled for the great third Forum on
China-Africa Cooperation in November 2006, Shanghai providing
the venue for the latest meeting of the African Development Bank,

---

2   Headline of article in *Wall Street Journal*, 29 September 1967, quoted in
    Jamie Monson, 'Liberating Labour? Constructing Anti-Hegemony on the
    TAZARA Railway in Tanzania, 1965-1976', p. 198 n. 4 below.

3   Remark of President Maurice Yaméogo quoted in Wei Liang-tsai, *Peking
    versus Taipei in Africa, 1960-1978* (Taipei: The Asia and World Institute,
    1982), p. 147.

4   Official Chinese figure announced in *South China Morning Post* (*SCMP*),
    Hong Kong, 31 January 2007 and *Financial Times* (*FT*), London, 1 February
    2007.

5   Official Chinese figure cited in *SCMP*, 18 May 2007 and *The Economist*, 19
    May 2007.

6   Chinese government estimates for late 2005 cited in *The Economist*, 28
    October 2006, *SCMP*, 2 November 2006, *FT*, 25 January 2007 and *SCMP*,
    15 May 2007.

the Chinese government taking on the construction of an expanded headquarters for the African Union, and Confucius Institutes arising to disseminate Chinese language and culture in centres ranging from Nairobi to Stellenbosch, it has been hard not to think in terms of something resembling the emergence of a Chinese Commonwealth.

Local and outside interest in this phenomenon has correspondingly been greater than anything ever seen in the past. Earlier, even in the Maoist period, China's presence in Africa was largely mulled over by specialists; now it has become a major world issue, a burning question about which over thirty international conferences were held in 2006 alone, on which every self-respecting columnist finds it necessary to express an opinion, French ministers draw up reports and US congressmen address joint letters to the Beijing government. And once again the response has been characterized by extremes of delight and hostility. While President Mugabe of Zimbabwe has unveiled his 'Look East' policy and urged his subjects to acquire Chinese language and cookery skills, and former President Obasanjo of Nigeria has informed Chinese guests, 'When you're leading the world, we want to be very close behind you',[7] the fear of demonstrations by disgruntled local employees has forced Hu Jintao to cancel a visit to a Chinese-owned mine in the Zambian Copperbelt, Chinese workers in several countries have been victims of murder and kidnapping, and Western activists holding China responsible for the Sudanese government's genocidal repression in Darfur have threatened to derail the Beijing Olympics.

Here, not before time, is a book designed to explore the hugely expanded dimensions of this subject. Earlier volumes, including my own *The Star Raft: China's Encounter with Africa* (1988), were for the most part general surveys aiming to awaken interest in the broad Sino-African relationship and to compare the apparent patterns of Chinese conduct in Africa with the record of the European powers. Detailed reports were, of course, compiled on occasion by Western aid or intelligence personnel working locally in Africa, but these

---

7   Declaration made to President Hu Jintao and his entourage during their visit to Nigeria, quoted in *SCMP*, 28 April 2006.

went unpublished. Now at last we have a collection of in-depth essays cutting and slicing the subject in numerous ways. Case studies of Chinese interaction with individual African countries, regions and post-colonial groupings; analyses of the impact the Chinese upsurge has made on various sectors of African business and industry; viewpoints of the different external powers including—a bonus unthinkable twenty years ago—an informed contribution from China itself.

And here too is a much needed effort to take some of the heat and mystery out of the study of China's role on the continent. Time and again, in their close-focus chapters, the authors demonstrate that the new Sino-African encounter doesn't lend itself to easy generalization. On the Chinese side we find a diversity of actors who were simply not present a generation ago: provincial governments, giant oil and construction firms and the great new wave of individual retailers, doctors, restaurant operators and other entrepreneurs—not all of them by any means under the day-to-day micromanagement of Beijing. We also find reports of debate and discord among Chinese policymakers, of a kind not observable a generation ago even if it went on, over China's role in the Sudan and the social and environmental responsibilities of Chinese companies. In Africa the cast of characters ranges from the political and business elites to the ever more vocal NGOs and trade unions and the ordinary townspeople who buy their necessities at Chinese shops. Even among the Western powers a contrast emerges between the agitated reaction of US government circles to China's resurgence on the continent and the laid-back attitude of French officials who detect no immediate challenge to their country's interests.

As the actors vary, so does the action from place to place. We find Chinese oil firms displacing local communities in the southern Sudan and drilling without a permit in a Gabonese nature reserve, while Chinese construction firms rebuild large parts of the infrastructure of postwar Angola and other states (not always resource-rich ones) where the West has hung back; Chinese interests investing in an industrial take-off in Mauritius but not in Nigeria; China's thirst for resources improving commodity prices and terms of trade for most countries while competition from Chinese exports cripples the nascent textile industries of South Africa and Lesotho. We find Chinese shopkeepers appreciated in Cape Verde and Senegal but not in Namibia. We find the Chinese ambassador to Zambia crudely threatening that diplomatic ties will be broken off if a hostile candidate wins the presidential election, while Beijing's top leaders tour Africa with an assiduity never shown by their Western opposite numbers and the Chinese media talk up Africa's promise in positive tones far removed from the Western press's monotonous preoccupation with African gloom and doom. Some of the authors also inject into the current excitement a helpful dose of relativism. China's lunge for resources, they remind us, is not directed solely at Africa but is taking place right across the globe. The intimate ties cultivated by Beijing's oil majors with accommodating African despots in order to 'lock up' supplies is not a uniquely Chinese piece of devilry but has been standard practice in the Western oil industry in Africa for many years.

So where is the Chinese Commonwealth headed? Given the conflicting nature of the evidence the outlook of the authors is, not surprisingly, mixed, with some emphasizing the scope for friction and the risks to both China and its African partners while others write in a spirit of what one of them terms 'realistic optimism'. Looking from the historical angle one point ought perhaps to be kept in mind. Beijing has now accumulated half a century's worth of experience in dealing with post-colonial Africa. Egregious mistakes have been made, but the learning process has been constant, and the Chinese have shown a consistent ability to adjust their policies where adjustment has plainly been called for. At the end of the 1960s, for instance, after Maoist attempts to subvert conservative, Western-leaning governments had resulted in a series of diplomatic debacles, the decision was made that Beijing should from now on stand back and 'support whoever is the leader'.[8] Over the last few years this policy of 'non-interference' has landed the Chinese leaders in trouble of the opposite kind, as large swathes of African opinion condemn their support for despotic regimes in the Sudan and Zimbabwe and the once sainted People's China ironically finds itself viewed in many

---

8   Phrase used by Chinese Foreign Ministry official in interview granted to author on 21 July 1982.

countries as the champion of corrupt vested interests against the African poor; but we are now seeing signs that Beijing has become aware of the damage and is seeking ways to reach out once again to a broader constituency.

A similar adaptability may be found in Chinese approaches outside the political sphere. By the early 1980s it was clear from the floundering performance of TAZARA and other much publicized aid projects that Chinese skills were not getting transferred to the African recipients on the lines once laid down by Premier Zhou Enlai. The Chinese leadership took note of this shortcoming, and by the end of the decade had already begun to embark on the new programme of professional and technical training for Africans both at home and in China that has been so conspicuous in recent years. Again, in the early 1980s it was possible to pick up mild but unmistakable murmurings in some African quarters—why was it always *China* teaching *Africa*, didn't the Chinese feel the continent had anything to teach *them*? Even to this Beijing has replied in some measure, with the marked increase in African studies that has been arranged since that time in Chinese institutes and universities, and the assertions of some Chinese Africa hands that much more must be done to address the 'educational deficit'.[9] Harder to alter may be certain ingrained patterns of grass-roots behaviour. Will Chinese enterprises in Africa be able to overcome their reluctance, apparently as widespread and resented as it ever was, to employ local people in responsible posts, and their preference to do things by themselves?

One still more imponderable question is raised by the series of meditative articles with which the book closes. What will China's future role on the continent be vis-à-vis its competitors? Will China, maybe followed by India and Japan, nudge the Western powers to the sidelines, so that its current burst of activity indeed proves to mark a watershed in African history; or will its approach to the continent lose its distinctiveness and appeal in the face of the inevitable compromises that day-to-day dealings in Africa impose? Are

---

9 Phrase used by Professor Li Baoping of Beijing University in paper submitted to China-Africa Links workshop held at the Centre on China's Transnational Relations of the Hong Kong University of Science and Technology on 11-12 November 2006.

we bound for a collision between the United States and China over African resources, with local governments exploiting the conflict as best they can; or is there hope for the more constructive scenario that some at least of the Western actors profess to want, in which Africa's Western and Chinese partners team up and draw on each other's strengths to help the continent forward in a wide range of areas, from offshore oil extraction to public health care? Whatever the outcome, China's resurgence in Africa has to rate as one of the most striking developments of the early twenty-first century—and this thorough and balanced study provides the right equipment with which to assess it.

Hong Kong, September 2007

INTRODUCTION

Chris Alden, Daniel Large and
Ricardo Soares de Oliveira

We had a memorable yesterday...We enjoy a splendid today. The flower of Sino-African friendship is blooming with the care and nurturing of the Chinese and African peoples. We will greet a flourishing tomorrow...China, the biggest developing country in the world, is ready to join hands with Africa, the biggest developing continent in the world, to...march into the 21st century full of confidence.[1]

China's expanding relations with Africa are the most important dynamic in the foreign relations and politics of the continent since the end of the Cold War. The nature and implications of China's renewed engagement with Africa are only beginning to be appreciated, but it is already clear that this is a process of profound significance. The unprecedented interest among the media, academic quarters, and a range of governments and international organizations that has gathered momentum since 2006 recalls, and has already exceeded, the last comparable episode of attention following Premier Zhou Enlai's African 'political safari' in 1963-64. Rather than revolutionary prospects being 'excellent', as Zhou (in)famously declared in Mogadishu, some regard China's 'new strategic partnership' with Africa as bearing such potential in terms of common prosperity through 'win-win' cooperation, while others see mixed benefits and the potential for threat.

---

1 President Jiang Zemin, speech to the Organization of African Unity, Addis Ababa, 13 May 2006. *ChinaAfrica*, 66 (June 1996), p. 24.

1

China's 'Year of Africa' in 2006 saw China-Africa relations attain an unusual prominence. In January the now-traditional New Year's tour of Africa by the Chinese Foreign Minister Li Zhaoxing, who visited Cape Verde, Liberia, Mali, Senegal, Nigeria and Libya, was followed by the release of China's first Africa policy statement and tours by President Hu Jintao (Morocco, Nigeria and Kenya) in April and Premier Wen Jiabao (Egypt, Ghana, Democratic Republic of Congo, Angola, South Africa, Tanzania and Uganda) in June. The wide geographical extent of these tours was reinforced by regional meetings of the Macau Forum and the Conference of Sino-Arab Friendship. However it was the Forum on China-Africa Cooperation on 4-5 November 2006 (FOCAC or *Zhong Fei Hezuo Luntan*) that showcased China's new 'strategic partnership' with Africa. Beijing was painted with a selection of images of Africa and a profusion of public banners proclaimed 'Friendship, Peace, Cooperation and Development' (*youyi, heping, hezuo, fazhan*). As the third ministerial and first heads of state summit, FOCAC was attended by 'leaders of China and 48 African nations'.[2] It amounted to a public declaration of China's arrival in Africa, and sought to impress this upon the African guests and the world at large.

The recent visibility of China-Africa relations has been accompanied by grand pronouncements about the new 'age of the dragon' in Africa. External coverage at times has suggested that China has suddenly exploded into and is now 'conquering Africa'.[3] There have been sweeping calls for Africa to 'Look East' in a new, more optimistic age of economic growth and apparent political opportunity. As one Kenyan newspaper asked: 'With China calling, is it time to say goodbye to [the] US and Europe?'[4] At the same time there have been growing concerns, sometimes articulated as fears of 'neo-colonialism', that China's relations with Africa replicate and reinforce established patterns that are unfavourable to African development. Such questions are important and are set to be considered for some time. However,

2 See www.focac.org.

3 Andreas Lorenz and Thilo Thielke, 'China's Conquest of Africa', *Der Spiegel*, 30 May 2007.

4 Mark Sorbara, *The Nation* (Nairobi), 13 April 2006.

rather than 'the age of the dragon descending upon Africa',[5] or indeed a new 'panda menace' looming over the continent,[6] Chinese engagement with Africa today represents the continuing development of relations that were revived in a more concerted manner under state direction from Beijing after 1989 and, in turn, have been cultivated by different African governing elites. While China's inward focus on the daunting task of modernization preoccupied its leadership after 1978, Africa found itself downgraded in China's official foreign relations, although it was by no means forgotten. China repositioned itself and reached out to Africa again in a new phase during the 1980s (which began, for example, with Beijing's support for Salim Salim's bid to become UN Secretary General in 1981). Following the repression of the pro-democracy movement in Tiananmen Square in June 1989, Beijing looked to Africa for political support and increasingly as a source of resources and a potential market. The post-colonial Chinese engagement with Africa may have been episodic as a result of a combination of domestic politics and China's own foreign relations, but unlike 1433, when Chinese sea voyages to Africa stopped, there was an underlying continuity of ties.[7]

Historical background

The historical background to China's longstanding connections with different parts of Africa can only be very generally summarized here.[8] The example of the Ming Dynasty diplomatic missions seeking trade and recognition on behalf of the Chinese Emperor, as opposed to conquest or occupation—famously Zheng He's seven voyages be-

5   Lorenz and Thielke, 'China's Conquest of Africa'.

6   Antoine Halff, 'The Panda Menace', *The National Interest*, July 2007.

7   As one title, capturing part of the high interest generated by the latest phase of relations, asserted: 'China in Africa: They're Back!' George Moose, *Africa Policy Journal*, 2 (2006).

8   See Philip Snow, *The Star Raft: China's Encounter with Africa* (London: Weidenfeld and Nicolson, 1988); Teobaldo Filesi, *China and Africa in the Middle Ages* (translated by David. L. Morison) (London: Frank Cass, 1972); J.J. L Duyvendak, *China's Discovery of Africa* (London: Arthur Probsthain, 1949); Gao Jinyuan, 'China and Africa: The Development of Relations over Many Centuries', *African Affairs* 83, 31 (1984), pp. 241-50.

tween 1405 and 1433—continues to be regularly invoked to demonstrate a contrast to European exploration and conquest in Africa.
Together with shared colonial experience, it remains an important
part of the basis for claims that China is different in the manner
in which it relates to Africa. As Philip Snow has documented in
his pioneering work *The Star Raft: China's Encounter with Africa*, the
historical backdrop is important. It imbues China's approach to its
Africa relations, and the use of history is a notable aspect of China's
connections with the continent. The third FOCAC, during the
fiftieth anniversary year of the PRC's establishment of diplomatic
relations with Egypt, was underpinned by historical recollection
emphasizing the commonalities between China and Africa: cradles
of civilization, victims of colonialism, a developing country and developing continent.[9]

The PRC's engagement with Africa waxed and waned according
to its domestic situation, Cold War politics and its dispute with the
Soviet Union.[10] Beijing rhetorically championed Third World causes
during the different phases of its involvement with Africa, including
the revolutionary 'national liberation' struggles of the 1960s and 'self-
reliant development' of the 1970s. China sought to use its relations
with Africa to enhance its position vis-à-vis the US and Taiwan, as it
previously had done vis-à-vis the Soviet Union.[11] The PRC's involvement in Africa took different forms—including support for liberation

---

9 See, for example, Yuan Wu, *China and Africa* (Beijing: China Intercontinental
   Press, 2006) (trans. Li Guoqing).

10 Emmanuel Hevi, *The Chinese Communists and Africa* (New York: Praeger,
    1966); Bruce D. Larkin, *China and Africa 1949-1970: The Foreign Policy of
    the People's Republic of China* (Berkeley: University of California Press, 1971);
    Alaba Ogunsanwo, *China's Policy in Africa, 1958-71* (Cambridge University
    Press, 1974). George T. Yu, *China and Tanzania: A Study in Cooperative
    Interaction* (Berkeley: University of California, 1970), Yu, *China's African
    Policy: A Study of Tanzania* (New York: Praeger, 1975); Alan Hutchison,
    China's Africa Revolution (London: Hutchinson, 1975); Steven F. Jackson,
    'China's Third World Foreign Policy: the Case of Angola and Mozambique,
    1961-93', *The China Quarterly*, 142 (June 1995), pp. 388-422.

11 Peter Van Ness, 'China and the Third World: Patterns of Engagement and
    Indifference', in Samuel S. Kim (ed.), *China and the World: Chinese Foreign
    Policy Faces the New Millennium* (Boulder, CO: Westview Press, 1998), p.
    151.

struggles and aid programmes—but its foremost motivation was not based on resource needs. As Larkin observed in 1971: 'For the most part strategic minerals do not figure prominently in China's quest for economic relations with Africa.'[12] Rather, it was driven by the combination of a desire to pursue prestigious aid work and geopolitical exigencies, including strategic competition with Taiwan before and after Beijing's successful entry into the UN with the support of African votes in October 1971.[13] More limited Chinese engagement in Africa during the 1980s reflected China's changed internal development and modernization priorities under Deng Xiaoping, as did the reorientation of Chinese aid in Africa during the 1980s when its political philanthropy developed into more commercially oriented involvement. China's aid programme in Africa may have been scaled back in the 1980s, but commerce continued. Chinese business ventures or infrastructure projects may not have proceeded on a comparable scale to today but were active in a number of contexts. Zhao Ziyang's tour of eleven African countries in late 1982 and early 1983, designed to repeat Zhou Enlai's ground-breaking tour, sought to reinvigorate relations and assert shared Third World identity.[14]

Facing international isolation after the Tiananmen Square crackdown, China reinvigorated its political interest in Africa and embarked once again on proactive Africa diplomacy. This was catalyzed by President Jiang Zemin's tour of Egypt, Kenya, Ethiopia, Mali, Namibia and Zimbabwe and his address to the Organization of African Unity in May 1996. In calling for the rejuvenation of 'traditional projects aided by China', increased political cooperation and expanded economic ties, Jiang offered an optimistic vision of flourishing

---

12 Bruce D. Larkin, *China and Africa 1949-1970*, p. 93.

13 See, among others, George T. Yu, 'Peking versus Taipei in the World Arena: Chinese Competition in Africa', *Asian Survey*, 3, 9 (1963), pp. 439-53; George T. Yu and David J. Longenecker, 'The Beijing-Taipei Struggle for International Recognition: from the Niger Affair to the U.N.', *Asian Survey*, 34, 5 (1994), pp. 475-88.

14 See Deborah Bräutigam, *Chinese Aid and African Development: Exporting Green Revolution* (London: Macmillan Press Ltd, 1998). George Yu, 'Africa in Chinese Foreign Policy', *Asian Survey*, 28, 8 (1988), pp. 849-62.

relations. Even then, however, with a trade volume of $3.5-4 billion, China's share of Africa's trade was comparatively small. The Chinese government was keen to address its trade surplus with Africa: 'China only exports but imports little' from African countries.[15] At this stage, recognition that 'Africa is a market with great potential' was accompanied by increased government and enterprise interest in economic engagement, the entry of Exim Bank and establishment of Investment, Exploitation and Trade Centres in Egypt, Gabon, Cameroon, Côte d'Ivoire, Guinea and Mali which were intended to combine investment, resource extraction and trade functions. The impressive thickening of ties that has been evident since 2000 has thus followed on from the 1990s, but through a more concerted drive to expand China's engagement in Africa.[16]

China's African engagement

Current relations are developing in a markedly different context from previous periods of Chinese involvement in Africa. China's engagement today is occurring under new circumstances in which a more developed China operates under conditions of growing interdependence and plays an increasingly important role in the global economy. The ideological disagreements of the Cold War have been superseded by economic competition and political differences, as China participates in the global economy and pursues better trade terms rather than an alternative socialist vision. Beijing's engagement appears to be predicated upon a longer-term timeframe and driven by economic diplomacy rather than the ambitious ideology of the past.

The key factors propelling Chinese engagement in Africa can be summarized as a combination of domestic Chinese dynamics, desire to expand into new markets and international political factors.[17]

---

15 'Economic and trade relations between China and African countries in 1996', *Almanac of China's Foreign Economic Relations and Trade 1997/1998*, p. 430.

16 See Ian Taylor, *China and Africa: Engagement and Compromise* (Abingdon: Routledge, 2006).

17 See Chris Alden, *China in Africa* (London: Zed Books, 2007) and Denis M. Tull, 'China in Africa: Scope, Significance and Consequences', *The Journal of Modern African Studies*, 44, 3 (2006), pp. 459-79.

The overarching driver has been the Chinese government's strategic pursuit of resources and attempts to ensure raw material supplies for growing energy needs within China, in part reflecting the country's position as a centre of global manufacturing. Most significant Chinese activity and investment in Africa is related to this demand, rooted in domestic economic and political changes in China and the changing profile of resource needs accompanying its economic development and role in the global economy. 'An unprecedented need for resources is now driving China's foreign policy.'[18] China's post-1978 determined focus on economic development contributed to an annual growth rate of over 9 per cent. From the 1990s, however, it became necessary to acquire overseas supplies, including energy.[19] China's energy diplomacy has become a notable foreign policy issue under President Hu Jintao, who has led expanded diplomacy not merely in Africa but around the world, including the Middle East and Latin America. The Chinese government's diplomacy with oil states is aimed to a considerable extent at enhancing its energy security.[20]

A further factor is Africa's status as a market with strong commercial potential for Chinese business. The Chinese government, businesses, and entrepreneurs have regarded (or, for many businesses, been financially encouraged to regard) Africa as a continent of economic potential populated by consumers. Explicitly rejecting 'Afro-pessimism', to date they appear to have not been overly encumbered by investment constraints or concern about political instability that have affected other investors. Central government support for Chinese state owned enterprises (SOEs) has been important in directing FDI in Africa, as opposed to other regions. Africa is a place for Chinese companies to gain experience as well as establish and expand business ventures into the global arena. While most business

18 David Zweig and Bi Jianhai, 'China's Global Hunt for Energy', *Foreign Affairs*, 84, 5 (2005), p. 25. See also Ian Taylor, 'China's Oil Diplomacy in Africa', *International Affairs*, 82, 5 (2006), pp. 937-59.

19 As Martyn Davies has argued, a longer-term (25-year) strategy of seeking to extract the Chinese economy from international commodity networks may well operate too. Chatham House 14 December 2006 (on record).

20 Erica S. Downs, 'The Chinese Energy Security Debate', *The China Quarterly*, 177 (2004), pp. 21-41.

and related political activity occurs at the state level, including SOEs, a further trend of increasing private entrepreneurial activity is evident in many locations (including, as detailed in this volume, Tanzania, Nambia and Cape Verde).[21]

Finally, there are political factors operating as part of what is styled 'win-win cooperation'. Since helping China gain admission to the UN, African states have supported China (including in the years following 1989) in different multilateral settings. China in turn styles itself as leader of the global South and champion of a progressive 'new international political and economic order featuring justice, rationality, equality and mutual benefit' and 'safeguarding legitimate rights and interests of developing countries.'[22] Efforts to work with and speak for Africa as part of the global South are intertwined in China's emerging role in international affairs. It has highlighted its development efforts in Africa, with attendant claims to international status.

Two additional political dynamics in China's wider foreign policy are also at work in the African context. The first is China's strategic competition with Japan as manifested in Africa. This is seen particularly in the underlying objective of opposing Japan's UN Security Council aspirations, in which African state votes would play a role. Beijing's ability to marshal African support against Tokyo's aims was seen at the Asian African Summit in April 2005, where Chinese lobbying blocked an endorsement of a Japanese seat. However, the second area is more prominent, even if it is receding in importance for Beijing. The One China principle, the fundamental exception to China's 'no-strings attached' policy,[23] has seen the Chinese government use African support in its cross-Straits campaign.[24] Inviting

---

21 This is assisted by such bodies as the China-Africa Business Council, established in 2004 to support China's private sector investment in Cameroon, Ghana, Mozambique, Nigeria, South Africa and Tanzania.

22 *China's African Policy*, January 2006, Part IV (5).

23 Zambian opposition leader Michael Sata discovered this to dramatic effect after calling Taiwan a 'sovereign state' during the presidential elections of September 2006. This prompted China's Ambassador to Zambia to denounce his interference in China's sovereignty in an episode that, rather than being taken simply as a transgression of China's non-interference framework, might be better regarded as anchored in China's 'internal' politics.

24 This was seen, for example, when China's African allies rallied behind its

Taiwan-recognizing African states to attend FOCAC 3 as observers demonstrated a new approach to winning over the remaining recalcitrant states. The Chinese government's aim to deny space to Taiwan in Africa is succeeding, though the subject remains a sensitive issue for Beijing and the possibility that African states can play the Taiwan card to exert leverage vis-à-vis Beijing remains. Taiwan's political prospects in the continent are nonetheless bleak and rest on a dwindling number of small, strategically insignificant states. Five out of a worldwide total of 24 states that recognize Taiwan are in Africa: Burkina Faso, The Gambia, Malawi, São Tomé and Príncipe, and Swaziland. The loss of Chad in August 2006 was a marked setback for Taiwan as, in contrast to Taiwan's other African allies, it represented strong potential in terms of resources. Taiwan's economic relations with Africa, facilitated by the Africa Taiwan Economic Forum, constitute a proportionally small amount of its foreign trade.[25] Overall trade with Taiwan's African allies amounted to just over $56m in 2006, with Swaziland the highest-ranking state (trade running at US$30.2m or 0.007 per cent of total trade).[26]

Taiwan, nonetheless, continues to promote its role in Africa. The first Taiwan-Africa Heads of State Summit was held in Taipei on 9 September 2007. It saw Taiwanese President Chen Shui-bian joined by King Mswati III of Swaziland, President Blaise Compaoré of Burkina Faso, President Fradique de Menezes of São Tomé and Príncipe, President Bingu wa Mutharika of Malawi, and Vice-President Isatou Njie-Saidy of The Gambia. The Taipei Declaration affirmed the 'great historical significance' of this 'new chapter in the history of Taiwan-Africa diplomatic relations'.[27] Five core areas were

---

Anti-Secession Law in March 2005. Formal support for the One China policy is routinely expressed in official exchanges.

25 According to data from the Taiwanese Bureau of Foreign Trade, it conducted the most business in 2006 with Angola, which ranked as Taiwan's highest trade partner in the continent with a volume of US$2.15bn (0.46 per cent of total trade, or 27th position) behind South Africa with trade volume of US$2.06bn or 0.44 per cent, in 28th place).

26 January 2006-January 2007, using data from the Taiwanese Bureau of Foreign Trade

27 First Taiwan-Africa Heads of State Summit Taipei Declaration, Taipei, 9 September 2007.

singled out as priorities: information and communications technologies, economic development; medical assistance, the environment; peace and security. Like FOCAC, the summit produced an Action Plan and established a Follow-up Committee for its implementation. Shortly afterwards, an assortment of politicians, academics and NGO representatives gathered for the 2007 Taiwan-Africa Progressive Partnership Forum. If development was the prominent public theme of the Summit, Taiwan's aspiration to join the UN was its key subtext. Taiwan's Foreign Affairs Minister, James Chih-fang Huang, had toured Taiwan's five African allies (plus Chad) in July 2007 to carry the torch for Taiwan's annual attempt to join the UN. China-supporting African governments have spoken out against the bid. One section of the Summit Declaration got to the heart of Taiwan's diplomatic objectives in Africa. It affirmed that 'Taiwan's African allies support Taiwan's legitimate right to join the United Nations and its specialized agencies'. They duly backed Taiwan's attempt to join the UN, but on 21 September 2007 the UN General Assembly's General Committee decided not to place the issue of membership on the UN's agenda, thus thwarting Taipei's fifteenth consecutive bid.[28]

Anatomy of current relations

The present phase of China's Africa engagement continues but departs from its past involvement in terms of its scope, scale and importance. Many commentators thought that the PRC's presence in Africa in the 1960s would endure and effect political change, while during the 1990s some went as far as to dismiss China's importance in the continent altogether.[29] However, the context of relations has altered in important ways. China's position in the world has shifted away from self-reliance and into an interdependent phase, as signalled and deepened by China's accession to the World Trade Organization in 2001.[30] The nature of China's state-backed thrust into Africa appears

---

28 *AP*, 'China thanks Africans for defeating Taiwan's bid to join UN', 28 September 2007.

29 Gerald Segal, 'China and Africa', *Annals of the American Academy of Political and Social Science*, 519 (1992), pp. 115-126.

30 See Alastair Iain Johnston and Robert S. Ross (eds), *New Directions in the*

to be predicated upon a medium-long term involvement in which China's diplomatic presence throughout Africa serves commercial objectives.[31] Furthermore, while primarily anchored in state-related forms, the growing diversity of engagement by a range of Chinese actors ensures that the objectives of state and new private actors are no longer necessarily coterminous as they once might have been.

Trade

Trade between Africa and China began to accelerate in 2000 when official two-way China-Africa trade stood at $10.5 billion. This rose to $29.5 billion in 2004, nearly $40 billion in 2005 and some $55 billion in 2006. In the first half of 2007, China-Africa trade increased by 25 per cent over 2006 to reach US$32 billion, according to the Chinese Ministry of Commerce.[32] It is projected to reach $100 billion by 2010, if not before. China's share of African exports rose from 1.3 per cent in 1995 to 9.3 per cent in 2004, and was accompanied by 'significant redirection' and decline of African exports to OECD countries between 1995 and 2004.[33] In the context of China's overall economic relations, the continent is a comparatively small trade partner for China: Africa accounted for 2.6 per cent of the total volume of China's foreign trade in 2004.[34] Overall trade in 2005 bore a deficit for China of some $2.95 billion. In practice, this meant an operating deficit with a small number of resource-producing states (including Angola, Sudan, Republic of Congo, and Equatorial Guinea).

The profile of China's imports from Africa reflects the unequally distributed geography of Africa's resources. China has become a

---

Study of China's Foreign Policy (Stanford University Press, 2006).

31 China's already considerable diplomatic presence in Africa, and its stress on having diplomatic representation in as many states as possible, is a contrast to Britain, among others; Britain is scaling back and regionalizing diplomatic representation, something the Chinese consider surprising. This reflects the fundamental statist orientation of the Chinese engagement with Africa.

32 *Xinhua*, 'China's direct investment in Africa hits $480 mln in first half', 29 August 2007.

33 Andrea Goldstein, H. Reisen, Nicolas Pinaud, and X. Chen, *The Rise of India and China: What's in it for Africa?* (Paris, OECD: 2006), p. 45.

34 MOFCOM, *China Commerce Yearbook 2005*, p. 126.

major market for key African raw and soft commodity producers: Angola, Nigeria, Sudan, Zambia, and the two Congos. Overall, five oil- and mineral-exporting countries account for 85 per cent of Africa's exports to China.[35] Oil is the most significant export, making up almost 100 per cent of Angolan exports to China, with timber also important.[36] Growing African exports to China correlate narrowly with the growth of its major commodity exports (oil, metals/minerals, agricultural products, woods, cotton) to China.

A leading illustration of the impact of Chinese competition is the case of African textile industry.[37] The Multifibre Agreement (MFA) quota systems and investment from Asia contributed to the development of the clothing industry in Southern Africa, including Lesotho and Swaziland, in the 1990s. When quota limits on Chinese exporters under the MFA were lifted in January 2005, the impact of this was considerable for African clothing and textile exporters benefiting from the US African Growth and Opportunity Act (AGOA). Overall African clothing exports under AGOA declined by 17 per cent in 2005. Lesotho's and Madagascar's exports fell by 14 per cent. The main casualty was South Africa, with a 45 per cent decrease in exports. The impact on employment in 2004-5 was tangible: employment in the clothing sector in Lesotho declined by 28.9 per cent, 6,000 textile workers lost jobs in Lesotho in January 2005 alone; in Swaziland employment in this industry fell by 56.2 per cent, and in South Africa by 12.2 per cent.[38]

China-Africa trade relations should be considered in world context and the differential impacts within Africa appreciated, as Kaplinsky has underlined.[39] China has significantly contributed to keeping an-

---

35 Harry G. Broadman, *Africa's Silk Road: China and India's New Economic Frontier* (Washington, DC: The World Bank, 2007), p. 12.

36 Combined with crude oil, these accounting for 97.1 per cent of Gabon's and 84 per cent of Cameroon's exports to China.

37 See Mike Morris, 'China's Dominance of Global Clothing and Textiles: is Preferential Trade Access an Answer for sub-Saharan Africa?', *IDS Bulletin*, 37, 1 (2000), pp. 89-97.

38 Raphael Kaplinksy *et al.*, 'The Impact of China on Sub-Saharan Africa' (April 2006), pp. 18-19.

39 Ibid.

nual world economic growth above the 4 per cent threshold deemed 'critical for improving the terms of trade for primary commodity producers'.[40] China is a key world net importer of commodities. Low US interest rates, assisted by Asian countries' recycling of their considerable foreign exchange reserves into US securities, stimulated raw commodity prices and benefited commodity exporters in Africa. The expansion of China's manufactured exports may have helped to reduce world prices for manufactured goods, but this translated into pressure on major African clothing exporters (Kenya, Lesotho, Madagascar, Mauritius, South Africa and Swaziland). Africa is benefiting in mixed ways from a worldwide growth cycle driven by China and reinforced by India. Real GDP in Africa grew at an annual rate of 4.2 per cent between 2001 and 2004 (compared with 3.3 per cent between 1997 and 2000). Sub-Saharan Africa's real GDP growth rate reached an eight-year high at 5.4 per cent in 2004, with rising commodity prices played a critical role in the increase.

Despite its overwhelming importance for Africa itself, Chinese FDI in Africa remains a comparatively small proportion of its overall outward FDI (some 3-5 per cent). UNCTAD reported that the level of China's FDI reached US$1.6 billion by 2005.[41] However, statistics vary. One report, noting that China's direct investment in Africa for the years 2000-2006 was US$6.6 billion according to China's Ministry of Commerce, suggests that 'official statistics may not fully capture the true magnitude of direct investment by Chinese entities in African countries.'[42] Not all investment is supported directly by the Chinese central government: there is an emerging dynamic of regional investment directed from lower levels of Chinese government, including the provincial level,[43] as well as private entrepreneurial

---

40 Goldstein *et al.*, *The Rise of India and China*, pp. 18-19.

41 See UNCTAD, *Asian Foreign Direct Investment in Africa: Towards a New Era of Cooperation among Developing Countries* (New York and Geneva: UNCTAD, 2007).

42 Jian-ye Wang, 'What Drives China's Growing Role in Africa?', IMF Working Paper August 2007.

43 In certain cases, these revive older connections. For instance Hefei, the capital of Anhui Province in eastern China, became a sister-city of Freetown in 1984, and the Anhui Foreign Economic Construction Corporation was

investment. The dominance of major resource providers in China's imports from Africa is reflected in Chinese investment patterns concentrated on resource-producing states. Chinese FDI to Africa appears predominantly resource oriented. In 2004 China became the world's second largest importer of oil after the US, and it sources some 30 per cent of oil imports from Africa. Angola is China's biggest supplier of oil in Africa, currently providing some 500,000 bpd, or 15 per cent, of China's imports. Chinese national oil companies are pivotal drivers of overseas oil investment. Natural resource rich countries continue to be main destinations, with 50-80 per cent of Chinese FDI in Africa in natural-resource exploitation and resource rich countries (Angola, Sudan, Chad, Equatorial Guinea, Nigeria, South Africa). However, concurrent with this concentration of investment and commercial activity in larger, resource rich economies, there are processes seeing Chinese business 'rolling out across the continent relatively evenly, positioning themselves in countries such as Sierra Leone with comparatively virginal markets and less rigid government control that presumably permit them to realize higher profits.'[44]

Investment relations have gained momentum and increasingly are subject to bilateral regulation. As well as state diplomacy, Chinese Trade Centres assist Chinese investment by providing information to both local and Chinese businesses considering investing or trading, and a degree of logistical support with business start-ups. Chinese Economic and Commercial Counsellors attached to Chinese embassies also provide information.[45] Investment is thus set to increase exponentially. China's African Development Fund, announced during the third FOCAC, was launched in June 2007 with $1 billion of a projected $5 billion fund to encourage and support Chinese business operating in Africa. The China Development Bank will oversee government equity support for Chinese corporations for

---

operating in Sierra Leone in 2006.

44 'China's Interest and Activity in Africa's Construction and Infrastructure Sectors' (Centre for Chinese Studies, Stellenbosch, 2006), p. 40.

45 Ibid.

commercial activities in Africa as a major part of China's 'economic cooperation'.

The established pattern of trade—China mostly importing African natural resources and exporting manufactured goods in return— shows little sign of being changed to any significant extent. While African business is stepping up operations in China, if from a very low starting point, continuing concern that China is replicating more established patterns of Africa's unfavourable relations with external partners has continued to be articulated and is recognized as a challenge by the Chinese government. The basic question facing Africa's trade with China (as indeed with the EU, for example) is what can be exported to China beyond resources? While Beijing seeks credit for expanding its zero-tariff policy, in practice this is of largely symbolic value. In 2004, African exports corresponded to just 72 of 190 zero-tariffs lines.[46] Nor do these translate to a significant amount: in 2006 China imported some US$350 million of goods under the zero-tariff policy, including US$180 million worth of sesame.[47]

Chinese companies have become the most confident investors in Africa.[48] This is especially the case in South Africa, but other important FDI destinations include Tanzania, Ghana and Senegal. The diversity of Chinese companies is considerable, ranging from major multi-billion dollar SOEs to small businesses run by individuals. The majority of Chinese companies in the initial phase of market entry have been SOEs but there are an increasing number of private Chinese construction companies. The major state-backed Chinese investors do not appear to have substantially integrated into African business communities yet, in contrast to entrepreneurial networks such as those in Mauritius with more embedded positions. China opened its first Economic and Trade Cooperation Zone in Zambia in February 2007. With it, and the others that were down to follow, the successful model employed in China is being transplanted into Africa.

---

46 Broadman, *Africa's Silk Road*, p. 170.

47 'MOC official answers questions on granting zero-tariff to least-developed African countries', 20 August 2007 from the MOFCOM website.

48 See Chris Alden and Martyn Davies, 'A Profile of the Operations of Chinese Multinationals in Africa', *South African Journal of International Affairs*, 13, 1 (2006), pp. 83-96.

A substantial amount of commercially oriented Chinese financial activity has been devoted to infrastructure projects.[49] Chinese companies have in a relatively short time attained a strong position, in part through a reputation for low costs and fast delivery and, with the notable exception of South African business, lack of competition (though competition between Chinese companies is a factor). Frequently financed by soft loans, state-linked Chinese companies run successful infrastructure construction projects across Africa. China's Roads and Bridges Corporation, for example, is active in various contexts such as Angola where it is rehabilitating 1,200 km of roads between Luanda and Uige. Chinese actors are also involved in dam projects.[50] Chinese FDI in services, particularly telecommunications, is also increasing across Africa. Huawei Technologies has expanded communications business to 39 Sub-Saharan African countries. Tourism is another area of expanding cooperation; 26 African countries are now officially approved destinations for Chinese tourists.[51]

An important dynamic facilitating investment is the role of state-backed Chinese banks. The Export-Import Bank of China (or Exim) has rapidly become the world's largest export credit agency with 'significant and expanding operations in Africa'.[52] Exim Bank operates in a manner that differs from the export credit rules prevailing in OECD economies. As a state-backed bank, it has been funding projects often linked to broader political aims.[53] A number of new

---

49 There is often a thickening of ties on the back of investments or new projects. For example, the China Southern Airlines air link between Nigeria and Beijing through Dubai will facilitate travelling by some 100,000 Chinese workers and engineers who are in Nigeria for railway construction.

50 Such as Ethiopia's hydroelectric dam and power plant on the Tekeze River, Sudan's controversial Meroe (Hamdab) dam, the Mphanda Nkuwa Dam in Mozambique, the Gangelas Dam in Angola, the Adjarala Dam between Togo and Benin, and the Imboulou Dam in Congo Brazzaville.

51 With the addition of Algeria, Cape Verde, Cameroon, Gabon, Rwanda, Mali, Mozambique, Benin and Nigeria. Action plan of the Beijing Summit of the Forum on China-Africa Co-operation. 5 November 2006.

52 Todd Moss and Sarah Rose, 'China ExIm Bank and Africa: New Lending, New Challenges', Centre for Global Development Notes, November 2006.

53 The former Nigerian President Obasanjo called for the establishment of an 'Africa-China Bank', a new regional institution, to promote investments

African borrower countries with Exim Bank, such as Ghana (with a projected $1.2 billion worth of new loans) and Mozambique ($2.3 billion for the Mepanda Nkua dam and hydroelectric plant), were granted debt relief under the HIPC initiative. Chinese companies, however, draw on a range of funding, not just that directly connected to the Chinese government.

Exim Bank and other Chinese banks have emerged as bilateral competitors for the established IFIs. This has provoked concerned reactions; the President of the European Investment Bank, for example, noting strong competition from Chinese banks in Africa, commented that 'they do not bother with social and human rights conditions', adding, 'We should continue to have conditionality, but we need to think about it.'[54] The announcement by the President of the African Development Bank, Donald Kaberuka, at its May 2007 meeting held in Shanghai, that Exim Bank had agreed to finance projects worth $20 billion over the next three years, would mean that it will be the single biggest financing agency over that period.[55]

Aid

Traditional altruistic aid is no longer at the forefront of China's African engagement, though the effects of Chinese aid to Africa may be visible in terms of high-profile infrastructure. Officially the Chinese government focuses on agricultural development, infrastructure, human resources training, and medical and health cooperation. Details of the quantity, concentration and terms and conditions of zero-interest or concessional loans, grants, technical assistance are however elusive, but such forms of aid appear to be bound up with infrastructure projects.[56] 'Tied aid' has been a source of controversy for a grow-

---

between China and African countries. 'Nigeria Proposes Africa-China Bank', *Nigeria First* (Abuja), 7 November 2006.

54 'Chinese loans to Africa dangerous' – EU Bank', *AFP*, 29 November 2006.

55 *Africa Confidential*, 'Year of the Pig – the New Scramble for Africa', 48, 11 (2007), pp. 6-7.

56 China's pledge to double its 2006 assistance to Africa by 2009, for example, was hard to gauge in the absence of adequate baseline data about current levels of assistance.

ing number of African trade unions and civil society activists. Some is rapidly disbursed according to political opportunity; in other cases it is bound to China's larger investments in resources. Aid is used in symbolic gestures assisting economic involvement. 'Prestige' projects are often linked to improving relations with states (constructing stadiums in Mali and Djibouti, or the houses of parliament in Mozambique and Gabon). The first of 10 anti-malaria centres due to be built in 2007—and a total of 30 pledged by 2009—opened in Liberia in February as part of a broader health sector training and cooperation programme. FOCAC 3 also pledged to expand Chinese support for scholarships for African students studying in China, education and agricultural aid, including Chinese technical assistance.[57] Aid is one area in which China looks set to expand not merely to enhance its interests but also to further claims to leadership and demonstrate constructive contribution to human development beyond narrowly extractive or profit-oriented activities. In recent years China has supported humanitarian aid, conflict resolution and peacekeeping in Africa as part of an apparent emerging and increasingly prominent role as humanitarian donor and development force.[58]

Debt relief has been a prominent area of Chinese aid and political relations. China has committed itself to cancelling some US$1.27 billion worth of debt from 31 African countries. Promises of further debt relief were made at the third FOCAC, followed by a number

---

57 The most recent FOCAC pledged that China would: 'Over the next three years, train 15,000 African professionals; send 100 senior agricultural experts to Africa; set up 10 special agricultural technology demonstration centers in Africa; build 100 rural schools in Africa; and increase the number of Chinese government scholarships to African students from the current 2,000 per year to 4,000 per year by 2009.' Around 1,100 students from 46 African countries were studying in China in 2006. An Egyptian-Chinese University was planned for Egypt.

58 The total number of Chinese military personnel and civilian police sent on peacekeeping missions in stood at over 1,800 in early 2007, with pledges of continent participation in peacekeeping missions and assistance to 'African regional organizations'. Some three quarters were supporting UN operations in Africa, mainly Liberia, Democratic Republic of Congo and Sudan. In November 2006, the World Food Programme welcomed China's first donation of US $1.75 million since it graduated from being a recipient of food aid at the end of 2005.

of other gestures early in 2007.[59] Media and culture are additional sectors of expanding cooperation. There are currently Confucius Institutes in Rwanda (at the Kigali Institute of Education), Zimbabwe, Madagascar and Egypt, two in Kenya and South Africa and three in Nigeria. China's new small volunteer programme started with a government pledge to send 300 'youth volunteers' to Africa.[60]

International politics

Looking at the broader canvas of international politics, China's developing relations with Africa have implications on a number of fronts. In the first instance, China's growing political clout in Africa is based on its surging economic presence across the continent, something that derives from the profound transformation of the Chinese domestic economic environment since 1978.[61] This enormously powerful economy in turn poses opportunities and challenges for Africa's own development prospects as well as the continent's economic ties and political orientation towards its traditional partners in the West. And, finally, the emergence of China as a leading actor in Africa is compelling precisely because it is the most prominent expression of emerging international trends that put China at the centre of contemporary global politics.

---

59 Chad receiving US$32 million in debt relief, Equatorial Guinea US$75 million and Sudan some $80 million.

60 In November 2006, 10 of a projected 50 Chinese professional volunteers were working the Ethiopian News Agency, Ethiopian Television, Press Agency and various sections under the Ministry of Information 'Chinese Volunteers Begin Free Service', *The Ethiopian Herald* (Addis Ababa), 10 November 2006.

61 For academic literature on Chinese foreign policy towards Africa, see various works by George Yu (op. cit.); Richard Payne and Cassandra Veney, 'China's Post-Cold War African Policy', *Asian Survey* 38, 9 (1998), pp. 867-79; Ian Taylor, 'China's Foreign Policy towards Africa in the 1990s', *Journal of Modern African Studies*, 36, 3 (1998), pp. 443-60; Ian Taylor, 'The "All Weather Friend"? Sino-African Interaction in the 21st Century', in Ian Taylor and Paul Williams (eds), *Africa in International Politics: External Involvement on the Continent* (London: Routledge, 2004), pp. 83-101; Marcel Kitissou (ed.), *Africa in China's Global Strategy* (London: Adonis & Abbey, 2007); Barry Sautman and Yan Hairrong, 'Friends and Interests; China's Distinctive Link with Africa', *African Studies Review* 50, 3 (2007).

For China itself, as the renewed engagement with Africa flows directly from the three decades of rapid development, the relationship holds implications for the course and conduct of China's transformation from socialist bastion to a fully market capitalist economy. At the sharp end of China's presence in Africa are its state-owned enterprises involved in resource extraction and infrastructure development. They are products of the CCP's decision to transform moribund state institutions into state-directed multinational firms able to compete against the best of the established international corporations. This 'going out' policy, formally launched in 2001, is supported by Beijing's astute 'no conditions' diplomacy as well as billions of dollars in foreign reserves, which have allowed companies like PetroChina, ZTC or Jiangsu International to gain a foothold in markets in a short period. As they establish their presence in Africa, their practices—derived from experience at home, where social and environmental legislation has been weak to non-existent—increasingly determine the shape of relations with Africa. Complicating matters is the decentralization of economic policies, which has reduced the central government's ability to influence the actions of private Chinese entrepreneurs.[62] With African resources becoming ever more important to the health of the Chinese economy, Beijing's domestic policy of delivering greater prosperity at home, on the back of sometimes painful economic reforms, without relinquishing significant political control is arguably in danger of becoming hostage to the fortunes of its international forays in places like Africa. Surely this is what is being seen in the diplomatic controversy over Chinese support for the pariah regime in Sudan.

While China-Africa relations are an important factor in Beijing's own domestic calculations, the burgeoning ties with China hold tremendous implications for Africa. Africa's development needs, as outlined in a host of initiatives such as the New Partnership for African Development (NEPAD), require an infusion of substantial foreign investment aimed at improving its physical infrastructure, the opening of new markets and better prices for its products, and an expan-

---

62 Bates Gill and James Reilly, 'The Tenuous Hold of China Inc. in Africa', *Washington Quarterly*, 30, 30 (2007), pp. 37-52.

sion of human capital, all of which would contribute to a sustained growth cycle that would allow the continent to meet its development aims for the next decade. China's engagement with Africa provides for many of these very conditions and that is why, irrespective of the concerns being voiced in some circles in Africa (see below), Chinese involvement is widely considered to be a positive-sum game.[63] For instance, diversifying sources of foreign investment, an explicit policy pursued by the oil producers like Angola and Nigeria, has contributed to opportunities to extract better terms from donors and lenders alike. At the same time, it should be noted that China's rapid insertion into Africa has benefited directly from the previous decades of neo-liberal restructuring of African economies, including the removal of barriers to investment and the privatization of state-owned assets. Moreover, their investment outreach commenced at roughly the same time as the West began to reduce its exposure to Africa (as illustrated, most notoriously, by the French-directed devaluation of the CFA Franc in 1994 and the Western shift to pursuing investment opportunities in, ironically, China).[64] In this context, China's rapid gains on the continent, far from being a sudden 'scramble for Africa', could be more accurately described as pushing on an open door, one which in any case the West had left ajar as it scrambled eastward.

The Chinese impact on governance in Africa, which has exercised Western and African minds alike, is arguably the most contentious component of its engagement. By actively courting 'pariah regimes' like those of Sudan and Zimbabwe, Beijing has not only irritated the West—which at least initially was not seen to be a particularly worrisome outcome by Chinese officialdom—but found itself at odds with an emerging consensus on the necessity of good governance within Africa itself. The voices arguing for improvements in accountability, transparency and democracy were not just civil society activists but some of the top leaders of the continent, like Nigeria's former President Olusegun Obasanjo and South Africa's Thabo Mbeki, and their

---

63 See, for instance, Garth le Pere and Garth Shelton, *China, Africa and South Africa: South-South Co-operation in a Global Era* (Midrand: Institute for Global Dialogue, 2007).

64 See Firoze Manji and Stephen Marks (eds), *African Perspectives on China in Africa* (Oxford: Fahamu, 2007) for a range of views.

concerns were reflected in the reformulation of the African Union and the NEPAD initiative. This unexpected development put China in an invidious position, opening it to criticism from African sources of its single-minded pursuit of profit over the needs and concerns of ordinary Africans. The paradoxical result of this has been seen in the case of Sudan, with a seemingly gradual shift away from its categorical support for non-intervention in domestic affairs to one in which it supports the African Union position (and with that the West) on the necessity of a peacekeeping operation in Darfur.[65]

The fast pace and changing dynamics of Chinese foreign policy towards the continent is a noteworthy feature of its engagement. For instance, China's Africa policy changed in three discernable ways after the Beijing Summit of 2006. It moved beyond its primary focus on resource acquisition into areas like financial services and an expansion of activity related to agriculture. It attempted to build islands of Chinese investment in the form of Economic Cooperation Zones in selected African countries; and it modified its conventional investment packages to include greater emphasis on social and community outreach. The bold foray into financial services—with the US$5.4 billion purchase of 20 per cent of South Africa's Standard Bank (its largest bank and the one with the most exposure in Africa) in November 2007 by the Industrial and Commercial Bank of China and, less than a week later, the announcement of a partnership between the China Development Bank and Nigeria's United Bank of Africa—signalled the deepening of its economic engagement. Building on its past history as a provider of technical assistance in this sector, Chinese sponsored agricultural centres are springing up across Africa and, when combined with an expanding Chinese role in financing, training and commercial farming, seem to presage a more substantive involvement.[66] Debates around the uncertain status of the structure of the Economic Cooperation Zones, stalled their

---

65 See 'Arms, Oil, and Darfur: The Evolution of Relations between China and Sudan', *Sudan Issue Brief* (Geneva: Small Arms Survey, 2007).

66 'Chinese team to discuss agricultural centre', Agência de Informação de Moçambique, 7 November 2007. Discussions are being held in Senegal and South Africa, while Chinese farmers are establishing themselves in Zambia and Zimbabwe.

development in other regions. The now conventional approach of Chinese FDI in resource rich countries was adjusted, as seen in the over US$5 billion package for the DRC announced in September 2007 which included US$3 billion for infrastructure rehabilitation and US$2 billion to develop mines in Katanga, Ituri and the Kivus, while 31 hospitals and two universities are to be built. A new 'social clause' has come into Chinese investment in Africa.

Finally, China's deepening presence in Africa holds wider implications for the international system. It has challenged Western pre-eminence in a region that had long served as Europe's *'chasse gardée'* and, for the United States, as an increasingly important source of its energy needs. Moreover, China's ability to command colossal financial resources, from revenues arising from its arrival as the premier global manufacturer and a leading trading nation, in the service of its foreign policy interests gives it an easy position that Western states can only envy. Just as America's shift from debtor to creditor nation after 1919 is marked by historians as a turning point in the distribution of power in the international system, so too China's status as a top international creditor is a signal that power is moving East. The shock induced by Africa's dwindling interest in borrowing from the World Bank and European Investment Bank, which has caused both institutions to decry Chinese lending practices as well as questioning their own relevance, is seemingly another indicator of the West's putative marginalization on the continent.[67] China's capturing of markets through the unbeatable combination of aggressive diplomacy, financial largesse and low costs, coupled with African aptitude in playing one suitor off of the other, only fuels this sense of impending relegation in Western capitals. Faced with this new challenge to their established international standing, the leading industrial countries have sought to respond through a strategy of heightened public criticism and grudging collusion with China. China in turn, belatedly recognizing the dangers posed by an aroused Western perception of threat to established interests, has sought to counter this discourse of fear with its own declaration that China's rise to prominence would

---

67 'China treads on Western toes in Africa', *Financial Times*, 12 January 2007.

be peaceful.[68] In this context, Robert Zoellick, the former US Assistant Secretary of the Treasury, has called on China to assume a role as 'responsible stakeholder' in the international system commensurate with its economic importance.[69] Africa, again, is held to be a litmus test for Beijing's commitment to a largely Western-inspired agenda on governance and accountability.

China's return to a position of significance in African affairs is set to have a sustained impact on the continent. Whether this engagement redefines many of the traditional shibboleths of African international relations, as the rhetoric of 'win-win' partnerships suggests, remains to be seen. In any case, as the proving ground for a new activist China, Africa provides an important insight into the conduct of a resurgent China in regions and markets such as Central Asia, Latin America and the Middle East. The 21st century is indeed being made in Africa.

Overview of the book

The overarching aim of this book is to contribute towards deepening and broadening analysis of 'China in Africa', here referring to sub-Saharan Africa, through analysis of key themes in contemporary relations and more detailed case-studies. The book is structured as follows. The first section addresses China-Africa trade linkages and the political economy of China's recent involvement in the continent. Chapters examine the nature of trade relations, the impact of Chinese entrepreneurs on African manufacturing, China's Lusophone Africa strategy, the geopolitics of Chinese oil investment, and the political consequences of Chinese economic involvement in Africa. The second section considers China-Africa relations today from different regional perspectives and seeks to explore the very different, indeed opposing, ways in which the growing presence of China is perceived

---

68 Bates Gill, Chin-hao Huang, J. Stephen Morrison, *China's Expanding Role in Africa: Implications for the United States* (Washington, DC: Center for Strategic and International Studies 2007), pp. 159-60.

69 See Robert B. Zoellick, 'Whither China: From Membership to Responsibility?' Remarks to National Committee on U.S.-China Relations, 21 September 2005.

in Africa, China, Europe and the US. Country case-studies are the focus of section three. This is anchored by two chapters engaging the historical lineages of the PRC's aid programme in East Africa through analyses of the TAZARA railway and the presence of Chinese medical practitioners, which both show some of the important continuities in these programmes as manifest today and, in their different ways, testify to some of the pronounced changes in China's approach over time. The selection of case-studies makes no attempt at being fully representative. This section aims, rather, to provide detailed analyses of current relations featuring more high profile instances of Chinese involvement (Angola, South Africa and Sudan) as well as detailed studies of less prominent but revealing cases (Cape Verde and Namibia) where the Chinese presence is characterized by small-scale, entrepreneurial migration. The final section begins by serving up a cautionary note about considering relations today, before presenting two alternative readings of the potential impact of Chinese involvement for Africa: the first concludes that China's growing role could be part of an Asia-centred shift with profound and potentially transformative implications for Africa, while the second points to deep structural constraints that have historically shaped African interactions with the outside world, and postulates the Chinese presence as following this established path.

SECTION 1
POLITICAL ECONOMY

1
CHINA'S BOOM: WHAT'S IN IT FOR AFRICA? A TRADE PERSPECTIVE

Andrea Goldstein, Nicolas Pinaud and Helmut Reisen

China and India, the so-called Asian Drivers, are rapidly catching up with industrial countries and reclaiming their historical roles as world economic powers. Is this good news for the economic development of sub-Saharan Africa? This chapter explores two sets of interactions between Africa and China.[1] At the *global* level, China's ascendancy appears to have implications for raw material price levels and volatility, exchange rate dynamics, and income distribution.[2] In *bilateral* terms, competition from China in the production of labour-intensive goods affects resource allocation (de-industrialization, input

---

1　This chapter is based on a longer study that also considers the impact of India's ascendancy on Africa. Andrea Goldstein, H. Reisen, Nicolas Pinaud, and X. Chen, *The Rise of China and India. What's in it for Africa?* (Paris: OECD Development Centre Studies, 2006). 'Africa' refers to sub-Saharan Africa unless otherwise stated.

2　See also H. Reisen, M. Grandes and N. Pinaud, 'Macroeconomic Policies: New Issues of Interdependence', OECD Development Centre, Working Paper, No. 241 (2005).

linkages, and vertical integration), while demand complementarities have capital-flow effects (such as through FDI and project finance), which in turn may constrain the range of industrialization strategies available.[3]

The chapter begins with the indirect global macroeconomic effects of China's growth on raw material markets, through which Africa's economies are most prominently linked to the world economy. In order to explore possible allocative consequences (the so-called Dutch Disease effects), it then looks at changes in the terms of trade of African countries that are influenced by lower prices for manufactured goods and higher raw material prices. It goes on to study the intensification of trade between China and Africa and identifies the corresponding policy challenges that arise from the fact that, firstly, China is a 'swing importer' in certain raw material markets; and, secondly, China is exerting severe competition on local African and third markets for low value-added and labour-intensive manufacturing goods.

As the present study documents, African economies are affected differentially by Chinese economic growth. Complementary effects are possible in certain cases, as African producers benefit from increased Chinese demand. Further, China and other Asian countries may want to secure more raw materials, to improve export infrastructure in selected African countries, while offering project finance, FDI and other forms of trade-linked capital flows. In other cases where Asian economies indirectly divert investment resources away from African economies and compete with nascent local manufacturing sectors (e.g. clothing), interests may be competitive rather than complementary. While on balance the short-term opportunities of Asia's ascendancy and the concomitant effects on South-South trade may outweigh the economic costs for Africa (in particular for its raw material and energy exporting economies), serious long-term risks may be involved. These risks are related to inadequate institutions and governance systems which may lead to the misallocation of revenues from higher raw material prices and disincentives for investment in tradable activities in the non-traditional sector, which are required

---

3   See also Andrea Goldstein, *Emerging Multinationals in the Global Economy* (London: Palgrave, 2007).

in order to distribute more equitably between sectors the benefits of global trade.

China's global impact

The sheer size of China's economy, its phenomenal rate of growth, its appetite for natural resources, and its growing economic and political power augur that it will reshape the world economy and provide both competition and opportunities across the board to major trading partners in OECD countries, to developing countries and to other emerging economies.

The Chinese boom and its global impact: the channels. Between 2000 and 2006, China contributed 23.7 per cent of global output growth, compared to 19 per cent between 1990 and 2000, and 7.8 per cent between 1980 and 2000.[4] This contribution has helped to hold world growth above the 4 per cent threshold which is critical for improving the terms of trade for primary commodity producers. A recent estimate finds that world commodity prices rise 1.5 per cent for every one per cent increase in world industrial output, with a one-quarter lag at the most (Bloch *et al.* 2004). If world industrial growth exceeds 4 per cent, the *barter terms of trade* of primary commodity to finished goods rise. High global growth has recently halted and reversed the secular decline of raw commodity prices since the Second World War, caused by the uneven effects of technological progress on the production of manufactured goods and raw materials.[5]

On the financial front, Asian investors have been recycling foreign exchange reserves into US securities (the *Asian bid)* which in turn has contributed to low interest rates in the US. That much of Asia is explicitly or implicitly pegged to the dollar (whatever may be officially

---

4   Authors' own calculation based on IMF World Economic Outlook Database (April 2007), i.e. on purchasing-power-parity (PPP) valuation of country GDP.

5   R. Prebisch, *The Economic Development of Latin America and its Principal Problems* (Lake Success, NY: United Nations Economic Commission for Latin America, 1950); H. Singer, 'The Distribution of Gains between Investing and Borrowing Countries', *American Economic Review,* 40, 3 (1950), pp. 473-483.

pronounced) is well known.[6] Besides, exchange rate targets have been repeatedly set based on basket pegs, reserve volatility, or interest rate volatility (Branson 2001). What is new, however, is the sheer scale of official reserve accumulation. By the end of 2006, China and Hong Kong had accumulated 1.2 trillion dollars in foreign exchange reserves, of which 37.7 per cent were invested in US Treasury Bills and Bonds. China and Hong Kong have therefore become the second largest holder of US Treasury securities (US$451 billion at the end of 2006), only second to Japan (US$623 billion): China is now holding 9.2 per cent of outstanding US Treasury securities held by the public and 21.4 per cent of those in foreign hands.[7]

Regardless of the currency regime, sustained growth differentials in China vis-à-vis its main trading partners will imply a trend appreciation in the real effective exchange rate (the *Balassa-Samuelson effect*). This will raise China's purchasing power, while it will negatively affect its export competitiveness. Africa's primary commodity exporters would be likely to benefit from a (real effective) renminbi appreciation. To be sure, such appreciation amounts to a tightening of monetary conditions in China, and therefore could initially slow down the country's economic growth and its demand for commodities. As China's demand for commodities would shift away from domestic suppliers to cheaper foreign supplies (including supplies from Africa), domestic prices would gradually adjust downwards and international US dollar prices upwards, depressing the profitability of China's producers and boosting that of foreign competitors.[8]

---

6   Targets of slightly undervalued real effective exchange rates can be rationalised in the development context on the basis of the fact that they provide a bias towards exports and may thus stimulate growth in countries where the lack of sound financial institutions, and distorted local prices, would otherwise provide inadequate signals for the efficient allocation of resources R. McKinnon and G. Schnabl, 'China: A Stabilizing or Deflationary Influence in East Asia? The Problem of Conflicted Virtues,' mimeo, Stanford University (2003).

7   According to figures from the US Treasury (www.treas.gov/tic), the Hong Kong Monetary Authority and the PRC's State Administration of Foreign Exchange (SAFE).

8   Deutsche Bank, 'China Macro Strategy: 18 Ways to Play the RMB', Deutsche Bank Research, 20 May 2005.

An analysis of the determinants of growth in China suggests that rapid growth should continue for the foreseeable future, albeit at a somewhat slower rate.[9] Not only has the output growth potential of the Chinese economy been increasing since 2000, but thanks to capital accumulation (investment growth) it has accelerated to reach 9.5 per cent in 2005.[10] As more capital is accumulated, its marginal product will fall, resulting in a smaller contribution of capital to growth. Nonetheless, there is considerable room for further increases in efficiency through institutional and trade reforms, the second most important growth determinant in China.[11] The continued reallocation of labour from agriculture to manufacturing is another major stimulant of productivity growth. With large sections of the Chinese population, unemployed or underemployed, still living in the rural areas, and with relatively low productivity, the growth potential is almost unprecedented.[12] In China, in the presence of large labour reserves, growth will not be labour-constrained for some time and the productivity of capital will remain high in the industrial sector despite a vibrant pace of capital accumulation.

Global commodity markets and China's appetite for raw materials. The current process of increasing capital intensity has spurred the drastic increase in both energy and metal use in China.[13] The average annual

9   C.Holz, 'China's Economic Growth 1978-2025: What We Know Today about China's Economic Growth Tomorrow,' mimeo (2005), http://ihome. ust.hk/~socholz/ Projecting real GDP growth rates into the future, Holtz finds the size of the Chinese economy will surpass that of the US in terms of purchasing power between 2012 and 2015. By 2025, China is likely to be the world's largest economic power by almost any measure.

10 OECD, *2005 Economic Survey – China* (Paris: OECD, 2005).

11 M. Francis, F. Painchaud and S. Morin, 'Understanding China's Long-Run Growth Process and its Implications for Canada', *Bank of Canada Review* (Spring 2005), pp. 5-17.

12 In China, total labour force is reckoned at 740 million people; no more than 370 million currently work in the industrial segment of the economy, and the number of those who would potentially abandon their agricultural activities to find a job in the urban-based industrial sector is estimated at around 150 million or more: OECD, *2005 Economic Survey – China*.

13 Energy use is measured by the equivalent of kilotons of oil. Metal use is measured by the apparent consumption of crude steel (thousand metric

growth of energy consumption was 1.2 per cent between 1996 and 1999, before rising steadily to 14.5 per cent in 2003 with an average annual growth rate of 6.2 per cent during the period 2000-3. Meanwhile, Chinese energy production also increased at an annual rate of 6.2 per cent (2000-3). Similarly, the growth rate of crude steel consumption surged to a nine year high from 1.7 per cent in 2000 to 25.2 per cent in 2003, while the growth rate of crude steel production increased at an average annual rate of 15.7 per cent.

Although the shares of commodities in China's overall imports are not high (8.4 per cent and 5.6 per cent for crude oil and metalliferous ores respectively in 2006), China has nonetheless become a first-rank world commodity *net importer*[14] because of the rate at which its economy has grown. Table 1 highlights the fact that China has contributed tremendously to world import growth for selected commodities.

Kennan and Stevens find that six categories of Chinese imports relevant to African exporters—for the most part over the period 1998-2003, commodities—have grown 1.5 time faster than the average growth of Chinese overall imports: feed from Burkina Faso, Ethiopia, Nigeria, Sudan, Tanzania; cobalt from South Africa and the Democratic Republic of Congo; copper from Zambia and South Africa; alumina from Guinea; ferrous metals from Mauritania, South Africa and Zimbabwe; chemicals from Niger.[15] Note that for the rest of the world the growth in commodity imports is far slower than in China over a similar period (1999-2004, Table 1). For example, in the case of cotton, had it not been for China's strong demand, world demand would have receded (-0.05 per cent) between 1999 and 2004. China's contribution to the growth of world demand for cotton was indeed over 100 per cent over the period. This can also be verified by the rise in China's share of global imports for major commodities: China's share in world imports of crude oil, metalliferous

---

tonnes).

14 From the perspective of Africa's raw commodity exporters, it is China's *net demand* that influences prices and export volumes.

15 J. Kennan and C. Stevens, 'Opening the Package: the Asian Drivers and Poor-Country Trade', mimeo, Institute for Development Studies, Sussex (2005).

	Average annual growth of world demand excluding China, %	Average annual growth of China's demand, %	China's contribution to growth of global demand, %
Crude Oil	19.1	48.8	7.0
Metalliferous ores	14.2	47.4	28.9
Woods	3.6	17.0	20.7
Cotton	-0.05	98.6	100.7
Precious stones	5.9	28.5	5.6

Table 1: China's contribution to growth of world imports of selected commodities, 1999-2004[1]

Sources: Authors' own calculations based on UN Comtrade database

---

1 The chosen commodities are major commodity exports from Africa to China.

ores, woods and cotton rose from 1.9 per cent to 6 per cent, 6.4 per cent to 24.8 per cent, 2.5 per cent to 9 per cent and 4 per cent to 33.2 per cent respectively between 2000 and 2005.[16]

Africa's integration in global trade: does China's ascendancy make a difference?

Many African economies are prominently linked to the world economy as important producers of raw material and soft commodities.[17] The emergence of China over the last decade as a key net importer of commodities means that global commodity markets are likely to be

---

16 Figures from UN Comtrade.

17 For a detailed description, see Goldstein et al., The Rise of China and India, Appendix A.

the main channels through which the impact of China's ascendancy has been (and will be) felt on the African continent.

Figure 1 below shows considerable correlation between China's macroeconomic performance (GDP and industrial growth rates) and African commodity exports.[18]

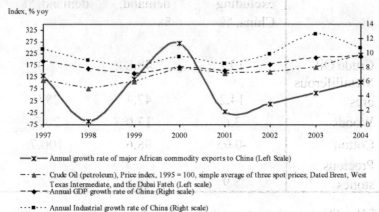

Index, % yoy

Figure 1: The Influence of China Growth Performance on African Commodity Exports

Source: UN Comtrade, World Bank Commodity Price Data (Pink Sheet) and *World Development Indicators*

Africa is indeed linked to China's demand for primary commodities via two channels: first, *the international price of commodities*: exchange rates, global inflation, interest rates, bond yields, house prices, wages and profits are increasingly being driven by the state of the economy in China. So are international raw material prices. It is useful to study how export prices of commodities, terms of trade and potential Dutch Disease effects will impact on Africa. Second, *the direct trade dependency of Africa on China and India*: very simply, is Africa, as a commodity exporter, becoming more (perhaps too) dependent on China? Has Africa simply succeeded in redirecting its commodity

---

18 The major African commodity exports to China are: crude oil (UN Comtrade SITC-Rev.3 code: 333), metalliferous ore, scrap (28), cork and wood (24), cotton (263), pearls and precious stones (667).

exports towards China, currently the world's most dynamic markets? Or has Africa also become more dependent on the vagaries of the international markets for such commodities?

Africa's terms of trade. The long-run tendency for prices of primary products to decline vis-à-vis those of manufactured products has resulted in a deterioration of the net barter terms of trade for many developing countries dependent on the export of raw materials and imports of manufactured products.[19] This led to the influential policy suggestion that developing countries industrialize and diversify their exports into manufactured goods.[20] As already suggested, the performance of China has presumably helped reverse this secular trend.

Figure 2 shows the *net barter terms of trade* and purchasing power of exports (income terms of trade) for Africa and Asia from 1980 to 2002. Insofar as the majority of African countries are still exporters of primary commodities with little diversification into manufactured exports, recent market trends have positively affected prices and improved the terms of trade.

Conversely, terms of trade for exporters of manufactured goods have displayed a downward trend. The rapid export growth of low-skill and labour-intensive manufactured goods has increased the market competition for these goods and hence exerted a downward pressure on their prices. Yet Figure 2 underlines that the purchasing power of Asian countries has grown sharply even if their terms of trade have been declining since 2000. This largely reflects their rising productivity and also the gains in the world market share of manufactured goods requiring low-skilled labour. The *volume* of exports expands significantly and outweighs the decline in barter terms of trade.

In this context, Africa's income terms of trade may well have benefited from Asia's emergence, through various channels: as suggested, a net rise in the demand for raw commodities translating into higher export unit prices and volumes; and urban consumers

---

19 The net barter terms of trade are measured by the ratio between the unit value (price) index of exports and that of the imports. The purchasing power of exports is defined as the value index of exports deflated by the unit value of imports.

20 Prebisch, *Economic Development of Latin America;* Singer, 'The Distribution of Gains'.

Africa

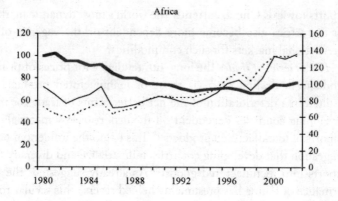

Asia

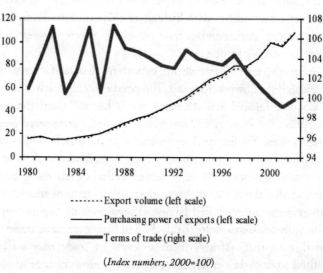

········ Export volume (left scale)

——— Purchasing power of exports (left scale)

━━━ Terms of trade (right scale)

(*Index numbers, 2000=100*)

Figure 2: Terms of Trade, Export Volumes and Purchasing Power of Exports in Africa and Asia, 1980-2002

Source: UNCTAD *Handbook of Statistics* (2005)

gaining from cheaper consumer goods and investors benefiting from cheaper capital goods. Exporters and urban consumers may indeed enjoy higher purchasing power as import prices are lower compared to prices of previous import sources or domestic producers.

Figure 3 shows the barter terms of trade and purchasing power of exports for the twelve major African trading partners of China.[21] Since 2000, African economies with a large share of oil, metals and agricultural products in their total exports have gained the most from the recent changes in the global economy. In general, both net barter and income terms of trade have improved substantially since 2000. Oil exporters experienced the biggest improvement in the terms of trade, 14.5 per cent on average in 2000-2. Despite a more diverse export product composition and large differences in price trends for individual commodities, agricultural exporters also improved their terms of trade by 6.9 per cent on average.

The benefits of China's rising global demand (net imports) for commodities relevant to Africa may, nevertheless, be attenuated by the *volatility of demand* on the part of the Asian giants. This is caused partly by cyclical variations and is also due to arbitrage between domestic production and imports. Moreover, as approximately 70-80 per cent of manufacturing exports from China is produced by multinational corporations, high demand for raw materials partially reflects relocation of raw material demand from production sites elsewhere. Such adjustments do not occur without friction, which in turn could have fuelled demand volatility. Consequently, rising raw material demand from China is not necessarily an unfettered blessing for Africa.

China's *net imports* of the most important commodities relevant to Africa's exports (oil, metals, wood and cotton) have actually recorded large swings between 2000 and 2005. And, although all four commodities have recorded price increases since 2000 (cotton notwithstanding), their prices have been very volatile over the period. Table 2 compares the volatility (measured as standard deviation around the trend) in commodities relevant to Africa for two time periods.

---

21 They are classified according to the major product category in their exports: oil, metals, agricultural products, or manufactures. The classification for some exporters is not straightforward. For example, those classified as agricultural products exporters often have a more diversified export structure and majority of them also have a respectable share of metals exports. This would certainly imply that their terms of trade are also sensitive to changes in the prices of the remaining primary commodities in their export bundles.

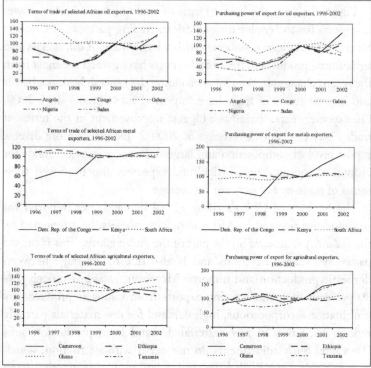

Figure 3: Terms of Trade of Major African Oil, Metal and Agriculture Exporters, 1996-2002

Source: UNCTAD *Handbook of Statistics* (2005)

Volatility rose for all commodities except copper. Although it is difficult to separate the relative contribution of different factors,[22] increased volatility between 2000 and 2005 (compared to the 1995-99 period) may have *been partly due* to the fact that China is a *swing producer*—exporting when prices are high and stockpiling when (be it for cyclical or exceptional reasons) they are not as attractive. Given

---

22 *World Energy Outlook* mentions a combination of factors that stretch the market and prompt widespread speculation by hedge funds and other investment vehicles, including increased terrorist attacks against energy infrastructure, political uncertainty in oil producing countries, and the rise in China and India's demand (IEA 2004).

	Volatility in Prices*		
	1995-1999	2000-2005	Difference
Oil (crude)	7.66	8.48	+ 0.92
Iron Ores	1.90	2.76	+ 0.86
Copper	5.48	4.23	- 1.25
Cotton	4.26	5.12	+ 0.86

Table 2: Volatility in Commodity Prices Relevant to African Countries

Note: * Standard deviation of monthly percentage changes

Source: Authors' own calculations based on World Bank data

its large economy, any behavioural change is likely to translate into volatility in world prices.

In turn, swings in prices of commodities relevant to Africa have resulted in substantial terms of trade variability which has in turn induced large movements in gross domestic income (Table 3). This illustrates that dependence on exports of primary commodity with little diversification involves a considerable developmental risk. China has diversified into the manufacturing sector to a greater degree. This has resulted in relatively low terms of trade variability, in spite of the fact that China is one of the most open economies in the world with a high export to GDP ratio of over 30 per cent in 2003.

Moreover, not all African countries are on an equal footing when it comes to reaping the benefits of higher commodity prices spurred by China's and India's demand for commodities. Far from Africa being homogeneously rich in natural resources, there are big differences among African trade patterns at the country level. A large number of African countries are net importers of mineral fuels, oils and distillation products and some of them (although in limited number) are net importers of raw materials. In this context, in their search for

	Terms-of-trade variability for each country*, 1997-2003	Terms-of-trade variability (average) for each group, 1997-2003	Terms-of-trade effects on GDI** for each country (per cent), 1997-2003	Terms-of-trade effects (average) on GDI for each group (per cent), 1997-2003
Oil exporters:		30.03		7.48
Angola	41.15		16.80	
Gabon	39.92		4.46	
Gabon	22.75		7.76	
Nigeria	38.44		0.92	
Sudan	7.90		..	
Metals exporters:		10.5		2.29
D. R. Congo	23.72		4.22	
Kenya	5.72		2.12	
South Africa	1.90		0.54	
Agricultural exporters:		13.21		2.11
Cameroon	19.73		4.47	
Ethiopia	15.19		1.69	
Ghana	9.16		1.08	
Tanzania	8.78		1.22	
Manufacturing exporters:		6.61		0.91
China	3.51		0.77	

Table 3: Terms of trade variability and effects on GDI, 1997-2003

Notes:

* Standard deviation of the annual rate of change of the net barter terms of trade

** UNCTAD calculates the average annual impact of terms of trade changes on GDI (Gross Domestic Income) as a percentage of GDP (Gross Domestic Product), in absolute value, 1997-2003, as the difference between the growth rates of GDI and GDP in real terms. GDI is the sum of all income earned in the domestic production of goods and services, while GDP measures the total market value of goods and services produced domestically during a given period.

Source: Authors' own computations based on UNCTAD *Handbook of Statistics* (2005).

commodities, resource-poor African countries may regard China as a competitor. Some African countries may even bear the brunt of rising commodity prices (oil prices in particular). In fact, gains from rising commodity prices have mostly accrued to oil exporters, followed by exporters of metal ores (Nigeria, Chad, Equatorial Guinea, Gabon, Congo, Angola, Zambia, and to a lesser extent, Mauritania, Mali, Guinea, Democratic Republic of Congo and Sudan).[23]

---

23 IMF, *World Economic Outlook* (Washington, DC: IMF, April 2004).

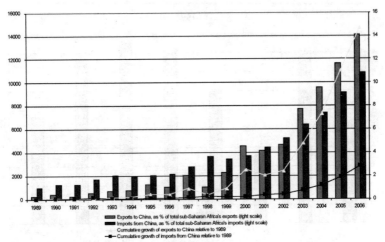

Figure 4: Africa's Trade with China, 1989-2006

Cumulative Growth and Share in Total sub-Saharan Africa's Trade, as %

Source: Authors' own calculations based on IMF Direction of Trade Statistics

China, an ever larger outlet for African exports. China's growing demand for commodities has not only resulted in higher commodity prices and a subsequent improvement of most African countries' terms of trade, but has brought about a significant redirection of African exports towards Asian markets and away from OECD markets.[24]

African trade with China has shown striking dynamism since 2000 (Figure 4). Sub-Saharan African exports to China started accelerating around 2002, and have since risen at an annual growth rate of 56 per cent. By 2006, African exports to China stood at $20.4 billion. This was almost six times the exports in 2002, and accounted for 14 per cent of total sub-Saharan African exports to the world. Since 2002, the average annual growth rate of African imports from China (54 per cent) has shown similar dynamism.

However, this reorientation has not led to a change in the composition of the African export mix, which remains biased towards the export of raw and, though to a lesser extent, soft commodities.

---

24 Though this is also in part due to the relatively slower GDP and export growth in OECD countries in the past few years, as well as to the reduced commodities intensity of OECD economies.

41

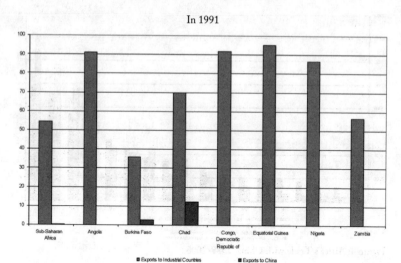

In 1991

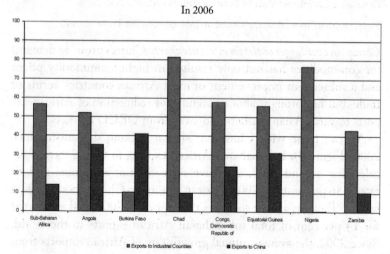

In 2006

Figure 5: The Reorientation of Africa's Exports Towards the Asian Drivers: Destination of African Exports (% of total exports).[1]

Source: Authors' own calculations based on IMF Direction of Trade Statistics

1   Industrialized countries, as defined by the IMF Direction of Trade Statistics, include the United States, Canada, Australia, Japan, New Zealand, Austria, Belgium, Luxembourg, Denmark, Finland, France, Germany, Greece, Iceland, Ireland, Italy, the Netherlands, Norway, Portugal, San Marino, Spain, Sweden, Switzerland, and the United Kingdom.

Chinese imports from Africa indeed show a very clear pattern in terms of commodity structure which is consistent with the latter's Ricardian advantage in commodity production (Table 5). Extractive mining and forestry in particular make up the bulk of African exports to China, as of African exports to the whole world: 'Product A, B and C', i.e. the top three items in total exports to China from each African country, closely correspond to Product I, II and III, each African country's biggest exports to the world. Crude oil (i.e. Product I for Angola, Sudan, Nigeria, Congo and Gabon) also comes first as a share of their exports to China with almost 100 per cent, 98.8 per cent, 88.9 per cent, 85.9 per cent and 54.8 per cent respectively. Metals rank first in exports of the Democratic Republic of Congo, Ghana and South Africa to China (with 99.6 per cent, 59.8 per cent and 45.6 per cent of their exports to China respectively), and they are key products in exports of these countries to the world. Woods come second in Chinese imports from Gabon and Cameroon with a share of 42.3 per cent and 39.7 per cent respectively, while they similarly account for the lion's share of those countries' exports to the world. Overall, woods and crude oil together account for 97.1 per cent and 84 per cent of Gabon's and Cameroon's exports to China respectively.

According to Table 5, the only other products to feature significantly in China's imports from the selected African exporters are cotton from Cameroon and Tanzania and cocoa from Ghana.[25] Exports of cotton to China have been boosted by the Multi-Fibre Agreement (MFA) phasing out and by the rapid build-up of the Chinese textile industry. Moreover, Chinese domestic supply of cotton remains in a state of flux and not always able to cater for domestic demand. The aforementioned figures suggest that labour-intensive agricultural (except cotton) and manufactured goods do not feature significantly in the exports of any African country.[26]

---

25 Cocoa actually comes second to metals among Ghana's exports to China (31.6 per cent). While cotton accounts for more than half of Tanzania's exports to China, China absorbs no more than 4.2 per cent of Tanzania's overall exports of cotton.

26 Africa-India trade patterns are a bit different. African exports (oilseeds, cotton, edible vegetables and fruits, hides, nuts) to India are a bit more

Table 4 shows that African countries have not only been exporting mostly commodities to China over the last years, but have also succeeded in turning China (and India[27]) into significant markets for their commodities. China has largely driven the growth of world demand for African commodities: it accounted for more than 100 per cent of the growth in the world demand for commodities exported by Congo and the Democratic Republic of Congo. In other words, world demand for Congolese exports would have decreased had it

| | China's | |
	Share in aggregate commodity export of each country in 2002	Contribution in 2003
Angola	14.1	73.3
Cameroon	7.9	0.1
Congo	11.7	118.7
D R Congo	9.7	178.1
Ethiopia	..	..
Gabon	4.5	12.6
Ghana	2.6	3.0
Kenya	0.1	0.5
Nigeria	0.4	0.7
South Africa	3.2	5.2
Sudan	80.0	74.0
Tanzania	0.1	0.4

Table 4: China's Contribution to Growth of Commodity Demand for African Exporters in 2003

Source: Authors' own calculations based on ITC Trademap (UNCTAD)

Notes: Table 4 indicates China's contribution to the growth of world demand directed to African countries in 2003.

---

diversified and labour-intensive than those to China (see Table 12 in Goldstein et al., The Rise of China and India).

27 India absorbs almost half of Sudanese and Cameroon exports of metals while being by far the biggest importer of Tanzanian edible vegetables (68.7 per cent). The Senegalese production of phosphoric acid is almost fully exported to India.

Country	Share of China in Total Exports in 2003	Main Exports (in order of importance)	Crude Oil			Metals			Cotton			Woods			Oil Seed/rubber /cocoa			Textile		
			(1)	(2)	(3)	(1)	(2)	(3)	(1)	(2)	(3)	(1)	(2)	(3)	(1)	(2)	(3)	(1)	(2)	(3)
Angola	23.2%	Product I	25	99.9	7.5															
Cameroon	4.4%	Product I	4.4	44.2	0.2															
		Product II										8.6	39.7	1						
		Product III							17.4	15.9	0.4									
Congo	30.3%	Product I	31	85.9	2.4															
		Product II										37	9.8	1.7						
		Product III				72.5	4	0.4												
DR Congo	2.2%	Product I				41.4	99.6	0.4												
Gabon	5.5%	Product I	3.4	54.8	0.3															
		Product II										32	42.3	1.4						
Ghana	1.6%	Product I				13.2	59.8	0.12												
		Product II													1.2	33	0.2			
Kenya	0.3%	Product I																8.6	42.8	0.1
		Product II				2.48	29.1	0.01												
Nigeria	0.5%	Product I	0.5	88.9	0.4															
South Africa	4.6%	Product I				7.11	45.6	1.05												
		Product II										11	4.4	1						
Sudan	40.9%	Product I	81	98.8	5.5															
Tanzania	2.6%	Product I							4.2	53.8	0.1									
		Product II													14	23.4	0.02			

Table 5: China as Market for African Exports in 2003[1]

Notes:

(1) Each export item to China as a percentage of total exports of that item to the world. For example, China imports 25 per cent of Angolan oil exports to the world.

(2) The percentage share of a given item in a country's total exports to China. For example, oil accounts for 99.9 per cent of Angola's exports to China.

(3) Percentage share of export item from a given country in China's total imports for that item. For example, Angola's oil accounts for 7.5 per cent of China's total imports of oil.
Source: Authors' own calculations based on ITC Trademap (UNCTAD)

---

1   Selected countries are those for which trade with China represents the highest share in total export of each African country in 2003. Selected commodities are major exports of those countries to China as shown by the percentage share of a given item in a country's total exports to China (these commodities are main African exports as well). Commodity code classification is based on HS-Rev. 3.

not been fuelled by strong Chinese demand. China also accounted for 73.3 per cent and 74 per cent of the growth of world demand for Angola's and Sudan's oil respectively. As a consequence, China absorbed one quarter, one third and four fifths of Angolan, Congolese and Sudanese oil exports respectively in 2003 (Table 5). It also buys 32 per cent and 37 per cent of Gabonese and Congolese exports of timber respectively (idem).

China and Africa: prospects, risks and opportunities

China's growing demand for commodities has meant a significant redirection of African exports away from OECD markets, towards Asian markets in general and China in particular. But, as expected, Chinese imports from Africa show a very clear pattern in terms of commodity structure which is consistent with the latter's comparative advantage in commodity production (oil and metals in particular). In parallel, China (together with India) is currently integrating more than one billion people into the global labour pool, and competition is intensifying in tradable labour-rich goods, the relative prices of which are dropping.

On the face of it Africa, which is mostly integrated in global trade as a supplier of commodities, should be benefiting from this economic environment. It is selling larger volumes of its raw commodities at higher prices. As already suggested (Figure 4), the continent has also been importing increasing volumes of ever cheaper manufacturing goods from Asia, specifically from China, thus enhancing the purchasing power of its consumers.

This is no time for celebration, though. Firstly, Africa's trade reorientation may imply some disadvantages. It may derail the endeavours of African commodity producers to diversify away from traditional exports. Increasing reliance on capital-intensive commodity industries may be incompatible with poverty reduction[28] and trap African economies into the corner of high-risk price-volatile raw materials. Also, the presence of the Asian giants in resource rich African countries may increase the rents earned by an elite that commands access to these resources. It is important to note, however, that China's increasing presence in the natural resources-related sectors has not been evidently conducive to deterioration in transparency

---

28 See Goldstein *et al.*, *The Rise of China and India*, Chapter 6, for a discussion of whether the Dutch Disease theory and Leamer's framework of analysis are relevant to African economies (E. Leamer, 'Paths of Development in the Three-Factor, N-Good General Equilibrium Model', *Journal of Political Economy*, 95, 5 (1987), pp. 961-99; E. Leamer, H. Maul, S. Rodriguez and P.K. Schott, 'Does Natural Resource Abundance Cause Latin American Income Inequality?', *Journal of Development Economics* 59, 1 (1999), pp. 3-42).

and corruption scores.[29] Secondly, China has emerged as a formidable competitor in local and third markets (the US and Europe in particular), in the very few labour-intensive low-skill sectors where Africa could diversify away from commodity production. Certainly, labour-intensive manufacturing industries are less prominent in Africa than in other developing regions and Africa exports very few manufactured products.[30] Yet, such an analysis ignores opportunities for diversification away from traditional exports, i.e. *potential* rather than *actual* competition. In other words, China may nip in a bud whatever *attempts* by African economies to diversify away from traditional sectors. The effects of Chinese competition on third markets take on special importance because of trade preference erosion. The latter tends to undermine the competitiveness of African countries on markets in developed countries, vis-à-vis their Asian competitors. In a context of the end of Multi-Fibre Agreement protection, the case of clothing is particularly illuminating.[31] As regards the influx of Chinese imports in local African markets, there is little empirical evidence as to whether the purchasing power gains for the African consumer and the lower costs of inputs for African producers outweigh the losses which might be and have already been incurred by

---

29 Goldstein *et al.*, *The Rise of China and India*, p. 53.

30 An analysis based on the calculation of Export Similarity Index shows limited competition between Africa and China, South Africa notwithstanding (Goldstein *et al.*, *The Rise of China and India*).

31 The quotas associated with the long-lived MFA combined with the AGOA scheme to support the emergence of a sizeable (by African standards) garment industry on the continent (in the COMESA and SADC regions in particular). For further analysis see Goldstein *et al.*, *The Rise of China and India*, Appendix B; R. Kaplinsky and M. Morris, 'The Asian Drivers and SSA; MFA Quota Removal and the Portents for African Industrialisation?', paper prepared for the OECD Development Centre *Asian Drivers* project (forthcoming); and presentation entitled 'Nipping African Clothing in a Post-MFA Bud?' made at the joint OECD Development Centre-Standard Chartered seminar *Africa and China: Economic and Business Perspectives*, Shanghai, 16 May 2007 (http://www.oecd.org/dataoecd/55/7/38659120.pdf).

local producers.[32] Its overall welfare impact has been insufficiently investigated to date and existing work remains inconclusive.[33]

In this context still, trade opportunities ensuing from China's increasing presence on the continent are to be seized. Considerable room for improvement exists with respect to exploiting African natural resources in a sustainable manner. Making the case for diversifying African economies should not indeed preclude a more efficient exploitation of available natural resources on the African continent, especially once African relative factor endowments are factored in.[34] A sizeable commodity potential remains untapped on the continent, because these resources are costly to extract. But investment has recently become feasible as the prices of commodities have recovered thanks, *inter alia*, to the demands of the Asian drivers. The latter are also providing investments of resource-seeking nature that are complementary to imports from Africa and that could help unleash the African commodity potential. There is also considerable room for improving the efficiency and productivity of primary agricultural production in Africa (e.g. through greater use of fertilizers and modern techniques). At this stage, Africa's primary agricultural exports exhibit no obvious complementarities with China's current imports of primary agricultural goods. Yet, things might evolve with changes in Chinese dietary habits. As a result, opportunities might be seized

---

32 On competition exerted by Chinese products in African regional markets vis-à-vis local producers, see P. Kamau, 'The Developmental Impact of Asian Drivers on Kenya with Emphasis on Textiles and Clothing Manufacturing', paper prepared for the OECD Development Centre *Asian Drivers* project (forthcoming).

33 C. Edwards and R. Jenkins, *The Effect of China and India's Growth and Trade Liberalisation on Poverty in Africa* (IDS/Enterplan, 2005); J. Kennan and C. Stevens, 'Opening the Package: the Asian Drivers and Poor-Country Trade', mimeo, Institute for Development Studies, Sussex, 2005).

34 While initial patterns of relative factors endowments are not governed by inexorable fate, Mayer and Fajarnes point to the very limited changes in them in Africa (in particular relative endowments of land, labour and skilled labour) over time, and do not expect a dramatic decline in the share of commodities in African exports. J. Mayer and P. Fajarnes, 'Africa's Exports of Primary Commodities: Endowments, 'New' International Trade Geography and 'Old' Market Access and Entry Conditions', mimeo (Geneva: UNCTAD, 2005).

by African countries in agriculture and agro-processing. For instance, should the expected growing Chinese demand for meat materialize and part of it be met by local producers, China's imports of animal feed would increase. They may also be broadened from soya beans to maize, a commodity produced by several African countries.

Finally, the policy framework must be adjusted to the emergence of China as a significant trade partner of the African continent as well as a strong competitor on third markets. China may directly and indirectly help Africa unleash its commodity potential, but without improved management of its revenues, this would fail to foster sustained development. Countries rich in natural resources should regard the latter as assets that are certainly exhaustible but which may be used to develop new areas of competitive advantage, diversify the economy, create linkages with other productive sectors, and remove development bottlenecks.[35]

If unleashing the existing commodity potential is the most feasible and judicious option in the short/medium term, the persistent volatility in commodity prices and the exhaustibility of natural resources underline the urgency of diversifying the bases of African economies. Rethinking diversification strategies with the objective of avoiding direct competition with Chinese products and bolstering sectors that are complementary to Chinese growth should be encouraged. Improved access to the Chinese market for African products will be essential in this respect. China's at-the-border protection is now low and its tariff profile is relatively favourable to African products. But access to the Chinese market for African products is still impeded by tariff escalation in such key sectors as food, beverages and tobacco or textiles and leather, and by significant non-tariff barriers.[36] Also, supporting diversification strategies should translate into a clear

---

35 F. Bonaglia and K. Fukasaku, 'Export Diversification in Low-Income Countries: An International Challenge after Doha', *OECD Development Centre Working Papers*, No. 209 (Paris: OECD, 2003).

36 See Phil Alves, 'Trade and Market Access: Can China and Africa Cooperate?', presentation at a seminar entitled 'China in Africa in the 21st Century: Preparing for the Forum on China-Africa Cooperation', convened by South African Institute of International Affairs, Johannesburg, 16-17 October 2006.

commitment of OECD countries to uphold trade preferences. In clothing, for instance, a comprehensive revision of rules of origin should be undertaken so as to increase the effectiveness of such schemes as the AGOA and Everything But Arms, and ensure their ability to cushion effectively the impact of China's competition. G-8 countries should provide effective duty free and quota free access to all African goods, thereby providing African countries with a genuine competitive edge over intrinsically more competitive Asian competitors.

2

'FLYING GEESE' OR 'HIDDEN DRAGON'? CHINESE BUSINESS AND AFRICAN INDUSTRIAL DEVELOPMENT

Deborah Bräutigam

China's economic interest in Africa has generated considerable interest among analysts of development in those two world regions. Unease with China's expanded presence on the continent is reflected in comments such as that made in 2006 by Trevor Ncube, a Zimbabwean newspaper publisher living in South Africa: 'They are all over the place. If the British were our masters yesterday, the Chinese have come and taken their place.'[1] Newspaper headlines focus on the costs and benefits of China's investment in Africa's extractive industries—petroleum, copper, timber, platinum, and iron—or on China's contribution to the arms trade and the supply of inexpensive consumer goods that offer tough competition for African manufacturers.[2] Chinese leaders have tried to put these fears to rest. During

---

1 Craig Timberg, 'In Africa, China Trade Brings Growth, Unease,' *Washington Post*, 13 June 2006, p. A 14.

2 See, for example: Joseph J. Schatz, 'Zambian Hopeful Takes a Swing at China: Presidential Challenger Stirs Resentment at Asian Power's Growing Influence in Africa,' *Washington Post*, 25 September 2006; Frank Ching, 'China's African Empire,' *The Globe and Mail* (Canada), 4 January 2007;

his 2006 tour of Africa, Chinese President Hu Jintao told Nigerians that 'China's development will not bring a threat to anyone, but, instead, will only bring more opportunities and space for development to the world.'[3] Might the increased Chinese presence play a positive role by providing a model for low-tech industrial development, stimulating the spin-off of manufacturing, or acting to jump start local investment?

There is ample precedent for such a role. Japanese firms sparked an industrial boom in Southeast Asia in just this way, and Korean firms were central to the rapid expansion of manufacturing in Bangladesh.[4] The international product cycle operates in a manner whereby countries transit from the production of lower technology goods to higher technology goods, over time. Countries move from textiles and simple assembly to more complex products, as they move up the learning curve. As an illustration, after the Second World War Japan began producing textiles and auto parts at home and exporting them to Thailand where Chinese business networks distributed and sold the goods. By the 1960s, higher labour costs and trade quotas pushed the Japanese to move into direct production in Thailand, where they provided a stimulus for investment by example, and where they established joint ventures with their ethnic Chinese distributors. Finally, by the 1980s, few Japanese firms were producing textiles in Thailand: they had been bought out by their ethnic Chinese partners who by then dominated the industry.[5] Auto parts have been slower to make such a transition, but here too ethnic Chinese firms in Thailand have accelerated production. In Asia, Japan was the leader of this 'flying geese' model.[6]

'China Denies Charges of Milking Africa of its Rich Resources,' *The Press Trust of India*, 12 March 2007.

3   Quoted in Timberg, 'In Africa, China Trade'.

4   For discussions of these earlier Asian experiences, see Kunio Yoshihara, *The Rise of Ersatz Capitalism in South East Asia* (Oxford University Press, 1988) and Yung Whee Rhee, 'The Catalyst Model of Development: Lessons from Bangladesh's Success with Garment Exports', *World Development* 18, 2 (February 1990), pp. 333-46.

5   Yoshihara, *Rise of Ersatz Capitalism*, p. 19.

6   On the 'flying geese model', see Kiyoshi Kojima, 'The "Flying Geese" Model of Asian Economic Development: Origin, Theoretical Extensions, and Regional Policy Implications', *Journal of Asian Economics* 11, 4 (Winter

As the research reported below illustrates, the origins of some of sub-Saharan Africa's manufacturing success stories can be traced to the catalytic effect of investment by and the example of Chinese industrialists. Will Chinese firms in Africa be catalytic 'flying geese' or is China more likely to play the role of a 'hidden dragon', with Chinese exports helping through competition to complete the process of de-industrialization that some argue has been the result of the African continent's trade liberalization? This chapter sheds light on these questions.[7] It draws primarily on the author's research in Mauritius and in Nigeria, but adds examples gleaned from other research on this topic. In the first case, ethnic Chinese entrepreneurs living in Mauritius helped persuade the government to establish an export processing zone, and then travelled to Asia, inviting co-ethnics from Taiwan, Hong Kong, Malaysia, and (later) mainland China to join them in joint ventures. These investments exposed Mauritians (both Chinese and non-Chinese) to the intricacies of global production and export processes, which led to dynamic, export-oriented manufacturing growth. In the second case, Nigerian entrepreneurs in the eastern Nigerian town of Nnewi used their connections to ethnic Chinese trading networks (first in Taiwan, but later across Asia) to assist in the transition from importing auto spare parts to producing them, creating a small industrial boom. Both cases suggest that important, positive externalities can result from Chinese business linkages with Africa. However, while the Mauritius case can be seen as an extra-Asian example of the global reach of Chinese business networks and their stimulating impact, the Nigerian (and Lesotho) cases suggest that domestic factors may still present significant obstacles to any transfer of the Asian 'flying geese' model to African industry. Furthermore, both Mauritian and Nigerian firms have been hurt by competition from

2000), pp. 375-401. For a critical perspective on the model, see Martin Hart-Landsberg and Paul Burkett, 'Contradictions of Capitalist Industrialization in East Asia: a Critique of "Flying Geese" Theories of Development', *Economic Geography*, 74, 2 (April 1998), pp. 87-110.

7   The cases in this chapter are drawn in part from on an earlier article of mine: Deborah Bräutigam, 'Close Encounters: Chinese Business Networks as Industrial Catalysts in Sub-Saharan Africa', *African Affairs* 102, 408 (July 2003), pp. 447-67.

China, which has led some to fear that Chinese business indeed poses more of a 'hidden dragon' threat than an opportunity.

The context: Chinese investment in Africa

In the 1970s and 1980s, Chinese firms from Taiwan and Hong Kong began to establish closer business ties in Africa, leading in some cases to investment. After 1985, when China relaxed its emigration policies, and particularly after 2001, when Beijing promoted the 'Going Global' policy, they were joined by firms from the Chinese mainland. By early 2007, the Chinese reported that there were more than 800 mainland Chinese companies operating in Africa; some 700 of these were run by private individuals and the rest were medium to large state-owned firms.[8] Although Chinese investments in natural resources have gained more media and scholarly attention, manufacturing firms are also important. Between 1979 and 2001, before the current boom, Chinese firms had already established 230 manufacturing investments in Africa (including North Africa).[9] South Africa received the main share, 83 investment projects, but there was already a significant mainland Chinese presence in Nigeria (33), Kenya (21), Mauritius (20), Ghana (17) and Zambia (17). The Chinese mainly invested in light industry, but there were also significant concentrations in electric appliances and spinning and weaving. Companies from Guangdong Province produced ethyl alcohol in Benin, sewing machines in South Africa, motors in Angola, and batteries in Mozambique.[10] A Zhejiang Province firm, Hasan Shoes, has produced a quarter of its output in Nigeria since 2006, and a Chinese factory is producing paper in Tanzania.[11] The pioneering Chinese white

---

8 'Africa to be more attractive for Chinese investors', *Xinhua*, 2 February 2007.

9 The information in this and the next few sentences is from World Bank, 'Patterns of Africa-Asia Trade and Investment: Potential for Ownership and Partnership', Africa Region, Private Sector Unit, prepared for the Asia-Africa Trade and Investment Conference (AATIC), Tokyo, 1-2 November 2004, p. 63.

10 'Chinese Companies Encouraged to Invest in Africa', *People's Daily*, 31 October 2000.

11 'When 'Made in China' become [sic] 'Made in Africa', *Xinhua*, 22 December

goods firm Haier (a worker-owned 'collective') produces household appliances in an Angolan factory with 700 employees.[12] Since 2005, investors from Henan province have filled the Guoji [International] Industrial Entry Zone in Sierra Leone, where factories produce mattresses, roofing tiles, and hair lotions in a factory zone jointly established by the local government and the Henan Guoji Industry and Development Corporation.[13] The Hisense group from Qingdao Province began by exporting black and white televisions and electrical appliances to South Africa in 1993, moving into a joint venture to assemble televisions and DVD players in 1997. In 2007, Hisense announced that they would build Hisense Industrial Park in South Africa to expand their production of colour televisions, refrigerators and washing machines for the southern Africa market.[14]

These manufacturing investments are set to increase. The Chinese are convinced that Africa is ripe for opportunity, and 'the early bird catches the worm.'[15] At the Beijing Summit of the Forum of China-African Cooperation in November 2006, the Chinese announced the establishment of a $5 billion development fund to encourage Chinese firms to invest in Africa. The Chairman of the Sichuan Hongda Group commented that competition in China is now 'so fierce' that new businesses find it 'difficult to get a toehold, but Africa is a huge market and the investment environment there keeps improving.'[16] A 2005 World Bank survey of 150 Chinese firms in eight Chinese

---

2006.

12 Renato Eguilar and Andrea Goldstein, 'The Asian Drivers and Angola', unpublished paper, March 2007, p. 12.

13 Andrew Child and David White, 'Chinese Investors Target Virgin Markets', *Financial Times* 15 March 2005, p. 12; 'Sierra Leonean President expects more Chinese investment', *Xinhua News Agency* 7 November 2006.

14 'China's Hisense to Build Industrial Park in South Africa', *Xinhua News Agency*, 21 January 2007; China Facts and Figures, 'Chinese Enterprises in Africa', 10 December 2003, http://www.china.org.cn/english/features/China-Africa/82043.htm [accessed 10 January, 2007].

15 Zhao Zhongqui, China's Economic and Commercial Counsellor in Freetown, quoted in Child and White, 'Chinese Investors Target Virgin Markets'.

16 'China, Africa to encourage co-op in private sector,' *Xinhua*, 23 October 2006.

cities with plans to invest abroad found that 18 per cent of them were planning to invest in Africa, and of these, 45 per cent were interested in manufacturing.[17] Will this new wave of investment displace existing industries, or will these firms form forward and backward linkages and stimulate technology transfer in the 'flying geese' model? The case of Mauritius provides a positive example.

Ethnic Chinese business networks and industry in Mauritius

Chinese business networks are responsible for some of the information, ideas and capital that helped launch Mauritius, a small island nation in the Indian Ocean, as an important centre for export-oriented industry in Southern Africa. Chinese were among the earlier settlers in multi-ethnic Mauritius, a country that was uninhabited when it was first discovered and settled by Europeans. Some of the region's earliest factories were established by Chinese: tobacco processing (1874) and alcohol distillation (1897).[18] By 1925, Chinese manufacturers were producing shoes and boots, rum, and aloe bags for shipping sugar.

Chinese entrepreneurs in Mauritius maintained close ties with their homeland and unlike the bulk of the population (descendants of enslaved Africans and former indentured workers from the Indian subcontinent), they had the resources to make visits back to their ancestral places of origin, often to find spouses. The case of Sir Edouard Lim Fat demonstrates how helpful these ties were for the industrial transition in Mauritius. In 1970, Mauritius became one of the first developing countries to establish a duty-free, tax-free export processing zone (EPZ). An engineering professor at the University of Mauritius and also a businessman, Dr Lim Fat was one of the early visionaries pushing for the establishment of an EPZ.[19] The Lim Fat family was originally from the Canton area, and Dr Lim Fat's in-

---

17 Harry G. Broadman, *Africa's Silk Road: China and India's New Economic Frontier* (Washington, DC: World Bank, 2007), p. 99.

18 Lim Fat, 'Contribution of the Chinese'.

19 Interview, Professor Sir Edouard Lim Fat, Port Louis, Mauritius, 19 April 1999; see also Dick Chan, 'Mauritius wants to be Hong Kong', *South China Morning Post* (Hong Kong), 23 January 1995.

laws were mainland Chinese who fled to Taiwan after 1949; it was there that Dr Lim Fat became interested in the export processing zones through his diaspora connections and social networks.

Shortly after the Export Processing Zone Act was passed in 1970, Sino-Mauritians such as Dr Lim Fat travelled to Asia, 'taking advantage of [their] numerous personal contacts in these Far Eastern lands' to promote the EPZ 'with ceaseless missionary zeal.'[20] Other Mauritian Chinese moved to invest in the EPZ, often with joint ventures forged through their networks in Asia. The success of Sino-Mauritians business networks showed in the percentage of Hong Kong equity capital invested in the EPZ: more than 90 per cent in the early years.[21] By 1982 there were more than 115 EPZ firms, and 59 per cent of the capital invested in the EPZ was from Hong Kong Chinese.[22] The EPZ boomed again after 1983 when uncertainty gripped Hong Kong as Great Britain negotiated the return of Hong Kong to China. The appeal of the Chinese overseas network in making Mauritius a destination for Hong Kong capital was clear: 'The Hong Kong investor who comes here does not feel so much like a stranger as he would in Africa. He sees Chinese faces, he eats Chinese food, his wife has someone to talk to.'[23]

Early in the life of the EPZs, joint ventures between East Asian and local investors were common, although this was not a requirement for foreign investment. Joint ventures appealed both to local whites (Franco-Mauritians) who had amassed capital in the sugar

20 L.M. Lim, 'Hong Kong and the free zone', *L'Express* (Port Louis, Mauritius), 11 July 1997. See also Michael Young, 'Mauritian development strategy: Hong Kong is the model', *The Financial Times*, 5 May 1971.

21 Many of the Asian industrialists brought in used machinery from Asia, but valued it at the price of new equipment; thus the value of this Asian investment may have been inflated (personal communication, anonymous reviewer).

22 Roland Lamusse, 'The Breakthrough in Export-processing Industrialization in Mauritius', Boston, African-American Issues Center Discussion Paper No. 13, no date, c1985.

23 Comment by Philippe Chan Kin, former chairman of the Mauritius Export Processing Zone Association, in Blaine Harden, 'Mauritius breaks out of Africa's poverty: free export zone works wonders for tiny island', *Los Angeles Times*, 21 November 1988.

industry and Sino-Mauritians who had become wealthy through trade and local manufacturing. Because Mauritians had the desire to learn the business, while the Asian firms needed risk-sharing and the local knowledge and contacts, joint ventures were genuine, not 'paper' partnerships. The importance of the initial capital and information links with Chinese businesses clearly made the EPZ concept a success. Those links were critical for transferring information that would lower the risks and costs to Mauritians of embarking on export-oriented industry. A Sino-Mauritian analyst pointed this out in a 1997 article: 'Most of [the local investors] were ex-partners or employees of EPZ firms who over the years had acquired the necessary experience and know-how from the Hong Kong industrialists in such vital areas as international marketing, the latest technology and large scale industrial production and management, and felt confident enough to start their own EPZ enterprises.'[24]

This was the 'flying geese' model in action. In time, many local Mauritians invested in the EPZ. By the late 1980s, more than half of the equity in the EPZ was local (mainly Franco- and Sino-Mauritian, but with important Muslim and Hindu participation) and Mauritius had become the third largest exporter of 'Woolmark' knitwear in the world. Support industries producing boxes, thread, buttons, and packaging materials for export firms had also grown. By 1997, Mauritian owners accounted for about 60 per cent of the capital invested in export manufacturing in Mauritius.[25]

As mainland Chinese firms began to increase their investments in Africa, they explored possibilities in Mauritius, assisted in many cases by their government. In 1999, for example, Chairman Li Peng brought a delegation of 125 people to Mauritius, including a number of business owners. Table 1 shows that between 1990 and 1994, and in the years 2001-5, investments by Chinese mainland firms in Mauritius overtook those from Taiwan, Hong Kong, and Singapore. In 2003, a mainland Chinese company (Shanxi Province's Tianli Group, Ltd) invested more than US$10 million to open a cotton yarn spin-

---

24 Lim, 'Hong Kong and the free zone'".

25 'L'Apport Hongkongais Dans La ZF', *L'Express* (Port Louis, Mauritius), 1 July 1997.

ning mill in Mauritius to supply export companies with locally made raw materials. When investment from Hong Kong, Singapore, and Taiwan fell, that from mainland China rose (Table 1).

(Rs million)

	1990-95	2000-06
Hong Kong	185	50
Singapore	40	14
Taiwan	92	0
China	35	89
Total FDI in EPZ	981	513

Table 1: Foreign Direct Investment in Mauritius by China and Chinese Diaspora
Source: Bank of Mauritius, *Annual Report*, 2005-2006, p. 258.
Note: not all of the Asian FDI goes to the EPZ sector.

Overall, the nature of these ethnic Chinese ties was clearly one of close connections leading to a transfer of technology through investment and its accompanying training, and the diffusion of trained personnel and managers to other firms in the EPZ sector. Ethnic Chinese have served as 'flying geese' for Mauritians, often bringing as part of their investment in used factories from areas where labour had become more expensive or political conditions less certain. But has China also been a 'hidden dragon' in Mauritius, withering local industry under the competition from its low-cost products?

The Chinese competition that opened up with the December 2004 ending of the Multi-Fibre Arrangement has had a painful impact on the textile industry in Mauritius. Between 2000 and 2005, the sector contracted by about 30 per cent. Firms closed and up to twenty-five thousand workers lost their jobs.[26] By 2006, there were almost no Hong Kong Chinese investors left, although some of their factories

---

26 Government of Mauritius, Central Statistical Office. In December 2004, some 13,792 employees in the sector were expatriates, most being Chinese nationals.

had been bought out by Mauritian entrepreneurs. Mauritians were claiming that the restructuring had largely been completed by 2006, with the remaining Mauritian firms moving upmarket or, in the case of several, building factories in lower cost countries: Madagascar, India, and even China itself.[27] These firms had looked the dragon in the face and decided not just to fight it, but to join it. Several of the large, competitive and vertically integrated textile companies had made significant new investments in China itself: Star Knitwear and Compagnie Mauricienne de Textile. In March 2007, the Chinese and Mauritian governments announced that Mauritius (Riche-Terre) had been chosen as the site of the second of three to five Chinese industrial export zones to be constructed in Africa between 2007 and 2010 (the first was launched in Zambia).[28] In this case, the 2 km square zone will be constructed by the same Tianli Group, which will spend €350 million (with help from the Chinese government).

The early industrial investments by Chinese manufacturers in Mauritius fostered a local industry that grew rapidly and over thirty-five years was gradually transformed into a shared foreign/local affair. However, in another case of Chinese catalysts, industrialization relied more on indigenous Africans, who took steps to travel to Asia and brought the information and resources they needed to make their own moves into industry. The case of auto parts in Nnewi, Nigeria, illustrates how this happened without any foreign investment on the part of the Chinese.

Ethnic Chinese business and industry in Nnewi, Nigeria

Until the 1980s, generally motor spare parts sold in Nigeria either came from the 'original' manufacturer (Peugeot, Mercedes, etc.) or were counterfeit copies made in Taiwan. However, early in that decade, a number of factories sprang up in the eastern region of Nigeria,

27 Author's Interview, General Manager, Floreal Textile, July 2005; David White, 'In search of a new league', Mauritius Report, *Financial Times*, 14 March 2006. David White, 'Survival in a cut-throat world', Mauritius Report, *Financial Times*, 14 March 2006.

28 Sithanen, 'Le projet de Tianli realise à partir de cette année', *L'Express* (Port Louis, Mauritius), 12 March 2007.

particularly in the town of Nnewi, whose large Nkwo market for used and new motor spare parts had grown into one of the largest in the country, with offshoots in many other towns and cities across Nigeria. By 2004 there were more than 17 modern, large and medium-sized factories in Nnewi, using imported technology and producing a wide variety of spare parts for cars, lorries, and motorcycles.[29] Together with engineering firms and machine shops, a number of aluminium foundries, and 68 smaller, less formal factories also producing spare parts, these businesses employed some 8-9,000 persons.[30] Some of these factories exported to neighbouring countries in West Africa, to the Middle East, and even to Europe. One advertised in the Abidjan, Côte d'Ivoire phone directory. The manufacturing boom attracted attention both in and outside Nigeria.

Contacts between Nnewi traders and their Chinese counterparts in Taiwan proved the major catalyst to industrialization. Spare parts for the Nnewi market network were imported primarily from Europe at first, but by the 1960s Asian distributors began to frequent the Nkwo market, offering to produce copies of the European 'original' brand name parts. The first Asian firms were Japanese, but they were rapidly supplanted by Chinese traders from Taiwan. Over time, Nnewi motor parts traders arranged to have their own brand name products made in Taiwan. During the 1970s, many Nigerian traders travelled to Asia to meet their suppliers, and were thus exposed to the industrial dynamism of the Asian newly industrialised countries, as well as the many small and medium firms still operating in Taiwan. The contrast with Dr Lim Fat's travels to Taiwan from Mauritius is instructive, however. Dr Lim Fat noticed export processing zones, and eventually persuaded the government in Mauritius to pass legislation establishing such an institution in Mauritius. He and other Sino-Mauritians travelled to Asia in part to persuade Chinese

---

29 For an extensive discussion of the Nnewi industrialization experience, see Deborah Bräutigam, 'Substituting for the State: Institutions and Industrial Development in Eastern Nigeria', *World Development* 25, 7, (1997), pp. 1063-80 and Banyi Oyelaran-Oyeyinka, *Nnewi: An Emergent Industrial Cluster in Nigeria* (Ibadan: Technopol Publishers, 1997).

30 Ikenna Emewu, 'Nigerian Government is Anti-Industry, Say Manufacturers', *Daily Sun* (Nigeria), 4 December 2004 [www.sunnewsonline.com].

co-ethnics to invest in Mauritius. Many did, reassured in part by the extended family and professional connections made through the Chinese diaspora. On the other hand, the Nnewi traders used their contacts with the Chinese in Nigeria to locate distributors and producers in Asia, with whom they could trade and, later, from whom they could purchase machinery and technical assistance. Without those contacts, the transition to manufacturing might not have happened, but in contrast to Mauritius, there have been no joint ventures of Chinese and Nigerians and no Chinese investment in Nnewi, and the Nnewi traders made no effort to change an unfavourable national level policy regime.

The contacts between the Nnewi manufacturers and the Chinese traders and manufacturers in Taiwan and elsewhere primarily enabled the diffusion of information and example. As the CEO of Edison Auto Industries, a manufacturer of brake linings and brake fluid commented, 'For eight years I imported these things [from Asia] and saw how simple they were to make.' He moved into manufacturing after studying machinery and processes in use by his supplier firms in Asia. All of the traders who established factories between 1983 and 1996 continued to maintain their trading business and distribution networks in Nigeria, and simply added their new brands to existing lines that they continued to import from Taiwan and elsewhere in Asia.

The networks of contacts established during years of trade eased the Nnewi entrepreneurs' task of gathering information about production. One manufacturer who had imported many lines of spare parts made in Taiwan solicited bids for machinery from a number of Chinese firms in Taiwan with which he had grown familiar. In other cases, the Nnewi entrepreneurs asked for recommendations from their Chinese networks for technical advisers to install the factories and train local people. Some companies, such as a producer of melded plastic components, sent groups of workers to Shenzhen and elsewhere in Asia for on-the-job training in Chinese factories. Others used their contacts with trading companies to identify Chinese manufacturers who were ready to sell used equipment, such as the oil filter manufacturer who purchased the entire plant of his Singapore supplier.

The Nnewi case demonstrates that it is possible for ideas and information about industry to be transferred from Chinese firms in Asia to African entrepreneurs, facilitating the development of dynamic manufacturing sectors. The relationship between the network of Nnewi spare parts traders and the Taiwanese manufacturers in the 1960s and 1970s resembles closely the early 'flying geese' relationship between Japanese manufacturers and Chinese business networks in Southeast Asia described above. However, in the absence of significant Chinese investment in the region, there were limits to the transfer of knowledge and the building of the kind of multiple strands (family ties, social and cultural celebrations, exchanges of credit, etc.) that characterize business networks among people from the same cultural group, as in Mauritius. Because of this, the Nnewi trader-industrialists lacked the extra advantage of the kind of learning opportunities possible for Mauritians, who had many joint ventures with, and professional opportunities to work in, overseas Chinese firms set up in the Mauritian EPZ—although they have compensated for this in part by a widespread practice of using foreign technical assistance. In 2004, for example, Nnewi firms each hosted an average of four foreign technical staff.[31]

How have firms in Nnewi fared against the competition of Chinese imports? Auto spare parts do not receive much protection from the Nigerian government, unlike textile manufacturers, for example, who have operated under a nearly complete ban on imports. The average tariff on auto parts was reduced to approximately 5 per cent in the trade liberalization of the country's structural adjustment programme (SAP) in the early 1990s. Even with local manufacturing firms close by, the Nkwo market in Nnewi continued to host visits from Asian traders who offered to copy 'original' spare parts in their home factories, increasingly located in China's special economic zones. Branded counterfeit parts, or those that are close copies but made in China, sell at very competitive prices. For example, in 2006, spark plugs made in China, counterfeit copies of those made by Toyota

---

31 Boladale Abiola, 'Knowledge, Technology, and Growth: The Case Study of Nnewi Auto Parts Cluster in Nigeria', Knowledge for Development (K4D) Program, World Bank Institute, World Bank, Washington, DC, 2006, p. 14.

or the American firm Motorcraft, sold at N55 compared with N220 for the original. Chinese branded parts intended to compete with the original manufacturer were also sold at prices less than half the original: China's 'Super Filter' sold for N200, while the original 'Bolus' or 'Dorian' oil filter sold for N550.[32] Local manufacturers have accused these Asian exporters of 'dumping' when they are able to consistently offer products at prices lower than the Nigerians can match. A 2006 study of Nnewi manufacturers found that 75 per cent of the firms ranked the Asian challenge as 'very severe'.[33] By 2006 China was Nigeria's largest source of imports, and the competition looked set only to increase. At the same time, some sixty Chinese firms had invested in Nigeria, in textiles, agro-processing, and a number of other sectors in addition to resource extraction.[34] The governments of Anambra, Benue, and Taraba States in Nigeria have entered into joint ventures to produce cement, woven bags, sugar, purified water, and machine tools with the Gongji Cangxi Industry and Commerce Development Company (a Henan province township enterprise that produces machinery for juice and vegetable oil extraction, concrete, and nails).[35] These new investments may have more potential for 'flying geese' spin-offs, given the rich entrepreneurial culture and skills in Nigeria.

Discussion and conclusions

As of 2007, there has been very limited fieldwork on the impact of mainland Chinese investment in Africa, but we do have other studies of ethnic Chinese investment (mainly Taiwan). These suggest that the catalytic effect of industrial investment may be limited to

---

32 Olatunji Ololade, 'A Fake Way to Die', *Tellmagazine* (Nigeria) http://www. tellng.com/news/articles/060629-4 /news/Sprep_deathtyres.html [accessed 19 October 2006].

33 Abiola, 'Knowledge, Technology, and Growth', p. 21.

34 'Nigeria-China Business and Investment Forum 2006,' http://www.invest. net.cn/news/ni2006/interview/index-2.html

35 Gongji Cangxi Industry and Commerce Development Company website, http://chinacangxi.com/english/ [accessed 31 March 2007]. Among these, the foundry and machine tools project was considered 'foreign aid', and supported by China's Foreign Trade Economy Cooperation Department [sic] according to the company's website.

countries and regions where conditions are particularly conducive. Sanjaya Lall's study of Taiwanese investment in the apparel industry in Lesotho found that not a single local entrepreneur followed the Asian investors into manufacturing:

...knowledge spillovers or backward linkages [are] almost wholly absent in Lesotho ... even 15 years after the first garment factory was established, almost no local firms have emerged to compete with the foreign firms, subcontract from them, or supply them with inputs like packaging or accessories ... Family owned and controlled East Asian firms have a culture that does not conduce to local skill creation or local participation at high levels. Work at these levels is conducted almost wholly in Chinese. The tendency to bring in textile workers from China reduces skill transfers and promotion at the shop-floor level ... suspicion and hostility on the part of the local population to the Chinese ... prevents the creation of greater trust and social capital.[36]

On the other hand, Gillian Hart's research on Taiwanese networks in South Africa provided an anecdote of a black South African entrepreneur, a technician who set up an informal company to subcontract to his former Taiwanese employer.[37]

The 'flying geese' model of dynamism that underpinned industrialization in Southeast Asia depended on several factors that are only unevenly observed across Africa. First, it required local investment by the 'lead goose' and joint ventures that spread knowledge to capable local entrepreneurs. We see some of this in Mauritius, none in the case of Nnewi, and while there is some evidence that joint ventures are on the rise, they seem to be primarily with governments, not indigenous entrepreneurs (this could be changing, however). Second, it required a 'push' from the home country: in the case of Japan, it was sharply rising labour costs that created an additional incentive to seek sites for offshore production. Chinese labour costs are similar to those prevailing in many African countries, and productivity is a good deal higher. However, there are some countries where com-

---

36 Sanjaya Lall, 'FDI, AGOA and Manufactured Exports by a Landlocked, Least Developed African Economy: Lesotho,' *Journal of Development Studies* 41, 6 (August 2005), pp. 998-1022.

37 Gillian Hart, *Disabling Globalization: Places of Power in Post-Apartheid South Africa* (Berkeley: University of California Press, 2002).

parisons indicate some potential for competitive advantage. In the spinning and weaving industry, for example, average 2004-5 costs per operator hour in coastal China were US$0.76, in Mauritius they were US$1.57, but in Kenya costs were only US$0.67.[38]

Another requirement for a 'flying geese' model to work is the policy environment in the host country. The rapidly growing Southeast Asian countries had a variety of policy frameworks, but all were investment- and export-friendly. Without supportive investment policies, relationships between Chinese entrepreneurs and those in Africa will generally be limited to trade, and when investment is shunned, the transfer of technology and learning is made much more difficult. Mauritius has implemented policies very similar to those in place in East and Southeast Asia's most dynamic countries. A well-working export processing zone is one aspect of this policy framework, but EPZs do not work in a vacuum. General economic policies also mattered. Mauritius and the Southeast Asian examples highlight the fact that although an economy with a high proportion of trade is often labelled 'open', these 'open' trading economies are not necessarily 'liberal' in the sense of 'free markets'. In both, exchange rate policies and other, more interventionist policies strongly encouraged exports, while at the same time many aspects of production for the domestic market were protected. Trade and capital account liberalization has happened in most of the Southeast Asian countries (and in Mauritius), but it has been for the most part quite gradual, and does not characterize the early years when export-oriented industry was first established. On the other hand, Nigeria and many other African countries have generally failed to establish an environment that would allow either domestic industry or export-oriented firms to thrive and grow. This may also be changing. The Chinese have repeatedly said that they believe conditions to be favourable for investment in much of Africa. In Sierra Leone, Chinese entrepreneurs commented favourably on the preferential tax policies adopted by the

---

38 Werner International, 'Spinning and Weaving Labor Cost Comparisons, Winter 2004/2005', Werner International Management Consultants, Herndon, Virginia, 2005.

local government.[39] At the same time, however, trade liberalization that exposes inefficient local industries to competition with Chinese imports may pose stark difficulties for infant industries. In one case, ironically, a Zambian textile factory established three decades ago with Chinese aid was forced out of production by a wave of Chinese textile imports.[40]

Over the past three decades, Chinese businesses from Hong Kong, Taiwan, the diaspora, and now mainland China have made increasingly visible forays into sub-Saharan Africa, forging links with African capitalists and stimulating industrial transitions in areas, such as eastern Nigeria and Mauritius, that had shown little industrial development before. A World Bank study published in 2007 found that most of the mainland Chinese investment has occurred since 2000; it is primarily 'greenfield' investment, which creates new jobs; investors are mainly branches of parent firms with headquarters in China's provinces, and many of the firms are more vertically integrated than other companies operating in Africa—a finding that may make skill and technology transfer more difficult.[41] In a reflection of the close business-government ties characteristic of Asian capitalism, the government in Beijing has fostered the growing interest in Africa, inviting private sector representatives to join high level government officials in delegations that have visited African countries (like Mauritius) and deepened the contacts between businesses in the two regions.

The case of Mauritius shows that Asian networks in a remote Indian Ocean island can have a powerful impact on a country's economic development, when the resources and information of networks are combined with supportive economic policies. Even though the early 'geese' have long since left Mauritius, the joint ventures they formed with local entrepreneurs persist and have expanded under sole Mauritian ownership. The establishment of a new enterprise

---

39 'Sierra Leone President expects more Chinese investment', *Xinhua* (Zhengzhou), 7 November 2006.

40 Chris McGreal, 'Thanks, China, now go home: buy-up of Zambia revives old colonial fears', *The Guardian*, 5 February 2007.

41 Broadman, *Africa's Silk Road*, p. 311.

zone in Mauritius will reinvigorate the networks, although the formation of an enclave will make technology transfer more difficult. The contrasting cases of Taiwanese investment in Lesotho and South Africa suggest that a supply of technically skilled local entrepreneurs will be a necessary prerequisite for the transfer of technology and the start-up of new firms. The Nnewi case shows that skilled indigenous African entrepreneurs can take advantage of contacts with Chinese firms to produce an industrial transition. However, these connections are unlikely to produce the kind of export dynamism found in Mauritius, until the policy environment becomes more conducive to exports.

3

CHINESE ECONOMIC DIPLOMACY IN AFRICA: THE LUSOPHONE STRATEGY

Ana Cristina Alves

After decades of support for local communist leaders, there are clear signs that the traditional ideological motivation behind China's African diplomacy has been replaced by a much more pragmatic one founded in its economic needs. Beijing is developing very successful economic diplomacy through cooperation, investment and trade in the African continent and by doing so is simultaneously reinforcing its role in promoting South-South dialogue and its 'soft power' in international relations. Indeed, by further advancing South-South cooperation, China may become a very important player in Africa in the near future, especially if it succeeds as an agent of development, an area where Western countries have failed for decades. China cleverly plays its assets in Africa by concurrently developing multi-dimensional strategies. One important illustration of China's regional approach to Africa is its relations with Portuguese speaking countries of Africa, or APSC: Angola, Mozambique, Guinea-Bissau and Cape Verde. Through Macau, China has established a supplementary link with these countries by using the Lusophone network left behind by the former colonial power, Portugal.[1]

The Portuguese speaking world

The legacy of Portuguese colonialism is not comparable to that left by other former colonial powers such as the United Kingdom, France or Spain, but as it encompassed four continents and Portuguese, the world's fifth language, is spoken by more than 240 million people, its imprint is nonetheless significant. There are eight Portuguese speaking countries around the world—Angola, Brazil, Cape Verde, East Timor, Guinea-Bissau, Mozambique, Portugal and Saint Tomé and Príncipe—and a few territories where Portuguese or a Portuguese dialect is also spoken (such as Macau, Goa, Damão and Diu, Melaka, or Galiza). However, from a *Realpolitik* perspective, the importance of the Portuguese speaking 'world' at the beginning of the 20th century has less to do with language than with the economic performance and resources of some of these countries. Together with Russia, India and China, Brazil is one of the four major emerging economies in the world while Angola, which has vast oil and diamond resources, was one of the fastest growing economies in the world in 2006 and 2007.

Five of the eight Portuguese speaking countries are located in Africa and only became independent in the mid-1970s. The lingering resentment against the former colonial administration is one of the reasons that explains the late creation of the Comunidade de Países de Língua Portuguesa (CPLP,[2] or Community of Portuguese Speaking Countries) in 1996, under the initiative of a Brazilian diplomat, Ambassador J. Aparecido de Oliveira, and with the support of the Portuguese government. After ten years of existence, however, despite the common heritage and goals of member states, several factors have hindered the progress of this community.[3] All member

---

1   São Tomé and Principe does not have diplomatic relations with China because of its diplomatic recognition of the Taipei government in 1997.

2   http://www.cplp.org

3   For a detailed analysis see Adelino Torres and Manuel Ennes Ferreira, 'A Comunidade dos Países de Língua Portuguesa no contexto de globalização:

states belong to different regional organizations, for instance, and those states that are expected to act as leaders cannot maximize their potential since they have diverse priorities (Brazil still faces serious issues with respect to its domestic development, while Portugal does not have extensive resources to propel its own development). Thus, the absence of political leadership and economic dynamism in a post Cold-War world framework dominated by 'market theology' mainly accounts for the modest achievements of this organisation.[4]

China's renewal of an old commitment

The end of the bipolar system of the Cold War had a deep impact upon foreign policy priorities, and one of the most obvious areas where this was apparent was the revitalization of economic issues.[5] During the 1990s, world trade grew about twice as fast as world output and FDI flows grew twice as fast as trade.[6] The process has been stimulated by new technologies that shrink distances and speed up transactions. Economies are losing their national character and public and private agents are becoming increasingly global, assembling a transnational system of production based on an international division of labour. In this new framework, economic diplomacy as a tool to promote and protect national interests has gained new importance in foreign policy strategies.

After more than two decades of economic reforms and phenomenal growth rates, China's economic diplomacy started making its first steps overseas through investment, and trade and by further regional and global engagement. China's status as a developing country and its history of exploitation by European powers, coupled with the fact that it does not attach any particular political conditions to its financial

problemas e perspectivas', in Adriano Moreira (ed.), *Comunidade dos Países de Língua Portuguesa - Cooperação*, (Coimbra: Almedina, 2001), pp. 23-119.

4   Adriano Moreira in a radio interview (TSF) on the 10th anniversary of the CPLP, 17 July 2006.

5   Although security issues have again become a matter of international importance after September 11.

6   Nicholas Bayne, 'Current Challenges to Economic Diplomacy', in Nicholas Bayne and Stephen Woolcock (eds), *The New Economic Diplomacy* (Hampshire: Ashgate, 2005) (3rd ed.), p. 86.

aid (with the exception of its 'one China' policy), gives Beijing a good hearing among African elites which regard the Chinese government as being more closely aligned to the needs of the Third World.

The new Chinese foreign policy engagement in Africa became more visible during President Jiang Zemin's tour of six African countries in May 1996. He proposed the development of a long-term, more structured cooperative relationship between China and African countries. This gave birth to the Forum for China-Africa Cooperation (FOCAC), formally institutionalized in Beijing in October 2000. The strong commitment of the Chinese central government in the creation of the Forum clearly illustrates the growing importance of economic affairs in China's relations with Africa at the beginning of the 21st century. FOCAC aims to promote cooperation in a wide range of fields: political affairs, peace and stability issues, multilateral cooperation, economic and social development.[7] Economic matters, however, have been the strongest component of the Forum since it founding. In the first six years of existence, China cooperation has become widely visible all around Africa, particularly in agriculture, infrastructure construction, trade, investment, development aid, human and natural resources development and debt relief.

The Lusophone strategy within China's foreign policy towards Africa

The existence of FOCAC, however, does not constrain Beijing in developing additional strategies to deepen its relations with specific countries, and this is illustrated well in the case of the African Portuguese speaking countries: Angola, Mozambique, Cape Verde and Guinea Bissau. These countries, which are also part of FOCAC, in fact share a very old connection with China through the centuries of Portuguese colonial rule over the enclave of Macau that left behind a bond based on the Portuguese language and culture as well as administrative structures and a legal framework.

Portugal's African colonies were the last to achieve independence in Africa, right after the military coup in April 1974 that brought the

---

7 'China-African Forum reaches action plan', www.china.com.cn/english/international/82640.htm

dictatorship in Portugal to an end. China, however, did not accept the handover of Macau at that time. The Chinese leaders did not consider Macau to be a colony but a territory under foreign rule like Hong Kong, and favoured the handover of the British controlled territory first as it was more important to them. China's negotiations with Portugal to return Macau to Chinese sovereignty followed the pattern established by the China-Britain talks. Under the principle of 'one country, two systems', Macau's handover took place on 19 December 1999, two years after Hong Kong's.

The new executive government of Macau was initially very cautious in handling the Portuguese heritage and was afraid that it could somehow damage its relation with the central government in Beijing.[8] In 2002, the Chinese central government itself directed Macau's Chief Executive to reinforce and take advantage of the Portuguese identity of the territory. In fact, it was under the initiative of the Chinese Ministry of Commerce that Macau became the headquarters of the Forum for Economic Cooperation and Trade between China and Portuguese Speaking Countries in October 2003. This new framework gave China the formal institutional means to maximize the potential of Macau as a special channel for cooperation and investment in those countries.

This trans-regional Forum aims at promoting mutual development by enhancing economic cooperation and trade between China and Portuguese speaking countries.[9] Eight countries were present at the founding meeting that took place on 12-14 October 2003 in Macau: China, Portugal, Brazil, Angola, Mozambique, Cape Verde, Guinea Bissau and East Timor, plus Macau as part of the Chinese delegation. Each country was represented by a delegation composed by governmental and business representatives, with China represented by the Deputy Premier, Wu Yi, and the Deputy Minister for Com-

---

8   According to interviews conducted in Macau in April 2001 and September 2003 among relevant local Chinese Macanese and Portuguese personalities, for a research project on the first five years of Macau as a Special Administrative Region.

9   According to the Chinese Deputy Minister for Commerce discourse at the closing session of this first Ministerial Conference in October 2003. http://www.ipim.gov.mo/pt/relation/r1.htm

merce, An Min. The ministerial meeting approved an action plan based on information exchange, improving the investment environment, promotion of trade and joint ventures, and the diversification of cooperation to agriculture, infrastructure construction and natural and human resource development.[10] It also decided that a ministerial meeting of the Forum would take place in Macau every three years and called for the creation of a permanent secretariat based in Macau, which came into existence in April 2004. The organizing committee was jointly presided over by the Chinese Minister for Commerce and Macau's Chief Executive.

The Permanent Secretariat (PS), based in Macau, is made up of staff from Macau's executive government and MOFCOM cadres and is responsible for the coordination and implementation of the agreements. The PS reports directly to Taiwan, Hong Kong and Macau Affairs department in MOFCOM and is headed by a Secretary General[11] (SG) appointed by the Ministry of Commerce in Beijing after consulting the PSC. The SG is assisted by a support office based in Macau and a Liaison Office in Beijing.[12] The support office reports to Macau's Executive Government through the Secretariat for Economy and Finance, from which it receives the funds to pursue its activities. The Support Office initiatives includes promotion of high level visits, entrepreneurial meetings, trade, investment and economic and technological cooperation, human resources training, and advertising of the Forum.[13] Within the scope of this forum, the same kind of activities are also promoted from Beijing, in which case they are funded by the MOFCOM. In 2005 all member countries agreed on the need to create a fund within the Forum to finance development projects especially in the African Portuguese Speaking Countries and East Timor, which is now (2007/8) in the process of

---

10 This first action plan was adopted on 13 October 2003. Full text available online at: http://www.forumchinaplp.org.mo

11 Presently the Secretary General is Wang Cheng An, who is supposed to complete his term of office (three years) in early 2008.

12 Although there the coordinator has an office in the PS facilities in Macau.

13 Information concerning PS organization is according to the PS statutes (which are in process of revision, 2007/2008) and interviews conducted in the PS in Macau in September 2006 and October 2007.

being created through a consortium of private and public banks from all the member states.[14]

For both historical and practical reasons, Macau is a privileged platform to serve as the locus of this endeavour. This fact was underlined by most of the official representatives who attended the first meeting of the Forum.[15] Since the 16th century, Macau has been the contact point between China and the Portuguese speaking world.[16] It has accumulated human connections and trade networks that survived the handover to China. Portuguese language and culture have also left behind institutional ties: Macau retained its membership of the 'Union of Portuguese Speaking Cities', the 'Meteorological Organisation of Portuguese Speaking Countries' and the 'Association of Portuguese Speaking Universities'. Macau has also acted as an open gateway into China for several centuries, and today has a special relationship with the Central Government and large economic and political autonomy.

Macau owes much of its importance within the PRC to this pivotal role between mainland China and Portuguese speaking countries. Portuguese language and culture, even if not as well disseminated in Macau as in other former Portuguese colonies, have indeed acquired great importance for Beijing as a bridge to these countries. There are at present twelve universities in Macau. Most have established cooperation protocols with their counterparts in Lusophone countries for exchanges and also with universities in mainland China, mostly for Portuguese language teaching. This trend has become even more evi-

---

14 According to interviews conducted in Macau (October 2007) and among PSC embassies in Beijing (November 2007).

15 As stated in public declarations during the Forum meeting, namely, by the Chinese Deputy Prime Minister, Wu Yi; the Chinese Deputy Minister of Commerce, An Min; Macau's Chief Executive, Edmund Ho Au-wah; the Portuguese representative of the Portuguese Minister of Economy, Franquelim Alves. African representatives, not surprisingly, emphasized the role of Chinese assistance during the anti-colonial war. A complete collection of the discourses proffered during this first meeting in 2003 are available in a publication edited by the PS in Macau.

16 About Macau's historical role in linking China with the PSC see António Vasconcelos de Saldanha, *Estudos sobre as Relações Luso-Chinesas* (Lisbon: ISCSP, 1996); Jorge Alves, *Um Porto entre Dois Impérios: Estudos sobre Macau e as Relações Luso-Chinesas*, (Lisbon: IPOR, 2000); Ângela Guimarães, *Uma relação especial: Macau e as relações luso-chinesas, 1780-1844*, (Lisbon: 1996).

dent after the handover, much of it under the initiative of the Chinese authorities.

The second Ministerial Meeting took place on 24-25 September 2006 in Macau and was attended by the Ministers of Commerce from Angola, Mozambique, Cape Verde and Guinea Bissau and East Timor, the Brazilian Deputy Minister of Commerce, Macau's Chief Executive and the Chinese Minister of Commerce, Bo Xilai. The Minister of Commerce of São Tomé and Príncipe also attended the meeting as a special invitee, having the same category as the invited representative of UNCTAD. The Action plan adopted at this meeting further extended cooperation areas mentioned in the previous one to include tourism, transportation (aerial and maritime links), sanitary, science and technology, media, culture and the creation of its own financial cooperation mechanism.[17]

Despite the fact that during 2006 most of the member countries of this Forum established a resident representative in the Permanent Secretariat in Macau,[18] this Forum is not a traditional multilateral organization so much as an instrument of Chinese foreign policy. While the Action Plans of the Forum are negotiated in a multilateral setting in Beijing or Macau[19] prior to Ministerial Conferences (every three years), trade and cooperation agreements within this Forum are reached on a bilateral basis and China negotiates with each country separately.

The importance of Portuguese African countries for China

China's relations with the Portuguese-speaking world have been developing almost unnoticed by the rest of the world. The fact that

---

17 Full text available at: http://www.forumchinaplp.org.mo

18 As of November 2007 the East Timor representative alone was missing, but was due to be nominated soon. Portuguese and Brazilian representatives, however, are not based in the PS facilities.

19 The ministerial meetings, held every three years, are preceded by talks between the MOFCOM (Department of Taiwan, Hong Kong and Macau affairs) and the ambassadors from the Portuguese speaking countries, and chaired by the General Secretariat of the Forum. Meetings at this level also take place to discuss other issues, namely the present revision of the PS statute which has been under discussion since early 2007.

Macau has been moving closer to CPLP since 2002 is full of signifi-cance given that despite Portuguese efforts during the last years of its rule, Beijing never allowed Macau to join the organization. This fact clearly reveals China's interest in pursuing a closer relationship with the Lusophone world.

China has, indeed, several reasons to foster its relations with the Lusophone world:

First and foremost is energy security. Over the past few years, energy security, particularly oil supply security, has become a priority for the Chi-nese leadership. More than 60 percent of China's crude oil imports come from the Middle East, and Beijing views this dependency as a strategic vul-nerability because of ongoing political instability and US military prepon-derance in and around the region. China is, therefore, trying to diversify its energy imports away from traditional sources in the Persian Gulf. These include lusophone countries such as Angola, Brazil, Guinea-Bissau and Timor-Leste, [which, according to an online report by the British Petro-leum company are among the countries that had the highest growth rate in production in 2005 (Brazil and Angola)][20] (...) [Second], 220 million peo-ple represent a major market for Chinese manufactured goods. And finally, the Portuguese-speaking organization represents a diplomatic community, one that China can utilize to restrict Taiwan's international space.[21]

The total volume of trade between China and the APSC grew from US$11 billion in 2003 to more than US$34 billion in 2006,[22] testifying to the impulse given by the Macau Forum. It is important, however, to stress that the volume of Chinese imports from the Portuguese speak-ing countries was much larger than its exports in 2006—US$24.3 bil-lion and US$9.8 billion respectively, meaning a Chinese trade deficit of almost US$15 billion.[23] If we take into account the fact that Brazil is responsible for more than half of that trade volume (over US$20 billion in 2006)[24] and that it has a strong, established partnership with China (Brazil's third biggest commercial partner after the USA and

---

20 'Petróleos Lusófonos em crescimento', *Ponto Final*, Macau, 18 June 2006.

21 Loro Horta, 'China's Portuguese Connection', *Yale Global Online*, 16 June 2006.

22 MOFCOM Statistics online, http://english.mofcom.gov.cn/column/statisticsie.shtml, January 16, 2007.

23 Ibid.

24 Ibid.

Argentina), it seems reasonable to conclude that Brazil was not the main target when China first started to plan the Macau Forum.

Portugal, on the other hand, plays a minor role in real terms within China's Lusophone strategy. It is not a relevant trading partner for China, either within Lusophone countries or in the European Union. Its relevance to China is much more symbolic (historical and cultural links to Portuguese speaking countries) and instrumental, derived from its potential as an interface between the Lusophone community and the European Union. This approach is, indeed, the only explanation for Wen Jiabao having awarded Portugal the status of 'strategic partner' in December 2005 when he visited Lisbon.[25] What does matter for China, then, is the African Portuguese speaking countries and East Timor. Despite their small populations and weak or war-shattered economies, these represent a large pool of under-explored natural resources ranging from fisheries, agriculture, forestry and tourism to natural gas, coal, mining and oil.

Among the APSC Angola is undoubtedly China's most important trade partner, and is becoming China's key partner in the whole of the African continent. Bilateral trade grew from US$1 billion in 2002 to US$11 billion in 2006;[26] in that year it overtook South Africa as China's largest trading partner in the continent and Saudi Arabia as China's main oil supplier. Textiles, shoes and electrical equipment mainly constitute China exports but bilateral trade continues to be dominated by Chinese oil imports. China's second most important trade partner within the APSC is Mozambique. Bilateral trade experienced a fourfold growth after the creation of the Forum, rising from US$48.5 million in 2002 to US$197 million in 2006.[27] Cape Verde's bilateral trade with China grew from US$2.75 million in 2004

---

25 Together with the UK, France, Germany and Spain, Portugal is one of the five countries that have been granted this status in Europe.

26 MOFCOM Statistics online, http://english.mofcom.gov.cn/column/statisticsie.shtml, 16 January 2007.

27 MOFCOM statistics online cited above. Maputo and Beijing established diplomatic relations on 25 June 1975, signed a trade agreement and an agreement on reciprocal investment protection and set up a joint economic and trade commission in 2001.

to US$10 million in 2006.[28] Guinea Bissau[29] ranks fourth in this list, with US$5 million in 2006,[30] and São Tomé and Príncipe is at the bottom with a trade volume of US$1.22 million. Unlike Angola, in Guinea-Bissau, Mozambique, Cape Verde and São Tomé the trade balance is dominated by Chinese exports.

Chinese foreign direct investment in these countries has also increased sharply in recent years. The reasons why these countries are attracting public and private Chinese capital are related to the fact that all of them, despite having underdeveloped economies, are rich in natural resources. Angola is currently the second largest oil producer in Africa (after Nigeria)[31] and has one of the world's largest diamonds fields, as well as such other resources as gold, uranium, phosphates; Mozambique has coal, titanium, semi-precious stones, food crops (including cashews, maize, cotton, sugar, copra), fisheries, and is believed to have large reserves of untapped natural gas and oil; Guinea Bissau has bauxite, phosphates and offshore petroleum, food crops and fisheries as well; and Cape Verde, the poorest, has salt, limestone, food crops and fisheries.[32]

Apart from trade and investment, China has also been offering significant and much-needed financial assistance to these countries. Apart from debt relief (last time in September 2006, during the Ministerial Meeting in Macau), China is granting important financial aid and long-term loans at very low rates (grants, interest free loans and concessional loans through Eximbank), mostly for resource development and infrastructure rehabilitation.[33] China, however, is not

---

28 MOFCOM Statistics online cited above. China established diplomatic relations with the Republic of Cape Verde on 25 April 1976. In 1998 the two countries signed an investment agreement and a trade and economic cooperation agreement in 1999.

29 China and Guinea-Bissau established diplomatic ties on 15 March 1974. On 26 May 1990, however, the Bissau government set up diplomatic relations with Taiwan. Diplomatic relations with Beijing were restored on 23 April 1998.

30 MOFCOM Statistics online cited above.

31 Its production representing 1.6 per cent of world total output, according to BP data.

32 CIA, *The world fact book* online.

33 According to interviews with MOFCOM conducted in Beijing in November

motivated by philanthropic considerations as Chinese companies are providing the lion's share of goods and services as part of the loan deals. Indeed, not only Chinese enterprises but also Chinese labour have been leading the reconstruction projects, from schools and hospitals to roads, railways, dams, airports, refineries, social housing and telecommunications. By this means, Beijing is becoming a major cooperation partner of these countries and an influential agent within the Lusophone world, particularly in the African Portuguese speaking countries, using Macau as a hub to promote this purpose. Indeed, since 2003, China has been developing several initiatives to charm the CPLP, among them the creation of the Macau Forum, the Trade and Cooperation Agreement it signed with the CPLP that same year, the US$1 million it granted to Guinea Bissau to host the 10th CPLP summit in July 2006, and the Chinese aid for Macau to host the first ever CPLP Games in October 2006.

Conclusion

Despite all the risks involved, China may have the means to 'kick start' Africa's development take-off. It has the resources, technology, expertise and goods and, most important, the political will to pursue this purpose. China and African countries also seem to have a lot in common: most are developing economies, were subject to European colonialism, and have opaque political systems and markets. Most of all, and despite this background, China has achieved extraordinary economic growth, making it a very attractive development model for African countries. Within this framework, China's approach to the Lusophone world is a very interesting case study for a variety of reasons. It offers a window through which to study China's relations with Africa, but also demonstrates how pragmatism and a comprehensive strategy may lead China to make better and more efficient use of a regional organization than those who were expected to be doing so, namely Brazil and Portugal, but seem unable to act because of lack of initiative or the ghosts of neo-colonialism. Indeed, after a decade of existence, CPLP can hardly be described as a successful

---

2007.

organization and the economic and political benefits for its member countries have been marginal at best.

Having only a fragile link to this community through Macau, China is ingeniously using its observer status to become the economic engine of the Lusophone community. On the one hand, it is charming the less developed countries of this community by offering them development opportunities in exchange for access to their natural resources; on the other hand, it is soothing Portugal's and Brazil's reservations by awarding them a privileged status on a bilateral basis and promising investment. Although the importance of Macau may ultimately be more symbolic than real, the fact that Beijing lined up this 'Lusophone strategy' is itself evidence of the strategic thinking that is contributing towards making China's economic diplomacy so comprehensive and, up to the present, so prosperous in Africa.

4

MAKING SENSE OF CHINESE
OIL INVESTMENT IN AFRICA

Ricardo Soares de Oliveira

Over the past decade, Chinese investment in Africa's oil sector, in tandem with Chinese involvement more generally, has grown from residual levels to a major presence with important consequences for African politics and the continent's relations with the rest of the world. However, the level of research has fallen far short of an accurate reading of this momentous process. Recent discussions of Chinese oil investment in Africa have lacked factual precision, analytical clarity, and even a measure of sobriety.[1] Press coverage, particularly in the US, concentrates almost exclusively on the human rights and governance implications of China's so-called 'lack of a moral agenda', to the detriment of other, equally significant and poorly understood dimensions. In turn, this alarmist rendition is countered by a revisionist approach that sees China's demeanour in essentially positive terms and does not recognize the potential for negative consequences.

This chapter is an attempt at providing a succinct interpretation of this process. It does not aim to present an exhaustive account of

---

1   One exception is Ian Taylor, 'China's Oil Diplomacy in Africa', *International Affairs* 82, 5 (2006), pp. 937-59.

Chinese oil activities in Africa. Section one focuses on China's oil industry and its dual challenge of building world-class business firms and keeping the fast-growing economy provisioned with energy resources mostly unavailable domestically. This has resulted in the internationalization of Chinese national oil companies (NOCs). But the government's lingering distrust of international energy markets and US intentions towards China have led it to pursue a strategy of equity oil acquisition cemented by a proactive petro-diplomacy that, critics say, aims at 'locking up' oil reserves. Section two provides a summary of the present-day activities of Chinese oil firms in Africa, their business methods, and the challenges and opportunities they face. Section three discusses the likely implications of sustained, large-scale Chinese oil investment in the years to come for Africa, China and its Western would-be competitors.

The argument pursued is twofold. Firstly, I explain that the contrast between Chinese and Western oil business practice has been much exaggerated. The West does have a 'moral dimension' to its present-day Africa policies, but the oil sector—despite the 'oversold and underachieved'[2] campaigns on transparency and corporate social responsibility—has always been, and remains, conspicuously absent from it. Secondly, I argue that Chinese oil investment in Africa will indeed contribute to the tragic outcomes for the majority of African citizens that have been mooted by critics. However, this will not be due to the establishment of a new, hyper-exploitative and illiberal political economy of oil. Rather, the rise of China as an oil power in Africa will aggravate what is a much older political economy of oil extraction that for decades has exchanged political support and prosperity for local dictators against reliable provision of oil to consumers. In effect, Chinese NOCs will be joining in a form of time-honoured, if abysmally non-developmental, partnership long indulged in by African oil states, Western importer states, and Western international oil companies (IOCs). On account of Chinese technical backwardness and the resilience of Western oil companies, it is unlikely that the latter will be crowded out. The most probable overall outcome of

---

2 Michael Peel, 'Britain and Nigeria's half-hearted war on corruption', *Financial* Times, 17 October 2005.

the Chinese 'scramble for oil' is the *de facto* (if not rhetorical) erosion of Western 'progressive agendas'[3] and the full embrace by all players in the oil game of the *Realpolitik* approach needed for business success in the African oil sector.

Challenges for Chinese oil companies

Mirroring the centrality of oil provision for China's ongoing economic growth, NOCs are at the forefront of the Chinese government's attempts to construct globally competitive corporate players. This emphasis is due to two factors. The first is the understanding that successful late industrializers have always developed world-class firms, particularly in the 'commanding heights' of the economy,[4] and that China cannot secure its position in the world economy without them. As Deputy Premier Wu Bangguo put it, China's 'position in the international economic order will be to a large extent determined by the position of our nation's large enterprises and groups'.[5] The second factor is the overriding strategic importance of oil supplies and the concurrent desire of the Chinese government not to leave such a crucial task to the vagaries of the market and foreign intermediaries. Chinese 'national champions' in the oil sector are, in this vision, tasked with finding, extracting, transporting, refining and domestically marketing the oil needed to fuel China's growth. These factors also apply to NOCs of other fast-growing Asian economies and the Chinese bid for African oil must be seen as part of a wider pattern (see map).

To that effect, Chinese industrial policy has sought to gear up its three main oil firms, CNPC, Sinopec, and CNOOC, all of which

---

3 Discussed in Chapter 6 of Soares de Oliveira, *Oil and Politics in the Gulf of Guinea* (London: Hurst, 2007).

4 This includes sectors as diverse as aerospace, pharmaceuticals, oil and petrochemicals, power equipment, automobiles and components, steel and coal, consumer electronics, telecommunications, IT hardware and financial services. Peter Nolan, *China at the Crossroads* (Cambridge: Polity, 2003), p. 19.

5 Quoted in Peter Nolan and Jin Zhang, 'Globalization Challenge for Large Firms from Developing Countries: China's Oil and Aerospace Industries', *European Management Journal*, 21, 3 (2003), p. 287.

were established in the early 1980s.[6] CNPC and Sinopec were originally upstream and downstream companies respectively. Following restructuring of the Chinese oil sector in 1998, they became vertically integrated companies, although both remain stronger in their previous activities and more rooted in different regions of China.[7] CNOOC remains primarily an upstream company with offshore expertise. By 2001, all three had had subsidiaries successfully floated in the New York and Hong Kong stock exchanges, with some of the shares (10-30 per cent) listed.[8] Despite the subsequent presence of commercially minded minority shareholders, and the Chinese leadership's ambition to turn these firms into global corporate giants that can compete with Western oil majors, they remain principally the tools of Chinese government strategizing.[9]

For all the portraits in the Western media of Chinese oil companies as ruthless competitors, the Chinese outlook on these matters is altogether different. Chinese decision-makers are painfully aware of the inferior prowess of their oil firms in the global stage. They

6   Other companies have also shown an interest in overseas investment. Sinochem (China's fourth largest in the oil sector) has announced plans to spend US$2 billion in projects outside China over the next three to five years. See Deepa Babington, 'Chinese Sinochem looks to Africa in oil hunt', *Reuters News*, 23 April 2006. According to the *Financial Times*, Chinese companies have subsequently preferred to list in Hong Kong, but have avoided dual listing in the US, 'discouraged by the tough Sarbanes-Oxley corporate governance regulations and a Securities and Exchanges Commission investigation into insurer China Life following its IPO in 2003'. See Justine Lau, 'Chinese IPOs are bigger than those in US and Europe', *Financial Times*, 12 May 2006.

7   Robert E. Ebel, *China's Energy Debate: The Middle Kingdom Seeks a Place in the Sun* (Washington, DC: CSIS, 2005), p. 11.

8   'China's oil companies: drilling for the Party', *Economist*, 24 May 2003. Investors building up a stake in Sinopec and PetroChina (CNPC's internationally listed firm) included most Western oil majors as well as the known investor Warren Buffett. CNOOC for its part included Henry Kissinger among the members of its Advisory Board.

9   For a good overview of reform and partial privatization in China's energy sector see Philip Andrews-Speed and Cao Zhenning, 'Prospects for Privatization in China's Energy Sector', in Stephen Green and Guy S. Liu, *Exit the Dragon? Privatization and State Control in China* (London and Oxford: Chatham House and Blackwell Publishing, 2005), pp. 197-213.

possess neither the bountiful reserves of the NOCs of oil-producing states nor the technical expertise, financial weight and business savvy of European and American IOCs. 'The blunt reality is that after two decades of reform China's large firms are still far from being able to compete with the global giants.'[10] In their careful analysis of the challenges faced by China's oil industry, Peter Nolan and Jin Zhang conclude that its technological capability is 'relatively backward'.[11] Chinese oil companies are overstaffed and saddled with plenty of non-commercial obligations. While attempting to foster their character as commercial entities, state impingement frequently means that they commit to projects and policies that would not withstand commercial evaluation.[12] The internationally listed subsidiaries of the three companies are more agile, broadly appear to follow Western corporate governance principles, and are acquiring expertise at great speed. But even they are no match for their Western counterparts.[13]

10 Nolan, *China at the Crossroads,* p. 20.

11 Nolan and Zhang, 'Globalization Challenge for Large Firms from Developing Countries', p. 290.

12 This contradiction between commercial and non-commercial agendas is well illustrated by the distortions introduced by pricing policies in China. In order to protect consumers from high oil prices, the Chinese government keeps domestic prices artificially low. Suffering from squeezed profit margins, China's companies started to export their refined products in order to sell them at higher prices. This caused domestic shortages in 2005. Eventually, the Chinese government stepped in, prohibiting refiners from signing new export contracts and providing offsetting subsidies to compensate refiners such as Sinopec for their losses. Center for Strategic and International Studies and Institute for International Economics, *China: The Balance Sheet* (Washington, DC: CSIS and IIE, 2006), pp. 35-6.

13 The will to converge with Western levels of corporate governance and technical competence is a feature of these companies and some already portray themselves in such manner. Fu Chengyu, the CEO of CNOOC, for instance, suggested that China's major oil firms 'are not really like other Chinese companies. Our systems, models and processes are more like our Western counterparts.' See Francesco Guerrera, 'The maverick oil mandarin', *Financial Times,* 25 June 2005. On the occasion of CNOOC's failed bid for US oil firm Unocal, this passion for Western corporate standards did not prevent Fu from consulting with the Chinese government for approval *before* mentioning it to the company's board. See James Kynge, *China Shakes the World: The Rise of a Hungry Nation* (London: Weidenfeld and Nicolson, 2006), pp. 133-6.

This perceived fragility of Chinese corporate players in the global economy is echoed by the Chinese government's fear of dependence on foreign sources and transit lanes for keeping China's fast growing economy provisioned. China had been a net exporter until 1993; then its appetite for foreign oil grew so fast that, by 2004, it had become the world's second importer of oil. In tandem with this novel engagement with global energy markets, unsuccessful attempts at substantially increasing domestic production led to the realization that China is now irrevocably tied to energy supplies from abroad. Chinese decision-makers are deeply fearful of this. Not only do they know that all sea lanes leading to Chinese ports are controlled by the US Navy, and subject to disruption in the context of conflict or deteriorating relations. They also have bad memories of dependence on Russian energy supplies in the 1950s and early 1960s, which significantly curbed Chinese policy leeway even after the Sino-Soviet schism.[14] Yet for all the misgivings, the Chinese leadership has accepted this dependence as unavoidable.

Reflecting a significant and multifaceted debate on how best cope with its volatile energy supply situation,[15] China has engaged in the simultaneous pursuit of a number of policies (this is partly the result of a very fragmented policy process, as there is no central agency responsible for the energy sector). These include the diversification of foreign suppliers, increased domestic exploration for oil and use of China's plentiful coal reserves, the building of a strategic petroleum reserve, expansion of refining capacity, initial steps at energy conservation, etc.[16] For the purpose of this chapter, I concentrate

---

14 Erica S Downs, *China's Worldwide Quest for Energy Security* (Santa Monica: RAND, 2000), pp. 11-12. Distrust of foreign entanglements is heightened by China's own two decades-long experience as an energy exporter (from the early 1970s to the early 1990s), during which it successfully used its own 'oil weapon' to shape Japan's regional policies. See Downs, *China's Worldwide Quest*, pp. 43-4.

15 See, for example, Jonathan E Sinton *et al.*, 'Evaluation of China's Energy Strategy Options', report prepared for the China Sustainable Energy Program, 16 May 2005 and Erica S. Downs, 'The Chinese Energy Security Debate', *The China Quarterly* 177 (2004), pp. 21-41.

16 It should be emphasized that these policies have encompassed the partial opening up of China to foreign oil companies, mostly in joint ventures with

on the dimension that is most relevant for China-Africa relations: a concerted effort by Chinese NOCs to venture into foreign markets and acquire equity oil. While this was an unstated goal from the mid-1990s,[17] President Hu Jintao's embrace of a 'going out' policy in 2002 accelerated the drive for external involvement.[18] The objective is to increase Chinese control of supplies by subtracting a meaningful amount of oil from the international market. Through its vertically integrated companies, the Chinese government aims to 'control' a significant percentage of its oil needs while shielding the Chinese economy from potential price hikes or supply disruptions. As Erica Downs writes:

In the event of another oil shock, the Chinese government will be able to pressure state-owned oil companies to forgo windfall profits from higher international oil prices by requiring them to supply Chinese industries at artificially low prices, cushioning the impact of the shock on the Chinese economy.[19]

In outline, the main traits of China's 'mercantilist' approach to oil supply are: a) distrust of markets, especially in contexts of disruption or conflict; b) belief in ownership of oil resources through NOCs as the best guarantee of access; c) strong investment in friendly bilateral relations with oil producers.

This attempt at 'locking up' oil assets or, failing that, acquiring oil through fixed long-term contracts as opposed to the spot market,[20] while only a segment of an otherwise mostly market-based Chinese

---

the Chinese majors. According to Ebel (*China's Energy Debate*, p. 26) China plans to fully open up its domestic refined oil market to competition by 2007 in accordance with WTO commitments.

17 Zha Daojiong, 'China's Energy Security: Domestic and International Issues', *Survival* 48, 1 (2006), p. 180. According to the IEA (2000: 10), a May 1997 policy paper by former Premier Li Peng had already 'blessed Chinese involvement in the exploration and development of international oil and gas resources'.

18 Flynt Leverett and Jeffrey Bader, 'Managing the China-US Energy Competition in the Middle East', *Washington Quarterly* 29, 1 (2005), p. 193.

19 Downs, *China's Worldwide Quest for Energy Security*, p. 20.

20 While it is the upstream activity of Chinese oil companies that catches public attention, *African Energy* has pointed out the 'demand revolution shaking up the secretive trading market'. See 'China's long march to West Africa

approach to energy supplies, contrasts with current Western visions of well-functioning energy markets. The implicit role for Chinese NOCs—the subordination of commercial logic to the Chinese government's political imperatives—also contrasts with the maximization of shareholder value that drives Western IOCs. Far from opposing this impingement upon their commercial character, Chinese oil companies are the most strident advocates of a global equity oil strategy. They believe such immersion in the tough outside world of oil exploration and production can only provide them with a much-needed technical and managerial crash course in their grooming as 'global players'. While struggling for some autonomy from government political meddling, Chinese NOCs also count on state assistance through soft loans and petro-diplomacy to more than compensate for the uncommercial element encompassed by 'national interest' policies.[21] In pursuit of this vision, Chinese NOCs have fanned out into Central Asia, Latin America, the Middle East and Sub-Saharan Africa in a bout of frenzied negotiations and investment.

This means that, in addition to the complex challenge of attempted internationalization in perhaps the most competitive of business sectors, Chinese oil companies are perceived as poachers on someone else's turf. This is so particularly in the USA, where a veritable aca-

---

marked by increasing sophistication as well as big appetite', *African Energy* 95, February 2006.

21 Many analysts overestimate the extent to which Chinese NOCs are seeking independence from the Chinese state, which remains their biggest shareholder by far (author observation at a conference on the rise of China and India as energy consumers, Potsdam, January 2007). NOCs want the freedom to pursue commercial policies but would not want to lose the benefits of a close association with the Chinese state, which protects them from full international competition, grants them cheap finance, and can be counted on to advance company interests abroad. Furthermore, to think that the Chinese state would ultimately allow its strategic-sector companies the leeway to pursue completely independent policies is to misapprehend the nature of China's regime. The Communist Party remains responsible for all senior appointments; the main sources for capital remain the state-owned banks. A more possible medium-term outcome is a mixed company such as Brazil's Petrobras: on the one hand it is a competent, technologically advanced, and partly privatized firm; on the other, it remains one of Brazil's industrial 'jewels in the crown' which cannot conceivably pursue self-regarding policies in oblivion of the interests of the state.

demic and policy industry of concern for China's rise has come into being over the past years. Analysis and speculation on the behaviour of Chinese NOCs and their linkages with China's global strategy is a particularly fertile sub-genre. Among energy specialists, there is a virtual consensus that China's mercantilist energy strategy, itself the product of 'immaturity' and lack of understanding of energy markets, is bound to fail, as well as disbelief at the underlying 'paranoia'[22] of Chinese acquisitions. A number of arguments have emerged. First, that the foreign equity oil acquired (less than half a percentage point of world oil production) or likely to be acquired by China is not enough to make much difference. Second, that because of 'transportation and logistical costs', it will often make more sense to sell or swap oil cargoes in the international market than physically bring them into China,[23] which defeats the whole purpose. Third, that the Chinese 'shopping spree' fails to meet 'financial and commercial criteria acceptable to most IOCs':[24] Chinese companies overpay for their assets, either financially or through onerous 'packaged deals'. Somewhat illogically for a strategy so airily dismissed as amateurish, China's overseas energy policy is causing great anxiety in some quarters.[25]

---

22 'China's Splurge on Resources May Not Be a Sign of Strength', *New York Times*, 12 December 2004.

23 Downs, *China's Worldwide Quest for Energy Security*, p. 23. This was argued by a senior US-based Chinese scholar, who claimed that only about 10 per cent of Chinese foreign equity oil is actually sent back to China (conversation with the author, Potsdam, 18 January 2007, and subsequent email exchanges).

24 Ebel, *China's Energy Debate*, p. 41.

25 A prominent example was the attempted acquisition of the US oil company Unocal by CNOOC that led to a high-profile US backlash. While CNOOC claimed the acquisition was on commercial grounds alone, 'congressional and other critics in the United States charged that China as a country was using aggressive tactics to lock up energy supplies around the world and that CNOOC's bid represented a clear threat to US national security and should be blocked'. See CSIS and IIE, *China: The Balance Sheet*, p. 75. CNOOC withdrew its bid before this could happen. On the extensively covered Unocal-CNOOC affair see, e.g., Francesco Guerrera and Joseph Leahy, 'CNOOC considers $13bn for Unocal', *Financial Times*, 6 January 2005, Sebastian Mallaby, 'China's latest "threat"', *Washington Post*, 28 June 2005, Keith Bradsher, 'China retreats now, but it will be back', *New York Times*, 3 August 2005, and 'Giving China a Bloody Nose', *Economist*, 4 August 2005.

Are Chinese oil companies the storm troops of an aggressive foreign policy, then? No, but it is undeniable that Chinese decision-makers now link 'energy security with the much wider international political environment'.[26] As Rosemary Foot notes, the Chinese global strategy is characterized by two complementary dynamics. On the one hand, China's leadership understands the unipolar state of the international system, and wants to 'avoid open conflicts with the United States and not give it an excuse to shift its attention to [China] to pick quarrels that would result in extraordinary interference in China's endeavor to modernize': hence its attempts at accommodating US preeminence, foiling portraits of a 'China threat', and projecting the image of a conciliatory, peaceful and responsible presence in the international sphere. On the other hand, China's policy contains

an important 'hedging' element, or insurance policy, through which China seeks to secure its future. If it should be necessary […] China could try to use its newly formed bilateral and multilateral relationships to offset any serious deterioration of relations with America. The strong ties it has sought to establish around the world help ensure that Cold War-style containment […] simply could not occur in this era of interdependence.[27]

The mercantilist element of Chinese energy policy and its accompanying petro-diplomacy is one such instance of Chinese 'hedging' against possible worsening of the Sino-US relationship. Not wanting to 'put all its eggs in one basket',[28] the Chinese government believes that privileged access to oil and a dense political relationship with oil producers in the developing world will enhance its security. Whether or not it is mistaken in this belief—especially in regard to the fungible nature of the international oil markets, where no producer or consumer stands in isolation from others—is neither here nor there: the pursuit of this policy is itself consequential. And although recent developments may point towards partial convergence with a more

---

26 James Tang, 'With the Grain or Against the Grain? Energy Security and Chinese Foreign Policy in the Hu Jintao Era' (The Brookings Institution, Center for Northeast Asian Studies, October 2006), p. 28.

27 Rosemary Foot, 'Chinese Strategies in a US-hegemonic Global Order: Accommodating and Hedging', *International Affairs* 82, 1 (2006), p. 88.

28 Chung-lian Jiang, 'Le pétrole, nouvelle dimension des relations sino-africaines', *Géopolitique Africaine* (spring 2004).

market-based approach,[29] this is the political backdrop for much of China's policy towards Africa's oil resources in the past five years.

China's oil investment in Africa

The arrival and deepening involvement of Chinese NOCs in Africa over the last decade has taken place amidst revolutionary change in the continent's oil sector.[30] This is particularly so in the Gulf of Guinea region which in the past decade has witnessed a major (and still ongoing) reassessment of the magnitude of its petroleum reserves.[31] The estimate is now of over 50 billion barrels, or just under 5 per cent of world proven oil reserves,[32] roughly 80 per cent of which are in Angola and Nigeria alone. Technological breakthroughs in the form of ultra-deep water machinery and expertise have played a crucial role in this process. The first ultra-deep water discovery, Angola's giant Girassol oilfield, was made in April 1996. In less than three years, there had been 25 such finds, the fastest rate of discovery in the world.[33] The excitement over the ultra deep waters of the Gulf

---

29 The 2007 Chinese government's white paper on energy supply states that "worldwide search for oil and gas [...] will be carried out in a spirit of fair play and international cooperation so as not to disrupt sensitive international markets". This International Energy Agency—style language seems to point so some convergence with swestern approaches, as at least a wish to arrange the materials. That said, this has been the dominant Chinese approach until now. See http://www.cchina.gov.cn/WebSite/CChina/UpFile/FIle229.pdf (accessed 2 February 2008).

30 This distinguishes oil producers from African producers of other commodities, whose comparative prosperity over the past years is due directly to increased demand from the Asian Drivers and particularly from China. While the Chinese need for oil is one of the key demand-side reasons for current high oil prices, external competition for Africa's oil deposits predates it.

31 Soares de Oliveira, *Oil and Politics in the Gulf of Guinea*.

32 British Petroleum, *BP's 2005 Statistical Review of World Energy* (London: British Petroleum, 2005).

33 'Le point sur l'exploration/production dans le golfe de Guinée', *Marchés Tropicaux et Méditerrannéens* 502, 5 March 1999 and also Joseph M. Bruso *et al.*, 'Geology will support further discoveries in the Gulf of Guinea's Golden Rectangule', *Oil and Gas Journal*, 16 February 2004. Extending the analysis to deep waters (from 300 meters) there were 43 finds by late 1999, according to D. Harbinson, D. R. Knight and J. Westwood, 'West African Deep Water Developments in a Global Context', *The Hydrographic Journal* 98 (2000).

ASIA'S OIL INTERESTS IN AFRICA

ALGERIA
CNPC
Exploration: Block 112/102a (75%), Block 350 (75%) and Block 438b (100%).
Exploration, construction, marketing: Adrar Upstream & Downstream Integrated Project (70%).
Petronas
Exploration & production: Ahnet Block & Block 401C (interest).
PetroVietnam (PIDC) (40%) and Petroleum Authority of Thailand (PTTEP) (35%)
Exploration: Blocks 433a & 416b (Touggourt).
Teikoku (Japan)
Development: Ohanet, El Ouar I & II Blocks.

MAURITANIA
CNPC
Exploration: Blocks Ta 13, Ta 21, 12 & 20.
Production sharing: Blocks Ta 13, Ta 21 & 12.
Operation: Block 20.
Miscellaneous: engineering & technical services such as geophysical prospecting, well drilling & well logging.
Petronas
Exploration & production: Block 8 (interest), located NW of Nouakchott.
Operation: Chinguetti oil field.
Exploration: PSC A, PSC B; Offshore Blocks 2, 6 & 7; Blocks Ta 11 & Ta 12.

GAMBIA
Philippine National Oil Company
Exploration block (this deal had no tender or technical review, unsure of current status).

SENEGAL – GUINEA-BISSAU JOINT EXPLORATION BLOCK
Markmore Energy (Malaysia)
Exploration: Dome Flore Block (55% interest).

CÔTE D'IVOIRE
Joint exploration project, CI-112:
ONGC (India) (21%); Oil India (10.4%); Sinopec (27%).

TOGO
Petronas
Exploration: Togo offshore block (interest).

BENIN
Petronas
Exploration: Block 4 (20% interest).
Korea National Oil Company (KNOC)
Exploration & production: Blocks 2 & 3.

NIGERIA
CNPC
Blocks OPL 298, OPL 471, OPL 721 & OPL 732.
CNOOC
OML 130 (45%).
Sinopec
Interest in exploration project.
IndianOil
An onshore block.
Oil India Ltd (OIL)
Block OPL 205 (oil/gas; 25% interest).
Korea National Oil Company (KNOC)
Exploration & production: Offshore Blocks OPL 321 & OPL 323 (interest).

EQUATORIAL GUINEA
CNPC
Production: Block M (70%; operator).
China National Offshore Oil Company (CNOOC)
Exploration: offshore project (interest).
Petronas
Exploration & production: Block N, offshore Corisco Bay (interest).
Block P, Rio Muni Basin (interest).

GABON
IndianOil
Onshore farm-in arrangements in Gabon Oil India Ltd (OIL).
Exploration: Block Shakthi (FT-2000) (operator; 45% interest).
Petronas and Mitsubishi Petroleum Development Corporation (joint venture with Amerada Hess, operator)
Exploration & production: Moabi & Nguma Permits.

MOROCCO
Petronas
Exploration & production:
Timit Block, offshore (42.5%).
Exploration: Cap Drâa Haute Mer Permit Block (26.67%; operated by Energy Africa, 80% Petronas-owned).

LIBYA
CNPC
Exploration & production: Block 17-4 (interest).
Construction: crude/gas parallel pipeline in western Libya (2004).
Technical services: seismic crews, five drilling rigs & eight well logging crews.
IndianOil Corporation (IOC) and Oil India Ltd (OIL)
Exploration: Blocks 86 & 102-4 (18.4% interest in each).
Medco Energy (Indonesia)
Exploration: Area 47 (50% interest).
Korea National Oil Company (SK)
Elephant field, joint venture.
ONGC-Videsh (OVL)
Exploration & production: NC 188, NC 189 (49% interest in each); 81-1 & Contract Area 43.
Japanese consortium (Inpex, Japan Petroleum Exploration (JAPEX), Mitsubishi, Nippon Oil and Teikoku)
Exploration & production: Blocks 2-1/2, 40-3/4, 42-2/4, 81-2, 82-3 & 176-4.

TUNISIA
CNPC
Exploration: NK block.
Production: SLK Oilfield (50%).
Technical services: drilling.

NIGER
CNPC
Exploration, operator: Block Bilma (100%) & Block Ténéré (90%).
Technical services: geophysical prospecting, well drilling & logging.
Petronas
Exploration & production: Agadem Block (interest).

CAMEROON
Petronas
Exploration & production: Block PH 77 (interest).
Construction: Chad-Cameroon Pipeline (35% interest; completed).

CONGO-KINSHASA
Teikoku (Japan)
Production: Offshore Congo Block (32%).
CNPC
Reported to be interested in Lake Albert exploration & production.

ANGOLA
SSI (joint venture: Sonangol 45%, Sinopec 55%)
Exploration: Blocks 3/05 (25%), 15/06 (20%), 17/06 (27.5%) & 18/06 (40%).
Production: Blocks 3/05 (25%) & 18 (50%).
Petronas
Exploration: Block 24 (15%).
Teikoku (Japan)
Production: Cabinda North Block (17%).

EGYPT
Petroleum Authority of Thailand (PTTEP)
Exploration: Rommana Block (30%; not operator); Sidi Abd El Rahman Offshore Block (30%; not operator).
Petronas
Exploration: 4 blocks in Siwa, W Ghazalat, El Farafa, El Saloom (partnership with Tharwa Petroleum (Egypt)); Block E1 Burg (30% interest).
Exploration & production: NE Mediterranean Deepwater (Nemed) Oil & Gas Block (interest); West Delta Deep Marine (WDDM) Concession (interest).
LNG liquifaction plant (under construction; joint venture).
GAIL (India)
15% interest in NATGAS (gas company).
ONGC-Videsh (OVL)
Exploration & production: N Ramadan Block (interest).
AOC (Japan)
Exploration & production: NW October Block, Suez Gulf (interest).
Teikoku (Japan)
Interests in S October, N Qarun, W Bakr & SE July blocks.

SUDAN
CNPC
Blocks 1, 2 & 4 (40%), Blocks 3 & 7 (41%; operator; oil/gas), Block 6 (100%; Fula oil field & its pipeline), Block 15 (production sharing with Sudapet, Petronas & others), Khartoum Refinery (50%), Block 13 (co-operator).
Petronas
Refinery construction: Port Sudan (completion 2009).
Operates: service stations, bulk terminals, storage.
Exploration: Blocks 5A, 5B & 8 (interest).
Gas exploration & production: Offshore Block 15 (interest).
Sinopec
Exploration: Ogaden.
Ranhill International (Malaysia) and Petroneeds Services International (Sudan)
Development: Blocks 3 & 7.
Greater Nile Petroleum Operating Company (GNPOC) [CNPC 40%, Petronas 30%, ONGC 25% and Sudapet 5%]
Exploration & production: Blocks 1, 2 & 4 (joint operation).
Petrodar [CNPC 41%, Petronas 40%, Sudapet 8%, Sinopec 6% and Al-Thani Corporation 5%]
Exploration & production: Blocks 3 & 7.
White Nile Petroleum Operating Company (WNPOC) [Petronas, ONGC-Videsh (OVL) and Sudapet]
Exploration: Block 5A (Petronas 69%, OVL 24%); Block 5B (Petronas 39%, OVL 24%); & Block 8 (Petronas 77%).

ERITREA
Korea National Oil Company (KNOC)
Exploration & production: Dafnin Block.

ETHIOPIA
Petronas
Exploration & production: Ogaden Blocks 3, 4, 12, 16, 17 & 20; Gambela Basin Block G (interests).

CHAD
CNPC
Technical services Block H (100%);
geophysical prospecting, well drilling & logging.
Construction: N'Djamena Refinery.
China Petroleum Company (Taiwan) through overseas arm OPIC
Joint exploration: 3 blocks.
Petronas
Exploration & production: Doba Three-Field Development (Miandoum, Bolobo & Komé fields) (interest).
Exploration: Permit H (Doba, Doseo & Lake Chad Basins) (interest).

KENYA
CNOOC
Exploration: Lamu offshore region.

MADAGASCAR
Sunpec (HK, China)
100% owner of Madagascar Energy International Limited (MEIL) and its Madagascar Oilfield Block 3113 (gas/oil exploitation & operation).

MAURITIUS
IndianOil Mauritius Ltd
Operator: storage facility of 18,000 MT, Mer Rouge in Port Louis.

MOZAMBIQUE
Petronas
Exploration: offshore Zambezi Delta Block (interest).

SOUTH AFRICA
Petronas
Owns 80% Engen Ltd (Durban refinery, 1400 service stations).

Sources: EIA; Afroil; ENI; KNOC; Petronas; CNOOC; CNPC; Sinopec; IndianOil

Source: Africa-Asia Confidential, 1, 2 (14 December 2007, p. 5).

Credits: David Burles (cartographer), and Charles Moore (research).

of Guinea was such that a worldwide decrease in capital expenditure by oil companies during the 1998-99 drop in prices had no impact there: in fact, spending rose 10 per cent relative to the previous year.[34]

---

34 See Anne Guillaume-Gentil, 'Pétrole: la nouvelle donne', *Marchés Tropicaux et Méditerrannéens*, 10 March 2000 and 'Deep-Water Survey: Gulf of Guinea Development Work Set to Boom', *Petroleum Economist*, 23 October 2001.

Natural gas, still largely flared across the region, is increasingly being harnessed for production and exportation. Interest in onshore oil development has proceeded in tandem, despite political instability. At the forefront of this process are major Western IOCs that have dominated oil production in the region since the 1950s, such as Exxon-Mobil, Chevron, BP, Royal Dutch/Shell and Total. But scores of other companies of diverse sizes and origins are also taking part in this rush for business deals.

While Chinese oil companies have recently gained important footholds in high-profile Gulf of Guinea producers such as Nigeria, Angola and Equatorial Guinea, their first African stop was Sudan, a disreputable state mostly marginalized by the West since the 1990s. CNPC entered a partnership with Talisman, a Canadian oil company, and Malaysia's Petronas, and became the lead investor in the Greater Nile Petroleum Operation Co. From the Chinese point of view, there was no intrinsic sympathy for Sudan's exclusion by the West. China's objective was rather to explore the unique opportunity of putting down roots in the notoriously oil-rich Sudan while the country was still on the international blacklist. As John Ryle commented, 'the Chinese calculation [was] to consolidate and expand while Sudan is still a pariah state'.[35] In this, China was successful: not only is the country China's only major production site in Africa at the present time, but the end of the civil war in the south has also rekindled investors' interest in Sudan. China's willingness to engage with Sudan at a troubled time means it is in an ideal position to benefit from peacetime investment opportunities. Sudan's leadership has also benefited from this partnership, counting on oil revenues for regime survival and on China to deflect international criticism of the state-supported violence in Darfur. This could not conceivably take place without the resources made available to the Sudanese government by Chinese oil firms, even if at the political level Chinese complicity is matched by that of others such as the Arab League.[36]

---

35 Peter S. Goodman, 'China Invest Heavily in Sudan Oil Industry', *Washington Post*, 23 December 2004.

36 See the chapter by Daniel Large for a more detailed discussion of China-Sudan relations.

The Sudan case is exemplary of Chinese business methods in the African oil industry, not only because of China's willingness to get involved in rough spots and neglected regions, even if this is one of its hallmarks—notice, for instance, CNOOC's decision to enter the Niger Delta precisely when the insurgency there was expected to discourage new investors.[37] More importantly, the Sudan experience shows China's capacity for providing 'package deals' that promise aid, credit lines, and investment in infrastructure and other sectors that commercially minded companies would never contemplate, and that Western donors are not interested in. In Nigeria, for instance, CNOOC offered a US$2.7 billion development spending commitment on top of the US$2 billion-plus purchase of a 45 per cent stake in a Niger Delta oil block.[38] For its part, CNPC's acquisition of four drilling licenses came with its taking up of a controlling stake in the Kaduna refinery. That refinery's privatization had been decided in the 1990s but its poor condition and the impossibility of making a (legal) profit in Nigeria's downstream meant that serious investors had never before materialized.[39] Moreover, and although these deals were not tied up together, China's simultaneous offer to invest US$1 billion in Nigeria's crumbling railway system (yet another sure money loser) cemented Nigerian good will.[40]

As shown in the Nigerian case, a key feature of Chinese oil deals in Africa is that they are much more generous than those of other firms. Some analysts argue that this is a sign of inexperience, while others contend that this is because China is assuming that commodity prices will remain very high during the lifetime of its projects.

---

37 This elicited a bellicose reaction from MEND, the guerrilla group behind most of the attacks in 2006, which told Chinese oil companies to 'stay well clear' of the Niger Delta. See Dino Mahtani, 'Stay away from the delta, Nigerian rebels tell China,' *Financial Times*, 1 May 2006.

38 'It's definitive: CNOOC concludes its Niger Delta mega-deal—or so it thinks', *African Energy* 95, February 2006.

39 In a typical twist of Nigerian politics, CNPC subsequently lost the bid to a well-connected local group but reportedly remains keen on getting involved in the Kaduna refinery. See Wang Ying, "CNPC may expand its Nigerian oil refinery", *ShanghaiDaily.com*, 3 March 2008.

40 Rory Carroll, 'China extends its reach into Africa with $1bn deal for Nigeria's railways', *Guardian* 23 May 2006.

Whatever the case, Chinese oil companies can only afford to do so because they can access cheap finance through state banks in what critics have called 'predatory finance'.[41] As the *Economist* noted in a survey of Chinese foreign acquisitions, the fact that Chinese NOCs are linked to the state means that 'the cost of capital is close to zero': they do not always need to 'make a commercial return or perhaps even repay loans from state banks'. In turn, state bank loans are made available either at concessional loans with long maturities or 'at no interest at all'. Though 'clearly nonsense in a world of rational economics,' the *Economist* concludes, 'the abundant domestic liquidity and [...] foreign exchange reserves' means that 'it is [...] a nonsense that can go on for a long time'.[42] While there is disagreement as to the reasons for the Chinese willingness to pay so handsomely, the upshot from an African perspective is precisely that the Chinese will pay more and they are welcomed on that basis.

This is evident in China's involvement in Angola, which recently surpassed Saudi Arabia as China's number one source of oil imports during 2006.[43] As elsewhere, China's apparent willingness to overpay for assets is coupled with a readiness to leverage oil sector participation with a number of non-oil sector perks. In 2004, Sinopec outbid India's ONGC bid for block 3 and offered a major credit line and a commitment to the reconstruction of Angola's rail system. Sinopec also agreed to participate in a joint venture with Sonangol to finance and manage Sonaref's 200,000 bpd refinery in Lobito. The Lobito refinery had been a pet project of the Angolan leadership for more than a decade. But despite the involvement of major foreign consulting firms, its dubious economics meant that it could not garner enough interest from Western companies to see the light of day.

41 Peter Evans and Erica S. Downs, 'Untangling China's Quest for Oil Through State-backed Financial Deals', *Brookings Policy Brief* 154, May 2006.

42 'Chinese companies abroad: the dragon tucks in', *Economist*, 30 June 2005. An assessment by the respected oil consulting firm Wood Mackenzie noted that Asian NOCs 'have not drastically overpaid for asset acquisitions', especially in view of the consistently high oil prices of the past years. See 'Wood Mackenzie predicts establishment of Big Eastern Oil to rival Big Western Oil', Wood Mackenzie Press Release, 29 June 2006.

43 See the chapter by Manuel Ennes Ferreira for a more detailed discussion of Angola-China relations.

Sinopec's enabling of the refinery was thus far more momentous than a mere business deal.[44] It is also the tip of the Chinese iceberg in Angola. By opening up three credit lines totalling almost US$6 billion in a mere two years, the Chinese have enabled the Angolan government both to pursue its postwar reconstruction strategy in the absence of a Western donors' conference and to keep its distance from the IMF's transparency prescriptions although the subsequent increase in oil production and oil pries also played a key role. Moreover, China's willingness to partner with African NOCs gives it an edge over other companies when it comes to licensing rounds[45] and, through the sharing of technology and expertise, suggests the will to build relationships for the long haul.

It is true that Chinese NOCs are, for that time being, technically inferior to their Western competitors. Yet to stress the technical element excessively is to forget that African elites are as politically minded as the Chinese investors, and can do with less-than-stellar oil firms if they are bearers of other rewards. In other words, while still lagging behind Western companies in most areas, Chinese NOCs bring to the table the weight of the Chinese state, a willingness to pay for long-term engagements that would not be viable if perceived in the short term, and cheap finance to secure deals. As Robert Ebel notes, NOCs from importing nations, 'by their very nature, can offer terms far more acceptable to supplier nations than IOCs. In these instances energy requirements are often difficult to distinguish from political goals'.[46] This strategy is strongly underpinned by an activist petro-diplomacy, consisting of numerous visits by Chinese senior officials (including mostly recently China's President Hu Jintao and Premier Wen Jiabao). While a discussion of China's Africa diplomacy falls outside the ambit of this chapter, suffice it to say

---

44 The deal was called off in March 2007 by the Angolan government reportedly out of fear that Chinese investors wanted to corner the refinery' output for China's domestic market. See Lucy Corkin, 'Angola flexes newfound muscle', *Business Day*, 23 March 2007 and especially "Big oil, high stakes", *Africa-Asia Confidential*, 2 November 2007.

45 This was shown in the joint Sonangol-Sinopec acquisition of three deepwater blocs and many other instances of collaboration.

46 Ebel, *China's Energy Debate*, p. 84.

that China has provided oil producers with either implicit political support (as in the case of Sudan which, in part because of China, has been able to avoid full international opprobrium over Darfur) or the means to override external criticism (in the case of Angola and that of Chad, where recognition of mainland China in August 2006 allowed it access to Chinese aid and added support for its tussle with the World Bank). This largely accounts for the political, as opposed to merely economic, attraction of Chinese oil investment from the viewpoint of African incumbents.

Making sense of China's energy policy in Africa

I will now briefly discuss the likely impact of Chinese oil investment in Africa from the viewpoint of Africans, the Western companies and governments often described as rivals of the Chinese, and China and its NOCs.

The arrival of Chinese companies is welcomed by African elites both economically and politically. This is not necessarily the case with ordinary Africans who do not see any improvement upon the behaviour of traditional (mostly Western) oil investors and often resent Chinese employment practices. The same applies to political forces that are excluded from access to power-sharing and oil revenues: they have lost little time in demonstrating their hostility to Chinese oil firms as perceived accomplices of their adversaries. Already in the late 1990s, South Sudanese forces had deemed Chinese oil installations legitimate targets in their struggle against Khartoum. In the Niger Delta MEND,[47] an opaque rebel group with a separatist agenda, blew up car bombs in April 2006 as a warning to Chinese oil companies.[48] More seriously, nine Chinese Sinopec workers were slain in April 2007 during a rebel attack while prospecting in the Ethiopian-held Ogaden region.[49]

---

47 Movement for the Emancipation of the Niger Delta.

48 See Dino Mahtani, 'Stay away from the Delta, Nigerian Rebels tell China', *Financial Times*, 30 April 2006.

49 See Chris Buckley, 'China condemns Ethiopia attack amidst security fears', *Reuters News*, 26 April 2007, and 'Attack on Chinese-run oil field a reminder of dangers of China's interest in Africa', *International Herald Tribune*, 24

These sobering experiences have certainly demonstrated to the Chinese oil companies that they do not exist above local politics and that their elite pacts cannot provide a consistent degree of security for their operating conditions. But there is nothing new to this; Western oil companies have been labouring under these conditions for decades. Furthermore, the deep unpopularity of the oil industry in many oil-producing countries in Africa has never weighted decisively against its presence: even in areas such as the Niger Delta or Cabinda, where armed struggle has resulted from local grievances, this has not ultimately led to the ousting of Western oil companies. The same applies to Chinese NOCs. For them, the supporters they need to cultivate are still the domestic powerholders who alone control foreigners' legal access to oil resources. The subsequent problems caused by lack of legitimacy and the empirical demise of African states are perceived in security terms and addressed in the time-honored codes of an enclave extractive industry.

African elites understand that more investment and a plurality of investors can only increase revenues and their own negotiation leeway, both in oil industry terms and as states in the international system. In particular, the many associated Chinese businesses that come into an economy on the crest of oil investment constitute new business opportunities where African insiders can get involved in as the indispensable local partners.[50] Whether or not Chinese companies are at the cutting edge of environmental and labour practices does not rate highly in the concerns of decision-makers. The massive use of Chinese expatriate workers for the performance of non-skilled tasks in Angola has met substantial popular disapproval but next to no complaints by the political elite. The same applies to the environment: exposed while drilling for oil in the Luango Natural Reserve with unsuitable methods and without a permit, Sinopec could count on the support of the Gabonese government despite the public outcry against the company.[51]

April 2007.

50 See Manuel Ennes Ferreira's chapter in this volume for examples from Angola.

51 'China's Sinopec provokes conservation uproar in Gabon', *Agence France*

The point needs to be underlined: the most obvious consequence of the massive investment of Chinese oil companies is an increase in revenues for the governments of oil-rich states. Major decisions about how these revenues are spent will depend on Africans decision-makers, including the degree to which resource extraction is sustainable, the degree to which it is turned into a 'source of technology, skill formation and market access',[52] and the degree to which its rewards will be broadly shared. Unfortunately, an analysis of political and economic dynamics across oil-producing states—in terms of the self-serving, short-termist motivations of elites, the lack of capacity of institutions, and the feebleness of highly dependent economies—points to outcomes that are not markedly different from those of earlier oil windfalls.[53]

Politically, the effect of China's oil partnerships has been the strengthening of authoritarian, non-developmentalist governments and their avoidance of Western pressure in a number of key areas. This is not necessarily China's goal, but the political uses of its presence by self-serving incumbents are overwhelmingly negative. The latter perceive China's business-only approach as adding a degree of diversification to a landscape hitherto dominated by (at least theoretically intrusive) Western prescriptions.[54] This is especially the case with states such as Sudan, Angola or Chad, which faced a fairly unanimous stance from Western donors as to the reforms needed for engagement. African elites also appreciate China's understanding of,

---

Presse, 28 September 2006 and Philippe Alfroy, 'China's Sinopec 'illegally' destroying Gabon', *Business in Africa*, 29 September 2006.

52 Andrea Goldstein, Nicolas Pinaud, Helmut Reisen, and Xiaobao Chen, *The Rise of China and India: What's in it for Africa?* (Paris: OECD Development Center, 2006), p. 111.

53 For a study of this see Soares de Oliveira, *Oil and Politics in the Gulf of Guinea* and also Soares de Oliveira, 'Context, Path Dependency and Oil Based Development in the Gulf of Guinea', in Michael Dauderstadt and Arne Schildberg (eds), *Dead Ends of Transition: Rentier Economies and Protectorates* (Frankfurt: Campus Verlag, 2006).

54 Even before the establishment of the close Sino-Angolan partnership, officials of the NOC Sonangol could be heard salivating about the 'business-only' approach of the Chinese (author interview, Luanda, 24 January 2004).

and assistance to, projects that they feel are essential but Westerners tend to dismiss as 'prestige' or 'vanity' extravaganzas such as Angola's 'Nova Luanda' or Khartoum's new presidential palace. African elites do not want Western companies to go, of course: they know they need the West's essential technical expertise and certainly do not want to replace Western donors with a new dependence on China. But they do hope that heightened competition will make Westerners more pragmatic and less shrill about their conditionalities.

The West will deal with the rise of Chinese oil firms in Africa in a contradictory way. Western media and especially NGOs will mostly give their activities in Africa a bad coverage. The latter are the most evident losers in the process of China's expanding Africa role: in contrast with Western firms, which seek to be seen trying to address the criticism of civil society organizations, the Chinese government and oil companies often ignore NGOs.[55] But 'the West' is not a unitary actor trying to force 'transparency' and 'good governance' on wayward African oil producers. Beyond rhetoric, official Western reactions will be dependent on a Chinese engagement with international oil markets that is less equivocal and on a Chinese presence that does not detract from the business opportunities available to Western companies (which has not happened yet in most cases, as Roland Marchal argues in this volume). Chinese-Western relations over Africa's oil are therefore dependent on wider political dynamics. If these conditions for mutual adjustment are met, and China starts to behave like a mature energy importer (as most importer states

---

55 This view was expressed by several representatives of French NGOs at a seminar on China-Africa relations (Paris, 5 July 2007). Potential campaigning strategies for Western NGOs tackling Chinese activities in Africa are unlikely to be successful if framed in the same terms as those focusing on Western actors. Rather than direct lobbying in China, the more effective points of pressure are the Western regulatory agencies that Chinese companies want the approval of, such as the SEC, and would-be Western investors in subsidiaries of Chinese companies. In the case of Sudan, a heavy-handed campaign around the so-called 'Genocide Olympics' has nonetheless had the effect of concentrating Chinese decision-makers' minds as to the reputational damage of this close partnership. Initiatives such as the 'Publish What You Pay' campaign (www.pwyp.org, accessed 23 April 2007)—calling for standards that, if adopted, would apply to any company listed in Western stock exchanges—seem like a good place to start.

have tended to), governments in the West can only be happy at the Chinese willingness to pump more oil from inhospitable locations. The same applies to Western IOCs, which perceive their Chinese counterparts as much as an opportunity as a threat, especially when compared with the NOCs of oil producing countries. They will cry foul when state-supported Chinese bids thwart their own agendas, but will otherwise pragmatically go into business with the Chinese, as they have in Angola and Nigeria. As mentioned before, Western oil majors are strategic investors in the internationally listed subsidiaries of the three Chinese companies and cooperate extensively with them in China and elsewhere. Close partnerships with Chinese companies carry reputation risks, especially with activist constituencies in the West. But there are ways to go around this. The internationally listed, partially privatized subsidiaries of the three major companies are also tailor-made to fit Western expectations of accountability and corporate governance. When threatened with a Sudan-related investor backlash on the eve of being floated on the New York stock exchange, CNPC merely expunged from its soon-to-be-listed subsidiary, Petrochina, everything connected with Sudan operations. This ungainly wart removed, the company was highly attractive for would-be investors, and its flotation a success.[56] The *à la carte* system presupposed in this means that the subsidiaries of Chinese oil companies can move into the mainstream of Western capital markets while their differently-run parent companies continue to do business in states marginalized by the West.

The overseas activities of Chinese NOCs, their close articulation with Chinese state interests, and their initial scepticism towards the market mechanism as the solution for supply security are nothing new. China's policies are in fact 'no different' than those once pursued by 'other oil-importing countries concerned about the linkage between national and energy policy'.[57] Nevertheless, this politicized, market-

---

56 Goodman, 'China Invest Heavily'.

57 Ebel, *China's Energy Debate*, p. 5. According to the IEA, Chinese current policies 'mirror the classic moves of nations which found themselves in import dependency in the past' (International Energy Agency, *China's Worldwide Quest for Energy* (Paris: IEA, 2000), pp. 8-9). They are particularly reminiscent of the activities of European national champions such as France's

sceptic understanding of energy security[58] is at variance with that now broadly accepted by the industrial nations.[59] This approach is likely to continue for some time and Africa will play a key role in it. There is no doubting the stamina and competitiveness of Chinese oil companies. The leading oil consultancy Wood Mackenzie is right is stating that their presence is not a transient factor in Africa or elsewhere, and in heralding the arrival of 'Big Eastern Oil' to the continent.[60]

For the time being, Chinese NOCs are clearly inexperienced. But they learn fast and seem keen to emulate their Western counterparts in many ways, as a cursory look at their English-language websites will show. Might this mean that Chinese oil companies will end up

---

Elf Aquitaine (or Italy's ENI) until their privatization in the 1990s. The activities of these firms were informed by a paradigm—sometimes termed 'the French paradigm'—characterized by 'defiance towards the market and the willingness to put in place, under state initiative, a direct, concrete, and controlled link between national demand and the resources necessary for its fulfillment'. See Pierre Noel, 'Indépendance enérgetique versus marché mondial', *Revue de l'Énergie*, September 1999, pp. 2-3. France reacted to the 1973-74 oil crisis by primarily pursuing an aggressive campaign at energy independence that included the building up of one of the world's leading nuclear sectors. France only adhered to the EIA in 1992, and the primarily political running of Elf-Aquitaine was only halted by privatization in the mid-1990s and merger with TotalFina in 1999. The French convergence with the international oil market is therefore very recent and, some would argue, still to be completed.

58 Andrews-Speed *et al.*, 'Searching for Energy Security', p. 17.

59 US commentators who berate China for 'not understanding oil markets' also deny the eminently political, as opposed to merely commercial, nature of the international political economy of oil. (Ironically, these are the same commentators who chastise Venezuela, Iran and Russia for trying to score political victories on the back of their oil resources.) This reaction, often dressed up as an affirmation of the 'natural' character of oil markets as *markets*, is really a plea to the effect that oil *should* continued to be traded in the open market, not locked up. After three decades of OPEC price hikes, political upheavals, and wilful disruption of supplies (not to mention the frequent resort to the rhetoric of resource nationalism) it should be obvious that there is nothing natural about oil markets: as with all markets, they are a political construct, subject to decay and disruption. The implicit fear is that China's actions to secure its energy supplies may paradoxically contribute towards such a market deterioration.

60 Wood Mackenzie, 'Wood Mackenzie predicts establishment of Big Eastern Oil'.

supporting human rights, good governance, transparency, etc., at least to the grudging rhetorical extent that Western oil companies have? While rash observers assume that Chinese authorities simply do not care about being perceived as cavalier in this regard, in reality the Chinese government is extremely image-conscious. It makes consistent attempts at deploying 'soft power' and wants to be liked.[61] Note, for instance, the insistent disclaimers put out by Premier Wen Jiabao in his most recent trip to Africa to the effect that China was *not* pursuing a resource grab strategy in the continent,[62] or the reference in the Africa policy white paper to a need for 'competent Chinese enterprises' to invest in Africa.

There is certainly a nascent debate in some Chinese circles about corporate social responsibility. Some minor convergence may take place in the near future. A measure of PR-driven rhetorical acceptance of the Western-dominated discourse on how companies should behave will certainly occur. But this will not change the key operational features described above, for four reasons. Firstly, Chinese companies simply do not face the scrutiny of activist shareholders or a concerned civil society back home. There is an emerging pluralist debate on this in China, but if progressives in Western liberal democracies have not yet succeeded with their companies, why should Chinese critics get much further (or even that far)? Secondly, the fact that China tries to please does not mean that it is trying to please a minority of activists in the West. While Chinese oil companies do not want to be the targets of a media-driven smear campaign, the true constituencies they are seeking to charm are firstly, those of elites in the developing countries they are getting involved in, and secondly, those of regulatory bodies in the West that are essential for their international mainstreaming. In other words, Chinese companies may want to please the Sudanese government and the US Securities and

---

61 Bates Gill and Yanzhong Huang, 'Sources and Limits of Chinese "Soft Power"', *Survival* 48, 2 (2006), pp. 17-36.

62 See, e.g., Gavin Stamp, 'China defends its African relations', *BBC News*, 26 June 2006; Ana Dias Cordeiro, 'Primeiro-ministro da China em visita histórica a Angola', *Público*, 20 June 2006; 'China and Africa: for better or for worse?', *IRIN News*, 27 June 2006.

Exchange Commission, but not necessarily Human Rights Watch or Environmental Defense.

The third reason is that while they seek to placate some general criticism, Chinese companies will not want to become 'stakeholders' in Western progressive agendas that, if taken beyond mere window-dressing, could erode the meagre comparative advantage they currently possess. Even leaving aside the more demanding transparency and 'good governance' issues, forcing Chinese companies to abandon package deals, predatory financing, and overt support for ostracized despots might well be the death of them. And finally, to expect major changes in this stance is to misunderstand just how deep some of the Chinese government's assumptions run. Non-interference, mutual respect, the primacy of national sovereignty, etc., are not simply ploys to get ahead commercially, even if they do serve that purpose: they are coterminous with China's prevalent foreign policy values. Converging with something like the Western conditional approach to sovereignty would mark a sea change in Chinese policy that simply does not seem forthcoming in the short run.

It is important to keep China's oil partnerships and their consequences at the centre of any assessment. This said, one must not overstate the difference between the methods of Western companies and those of the Chinese newcomers. For many decades, the extraction of oil in Africa was structured around a *Realpolitik* relationship between oil-producing states, companies, and Western oil-importing states. The latter wanted energy security and did not mind partnering with questionable regimes for that purpose. (Arguably, they still don't.[63]) It is undeniable that Western policies towards Africa over the past decade have greatly improved, notably through the partial acceptance of agendas on transparency and the appropriate behaviour of corporations, and that there are powerful civil society actors in the West that simply do not exist in China. However, the apparent rhetorical victory in the West of the progressive agendas obscures the extent to which, on the ground, very little has changed.[64] It also fails

---

63 The nature of this decades-long partnership cannot be explored here in detail. See Soares de Oliveira, *Oil and Politics in the Gulf of Guinea*.

64 It must be noted that the absence of meaningful changes on the ground cannot

to shed light over the fact that many Western business actors did not willingly accept these new expectations upon their behaviour: rather, they caved in to international civil society pressure. In this sense, the Chinese presence and its unproblematic and very competitive embrace of the *Realpolitik* agenda may be just the right excuse for Western companies, under pressure to finally deliver on their rhetorical commitments, to bring about a return to previous forms of business-only engagement with Africa's oil that seemed on their way out. In a recent interview, for instance, the head of the European Investment Bank decried Chinese business standards in Africa but only as a cue to suggesting that, in order to stay competitive, Western companies will have to do likewise.[65]

Conclusion

While Chinese oil investment in Africa is a recent affair, the decade-long Sudanese case excepted, an interim assessment is possible. Firstly, Chinese oil investment in Africa is politically motivated and state-supported, a common enough historical occurrence among anxious import-dependent nations. Chinese NOCs often ignore short-term commercial considerations for the sake of the real bottom line of their majority shareholder, the Chinese state, which is energy security. It remains uncertain whether China will in time converge with the market approach favoured by industrial nations or deepen its 'strategic' understanding of oil supplies. This will most certainly be a function of broader developments in US-Chinese relations. Secondly, the operating procedures and investment choices of Chinese oil companies continue to show lack of experience. They are also technically backward in comparison with their Western counterparts and are unlikely to tackle some of the more challenging oil deposits in the deep and ultra-deep waters. But these companies have a steep

be attributed to oil companies alone: the lack of reformist constituencies amongst the empowered political actors in oil states such as Angola are just as consequential. A more serious effort was started by Nigerian reformists in the second Obasanjo Administration, but even there the results are highly problematic.

65 Victor Mallet, 'Hunt for resources in the developing world', *Financial Times*, 12 December 2006.

learning curve and are determined to succeed. Furthermore, African elites are as interested in the political rewards of the Chinese presence as in their investment and are unlikely to disfavour Chinese companies on that basis. Incumbents have skilfully used this Chinese presence to advance political agendas with negative developmental outcomes.

Third, harsh criticism of China and its oil companies is factually correct. Chinese oil companies are willing to partner with and shore up some of Africa's most brutal regimes; show little interest in 'good governance', human rights, transparency, or the environment; and provide a discourse that 'effectively legitimizes human rights abuses and undemocratic practices'.[66] However, most analysts who compare it unfavorably to Western practice tend to misunderstand how the political economy of oil in Africa works and has worked for the past 40-odd years. What is presented as an illiberal departure from Western procedure and prescription is in fact mostly the 'business as usual' approach followed throughout the region. This should not lead observers to be lenient about the Chinese deportment in Africa's oil sector: the idea that Westerners cannot criticize Chinese oil companies in contexts such as Sudan because theirs have a bad history in the region is nonsense. But that history may rather undermine the singular demonization that is widespread in some circles.

Finally, and tied to the previous point: how should one assess the likely impact of China's oil firms? It seems clear that they are not much of a progressive force in Africa. This does not presuppose a blanket judgment about the China 'threat' to the continent. Rather, the Chinese impact—like everyone else's—will be sector-specific. There is no doubt benign potential for Chinese investment in Africa. But when it comes to oil, it would be surprising indeed if Chinese NOCs were willing to act in a manner that is qualitatively different from that of Western operators, or better than their own very low domestic standards. It is also improbable that their actions will not lead to the tragic governance standards that are the consistent outcome of oil production throughout Africa. Whether one thinks Chinese NOCs will be more of the same, or will actually be worse—and

---

66 Taylor, 'China's Oil Diplomacy in Africa', p. 958.

the Sudan case seems to show that Chinese companies have until recently not cared for fig-leaf respectability—it is difficult to claim that there will be significant benefits for the majority of Africans from Chinese oil investment.

Of course, such negative, non-developmental consequences are not an inexorable outcome of petroleum economies, the activities of oil companies, or the presence of China, even if they all play a significant role. Although there are particular challenges to the proper management of oil revenues, it is undeniable that the resources made available by the present oil boom (according to some sources, the greatest inflow of money into Africa in history)[67] present the rulers of African oil-rich states with the opportunity to make consequential choices about the welfare of their citizens that are simply not available to the rulers of most of Africa's oil-poor countries. The role of African leaderships, and what they do with this opportunity, are therefore vital here. That the wrong choices are often made, and that the masses suffer immesurably from them, show the extent to which those in positions of power play a key role in fashioning the lives, and also the deaths, of their fellow Africans across the continent today.

---

67 Ian Gary and Terry Lynn Karl, *Bottom of the Barrel: Africa's Oil Boom and the Poor* (Baltimore: Catholic Relief Services, 2003).

5

THE POLITICAL CONSEQUENCES
OF CHINA'S RETURN TO AFRICA

Denis M. Tull

While the economic aspects of the PRC's growing involvement in Africa have received burgeoning attention, commerce, trade and related issues are not the only indicators of China's powerful return to the continent.[1] Beijing's political engagement with Africa has surged considerably over the last 10-15 years—although this fact is not captured by the neat measurement that economic indicators offer. For this reason, examining the political nature of the relations between China and Africa and the political impact this may have on the countries of the region is of paramount importance.[2] One can confidently assume that growing Sino-African interactions and the interests underpinning them are not limited to the economic realm—because, perhaps more than elsewhere in the world, economics and politics

---

1   This paper is based on Denis Tull, 'China's Engagement in Africa: Scope, Significance and Consequences', *Journal of Modern African Studies*, 44, 3 (2006), pp. 459-79.

2   A political aspect this chapter will not cover is the question of whether the growing interests of China and other emerging countries (Brazil, India, Malaysia etc.) in Africa could at least over the long term invalidate the received wisdom on Africa's international marginalization.

111

in Africa do not constitute clearly demarcated distinct spheres.[3] Instead they are intensely connected and determine the forms of authority and power (governmentalities) that are prevalent in Africa.[4] Therefore, even if one were to assume that the eagerness of African governments to build closer ties with China was primarily driven by anticipated economic benefits, this would be likely to have political implications too. Key to this are strategies of extraversion. For centuries Africa's political elites have used relationships of economic dependence vis-à-vis the outside world to assert claims on resources and thus consolidate their domestic authority.[5] To start from the assumption that Africa's emerging relations with China will mark a discontinuity in this regard would amount to a serious misreading of patterns that have characterized Africa's relations with the rest of the world for considerable periods of time.

To analyze the political dimension of China's growing interaction with Africa, this chapter addresses three questions: first, how does China's growing political involvement in Africa play out? Secondly, what are the factors that explain China's rising popularity with African governments? And finally, what are the political consequences of China's return for African countries and the region as a whole? The chapter is organized as follows: the first part will briefly sketch the general transformation of China's external relations, which provides the general background to the country's more dynamic foreign policy towards other regions of the world, including Africa. The second section will outline and summarize the evidence of China's increased political involvement with Africa. The interests and objectives underpinning this process will also be examined. In a third step, the recent evolution of Sino-African inter-state relations will be analysed by focusing on the key aspects that appear to make China an increasingly important and attractive political partner for African govern-

---

3   Robert Bates, *Markets and States in Sub-Saharan Africa* (Berkeley: University of California Press, 1981). Nicolas Van de Walle, *African Economies and the Politics of Permanent Crisis, 1979-1999* (Cambridge University Press, 2001).

4   Christopher Clapham, 'Governmentality and Economic Policy in Sub-Saharan Africa', *Third World Quarterly*, 17, 4 (1996), pp. 809-24.

5   Jean-François Bayart, 'Africa in the World: A History of Extraversion', *African Affairs*, 99, 395 (2000), pp. 217-67.

ments. The final part of this chapter will look at the political impact on Africa that can be deciphered so far from increasingly intense Sino-African relations.

The new parameters of China's foreign policy

China's increasing involvement in Africa is embedded in the general transformation of its foreign policy. It has embarked on a more active foreign policy over the last 15-20 years outside its own Asian neighbourhood. Abandoning its rather isolationist posture, China has developed legitimate claims to play a more active international role by expanding and intensifying its bilateral relations throughout the world, joining regional bodies dealing with security and economic issues and extending its involvement in multilateral organisations. Therefore most analysts agree that Beijing's foreign policy has become more dynamic, flexible and constructive than it was in previous decades.[6] The causes of this remarkable transformation of external relations are manifold: firstly, it is based on China's enormous economic success story over the past two decades. This has ushered in a more confident posture vis-à-vis the outside world, which in turn has undergirded the country's quest to be recognized as an important global player by the rest of the international community. Secondly, and strongly related, practical economic necessities convinced the Chinese leadership to embark on a more active foreign policy. The financial crisis in Asia in the late 1990s highlighted the vulnerability of China's economy to global shocks. Since much of China's economic success was based on its integration into the world economy, this interdependence exposed the country to dangers that were to be mitigated by a more active political posture. In other words, regional and international stability were increasingly perceived as a critical factor of continued domestic economic growth. Beijing conceived a more active foreign policy as the best strategy to defend and assert its national interests abroad. Thirdly, the emergence of the uncontested hegemony of the United States at the end of the Cold War also

6   Evan S. Medeiros, and M. Taylor Fravel, 'China's New Diplomacy', *Foreign Affairs*, 82, 6 (2003), pp. 22-35; Robert Sutter, 'Asia in the Balance: America and China's 'Peaceful Rise'', *Current History*, September 2004, pp. 284-9.

provided a stimulus for a reinvigorated foreign policy. Anxious that US supremacy in the international system might negatively affect China's 'peaceful rise' as a global power, Beijing developed the concept of *multipolarity*, which it defined as the forging of more or less flexible alliances to counter US hegemony and to build a fair global order. Putting this concept into practice necessitated the search for international, notably non-Western allies to enhance China's global leverage.[7] Furthermore, the conceptualization of China as a 'strategic competitor' by the US administration of President George W. Bush seemed to underscore that a *multipolar* world order, in which China was to present an important pole, was in Beijing's best interest.[8]

In summary, strategic considerations instigated a more active and globally-oriented foreign policy and, by extension, the search for allies, primarily in the southern hemisphere, on whom Beijing could rely in the pursuit of its national and international interests. The need to expand and strengthen China's bilateral relations with the states in sub-Saharan Africa was part of this strategy. From this perspective, China's fast increasing engagement in Africa is not so much a reflection of a singular or specific policy towards the continent. Instead, it is part of a general policy thrust that manifests itself similarly in Beijing's relations with other regions of the world (for example Latin America and the Middle East).

China's political involvement in Africa: an overview

Although China's engagement with Africa has surged over the last few years, the country is not a newcomer to the continent.[9] Throughout the post-independence period of postcolonial Africa, China fostered relations with the states of the region. Aside from Beijing's

---

7   Peter Hays Gries, 'China Eyes the Hegemon', *Orbis*, 49, 3 (2005), pp. 401-12.

8   Elizabeth Economy, 'Changing course on China', *Current History*, 102, 665 (2003), pp. 243-49.

9   Philip Snow, *The Star Raft: China's Encounter with Africa* (Ithaca: Cornell University Press, 1989); Roland Marchal, 'Comment être semblable tout en étant différent? Les relations entre la Chine et l'Afrique', in Roland Marchal (ed.), *Afrique-Asie: échanges inégaux et mondialisation subalterne* (forthcoming).

activities during the Cold War, African countries were always important in the race for international recognition with separatist Taiwan. The harsh reaction of Western states to the suppression of the pro-democracy movement in 1989 provided the impetus for renewed engagement with Africa, after a period of relative passivity starting in the late 1970s. The imposition of sanctions by the US and the European Union (EU) compelled the Chinese government to seek closer ties to countries of the developing world, including Africa. This spurred a massive increase in Chinese-African travel diplomacy, which still continues. Between 2003 and 2005 alone, more than 100 high-level meetings between Chinese and African envoys took place.[10] In the first six months of 2006, President Hu Jintao, Foreign Minister Li Zhaoxing and Premier Wen Jiabao undertook trips to Africa, where they visited 15 countries, including Nigeria, Ghana, Angola, Kenya and the Republic of Congo. For over a decade now, successive Foreign Ministers have made it a ritual to start the year's travel diplomacy with trips to Africa. Furthermore, and apart from the four states which entertain diplomatic ties with Taiwan (Burkina Faso, The Gambia, São Tomé e Príncipe, Swaziland), China has embassies in every African country. A rather novel part of diplomatic Sino-African interaction is the China-Africa Cooperation Forum.[11] Recently elevated from Ministerial level to a summit of heads of state, its third gathering occurred in November 2006. Finally, one of the most recent indications of China's renewed interest in Africa came in January 2006, when for the first time the Chinese government published an official paper outlining its policy towards Africa.[12]

Although an emerging economic superpower, China portrays itself, at least to African audiences, as a developing nation in order to underline the quasi-natural convergence of interests between China,

---

10 'Africa, China Growing Closer', *BBC Monitoring Newsletter*, May 2005.

11 Ian Taylor, 'The "All-Weather Friend"? Sino-African Interaction in the Twenty-First Century', in Ian Taylor and Paul Williams (eds), *Africa in International Politics: External Involvement on the Continent* (London: Routledge, 2005), pp. 89-91.

12 The paper ('China's Africa Policy') is available on the website of the Chinese Ministry of Foreign Affairs <http://www.fmprc.gov.cn/eng/zxxx/t230615.htm>.

'the biggest developing country and Africa, the continent with the largest number of developing countries' (Jiang Zemin). At the same time as stressing its attachment to 'South-South-solidarity', Beijing acknowledges its superior international standing and uses its permanent seat on the UN Security Council to position itself as a mentor of African countries on the global scene.[13] This includes China's claims to support fairer global trade and Africa's various reform-oriented institutions like the New Partnership for Africa's Development (NEPAD) and the AU, and an enlarged UN Security Council in which Africa should be represented.

While most of these pledges have remained extremely vague, China's increasing involvement in UN peacekeeping missions in Africa has been substantial. In 2004, for instance, some 1,400 Chinese participated in nine UN missions on the continent. The biggest contingent (558 troops) was sent to war-torn Liberia after the incoming Liberian government (2003) ended its diplomatic relations with Taiwan.[14] Likewise, a total of 1,090 Chinese soldiers have so far served in the UN Mission in the DR Congo.[15]

China's political involvement is matched or even overshadowed by its rising economic interests on the African continent. However, as will be shown below, there is plenty to indicate that China's political and economic interests and strategies in Africa go hand in hand. Fast expanding economic ties, dense travel diplomacy and a general discourse by both Chinese and African officials on the friendly ties between China and the countries of the region suggest indeed that Chinese influence in Africa is rising tremendously.

Growing engagement with Africa holds the promise of significant benefits for the Chinese government. With the exception of Nigeria and South Africa, most African countries are not heavyweights on the international political scene. However, the states of the region do amount to a quarter of the member states of the UN and thus are

---

13 'G8: Chinese Leader Urges More International Help for Africa', *Xinhua*, 16 July 2006.

14 However, China also provided 125 police officers for the UN mission in Haiti which recognizes Taiwan.

15 'China Sends Fifth Batch of Peacekeeping Troops to DR Congo', *BBC Monitoring*, 19 December 2005.

a source of considerable diplomatic support in international politics, particularly in international organizations with one country-one vote arrangements. For example, in the UN Commission on Human Rights, African countries have repeatedly—no less than 11 times, according to a Chinese diplomat—frustrated Western attempts to push through a formal condemnation of China's human rights policies.[16] Of late, intense courting led to China's recognition as a market economy by a good number of African states, a crucial status in the wake of China's WTO accession, to shield it from accusations of dumping practices.[17] Furthermore, African countries are said to have provided support for China's successful bid to host highly prestigious international events: the 2008 Olympic Games and the 2010 World Exposition.[18] African backing is also crucial in the Chinese pursuit of the concept of a multipolar world. As China has intensified its participation in international multilateral bodies, diplomatic assistance by African states has turned into a valuable asset of Chinese foreign policy. Finally, diplomatic support from African states pertains to the recognition of the principle of 'one China'. This remains an important issue for the Beijing leadership, even though it has lately lost some of its urgency as Beijing was considerably more successful than Taiwan in the quest for African recognition as the sole legitimate representative of China. Lesotho (1993), Liberia (2003), Senegal (2005) and most importantly South Africa (1998) all shifted recognition from Taiwan to the PRC in recent years. In August 2006, Taiwan suffered another blow when oil-producing Chad defected to Beijing, possibly to alleviate the pressure from Chadian rebels that President Deby had allegedly suspected to be backed by China via its allies in Sudan.[19] China's alleged support for the insurgents may

16 'L'Afrique Pro-Chinoise aux Nations Unies', *La Lettre du Continent*, 30 March 2006.

17 Thomas Rumbaugh and Nicolas Blancher, 'China: International Trade and WTO Accession', IMF Working Paper (04/36) (Washington, DC: IMF, 2004), p. 12.

18 'Premier Wen's Visit to Boost China-Africa Partnership: Official', *Xinhua*, 16 June 2006.

19 Keith Bradsher, 'Chad's switch to Beijing's side draws angry response in Taiwan', *Washington Post*, 8 August 2006.

not only have been linked to the Taiwan issue, but also had access to Chadian oil in mind.

What's in it for Africa?

But what about the political gains for African countries from increased interaction with China? The extent to which China appears to be welcomed with open arms by most African leaders clearly suggests that Sino-African relations are not a one-way street and that Beijing has benefits to offer its African partners, too. Indeed, mutual benefit is a recurrent subject of Chinese official jargon on Sino-African relations. As Chinese Premier Wen Jiabao restated: 'In cooperating with Africa, China is not looking for selfish gains. We are committed to two principles: equality, benefits both ways, and the non-interference in internal African affairs.'[20] According to Beijing, equality in Sino-African relations inevitably results in a 'win-win situation' for both sides. This stand is embedded in a discourse which posits China not only as an appealing alternative to the West, but also as a better choice for Africa. It is supplemented by Chinese references to the shared history of imperialism and colonialism that both China and Africa have suffered at the hands of Western states. Given the increasingly ambivalent relations between African countries and their former colonial powers, China makes a point of stressing its distinctiveness from Western countries and their policies towards Africa. Indeed, there is at least one major difference in the ways in which Beijing and Western governments approach their African counterparts.

This of course pertains to China's non-interference in internal African affairs, a policy based on unconditional respect for national sovereignty which makes any attempt to interfere into the domestic affairs of a state illegitimate. Needless to say, China's view on this issue does not specifically pertain to Africa. Rather, the notion of sovereignty and its corollary, non-interference, is a cornerstone of China's conception of statecraft and international relations as a whole. What makes the Chinese stance on sovereignty so particular

---

20 'China and Africa - for better or for worse?', *IRIN*, 27 June 2006.

in regard to Africa is the fact that perhaps nowhere else in the world has state sovereignty been more eroded than on that continent. This was largely the result of Western-prescribed policies over the past two decades, first in the guise of Structural Adjustment Programmes (SAPs) in the 1980s, then in the 1990s with demands for democratization. By tying development assistance to economic and political reform, well-intentioned Western donors sought to impose or support structural change in Africa's aid-dependent countries. Although not consistently carried out, the imposition of economic and political conditionalities progressively undermined the sovereignty of African states and put their governments under considerable stress. Unsurprisingly these demands for reform were not well received by African state elites who developed numerous strategies to evade them.[21]

China, in contrast, sticks to its state-centred orthodoxy. This is reflected in the fact that, apart from the Taiwan issue, no political conditions like respect for human rights are attached to the development assistance it provides to African countries. According to Premier Wen Jiabao, the Chinese government believes 'that African countries have the right and capability to solve their own problems'.[22] That this posture on the issue of sovereignty is gratefully acknowledged by African governments is hardly surprising. As a member of Djibouti's ruling party approvingly noted, China shows 'esteem of our sovereignty and freedom. That's why we African people always keep a friendly feeling toward China.'[23]

Comparing the non-intrusive attitudes of China with Western ones, other African officials are more candid. No doubt airing a common view among African governments, a spokesman of the Kenyan government observed: 'You never hear the Chinese saying that they will not finish a project because the government has not done enough to tackle corruption. If they are going to build a road, then it will be

---

21 Nicolas Van de Walle, *African Economies;* Nicolas Van de Walle, *Overcoming Stagnation in Aid-Dependent Countries* (Washington, DC: Center for Global Development, 2005).

22 'Premier Wen hails Sino-African ties of cooperation', *Xinhua*, 18 June 2006.

23 'African officials affirm China's aid for development in Africa', *Xinhua*, 15 June 2006.

built.'[24] Given the pervasiveness of corruption and autocratic structures in vast parts of Africa, China's lack of an ideological project in Africa and its pragmatic 'value-free' approach surely strikes a chord on much of the continent and explains to a large extent its rising popularity within African officialdom.[25]

Still, China's appeal certainly extends beyond Africa's hardened autocrats. The intrusive reform policies prescribed by Western donors are all too often at odds with the 'politics of the belly' in the vast majority of African countries where patronage and clientelist networks form the backbone of regime survival.[26] In this regard China's attractiveness to African governments may also be attributed to the fact that Chinese development assistance benefits the governments of receiving countries more directly than the policies of Western donors, who are preoccupied with the reduction of poverty. By the same token, Western donors for a long time perceived the African state as an obstacle to socio-economic development, often circumventing it and its elites by channelling aid through Non-Governmental Organizations. It was only at the end of 1980s that donors and the International Financial Institutions progressively abandoned their anti-statist policies, but Western development agencies still have an uneasy attitude towards the African state. This sharply contrasts with the state-centred concepts of the Chinese who, unlike Western countries, agree to finance grandiose and prestigious buildings (presidential palaces, football stadiums) that African leaders highly appreciate for their very own political reasons.

Similarly, China finances and builds infrastructure in many African countries, undertakings that—until recently—were out of fash-

---

24 See Tull, 'China's Engagement in Africa', op. cit.

25 By one measure, only 12 of the countries in Africa south of the Sahara are democratic whereas some 60 per cent of those states are hybrids or semi-democracies in which authoritarian practices and violations of human and political rights are still common. See Monty G. Marshall and Ted Robert Gurr, *Peace and Conflict 2005: A Global Survey of Armed Conflicts, Self-Determination Movements, and Democracy* (College Park: Centre for Inernational Development and Conflict-Management, University of Maryland, 2005: 43f.).

26 Jean-François Bayart, *The State in Africa. The Politics of the Belly* (London: Longman, 1993).

ion among the Western donor community. Since most infrastructure projects are public sector works, China conceives its investments as goodwill projects to woo the sympathies of African state leaders. This enables China to gain political influence, which often opens the doors for commercially or strategically more attractive businesses in other sectors, for example to win tenders for oil and mining concessions.[27] Somewhat exemplary in that regard is the decision by Chinese oil companies to invest in construction (e.g. Angola) or refurbishing of more or less defunct oil refineries (e.g. Nigeria)—steps from which Western investors have shied away but to which the governments of both those countries have attached great importance.[28] These are examples of the much touted mutual benefits in Sino-African relations, insofar as these investments enable China to lock up barrels while African governments can pursue their legitimate economic interests of building or reconstructing their moribund downstream sectors. In contrast to Western oil majors, which bid only for the juiciest stakes, the Chinese government and its companies thus provide economic know-how and relief that positively influence the attitudes of African elites towards China.

Returning to the politics of conditionality pursued by Western donors, it has not been lost on the Chinese government that a number of African governments have been unable to manage the political economy of reform imposed by Western donors over the past two decades, sometimes with devastating consequences such as outbreaks of violent conflict. In addition to the wholesale failure of economic reforms (SAPs), these setbacks, in Beijing's view, have merely confirmed its analysis that the poor record of Western-driven reform efforts in Africa will inadvertently facilitate Chinese advances

---

27 Karby Leggett, 'China flexes economic muscle throughout burgeoning Africa', *The Wall Street Journal*, 29 March 2005.

28 In Nigeria, CNPC was awarded rights of first refusal on a number of oil licenses in return for its commitment to acquire stakes in the Kaduna refinery. The same approach was taken by a Sinopec affiliate in Angola, where the investments in the building of a refinery is expected to provide the company with licenses for new oil blocks. For details, see the chapter by Ricardo Soares de Oliveira in this book.

on the continent. As *Renmin Ribao*, the official newspaper of the Communist Party, noted:

...owing to the general failure in the West's political and economic behaviour in Africa, African nations, which were only suspicious at first, are now negating Western-style democracy and have reinitiated "Afro-Asianism" and proposed "going towards the Orient". This has opened up new opportunities for further enriching the content and elevating the quality of China-Africa cooperation.[29]

The divergences between China's policy of non-interference and the intrusive approaches of Western states have nowhere been more evident than in African countries that have been denounced as so-called pariah states by the Western community.[30] Beijing's close ties to the regimes in Sudan and Zimbabwe have received particular attention. Increasingly isolated by Western states because of human rights abuses, both Khartoum and Harare have turned to China as an alternative source of aid, trade, investment and diplomatic backing. For example, China, as a member of the UN Security Council, repeatedly blocked Western-sponsored attempts to have sanctions imposed on the government of Sudan in relation to the conflict in Darfur.[31] It either abstained from casting its vote or threatened to make use of its veto right.[32] Similarly, China has opposed Security Council action against the government of Robert Mugabe in Zimbabwe. In 2005, it opposed discussion at the UN Security Council of a UN report into Zimbabwe's demolition campaign that left some 700,000 persons homeless.[33] More benign governments seek Beijing's diplomatic support too. For example, Senegal's recent shifting

---

29 Tull, 'China's Engagement in Africa', p. 467.

30 Chris Alden, 'China in Africa', *Survival*, 47, 3 (2005), p. 155.

31 *Reuters*, 'China threatens to veto Darfur UN draft—diplomats', 15 September 2004; Jasper Becker, 'China fights UN sanctions on Sudan to safeguard oil', *The Independent*, 15 October 2004.

32 Needless to say, China does not bear the sole responsibility for the international failure in Darfur. One has also to take into account the inconsistent positions of the US government and the ambiguous role of France. See Clough (2005).

33 'China, Tanzania Thwart Efforts to Put Zimbabwe Report on UN Agenda', *BBC Monitoring*, 26 July 2005.

of its recognition away from Taiwan to the PRC may well have been driven by the hope that China may support Senegal's bid to take one of the (to be created) African seats in an enlarged UN Security Council.

In the final analysis, and notwithstanding the peculiar cases of Sudan and Zimbabwe, the embracing of China by many African governments is an entirely rational and well-considered attitude. Beijing's rising political and economic interests provide Africa's countries with a rare opportunity to lessen their dependency on Western states and donor organizations by allowing them to diversify their relations with the outside world. As an alternative or additional source of diplomatic support, aid, investment and trade revenues, China is no doubt an attractive partner for African governments that perceive Western policies towards Africa as unduly intrusive and paternalistic. At the same time, China's popularity in Africa is also the flipside of Western neglect since the end of the Cold War, which resulted in a loss of Western strategic interests on the continent. Angola's President Eduardo dos Santos aired this opinion when he reportedly 'appreciated the fact that China assigns importance to Africa'—no doubt a reference to the relative withdrawal of the West from Africa.[34] By the same token, it can be argued that recent Western discourse on Africa, often focusing on the continent as a threat to international (i.e. Western) security, has done little to improve relations between African and Western governments.

The political consequences of China's return to Africa

To assess the political impact of China's growing involvement on the continent, it may be useful to distinguish three issues that are particularly relevant to specific groups of African countries today. First, the PRC's manifest return to Africa is occuring at a time when many countries of the region continue to undergo difficult political transitions from authoritarian to democratic political systems (*democratising/transition countries*). The assumption that China will make a constructive contribution to support transitions to democracy in Af-

---

34 'Chinese PM, Angolan President Discuss Ties, Stability in the Great Lakes Region', *BBC Monitoring*, 21 June 2006.

rica's fragile states appears far-fetched. In contrast to all other major donors in the region, except Libya, the promotion of democracy is obviously not an objective of China's foreign policy. Such a policy appears inconceivable to the extent that it does not square with Beijing's relativistic conception of individual human and political rights. In addition, the self-interest of the political elite of the Chinese one-party state contravenes the notion of supporting democracy abroad. Doing so would logically imply that China's Communist leadership would dent its domestic political legitimacy. This is one of the reasons why Beijing clings to the dogma of non-interference. Its defence of sovereignty, often to the benefit of unsavoury regimes, is likely to undermine existing efforts at political liberalization at large. For revenue from trade (and taxes), development assistance and other means of support (i.e. diplomatic backing) is likely not only to reduce the leverage of Western donors; it also widens the margins of manoeuvre of Africa's autocrats and help them to rein in domestic demands for democracy and the respect for human rights. In other words, Africa's autocratic or semi-democratic leaders will benefit from close relations with China while ordinary citizens are likely to be negatively affected by this relationship.

A second source of concern is China's impact on *mineral-rich countries*, which often happen to be conflict or 'post-conflict' states. The fact that Chinese companies are bringing much-needed investment to challenging countries like the DR Congo or Sierra Leone is positive.[35] However, these business activities can be problematic. Increased Chinese interests in African resources come at a time when Western NGOs, recently supported by governments, have initiated an increasingly prominent debate on the relationship between mineral wealth on the one hand and its detrimental effects on developing countries on the other. It revolves around possible options and regulatory frameworks to transform mineral wealth from a 'curse' into a vector of socio-economic development. In light of its rapidly growing reliance on imports, it seems unlikely that China will join these efforts, let alone subordinate its economic interests to international

---

35 Andrew Child and David White, 'Chinese investors Targeting Virgin Markets on the Cheap', *Financial Times*, 15 March 2005.

attempts to solve the structural problems of richly endowed countries, as these are likely to hold back its access to resources. What is more, Beijing has no economic incentive to fall in line with Western views on fiscal transparency and accountability. By rejecting regulation efforts on the grounds of non-interference, China can position itself as a free-rider and is likely to win the political favour of and, by extension, economic benefits from sovereignty-conscious governments. In that regard, the case of Darfur (Sudan) is illuminating in so far as it underscores the extent to which China is prepared to defend its economic interests. That the Chinese government donated $400,000 in support of the AU's mediation efforts to resolve the Darfur crisis in early 2005, a move that it hailed as a contribution to peace-building in Africa, appears disconcertingly cynical in that regard. If Sudan provides any clue for the future, it seems inconceivable that Beijing, not bothered by the humanitarian tragedy in Darfur, will compromise its interests for the sake of 'minor' (domestic) issues such as transparency.

A somewhat related question concerns the geopolitical implications that are likely to emerge if China continues its aggressive acquisition of energy in Africa and if—as many observers argue—the US also increases its energy demands in Africa over the next decade or so. Will this result in fierce competition for oil and gas between the two countries, or can political conflicts be avoided by mutual cooperation? At present the US administration claims to be fairly relaxed, while some voices in Congress warn of conflicts of interest in Africa.[36] Others even foresee a new scramble for Africa's resources, but one in which Africans, in the words of Kenya's Foreign Minister, 'are willing negotiators'.[37]

Finally, regarding *peace and security*, it is hard to come to the conclusion that China has played a generally constructive role in Africa. Firstly, China has become a major provider of arms and weapons to Africa. Between 2000 and 2003, for example, China was the second

36 US Department of Energy, *Energy Policy Act 2005*. Section 1837: National Security Review of International Energy Requirements (Washington, DC: February 2006).

37 Lionel Barber and Andrew England, 'China's scramble finds welcome in Kenya', *Financial Times*, 9 August 2006.

most important arms supplier of African states.[38] It is also discomforting that China provided weapons to both sides of the Ethiopian-Eritrean war. Secondly, China is supporting African militaries across the continent, often with little concern for the impact this may have on peace, security and human rights.[39] Thirdly, a number of reports suggest that China has not respected international arms embargos. Of course, as long as these are imposed by Western bodies, it has no legal obligation to respect them. But there are also indications that China has broken arms sanctions which were imposed by the UN Security Council.[40]

Conclusion

In summary, the evidence so far seems to indicate that overall China's return to Africa presents a negative political development that almost certainly does *not* contribute to the promotion of peace and democracy on the continent.[41] Even so, it is one thing to highlight some of China's egregious policies in Africa and quite another to echo the indiscriminate China-bashing that much of the media and other observers in the West are indulging in. Although Western policies towards Africa have come to reflect a more normative and reform-oriented edge in recent years and have broadly sought to promote appropriate objectives (democracy, human rights and conflict prevention), Western decision-makers have little reason to claim the moral high-ground vis-à-vis China. A fair number of flaws and criticisms that need to be levelled against Beijing's politics in Africa equally apply, though to a lesser extent, to Western policies towards Africa.

---

38 Richard F Grimmett, 'Conventional Arms Transfers to Developing Nations, 1996–2003' (Washington, DC: Congressional Research Service, 2004), p. 27.

39 Amnesty International, *People's Republic of China: Sustaining Conflict and Human Rights Abuses. The Flow of Arms Accelerates* (London: 2006).

40 Taylor, 'The "All-Weather Friend"?' p. 96. Amnesty International, *People's Republic of China: Sustaining Conflict and Human Rights Abuses. The Flow of Arms Accelerates* (London: 2006).

41 Taylor, 'The "All-Weather Friend"?', p. 99.

The broadly normative shift of Western policies towards Africa may be one of the reasons why the subject of Chinese-African relations has drawn such an extraordinary and often heated response since 2006 in many quarters. One is inclined to think that the attention the subject has received in the West has much to do with the attempts of Westerners to demarcate themselves from China and its 'value-free' politics towards a region that most Westerners falsely continue to see as a passive and helpless object of international politics. As regards the popular China-bashing, however, one cannot help thinking that Beijing's Africa policies are extremely *en vogue* if only because they provide Westerners with some respite from reflecting on their own deficient policies towards Africa. However, it needs to be clearly admitted that the study of China-African relations is in its infancy, and that accordingly the analysis presented in this chapter is merely a preliminary and tentative assessment. To learn about China's long-term and broad political impact on Africa, future research needs to pay much more attention to cases other than the few outrageous ones (notably Sudan) which are commonly cited as evidence of China's negative impact on Africa. This necessitates a closer look at Africa's Benins, Ethiopias and Rwandas, i.e. countries where China is present but where the political consequences of its involvement will be less evident and less obviously linked to the much touted hunger for resources and its attendant ruthless policies.

Ultimately, China's future role in Africa will be determined by African actors themselves, of whom a growing number seem to recognize that there are also downsides to China's growing involvement in Africa.[42] African actors, of course, are not a homogeneous lot. They include autocratic governments that have every interest to forge closer ties with China, if only to escape Western pressures for political and economic liberalization. Over the last decades, they have demonstrated deft skills in playing outside powers off against each other. But African actors also include the region's reform-minded organizations, namely the AU, NEPAD, and the Economic Community of West African States (ECOWAS). Recently these bod-

---

42 At present, however, it seems that these concerns are mainly focused on negative consequences in the economic realm.

ies have espoused procedures and principles which contravene the cornerstone of Chinese statecraft—state sovereignty. The progressive path taken by AU and ECOWAS in regard to the prevention and resolution of violent conflicts is particularly at loggerheads with Beijing's political concepts, for both organizations claim far-reaching prerogatives, including military intervention, to prevent or terminate large-scale human rights abuses and crimes against humanity. One may also recall that NEPAD's so-called African Peer Review Mechanism is, at least in theory, an instrument of political interference in the domestic affairs of states, which aims at promoting development and democracy in Africa. In the final analysis, it is not obvious how these competing conceptions can be squared—provided that Africa's regional bodies are determined to put their pledges for democracy and human rights into practice.

SECTION 2
INTERNATIONAL PERSPECTIVES

6

CHINA IN AFRICA: AFTER THE GUN AND THE BIBLE...A WEST AFRICAN PERSPECTIVE

Adama Gaye

Not since Senegal's independence in April 1960 has a major neighbourhood of its capital, Dakar, gone through such drastic transformations. No one who walks down the Allée du Centenaire fails to be amazed at the extent to which this thoroughfare has suddenly come to be teeming with people. Renamed Boulevard Général De Gaulle a few years ago in homage to one of the heroes of France, the former colonial power, today the Allée du Centenaire could ironically be dubbed *Boulevard Mao*. China has taken over the place and everything here now brings to mind the Great Helmsman who led the 1949 Communist triumph in China. In this city district hitherto known for its quietness, things changed overnight when Chinese men and women, as discreet as they were efficient, arrived just recently, in less than two decades. Pushing out the locals, they did not hesitate to rent most of the real estate in the neighbourhood at above-market prices. They quickly turned it into one of the many tropical Chinatowns that have multiplied recently throughout the African continent.[1]

This amounted to a slap in the face of traditional diplomacy in the case of Senegal. On the face of it, the presence in its capital of what one can term the 'Dakarois' Chinese contradicted the state of relations between the People's Republic of China and this West African state. The Senegalese government then led by President Abdou Diouf, tacitly supported by opposition parties (especially by the future President Abdoulaye Wade), decided to recognize Taiwan in January 1996. This decision had triggered the severance of relations with the PRC as Beijing's one-China policy was absolutely immovable.

At an early stage, very few African observers accurately gauged the true extent of Chinese migratory flows into Africa which started in the early 1990s. Such trends were themselves a consequence of the easing of restrictions on the movement of people out of their country that the Chinese traders were among the first to exploit. As a result, in Senegal and elsewhere in Africa where Taiwan had made diplomatic inroads, no one is surprised that Chinese from the PRC have come to reside in the same locations where the Taiwanese should have come to consolidate the basis of a still fragile relationship between their rebel island and several states across the African continent, where its diplomatic activism yielded important results.

Underestimated, even neglected, the Chinese 'quasi-diplomats' had an easy time pushing their agenda. They quickly turned numerous residential neighbourhoods in Africa into commercial areas. Not content with having bypassed the diplomatic obstacles, the Chinese of Dakar and those established elsewhere rapidly obtained their most precious goal: popular legitimacy. They took no time to gain the support of the poorest segments of the population. In the Senegalese capital, these did not take long to flow in the direction of the small retail outlets that flourish on both sides of the virtual *Boulevard Mao*.

---

1   See Adama Gaye, *Chine-Afrique: Le dragon et l'autruche* (Paris: Editions L'Harmattan, 2006) for a more indepth treatment.

Everything is available there: glittering ornaments, clothes for children and adults, gadgets, belts, scarves, handbags or shoes, and all sold at unit prices that defy all potential competition. By selling their wares at package prices between CFA francs 300 and 2000 (that is, a maximum of €6) the Chinese merchants guarantee the elimination of rivals. They give no chance to their local competitors, be they Senegalese or Lebanese. Besides dethroning them, the Chinese also outdid their rivals in the battle for public opinion: protests, strikes, and demonstrations of hostility against Chinese traders have thus far proved useless. This is because the bulk of the Senegalese population has consistently raised its voice to demand that the detractors 'allow the Chinese to continue to *work*'. Even the powerful National Union of Senegalese of Traders and Operators could not successfully impose the 'national preference' it sought against the Chinese influx. The Union was simply overtaken by the turn of events.

Taken aback by the hostility of other Senegalese, many of whom did not hesitate to call their manoeuvres xenophobic or even racist, the Senegalese traders and those of Lebanese origin had little choice but to buy from the new masters of local commerce and, if need be, to go and resell the same products elsewhere in Dakar or in the interior of the country. Some go even further. They come from neighbouring countries such as The Gambia, Guinea-Bissau and Mali with the idea that they no longer have to invest in long trips to Asia to seek out the merchandise now made available to them at their doorstep. They no longer have to confront the challenges of having to scramble to obtain a travel visa or plane tickets to acquire Chinese manufactured goods.

However, the presence of the Chinese in Dakar, as elsewhere on the continent, goes well beyond the simple anecdotal dimension. It represents the rapid growth of a Chinese diaspora that was previously negligible and mainly to be found in South Africa and Madagascar. What is the size of this population now? It is difficult to say with any accuracy. They numbered around 150,000 in 2004 and their number is likely to continue growing fast; a recent figure is 750,000.[2] In the

---

2   Howard French and Lydia Polgreen, 'Entrepreneurs from China flourish in Africa', 18 August 2007.

next five years, the number of these Chinese expatriates could double or even treble, even discounting the fact that the original estimates may be well below the real figures.[3] Whatever the case may be, this massive emigration of a Chinese labour force shows a political will that deserves deeper analysis, particularly in terms of the massive shake-up it presages. These men and women that one finds in the many corners of the continent are, perhaps, the new colonizers of Africa.

Even though the neo-colonial reference brings strong response from Chinese officials and scholars, the risk of domination of Africa by the rising Asian power cannot be dismissed outright as the relationship seems to be unilaterally driven by China and geared toward its own interests. This threat and many other legitimate questions hover around China's presence in Africa. Without doubt, the Chinese expatriates' show of resourcefulness brings to mind some of these questions: how did they manage to settle so easily in Senegal and in the rest of Africa? Are they part of a national project masterminded by China which could be reminiscent of an imperial drive? Why do they make such an effort to buy all the hard currency they can get their hands on, often at exchange rates that are far higher than those practiced by local banks? To what extent will the normalization of the African informal sector be put at risk by the unwillingness of Chinese traders to fulfil their fiscal obligations? What will happen if African-registered but Chinese-owned companies become the main source of taxes in the countries where they are based? Will they not use this financial clout as a blackmailing device or, at least, a source of undue influence over host states? Whatever happens, there is little doubt that the new Chinese presence will change the face of the continent.

Divergent African views

Various reactions are generated by the Chinese presence in Africa. The more optimistic are glad that they have come and perceive them first and foremost as potential investors in a continent starved of capital and which can only benefit from the technology and expertise

---

3   Pierre-Antoine Braud, 'La Chine en Afrique: Anatomie d'une nouvelle strategie chinoise', Institute for Strategic Studies-EU Analysis, October 2005.

they bring along. At the other end of the spectrum, however, there are those who do not mince their words to describe what they see as a dangerous phenomenon. 'We have to contain the Chinese, it is a life-or-death issue for our continent', states the fiery director of a West African democracy-promoting NGO.[4]

This feeling is shared by diverse sectors of African society. 'Africa gains nothing from the Chinese; there is no quid pro quo with them. Europe can at least sell their Airbus planes to the Chinese in order to recoup some of the damages that they bring about to other industrial sectors like textiles and manufacturing,' argues the President of the Chamber of Commerce of an African capital. 'I have not seen a single Chinese investment project that is productive in any way; they are content with building infrastructure, especially stadiums and congress halls to get Africans states to recognize the PRC.'[5] His views are corroborated by a West African banker, according to whom 'the Chinese create jobs that have next to no impact on the GDP of host states while the infrastructure projects they're involved in are short-lived and their products are poor quality.'[6] An even tougher statement came from Martin Abega, the executive secretary of one of Cameroon's employers' organizations. 'The Chinese', he says, 'do not respect the rules of the game; they are the champions of contraband'.[7]

Either negative or favourable, the views expressed do not change the reality of a Chinese presence that is most visible in the popular excitement that surrounds Chinese *boutiques*. Whether selling doughnuts in Congo-Brazzaville, second-hand garments in Nigeria, loincloths in Togo or African spices throughout the region, Chinese traders have concentrated on poor people with small incomes. No sector is neglected by them, not even music. They make the largely poverty-stricken African population happy, as happened in October 2007 during the Muslim Eid-el-Fitr festival marking the end of the Holy Month of Ramadan, when thousands of Senegalese thronged in the Chinese shops to buy gifts and clothes for their children.

---

4   Speaking anonymously to this author, Freetown, January 2005.
5   Interview in Paris, February 2005.
6   Interview, January 2006.
7   Interview, April 2005.

'Without them, we would have been dishonoured,' said one of them to the Senegalese Press Agency.[8]

There is another, bigger, picture to the business drive by Chinese firms and traders. The large Chinese businesses display an effective business acumen when they operate with prices that are so low as to raise rumours that their real goal is to get rid of competition. This was the case of a toll-road section under construction in Dakar. The Sino-Senegalese consortium that won the bid with a CFA 24 billion bid left behind a French firm that had made a CFA 40 billion bid. The entry of the Chinese into the game has changed the rules.

Whatever one thinks of Chinese methods, it must be granted that the Chinese have a perfect understanding of the liberal economy, including the huge opportunities it offers as well as the many flaws. This goes a long way to explain China's success on the continent. This assimilation of the fundamental rules of globalization is visible more broadly in the rising power's qualified engagement with the international sphere. Furthermore, while it is much too early to speculate on this, it seems that this new worldwide Chinese strategy is, from an African perspective, very different from earlier foreign penetrations of the continent. We are no longer in the era of the missionary wave of Arab and white conquerors that subjugated Africa in bygone centuries.

In today's very different context, one can consider the Dakar Chinese, despite their modesty, as the new 'Conquistadors' on African soil. In Senegal, they are leading the pack. In a way, through their action, one can witness the projection of Chinese power through consumer goods and a cheap labour force. *Exeunt* the Bible and the gun that allowed Western European nations to dominate Africa in earlier ages. While these Western nations continue to seek virtual control of African economies by means of the international financial structure, like the IMF and the World Bank, still under their domination, China for its part follows a multi-pronged strategy. In its approach, the work of its small traders is complemented by other industrial and political actors, including industrial and company ex-

8   13 October 2007.

ecutives as well as top political operatives, who have increased their presence and visits in Africa.

Every discerning observer can easily detect this new China project through the Dakarois Chinese on the Boulevard Général De Gaulle. The same applies to anyone visiting other major African cities. The fact is that no matter how much it aims at discretion, the Chinese diaspora has now become very conspicuous. This starts even before their arrival to Africa, aboard the planes bringing them to the continent. 'They completely book out our planes', says a disorientated European air hostess, before adding: 'Do you know that Chinese sends its convicts to Africa, just as [was done in] Algeria, to use them as labour?'[9] On the ground, the reality is even more compelling. In hotels, markets, mines, building sites and African streets, the Chinese are everywhere. Although they often keep to themselves and entertain very cold relations with local populations, they cannot go unnoticed.

Is there a hint of panic about this unexpected change? No doubt about that. Even if the extent of the Chinese presence and willingness to invest are still modest in regard to African needs, this presence carries important consequences, one of them being the potential possibility of a China taking over from the traditional foreign partners and actors on African soil. This is already suggested by a growing Chinese commitment: having reached US$55 billion in 2006, Chinese trade in Africa is expected to reach US$100 billion even before the set date of 2010. This growing trend is very connected with Chinese interest in oil and other mineral resources. In Algeria, Angola, Nigeria, Gabon, Sudan, Togo, Chad, Mauritania and many other oil-rich or potentially oil-rich locations, Chinese companies are actively seeking investment opportunities.

China as an alternative

The state of China-Africa relations was nowhere more evident than in the Forum for China-Africa Cooperation (FOCAC) Summit in Beijing in November 2006. African leaders flocked to this event

9   Interview, March 2005.

as if they had wanted to swear an oath of allegiance to the African continent's new tutor. Standing on a red carpet in the Great Hall of the People, President Hu Jintao could not hide his joy when, hand stretched out, he welcomed African heads of state one after another. Under the cameras of Chinese TV, attentive onlookers could discern the message that the Chinese President was aiming to send. Shortly after what recalled a traditional feature of China's relations with its neighbours in the past, the 'kow-towing' ceremony, Hu Jintao's announcement of a flurry of measures to help Africa showed that, behind the discourse of equality and the carnival atmosphere of the Summit, the Sino-African relationship is characterized by an undeniable asymmetry.

Yet African statesmen have not done much to redress this unbalanced rapport: they have merely adapted to it without much protest. Happy to have found shelter under the protective wing of a new patron, they have not hesitated to embrace the model that, while rejecting the term 'model', the Chinese are putting on the table. Ever since the demise of the Soviet 'model', many African leaders were longing for an alternative response to the Western neo-liberal political 'model'. The Chinese one is made more attractive by the fact that it also revives their power. It brings to a halt the decline of their role as leaders of African states emasculated over the past years by the combined action of the international financial institutions, the pressure of NGOs and the activities of various internal and external pro-democracy and human rights movements.

China is less concerned with promoting internal political changes, and democratization is not its main focus. It is not surprising therefore that, in addition to the financial aid promised by President Hu Jintao in his opening speech at the third FOCAC, the reaffirmation of China's policy of non-interference in the domestic affairs of sovereign states sounded like music to the ears of African rulers. This is the basis of the infatuation with China in the power circles of Africa. This discourse is articulated at a moment when the usual meddling foreign actors are going through major difficulties. Most of the Western nations are suffering from economic and financial woes and their international financial institutions have largely lost legitimacy owing to the poor results derived from the structural adjustment policies they have promoted in the world. In contrast, China can be credited with its successes in reducing poverty: it has pulled roughly 400 million of its citizens out of poverty. With over $1.4 trillion of foreign reserves, it now has considerable financial means to support its geopolitical interests in Africa. China's approach contrasts especially with the '*Diktat*' approach of the World Bank, the IMF and other traditional actors; it has imbibed the basic principles of public relations and comes with 'solutions', a message of respect and partnership, and a general deployment of 'soft power'.

China has therefore become an alternative choice for many African countries, political decisions-makers and intellectuals. It now occupies a political space that has for long remained vacant. This is the partnership African countries have been searching for since the end of the Cold War. It permits a rapprochement that is primarily articulated around state actors regardless of the anger this creates among the social forces that are excluded from it. These parallel social forces emanating from commercial, labour, and NGO segments of society look on with suspicion at the subterranean character of the new Sino-African relationship. The question has arisen whether China will have a positive impact on African development or, alternatively, its net result will be the rise of new oligarchies that will destroy the gains recently made across the continent in promoting multi-party democracy and good governance.

It is premature to make a definitive assessment of what the relationship between Africa and China will bring to the continent. At most, one can observe that in addition to its diplomatic efforts, China's presence in the continent is expressed through its companies that are showing an amazing dynamism. Specialized companies are on the ground in search of oil resources while others are pursuing efforts aimed at securing copper, iron ore or bauxite, those other mineral resources without which China cannot sustain its economical growth. Other Chinese groups are equally active in Africa; one example is the Bintumani hotel in Sierra Leone, which was built by Chinese businessmen even as that West African nation was going through a violent civil war in the 1990s.

There are three dimensions to China's strategy. The first is the necessity to secure long-term access to raw materials and resources like oil to avoid being dependent on the volatility of market prices and unreliable conditions to get these products. Another aspect explaining China's drive is the ambition to position the country in other territories with a view to implementing its outbound policy 'beyond China's borders'. The objective is to strengthen China's foreign trade and external market share in order to reinforce the position of Chinese multinationals. Last but not least is China's quest to get diplomatic support in Africa. Consolidating the positions it has built over the recent years, reversing Taiwan's diplomatic gains obtained in the mid-1990s and enhancing Beijing's new global geopolitical ambition are the main reasons behind the more dynamic foreign policy pursued across the continent.

China's interests are now more important than anything else. Its presence represents a sharp departure from issues like human rights, as it refuses to back the position held by many Western nations in Africa in the aftermath of the Cold War. Those nations even preferred to withdraw from Africa to showcase their contempt for human rights violations, but China's attitude is different. 'We don't believe that human rights should be above sovereignty issues,' says Wenping He, Director of the Africa Department at the China Academy of Social Sciences.[10] Not afraid of appearing as the accomplice of African dictatorships, and not bearing any regrets for its African policy, Beijing has allowed itself the means necessary to implement that policy relentlessly.

The long view

China's attitude is somehow dictated by memories of the breaking of relations with Moscow in the 1960s. Many in China have this in mind. It serves as a guide for Chinese leaders who understand the risks of being dependent on any powerful 'ally' able to become a 'rival', according to circumstances. Going to Africa offers another advantage to China as this move allows its companies to learn empirically how

---

10 Presentation at the conference 'A 'Chinese Scramble'? The Politics of Contemporary China-Africa Relations', Sidney Sussex College, Cambridge 12 July 2006.

to do business internationally. They gain experience which can be used elsewhere against American and other Western competitors. In this light, Africa is a guinea-pig continent for Chinese firms in their will to test their technological and industrial abilities with a view to successfully competing against their Western rivals, not just in Africa but elsewhere.

Above all, allowed so far to operate as they like, Chinese companies and officials have a unique opportunity to act in a close knit circle. Everything is done between them. Their interlocutors—or 'partners'—from the continent are marginalized in the management, running and profit of companies. Silence is the watch-word. There seems to be a Chinese *omertà* at work that is made more efficient by the legendary discretion of the Chinese people, and their effectiveness. 'We sell them our mineral resources and they sell us in return manufactured products with a predictable result: an imbalanced trade deficit that Africa will suffer from as the trade relations grow,' complains Moeletsi Mbeki, a leading South African business and academic expert of the South African Institute of International Relations.[11]

It is expected that China's return to Africa will increasingly draw attention. Although they are stealthy, China's efforts to conquer the continent, still under US and European influence, will be made difficult by the problems it will also encounter on the ground. Will China be able to root out the state and transnational actors that have been in place for so long? Its mission is almost like a dangerous gamble, despite the long relations of militancy that China built with several nations here from the mid-1950s. But the Chinese are always eager to say that nothing is new under the African sun and that their country has maintained relations with Africa for so long. 'This relationship dates back from the foundation of modern China' insist three Chinese experts from the China Institute of International Relations.[12]

Now China's relationship with Africa is no longer driven by militant international proletarianism as it was from the 1950s to the

---

11 Quoted by Paul Mooney, in *China's African Safari*, YaleGlobal, 3 January 3 2005.

12 Discussion in Beijing, March 2004.

mid-1970s. Today, following years of internal economic reforms, China has adopted a strategy mainly focused on its economic development and strategic long-term interests. This shift in priority, as in the past, was presented to African partners by the former Chinese Premier Zhao Ziyang on 13 January 1983 during a visit to eleven African nations (Algeria, Congo, Egypt, Gabon, Guinea, Kenya, Morocco, Tanzania, Zaire, Zambia and Zimbabwe). He explained that China would pursue equality and mutual advantage in sharing of profits, while refusing to make his country's cooperation dependent on any political conditionality apart from the 'One China Policy' which rules out recognition of Taiwan as a separate sovereign entity. After stating this stance, common in the Chinese approach to Africa, Zhao Ziyang said that efficiency in the execution of projects should be sought and these should not require a lot of investment. He also called for diversity in the forms of China cooperation, including the supply of technical services and the training of technicians, both top and low-grade ones. Zhao Ziyang also mentioned the idea of co-development not just for China but for its African partners, as the last aspect of the redefined African policy.

Keen observers of China were quick to understand that these measures would herald a new phase of realism. Gone was the time when China's support for 'African brothers' freed from colonial European rule was the main order of the day. Business and investment were now going to drive the relationship with Africa which began to be seen mainly as a market, if one put aside the Taiwan question. This evolution in China's relations with Africa was to be confirmed and enhanced later on, leading to a gradual 'normalization' of the China-Africa axis. Modernized, it now fits into the global framework of rational relations that China has managed to maintain with the rest of the world since the early 1980s.

Across Africa, from the busy shops of 'Boulevard Mao' in Dakar to the mining fields of Southern Africa, such as the Chambishi copper mine in Zambia, an assertive China has now made its mark in the continent. Its workers are building airports, railways and port facilities. Hospitals and museums or administrative buildings are made along the infrastructure geared towards facilitating the 'exfiltration' of the mineral and energy resources that China is seeking from Africa. To prove that this continent has become a key dimension to their national strategy, Chinese leaders, starting from the President, continue year after year to pay visit to African nations and institutions, not even hesitating to go to the most remote places. Clearly, China's return to Africa is powerful. Yet some challenging questions are beginning to be raised, in the light of negative spill-over effects of the new relationship between China and the continent—a relationship that seems to have been mainly defined, to its advantage, by the Asian nation pursuing an age-old tradition of national interest in foreign policy. Beijing must be aware that years of democratization attempts have left in many African minds a sense of justice and equity; one can therefore expect a backlash against what some in Africa see as the beginning of a unilateral Chinese takeover of the continent. Relying on the complicity of local government leaders alone will not ensure China's long-term interest in the continent: the recent recriminations against China's presence, which even forced Hu Jintao to cancel a visit to the Chambishi copper mine in early 2007, were a stark reminder that the 'Jamboree' of the Sino-African Summit has not yet penetrated down to the level of the ordinary African man. China is expected to match its nice win-win words with deeds that will show it is committed in practice to a relationship that has nothing to do with previous foreign forays in the continent.

This is a tall order. China, a world giant, faces a serious challenge in Africa: its easy return and the rapid gains made in less than a decade may be misleading. It must wake up to the realities of a continent better able than ever to realize what it should demand as a result of its growing inclusion in world business and politics. So far, China's African safari has not yet faced the tough challenges that lie ahead. They may soon become unavoidable, as one should expect Africa to wake up to the threats going with the opportunities offered by a smiling dragon too kind to be sincere in its promise to build a relationship beneficial to its African partner in equitable terms.

7

CHINA'S PERSPECTIVE ON CONTEMPORARY CHINA-AFRICA RELATIONS

Wenping He

A new milestone in the history of China-Africa relations was created when the first Forum on China-Africa Cooperation (FOCAC) took place in Beijing in 2000, a process that culminated in the Third Ministerial and first Heads of State Conference held in early November 2006. The year 2006 was significant in the diplomatic calendar of Sino-Africa relations; four major visits from China's top leaders cast China-Africa relations into the media spotlight at home and abroad. That year began with Foreign Minister Li Zhaoxing's tour of Cape Verde, Senegal, Mali, Liberia, Nigeria and Libya, which coincided with the release of China's first White Paper on its Africa Policy on 12 January. This was followed by President Hu Jintao's visit to the continent from 24 to 29 April, with stopovers in Morocco, Nigeria and Kenya. The final visit was made by Premier Wen Jiabao, who toured Egypt, Ghana, the Democratic Republic of Congo, Angola, South Africa, Tanzania and Uganda between 17 and 24 June. These high level visits underlined the importance that the Chinese government attaches to its African relations. Moreover, they indicate that following the establishment of official bilateral ties half a century ago, Sino-Africa relations have moved into an era of rapid development characterized by co-operation.

The end of the Cold War in the early 1990s saw Africa losing its much-valued geo-political status. In spite of this, China has remained committed to developing relations with the continent since it foresaw great value in fostering an across-the-board relationship with Africa by forging closer political, cultural and educational links. This was clearly demonstrated in the 1980s when Beijing began to cement and expand its economic and trade ties with the continent.

The importance of Africa in China's foreign policy agenda

The importance of Africa in Beijing's foreign relations can be best understood in the following two significant factors. *Politically, China has always regarded Africa as its most reliable ally in the international struggle.* The development of Sino-African relations has important political meaning for both China and Africa, as well as across the developing world. First, the strengthening of Sino-African relations is beneficial to unity and co-operation between developing countries. China's non-aligned foreign policy and its national commitment to socialism imply a promise that China will stand firmly and support the countries of the developing world despite what happened in the past or what the present and the future may bring. Unmistakably, the total strength of the developing world is increasing both in terms of its proportion of international trade and its right to speak on international affairs. China is the largest developing country in the world, and Africa is the continent that has the greatest concentration of developing countries. Therefore the development of Sino-African relations must be seen in this context, where it is Beijing's overriding goal to raise the international status of the developing world and establish a new international order by promoting South-South co-operation and the common prosperity of these countries. This is significant considering that current relations between the North and the South appear poor in certain respects. Thus, uplifting the collective prosperity of developing countries and enabling them to share in the fruits of globalization have far-reaching implications for world peace and development.

144

Secondly, Sino-African co-operation is considered important for strengthening a multi-polar world order and promoting both China's and Africa's international positions and influences therein. Since China adopted its economic reform path and opened up policy space for engagement, China's international image and position have improved remarkably, while its influence in international affairs has also simultaneously increased. In this regard, according to Beijing's view, Africa remains an important player in the global affairs of the current international system. Even though most African countries have suffered from political turbulence and economic recession during the early period of the post-Cold War era, most are now entering a period of political and economic stability, while their positions in the international setting have also improved. And this is where the synergies between China and Africa overlap. Clearly, China and Africa share a broad consensus on major international issues. They have traditionally co-operated and co-ordinated with each other on matters serving common interests. Both sides have collaborated to promote multilateralism and democracy in international relations and UN reforms aimed at peace and harmony in the world.

Finally, Sino-African co-operation can contribute to the success of the 'One China policy' and, most important, the culmination of China's reunification. In order to extricate itself from international isolation, Taiwan's leaders are taking Africa (especially West Africa) as the focus for developing its diplomatic relations. Although most African countries insist on the 'One China policy', there are still a few African countries who cannot resist the lure of money and maintain 'diplomacy' with Taiwan, which has a bad influence on China's African policy. However, with the dramatic increase in China's comprehensive national power, especially in the last decade, more African countries choose mainland China rather than Taiwan. The 'Taiwan factor' no longer has the same importance as before.

Economically, Sino-African relations can help strengthen China's path to sustainable development. Africa's rich deposits of natural resources and potential market advantages have great strategic meaning for China's economic development in the 21st century. With China's rapid pace of modernization and economic reform, China must expand into

145

new overseas markets and secure the supply of raw materials that is, indeed, critical for sustaining its growth trajectory with regard to national development and stability. Following China's accession to the WTO in 2001, the Chinese government has advanced further moves to expand the 'going out' strategy of Chinese enterprises to become globally competitive and enter new markets.

In fact, from the economic angle, China-Africa co-operation will bring each side's advantages into full play. There are 53 countries on the African continent, which has a total population of 850 million, abounds in natural and human resources, has great market potential and boasts huge potential for development. However, owing to long-lasting colonialist plunder and local conflicts, the continent remains economically backward, lacking capital, technology and expertise. On the other hand, China has acquired much economic strength and expertise over the past three decades since the country embarked on the road of reform and opening up in the late 1970s. At the same time, however, it is confronted with the problems of inadequate resources supplies and ever-fiercer competition in the domestic economic arena. Taking all this into account, China and Africa complement one another in resources, market, capital, technology and expertise. And much can be done in this regard.

While it may appear that China's intentions in Africa are intrinsically aligned to tendencies of mercantilist nationalism, China's current demand for natural resources has created a surge in the global commodity price index which has, to a large extent, seen Africa's economic growth level benefiting from the commodity windfall. Nevertheless, the real thrust of China's contemporary relations with Africa was felt in FOCAC which promoted a new impulse for future engagements.

FOCAC: a new initiative for promoting Sino-African relations

The emergence of a unilateral world order after the Cold War became an immediate concern for the vast majority of developing countries. The need to establish a new, fair and reasonable international political and economic order, so as to deal with the challenges of economic globalization and safeguard its legitimate rights and interests, was an overriding objective for the developing world to assert its independent voice in global affairs and extend its relations more broadly to include strategic partners from the South, especially in light of the experience of the Cold War. Seemingly, then, strengthening and institutionalizing relations between China and Africa was considered necessary to reflect the new impulses in the global South.

Hence the birth of FOCAC in 2000. At the end of the 1990s, some African countries proposed that as the US, Britain, France, Japan and Europe had established mechanisms for contact with Africa, it was necessary for China and Africa to establish a similar mechanism to fit in with the need to strengthen relations. After earnest study, China decided to echo the suggestions of African countries, and proposed to hold the Forum in 2000.

From a historical perspective, FOCAC must be seen as a continuation of the spirit of the Bandung Conference held in Indonesia in 1955. In essence, Bandung was about the spirit of common prosperity, respect for equality, justice, peace and the overall development of the developing world, based on its independent status. The relevance, today, of the Bandung Conference and what it stood for can be seen as one of the central pillars of China's foreign policy engagements with the developing world and, indeed, Sino-African relations. And this has become even more significant since FOCAC has become the platform where discussions on future co-operation and consultation in achieving a non-aligned and multilateral world order, which adequately reflects the developing world, can be held. In fact, the FOCAC Forum was the first of its kind in the history of Sino-African relations. It is a beneficial attempt as well as an important move for the Chinese government to further consolidate and strengthen friendly cooperative relations on the threshold of the new millennium.

The first Forum: Beijing 2000

In October 2000 the first FOCAC was held in Beijing. It focused on two major areas: how to promote and establish a just and equitable new international order, and how to further strengthen co-operation between China and Africa on economic and social development. The Forum reached consensus on a wide range of issues and adopted two important policy documents, the Beijing Declaration and the

147

Programme of Cooperation on Economic and Social Development. It also decided to hold a ministerial conference every three years, alternating between China and Africa.

During the Forum, the Chinese government offered to write off debts worth RMB10 billion owed by African countries within two years. In fact, the Chinese government completed ahead of schedule an even greater reduction of African debts. By June 2002, China had signed debt relief protocols with 31 African nations, cancelling 156 African debts totalling RMB10.5 billion. At the same time, China urged the international community to honour its debt reduction promises without further delay.

Moreover, the Chinese government committed itself to setting up special foundations for encouraging Chinese enterprises to invest in Africa and for a variety of training initiatives for African professionals. Since 1996, China has held training courses for middle- and high-ranking African diplomats annually, and launched annual seminars for African economic and management officials from 1998. China-Africa co-operation in higher and vocational education has also been enhanced. So far, China has trained 15,000 African professional personnel and offered scholarships to 20,000 students from 51 African countries studying in China. In addition, China will continue to dispatch training personnel to Africa to give short-term training courses. For example, China's Follow-Up Committee has sent Chinese experts to six African countries for regional training courses on malaria prevention and treatment, maize farming techniques, applied solar energy technology, etc. These courses have been aligned to the commitments that the Chinese government made at the 2000 Cooperation Summit.

The second Forum: the Addis Ababa 2003 Ministerial Conference

The second FOCAC was held in Addis Ababa on 15-16 December 2003, the first time that the meeting was held in Africa. Its main task was to review the implementation of the two documents adopted at the first Summit and to explore new ideas and measures to deepen co-operation. The meeting concluded with the adoption of the Addis Ababa Action Plan (2004–6), which reflected consensus of both sides on political issues and other important international issues of common concern. In particular, the Summit concretized ideas about strengthening of co-operation. Alongside the Addis Ababa Forum, the China-Africa Business Conference was also held. Representatives from nearly 100 Chinese enterprises held discussions on business opportunities and linkages with their African counterparts, which culminated in the signing of many contracts of intent to do business.

The major concrete measures that China promised to undertake included: granting some African countries tariff-free treatment for their exports to China; expediting increases in revenue and alleviation of poverty by exempting certain commodities of the least developed countries from import tariffs, to facilitate and expand the entry of exports from these countries into the Chinese market; and increased assistance and channelling of more resources into the African Human Resources Development Fund. The Chinese government decided to launch the 2004-6 China-Africa Inter-Governmental Human Resources Development Plan under the Fund.[1] Other measures include boosting tourism co-operation by encouraging more Chinese citizens to travel to Africa,[2] and holding a series of events to promote better understanding between the peoples, especially the younger generations of both sides.[3]

In addition, the Chinese government also promised to gradually increase development assistance to Africa. In September 2005, when President Hu Jintao attended the UN Summit on Financing for Development, he called for the UN to play a bigger role in development

---

1 A 33 per cent increase in the fund will allow China to hold 300 training courses in three years for some 10,000 African professionals in various fields, and raise the number of scholarships that China offers for African exchange students.

2 Apart from the original travel destinations of Egypt, South Africa and Morocco, China has decided to grant a further eight African countries Approved Destination Status: Mauritius, Ethiopia, Tunisia, Zimbabwe, Kenya, Zambia, Tanzania and Seychelles.

3 Including the '2004 China-Africa Youth Carnival', 'Meet in Beijing'—an international art festival focusing on African arts—and the'Voyage of Chinese Culture to Africa'.

assistance and declared that China would take important measures in such fields as tariffs, debt, preferential loans, public health and human resources to help other developing nations, especially African countries, to accelerate development. These measures included the following: China would write off debt or cancel interest payments owed, or provide assistance for servicing of low interest Chinese government loans made to poor and heavily indebted countries with which China had diplomatic relations but which had failed to service those loans by the end of 2004; train 30,000 people in various employment skills over the coming three years; and pledge US$10 billion of concessional loans over the next three years.

In short, the experience of FOCAC over the last six years has proven to be an important platform and dialogue mechanism for strengthening China-Africa co-operation and solidarity, and safeguarding common interests. At the end of 2006, the third Ministerial Meeting of the Forum, together with the first Sino-African Heads of States Summit, was held in Beijing on 3-5 November. According to China's Premier Wen Jiabao the Summit was intended to focus on 'China and Africa reducing...and remitting debts, economic assistance, personnel training and investment by enterprises.'[4]

The new-type China-Africa strategic partnership

The new initiative of China's strategic partnership with Africa was officially launched by two significant developments in 2006: the release of the 'China's African Policy' White Paper, and the speech by President Hu Jintao to the Nigerian parliament during his April visit. In both, reference was made to the concept of 'developing a new type of China-Africa strategic partnership'. Besides being clearly defined, it signalled the future course for Sino-African relations. During the Sino-African Summit, African delegations enthusiastically echoed the new concept and made clear that African countries were fully ready to build such a new-type China-Africa Strategic Partnership. The consensus on building this Strategic Partnership was regarded as the most important achievement of the Summit.

---

4   *Xinhua*, 'Chinese premier hails Sino-African ties of cooperation', 19 May 2006.

The central feature of the new partnership is consolidation of co-operation in the political, economic, cultural and security fields, as well as in international affairs, with emphasis on mutual trust and support. The real thrust of the new relationship is linked with China affording African countries respect and recognition of the right to choose their independent path of development. This is clearly stated in the language that China adopts towards Africa, which is non-intrusive and outlines continual support for African countries' efforts to seek renewal through strengthening unity. This is, undoubtedly, illustrated by the common mutual interests and collective international efforts to promote peace and development in Africa.

While strategically aligned to historical relations, the new type of China-Africa partnership is also about establishing benefits of mutual economic engagement. With China being the largest developing country and Africa comprising the largest concentration of developing countries, there is no doubt that each has a long road to sustainable development. Despite China's economic progress, it faces new problems such as a severe energy shortage and escalating competition in its domestic market. Given these factors, the Chinese government encourages Chinese firms to invest in Africa in various fields such as trade, agriculture, infrastructure building, mining and tourism, while offering an increasing amount of assistance to hasten the continent's development.

To date, China has spent RMB44.4 billion in assisting African countries with over 800 projects, including textile factories, hydro-electric power stations, stadiums, hospitals and schools. At present, trade between China and Africa is undergoing rapid growth. The bilateral trade volume rose from US$12.11 million in the 1950s to US$10.5 billion in 2000, US$29.4 billion in 2004, nearly US$40 billion in 2005, and over US$50 billion in 2006. In recent years China has increased imports from African countries and thus maintained a trade deficit with them, enabling these countries to earn a large amount of foreign exchange.

Moreover, Chinese firms have redoubled their efforts to penetrate the African market. At the end of 2006, Chinese investment in

Africa had reached US$11.7 billion.[5] Over 800 companies are currently operating in Africa, engaged in trade, manufacturing, natural resource exploitation, transport, agriculture and agricultural processing. Chinese companies have helped to create employment opportunities in African countries, increase their tax revenues, introduce practical technologies to these countries, enhance the competence of local workers and improve their productivity.

On the cultural front, China and Africa are aiming to become equal partners jointly promoting the prosperity and progress of human civilization. China and Africa are both origins of human civilization, boasting brilliant cultural heritages. In basic values, African culture has a lot in common with Chinese culture. For example, both value community spirit and the tradition of yielding personal gain to the interests of the community. Given these common values, China and Africa are expected to further strengthen their cultural linkages with a view to building a harmonious world where different civilizations coexist in the spirit of tolerance and equality, while also learning from each other. In a broader sense, cultural exchange is not only limited to exchanging students and teachers and holding artistic performances and exhibitions. Chinese medical teams, and flourishing programmes such as China's training of African workers and the exchange of experiences in pursuing development, are also part of the China-Africa cultural exchange.

In the field of security, China and Africa should enhance exchanges and consultation, thus raising the awareness of collective security in the international community, promoting a new security concept featuring mutual trust, mutual benefit, equality and co-operation, and shaping an international environment favourable for common development. Clearly, the future of China-Africa co-operation also holds significant relevance in non-traditional security fields, for example in preventing major infectious diseases including bird flu, and addressing cross-border crime, for joint response to the challenges posed by globalization. Hence, the new impulse in China-Africa re-

---

5   Jia Qinlin, head of Chinese Political Consultative Conference, opening ceremony speech at the China-Kenyan Economic and Trade Co-operation Forum in Nairobi on 24 April 2007.

lations can be felt on many fronts. This multi-dimensional approach to strengthening relations is markedly different from that which has prevailed between Africa and its traditional development partners.

At the opening ceremony of the Beijing Summit, President Hu Jintao unveiled eight major measures in the coming three years in a bid to promote the new China-Africa strategic partnership and facilitate bilateral co-operation in a wider scope and on a higher level. These involve expanding aid, offering preferential loans, encouraging Chinese firms to invest in Africa, constructing the AU conference centre, eliminating debts of some least developed African nations, extending zero-tariff treatment on 190 products from some of the poorest African countries to cover 440 products, setting up three to five offshore economic and trade co-operative zones in Africa, training professionals for African countries, and constructing 30 local hospitals. These show that China cares very much about Africa's development. All these measures, quantified and having very particular content, are easier to implement and fulfil than generally stated goals.

The experience and practice of FOCAC over the past six years indicate that it is not an empty-talk club. It is an important platform and effective mechanism conducting collective dialogue between China and African nations and exchanges in the field of governance, promotion of mutual trust, and pragmatic co-operation. President Hu Jintao's announcement indicates that the Chinese government gives top priority to the promotion of two-way investment. In contrast with the fast expanding Chinese-African trade in recent years, the mutual investment rate between the two sides still remains low. Mutual investment, however, is a vitally important factor benefiting both and assuring their sustainable development.

African countries prefer mechanisms which help tap their internal potential to those that merely provide one-way aid, which is like a blood transfusion. Only after they acquire the capability of supplying their own blood can they shake off poverty altogether. Obtaining investment to start businesses and industries is pivotal to Africa's industrialization and revival, as well as increasing employment, hastening technical know-how transfer to the continent, and facilitating the training of its own professionals. The Chinese government will therefore set up a US$5 billion China-Africa development fund to help Chinese companies invest in Africa. At the same time, a number of economic and trade co-operative zones in Africa and a China-Africa chamber of commerce are expected to be set up. All this is bound to bring Chinese investment in the Africa to new heights.

Problems emerging in China–Africa relations

Even though relations have been enjoying sound, rapid development, it is imperative that we pay great attention to the new problems and challenges and consider the ways and means to deal with them. In recent years, with accelerated economic globalization and China's economic expansion, issues have unavoidably emerged as China-Africa relations experience rapid development. Generally speaking, the major problems in recent years are the following.

Energy development and the issue of 'delivering benefit to the people'. With China's energy exploitation in Africa, some people in Western media and academic circles (and even political circles) began to question China's motives in Africa, suggesting that 'China is conducting energy diplomacy in Africa' and that 'China's energy plunder in Africa' is a type of 'neo-colonialism'. They hold that China's attention is based on its demand for oil and other strategic raw materials. They say that China has become the second largest oil consumer after the US, that Africa is rapidly becoming an important supply base of oil and that China's rapid economic development and its relative lack of domestic resources determine that it pays constant attention to production bases of natural resources. These arguments are clearly one-sided and bear the imprint of the Cold War mentality, but at the same time, they serve to remind us indirectly that we should avoid following the old path of the Western colonialist countries while seeking energy supplies in Africa.

Take Sudan for example. China has invested a great deal in oil exploration there. When I visited South Africa at the end of 2005 and met Sudanese people from religious and political circles, they had considerable reservations, expressing certain dissatisfaction about the benefits they got from China-Sudan oil cooperation.

Although a North-South peace agreement has been signed, there are still multiple contradictions and widespread social confrontation. China has already signed an agreement on oil exploitation with the Sudanese government in the north, but the oilfields are in Southern Sudan, leaving Chinese oil companies between the two sides and easy media targets. The South often complains that land acquisition for exploration led to displacement of people who have not been provided with employment. An influential Christian bishop in Upper Nile Province has always been quite friendly towards China, but on many public occasions he called on Chinese oil companies to pay more attention to environmental protection in oilfields of Southern Sudan, to have more exchanges with the local people, and to protect and improve the immediate interests and living standards of the local people.[6]

For historical reasons, the controlling rights to oil exploitation in African countries are in the hands of France, the UK, Italy, the US and other former Western colonial powers. Over the years, since Western oil companies have been only concerned with their own economic interests and have neglected environmental protection in oil producing areas and the local peoples' ability to develop their economy, the constant flow of 'oil dollars' has only filled the pockets of Western oil companies and some corrupt African officials, instead of bringing benefits to local people. On the contrary, the unequal distribution of wealth and 'black gold' resources has led to internal conflicts. For example, Nigeria, the largest oil producer with a daily output of 2.5 million barrels of crude oil, is facing a prolonged oil products shortage due to its poor oil refining capacity and has to rely on large amounts of imported petrol. In the Niger Delta, owing to their lack of access to oil wealth, local people often take great risks to steal oil from pipelines or kidnap foreigners.

Therefore, relying on the traditional friendship and the fact that both China and many African states are developing countries, African countries place high hopes in us. They hope that in exploring oil

---

6   See Daniel Deng, 'A Statement of the Current Situation in Northern Upper Nile', paper for the conference 'Afro-Chinese Relations: Past, Present and Future', 23-25 November 2005, Johannesburg, South Africa.

markets in Africa, a newly enriched China will abide by the principle of win-win cooperation, pay more attention to environmental protection and the improvement of people's living standards in the local area, and help oil producing countries in Africa to improve their ability of economic development. In a word, efforts should be made to enable the local people to benefit from their oil wealth.

Trade frictions and conflicts of economic interest. Certain African scholars hold that China's economic development constitutes both tempting opportunities and terrible threats to Africa.[7] Take, for example, the textile trade, where the sustained increase in exports from China to the US and the EU, the two largest markets for textile products, and the great increase in Chinese products to African countries where textile and apparel is a key industry have, to a certain extent, eroded these countries' international market share, affecting the development of the textile industry and leading to bankruptcies and unemployment.

Indeed, with ever expanding economic and trade cooperation between China and Africa, conflicts over trade and investment between the two sides are also becoming more prominent. China's absolute advantage in labour costs and resources has put the textile and light industries in some African countries in a helpless position. For example, in South Africa, a pair of trousers made in China only costs US$1 which includes long-distance transport costs and customs duty, while the same product locally produced costs ten times as much.[8] The influx of Chinese commodities such as textile products, clothes, shoes, and motorcycles objectively affected the development of the young manufacturing industry in Africa. Competition between the same types of products from China and Africa also weakens the export capability of African countries, indirectly undermining relevant industries in Africa as well the international community's enthusiasm

---

7 Represented by Mr Moeletsi Mbeki, Deputy Director of the South African Institute of International Affairs. See *China's Journey to Africa*, Yale *Globalization* 3 January 2005.

8 See 'Africa, Competition Not Only from China', by Lin Zhishen, special report on Cankaoxiaoxi: 'Friction, the Pain of Chinese Textile Products', 30 June 2005.

about making direct investment in Africa. According to the Chinese Ministry of Commerce, since the founding of the WTO the total number of cases concerning anti-dumping and safeguard measures brought against China by African countries is 48, accounting for 6.2 per cent of investigated cases of trade protection by foreign countries, which is much higher than the proportion of China–Africa trade in China's total foreign trade volume.[9] Experts have also pointed out that the end of the global textile quotas may lead to unemployment of about 30 million people, a large portion of whom could be in Africa. By 2007, US$42 billion of textile exports will be shifted from sub-Saharan and southern Africa to China. It seems that facts support this view. Following the end of global textile quotas on 1 January 2005, six textile factories in Lesotho went bankrupt within several months, leaving 7,000 people unemployed. Around the same period, seven textile factories in Kenya went bankrupt, causing wide unemployment.[10]

Certain African scholars also deem China–African trade relations to be a kind of unequal mode of 'North–South economic relations' because Africa mainly exports raw materials and imports manufactured goods. Indeed, although the volume of trade between China and Africa has increased, the trade structure where China exports machinery, electronic products, textile and light industry products to Africa and imports oil, timber, mineral products and other raw materials from Africa has not been changed.

Differences in political understanding and concepts of values. In recent years the process of political development and democracy has been quite rapid in Africa. In government documents and the daily talk of the ordinary people, words like democracy and human rights are frequently heard. The development of NGOs and civil society is also quite fast, and Africans are very proud of this. This may lead to some misunderstanding on the part of Africans about China's democracy and human rights conditions. Some even think that China has not

---

9   'Steady Development of China-Africa Economic and Trade Cooperation', by Zhou Jianqing, *West Asia and Africa*, 1 (2006), pp.17-18.

10   See Lin Zhishen 'Africa, Competition Not Only from China'.

paid due attention to the development of democracy and human rights in Africa.[11] Western countries have gone even further, claiming that China only pursues selfish interests in conducting economic and trade relations with Africa while neglecting the democracy and human rights conditions of recipient countries. They argue that China's unconditional economic aid has objectively supported the so-called 'failed states' in Africa, and that it is detrimental to the promotion of 'good governance' by Western countries and the progress of anti-corruption and human rights causes in Africa.[12]

As early as 1988 the African Commission on Human and People's Rights was established. Since the 1990s, 'good governance' has become a new concept very popular in Africa. Both the AU and the New Partnership for Africa's Development (NEPAD) deem good governance one of the indispensable preconditions for rejuvenation and development in Africa. Good governance, to put it simply, means enhanced governing capacity and responsibility as well as improved management standards and administrative efficiency. It emphasizes people's role in participating in political activities and civil society as well as decentralization and grass roots service. It promotes democracy, the rule of law and transparency of government, respects the independent role of legislative bodies and judicial bodies, and safeguards human rights and the rights and interests of women. To strengthen administration and promote good governance, African countries have also created a mechanism of democratic supervision—the African Peer Review Mechanism, an important part of NEPAD adopted in March 2003. A country joining this mechanism must make the running of its government, its economic policies and its human rights conditions public, and accept supervision and assessment of member countries according to set standards. If a member state is found to fall short of certain standards through checks and supervision, the specialized agency of the mechanism is entitled to demand that the country conducts reforms in the areas concerned and put forward concrete suggestions.

---

11 See Jean-Germain Gros, 'Chinese Economic Success and Lessons for Africa: Possibilities and Limits', *Nkrumaist Review*, May 2005.

12 'Africa: China's great leap into the continent', IRIN 23 March 2006.

If a member country has no means to reach certain standards, then it will not be able to benefit from NEPAD as other member states do. By April 2005, 24 countries had joined this mechanism.

Moreover, there are also some differences among African countries' stances on the issue of international intervention, and the principles like 'sovereignty coming first' and 'non-interference in internal affairs'. Although the principle of 'non-interference in each other's internal affairs' is maintained in the AU charter, the principle of 'non-indifference' is also confirmed. According to this principle, the AU Peace and Security Council has the right to conduct military intervention in case of events like 'war crime, genocide, crime against humanity and serious threats to law and order' in member states. It is also permissible to send peacekeeping troops to stop a war and safeguard peace when military conflicts occur.

How to promote 'all-round co-operation' between China and Africa

Over half of China's African Policy Paper is devoted to elaborating how China will further strengthen 'all-round cooperation' with Africa. It is fair to say that it was the first time for China to put forward the concept of 'all-round cooperation' clearly in the form of a government paper on China-Africa relations in recent years. To cope with the above-mentioned new problems and challenges in China-Africa relations, attention should be given to the following points in the process of promoting 'all-round cooperation' in the new era:

In the process of energy exploitation, commercial interests should be effectively combined with social interests, with attention paid to environmental protection and people's livelihood in the local area. In energy cooperation, China's approach is different in nature from the plundering mode of Western oil companies. It is clearly spelt out in the African Policy Paper that 'China will cooperate with African nations in various ways on the basis of the principle of mutual benefit and common development, develop and exploit rationally their resources, with a view to helping African countries to translate their advantages in resources to competitive strength, and realize

159

sustainable development in their own countries and the continent as a whole.'[13] For example, Chinese companies in Sudan began to be involved in energy exploitation from the mid-1990s. By the end of 2003, Chinese oil companies had invested US$2.7 billion in Sudan, built 1,506 km of pipelines and set up a crude oil refinery with the output of 2.5 million tons per year and several petrol stations. This has not only made Sudan an oil-exporting country, but also enabled it to have a comprehensive industrial system of oil prospecting, production, refining, transport and sales.[14] By contrast, Shell has been exploiting oil for over five decades in Nigeria, a country with rich oil resources in Africa, but the country still remains an exporter of crude oil and an importer of petrol effectively without its own oil producing and processing system, thus remaining an exporter of primary resources.

In the process of helping Africa promote its sustained economic development, more attention should be given to social benefits and people's livelihood in China-Africa energy exploitation and cooperation. Specifically, in the process of resources exploitation on the one hand, Chinese enterprises should pay more heed to establishing and maintaining a good image by devoting part of their profits to environmental protection, education, hospitals and other projects concerning people's livelihood. On the other hand, we can also combine our traditional foreign aid of sending medical teams, digging wells, cooperation in education and the 'volunteers' service, which has existed for several years, with work related to energy exploitation in order to help Chinese enterprises solve issues related to local people's livelihood.

At the same time, the Chinese government might also consider the drafting and, when conditions are ripe, the promulgation of a Law on Overseas Investment, with the aim of using law and directive orders to set compulsory provisions that an enterprise should devote a certain percentage of its profit to improving the livelihood of

---

13 'African Policy Paper', Chinese Ministry of Foreign Affairs. http://www. fmprc.gov.cn

14 See 'Energy Cooperation between China and Sudan', *China Oil and Petrol*, 16 (2005), p. 40.

the people. Strategically speaking, exploitation of resources and energy cooperation in Africa is not only the job of the individual or enterprise, but also the job of government concerning state interests and diplomacy.

In Sudan, for example, people in the South actually have no objection to oil exploitation by Chinese companies. They just want to benefit more from it. Therefore, China can hold negotiations with the Sudanese government so that each party allocates part of its profit to be used in relocation and employment, in order to win support from the local people. According to the peace accord, after a six-year transitional period, Southern Sudan will hold a referendum on whether it will become an independent state. Any failure to win people's hearts in southern Sudan will be detrimental to the unity of Sudan and the friendly relations between China and Sudan.

Acting in the manner of a benevolent power, China should help African countries in readjusting their textile industry so as to improve the competitiveness of their products and promote sustained development of China-Africa economic and trade cooperation. Trade frictions with African countries should be resolved within the framework of the new type of strategic partnership. After all, Africa is the continent that has the largest number of the least developed countries, as well as being our diplomatic cornerstone of traditional friendship. It represents reliable diplomatic resources and strength for us concerning a series of major international political and economic affairs. To properly handle issues concerning competition and frictions in bilateral economic and trade relations, we must be far-sighted, transcend the market rules of competition and 'survival of the fittest'. We should follow a competition mode that is different from our dealings with developed countries and adopt some protective and compromising measures for the textile industry and other related pillar industries in Africa. In June 2007, during his visit to South Africa, Premier Wen Jiabao declared that China would restrict our export quotas of textile products so as to help relevant African countries in restructuring their textile industry and improving the competitiveness of their products. This was warmly received by South Africa and other African countries.

The Chinese government should also actively guide the development orientation of Chinese industries that have comparative advantages by promoting their transformation from extensive growth to intensive growth featuring high added value and high technological content and encouraging them to follow a path of market diversification, thus leaving some time and space for the restructuring of relevant sectors and industries in Africa and the improvement of their competitiveness, so as to reach the goal of common development. To change the structure of commodity trade and resolve trade imbalances between China and Africa, the two sides should coordinate their strategies for future economic development with an eye to setting up more Chinese firms in Africa, improving African capacity of processing and product development, and diversifying their export varieties.

Stepping up aid and strengthening supervision on foreign aid projects. Aid is one of the most popular topics in Africa. In the 1960s and 1970s, despite its own economic difficulties, China devoted huge amounts of human and physical resources to help build the Tanzania-Zambia Railway. So far China has provided aid for Africa in various areas with a total sum of RMB44.4 billion and has assisted over 800 infrastructure and public welfare projects. In the past 20 years, with the rapid economic development in China, the expectation of African countries on China's aid has also increased. Therefore, we should properly increase the level of our aid for Africa on the basis of our increased comprehensive national strength.

As a matter of fact, with enhanced national strength and international influence, we have the obligation and capability to do it. In September 2005, at the summit celebrating the 60th anniversary of the UN, President Hu Jintao, on behalf of the Chinese government, made five solemn pledges to the least developed countries, including: China will grant zero tariff to some products from 39 least developed countries which have diplomatic relations with China; cancel the debt of all the heavily indebted poor countries that have diplomatic relations with China; provide US\$10 billion of preferential loans to developing countries; increase relevant aid to developing countries, to African countries in particular; and help developing countries train human resources in various fields. These pledges are not only a concrete demonstration of China as a big responsible country but also an important guarantee of further development of China-Africa relations and the strengthening of China-Africa 'all-round cooperation'.

Supervision and management of the capital flow and progress of all assistance projects under way should be strengthened to avoid misuse and embezzlement of capital. For implementation, projects can be categorized according to the amount of capital involved. For example, projects involving over US$100 million should be implemented by SOEs. Medium development projects involving less than ten million dollars can be open for bid among SOEs, qualified collective enterprises and private enterprises. Small projects under US$100,000 can be well open to private enterprises in the form of bidding. Diversified participation constitutes a new path for us to improve the efficiency of foreign aid projects.

Strengthening communications and mutual understanding and conducting dialogues on democracy through multiple channels. In this era of globalization and great diversity, it is natural for countries with different historical processes and national conditions to have differences in political understanding and values. However, these differences should be tackled through periodic communication and dialogue at various levels in order to promote mutual understanding and avoid a negative impact on overall diplomacy.

During visits by leaders at various levels and people from different circles, it is necessary to give more positive comments on the process of democratic development in Africa. More explanations should be given about China's 'bottom up' mode of democratic development which is determined by its national conditions; although it is different from the 'top down' mode of democratic development in Africa, they aim at the same goal, as should be explained to convince Africans and 'win their hearts'.

'All-round cooperation' between China and Africa in the new era is a trend. Diplomacy is not only the behaviour of the government and the leaders, but also the behaviour of the whole society. Citizens can be mobilized to cultivate an atmosphere of 'grand diplomacy' so as to integrate China-Africa friendly exchanges and cooperation at all levels. At present, there are multi-layered exchanges between China and Africa through various channels. In addition to the political and economic arenas, exchanges are also conducted in military affairs, education, health, medical care and culture and among youth, women and technical personnel and scholars. Currently, over 50 provinces and cities in China have established formal ties with their counterparts in Africa. Therefore, it is necessary for people from different trades to have full understanding about our national conditions and Africa's development so that they can serve as 'non-governmental envoys' in promoting China-Africa friendship in the new era.

Strengthening African studies. Africa has always been China's important ally. China and Africa have had over half a century of relations of traditional friendship. In the past we often said that China-Africa economic relations (a relatively small trade and investment volume) did not match our traditional friendly political relations. At present, after over a decade's development, China-Africa economic relations have been greatly strengthened. However, another thing that does not match the friendly relations has not aroused people's awareness: the limited focus on African studies in China does not match the tremendous demands of China-Africa relations.

In recent years, great changes have happened in African politics and society. Our research on Africa is far from enabling us 'to know ourselves and others perfectly'. Currently in the Chinese Academy of Social Sciences, the largest research institution on African studies, there are only around 20 researchers on Africa (nationwide the number of people engaged in studying and teaching of African affairs is less than 300). Facing 53 African countries, inevitably they cannot cover all of those and their research may be not as thoroughgoing as it ought to be. Therefore, I suggest that the research focus on African studies should be strengthened. Research teams in diplomatic and foreign trade-related government departments and those of academic institutions should be integrated so as to cultivate a group of experts on Africa, who can exchange views among themselves and provide reliable and timely information for decision-making at the central level.

All in all, 2006 is a year worth remembering in the history of friendly relations between China and Africa. Fifty years ago, China and Egypt established diplomatic relations at ambassadorial level, which started diplomatic relations between China and African countries. On the occasion of the 50th anniversary of the diplomatic relations between China and Africa, the Beijing summit and the third FOCAC ministerial meeting were held in 2006. Therefore, we have every reason to believe that the friendly relations of cooperation between China and Africa will have a brighter tomorrow.

8

CHINA-AFRICA RELATIONS: AN EARLY, UNCERTAIN DEBATE IN THE UNITED STATES

Bates Gill, J. Stephen Morrison
and Chin-Hao Huang

China, in its quest for a closer strategic partnership with Africa, has increasingly dynamic economic, political, and diplomatic activities on that continent. Following the high-profile summit of the third Forum on China and Africa Cooperation (FOCAC) in November 2006, senior Chinese officials, including President Hu Jintao and the then Foreign Minister Li Zhaoxing, visited a total of fifteen different African countries within the first quarter of 2007. The Chinese push forward in Africa raises the promise of achieving future gains to benefit African in significant, constructive ways, and hence hopes that China will seriously turn its attention to long-neglected areas such as infrastructure development and that its strategic approach will raise Africa's status globally, intensify political and market competition, create new choices in external partnerships, strengthen African capacities to combat malaria and HIV/AIDS, and propel the continent's economic growth, enabling African countries to better integrate with the global economy.

China's expansive engagement in Africa inherently carries significant implications for US interests in Africa and around the world,
as well as for US-China relations. Like China, the United States is
in the midst of an expansive phase of ever-greater engagement in
Africa, and it is now widely acknowledged that US national interests
in Africa have burgeoned to include substantial global energy stakes,
regional security and counterterrorism concerns, public health, and
intensifying competition with China, India, South Korea, and other
Asian countries that have significantly enlarged their engagement in
Africa.[1]

In light of these rapid developments, there seems to be an early,
growing sense of discomfort and uncertainty in Washington over
Chinese engagement in Africa. This uncertainty stems from four
main sources. First, there is limited understanding of the evolving
African opinion forming around China's expansive engagement in
the continent. Ultimately, sentiment within Africa will be a pivotal
driver in shaping China's future relationships with African partners.[2]
Second, while China's more ambitious and complex Africa policy of
today may in due course bring financial and political payoffs, alter the
playing field in Africa, and create pressures for changes in US policy
approaches, multiple risks also attend China's strategy. Given these
realities, it remains difficult to predict the relative success or failure
of China's approach in the near to medium term. Third, the Bush
Administration's approach to Africa, while featuring such signature
initiatives as the President's Emergency Plan for AIDS Relief and
the Millennium Challenge Corporation, is nonetheless consumed
with Sudan, and outside Africa the Bush Administration faces distractions from other widening challenges. It remains uncertain how
the next administration will carry forth US policy toward Africa and

---

1   For literature on the growing importance of Africa to US strategic interests,
    see Princeton Lyman and J. Stephen Morrison, *More than Humanitarianism:
    A Strategic U.S. Approach Toward Africa* (New York: Council on Foreign
    Relations, 2006).

2   The African Union has convened a task force examining the implications
    of China's, India's and Brazil's partnerships with Africa. The latest AU
    assessment (September 2006) on China's role calls for African countries to
    become more proactive in driving the agenda in future political and economic
    discussions and agreements with the Chinese.

whether China's engagement in Africa will be a priority consideration. Fourth, US-China relations overall—of which US-China engagement in Africa is but one second-tier concern—are themselves
uncertain and are vulnerable to simplistic, zero-sum calculation in
both Beijing and Washington. This situation will impede the near-
term formulation of an integrated, coherent US strategy that might
leverage areas of common interest while mitigating those areas where
US national interests and values are in conflict with Chinese approaches. Hence the time is ripe to generate new and longer-range
thinking about US policies to engage China productively in Africa.

China's expansive engagement in Africa

China's emergence as a rising global power is directing increasing attention to the activities and intentions of its expansive foreign policy
worldwide. While much of this attention focuses on China's growing
clout in Asia, China's increasing economic, political, and diplomatic
activities in Africa and other parts of the world are also coming under
greater scrutiny.

China's expanding engagement in Africa did not begin from
scratch. Beijing supported many liberation movements and other
insurgencies in sub-Saharan Africa and was quick to establish diplomatic ties and supportive economic relations with newly independent states as they emerged from the colonial era. Indeed, for more
than half a century, the Chinese systematically cultivated solidarity
and working relations with a range of African states. It was a profitable diplomatic investment which persisted into the post-Cold War
era when Western powers were more inclined, in the 1990s, to scale
back their presence.[3]

Today, China's Africa policy is carried out on a higher plane and
is more complex, multidimensional, ambitious and ultimately higher
risk. Its rising economic engagement is tied to conspicuously strategic goals, centred on access to energy and other scarce high-value
commodities. On the diplomatic front, Beijing has shown a new
determination to complete the process of eliminating bilateral ties

---

3 George T. Yu, 'Africa in Chinese Foreign Policy', *Asian Survey* 28, 8 (1988),
   pp. 849-62.

between Taiwan and a dwindling number of African capitals, and to use its accelerating entry to Africa to consolidate global allegiances and Beijing's putative leadership of the developing world. Beijing has also taken on a more active role in the security sphere: China's contributions of soldiers and police to UN peace operations, concentrated in Africa, have increased tenfold since 2001.[4]

China's policy in many instances is also tied to ambitious commitments to revitalize depleted critical infrastructures and invest on a substantial scale in strengthening human skills. It is not only official China that provides direct economic and diplomatic support. Chinese companies have become far more active as both importers of African energy and raw material resources and exporters of Chinese goods and services. China has deepened its commitments in non-traditional areas, such as helping African nations tackle public health problems. The China-Africa summit in Beijing in November 2006 featured 43 African heads of state in an effusive exchange with China's top leadership.[5] It also featured new economic and financial agreements, as well as significant debt relief and trade commitments.

The payoffs to China financially and politically may ultimately be very significant and alter our understanding of what kinds of intervention can achieve durable results. But multiple risks also attend China's expansive engagement in Africa. Business calculations on major investments are murky, and many will likely turn out badly. The bet that China can transform Africa's infrastructures where others have failed awaits proof of success, and challenges are surfacing for Beijing in translating its vision of a strategic partnership with Africa into a sustainable reality.[6]

---

4 As of February 2007, China had provided over 1,800 troops, military observers, and civilian police toward current UN peacekeeping operations. Three-fourths of Chinese peacekeeping forces are supporting UN missions in Africa (primarily Liberia, Sudan, and the Democratic Republic of Congo).

5 For greater details and content of the various official statements, documents, and declarations, see 'Beijing Summit and Third Ministerial Conference of the Forum on China and Africa,' November 2006, <http://english.focacsummit.org/documents.htm>.

6 Bates Gill, Chin-hao Huang and J. Stephen Morrison, *China's Expanding Role in Africa: Implications for the United* States (Washington, DC: CSIS, January 2007).

The expectation that China can have significant sway politically and displace the influence of others must take into account Africa's sensitivity to anything that smacks of neo-colonialism, and how callous and indifferent 'petropowers' in Africa have become as global energy markets tighten. In selecting energy-rich Angola and Nigeria as preferred partners, and choosing close support for Zimbabwe, China selected three of the most corrupt and difficult environments. In Sudan, Beijing finds a partner embedded in enormous political and moral controversies of its own making. In South Africa, it has entered a place of acutely high sovereign sensitivities.[7] Beijing is beginning to encounter serious challenges: criticism by a Zambian presidential candidate during the 2006 elections that China engages in unfair mine labour practices; South African trade union opposition to the flooding of South African markets by Chinese textiles. Some adjustments in approach, such as voluntary textile export quotas for South Africa, have now been set in place.

The unformed (and under-informed) US debate on China-Africa-US relations

China's dramatic moves on Africa have triggered an important debate in the United States over how to characterize Chinese intentions, policies, and practices in Africa. However, the American debate is still at an early and uncertain stage, and remains by and large unformed—and often under-informed.

Like China, the United States is in the midst of an expansive phase of ever greater engagement in Africa. US foreign assistance levels to Africa have more than tripled during the Bush administration. Signature White House initiatives have been launched that have had a predominant focus on Africa: the five-year, $15 billion

---

7   South Africa's President Mbeki delivered a stern warning to China in a public speech in January 2007, describing its approach to Africa as the threat of a new colonialism that would lock African in underdevelopment. That did not go unnoticed in Beijing, and during President Hu's speech in Pretoria in February 2007, he went out of his way to assure his audience that China would create new balances in trade relations as one demonstration of its sensitivity to African interests and opinion.

President's Emergency AIDS Relief Plan; the US Malaria Initiative; and the Millennium Challenge Corporation, which seeks to reward states that are well governed and performing well economically with substantial new aid compacts that will accelerate economic growth. Private sector engagement is steadily rising, concentrated in the energy field, and annual two-way trade reached $60.6 billion in 2005, up 36.7 per cent from 2004.

Since September 11, 2001, US military engagement has been enlarged substantially: through the Trans-Sahara Counterterrorism Initiative; a Gulf of Guinea maritime initiative now in development; and an ambitious Horn of Africa counterterror programme. The Combined Joint Task Force–Horn of Africa, based in Djibouti, is projected to be in place over the next 15 years. Following the Ethiopian military's intervention in Somalia in late December 2006, which routed the Islamic Courts government, the United States engaged directly in early January 2007 by attacking fleeing convoys suspected of transporting 'hard target' terrorists tied to the August 1998 al Qaeda attacks on the US embassies in Kenya and Tanzania and the subsequent attacks on Israeli tourists in Mombasa, Kenya in November 2002. In addition, it was announced in February 2007 that the United States would establish a dedicated, new military command—the Africa Command—in order to more effectively oversee US military-related activities on the continent. Such activities had previously been divided among three commands, the Europe Command, the Central Command and the Pacific Command.

This shift has called into question whether the United States has adequate personnel, resources and internal coordinating mechanisms to manage its rising interests. It has also called into question whether these relatively 'harder' interests will conflict with existing, long-standing commitments to the promotion of democracy and human rights, poverty alleviation, and conflict resolution. In the Bush years, a significant, sustained, high-level commitment has been made to ending Sudan's North-South war and, more recently, to ending the genocide in Sudan's western region of Darfur. The events leading up to the toppling of the Islamic Courts Union in Somalia and the post-conflict reconstruction since then have also demanded high-level US foreign policy attention.

At the same time that these developments have advanced, the clock on the Bush Administration is ticking ever louder. In particular, the hangover effects of Iraq on US credibility and legitimacy have at times constrained US engagement in areas like Sudan.

The American response to China's engagement in Africa will also be shaped by the overall US-China relationship. Broadly speaking, while US-China relations are generally stable, the American public, members of Congress, and executive branch officials are uncertain at best about the future with China, and at worst see China as an economic and security threat over the long term. This may inevitably limit the ability of forward-looking thinkers to build a more productive set of relationships for American interests in partnership with Chinese in Africa.

With regard to US views on China-Africa relations, a part of the problem lies in the lack of good information on the American side. US understanding of how Chinese motivations towards Africa are formulated and executed is thin at best.[8] Likewise, US understanding of evolving African sentiment toward China's expansive engagement is limited. There is a tendency on the part of the United States and China alike to mirror image one another. American critics often focus narrowly on China's pursuit of energy as the best explanatory lens through which to understand China's policies in Africa. Yet in Sudan, for example, oil is important but no longer the sole strategic factor in Chinese foreign policy calculations, and China faces increasing debates and complexities in its policy choices.[9] Progressives in the Chinese policymaking elite argue that Sudan's oil assets are not worth pursuing in the long run, and have suggested scaling back relations with Khartoum in an attempt to burnish China's image and international reputation. Inversely, there is a tendency among Chinese conservatives to argue that the United States and other Western

---

8   At a public statement at CSIS, Washington on 8 February 2007, Deputy Assistant Secretary of State James C. Swan noted that it was important to see China's role in the continent within a broader context of China's global foreign policy strategy and vision of the evolving international system.

9   See official Congressional record for written testimony of J. Stephen Morrison and Bates Gill on 'China and Sudan,' submitted to the US House of Representatives Foreign Affairs Committee on 8 February 2007.

countries are merely trying to force China out of Sudan to get to its oil.[10] The Chinese critics are also quick to point out that the United States—by dealing closely with such countries as Equatorial Guinea—is just as likely to engage in an uncritical embrace of autocratic, corrupt, and unstable regimes.

US insistence on bringing a new peacekeeping force into Darfur under a sweeping UN mandate without Khartoum's consent is seen by Beijing as a violation of Sudan's sovereignty that raises the risk that a UN force might be used to apprehend high-ranking Sudanese officials indicted by the International Criminal Court. These actions run counter to the long-held Chinese principle of 'non-interference' and partially explain its cautious approach toward Sudan.[11] To untangle this gridlock, the looming humanitarian crisis in Darfur should be elevated in the US-China agenda. Washington should work with Beijing to test Khartoum's willingness to honour a ceasefire, oversee disarmament, protect humanitarian corridors, and move forward an internal Darfur dialogue. It should explore ways that China might more meaningfully contribute to the hybrid UN/African Union operation.[12]

US knowledge of how African opinion is responding to an expansive Chinese presence is lacking. At a minimum, American approaches need to be sensitive to the many and long-standing positive legacies and images the Chinese have in various parts of Africa—particularly in comparison with past practices of colonial and other Western powers. There is a dearth of quality, informed analyses of China's multiple impacts in those places in Africa where China has made its greatest plays, and there is often missing from American writings an essential humility and care in estimating how

---

10 Simon Robinson, 'Time Running Out,' *Time*, 10 September 2006.

11 China has exercised much prudence and caution in a series of UN Security Council resolutions targeting Sudan. The concepts of 'non-interference' and 'national sovereignty' are important bedrocks of Chinese foreign policy and have been the basis for its conservative posture towards sanctions or other punitive measures against Khartoum since discussions in the Security Council on Darfur began in mid-2004. China's abstentions have allowed the Security Council to adopt Resolutions 1591, 1593, and 1706 targeting Sudan.

12 J. Stephen Morrison and Chester A. Crocker, 'Time to focus on real choices in Darfur', *Washington Post*, 7 November 2006.

US influence can be effectively brought to bear to shape Chinese approaches.

It is also true that in the long list of priorities in the US-China relationship, engagement in Africa occupies a second tier. Other pressing issues for Washington—from Iran to North Korea, and from East Asian stability to fending off China's economic challenge at home—will consume more time and energy in the formulation of China policy in Washington. Unfortunately, this also means that in return for Chinese cooperation on those issues, Washington may be less willing or able to expend the necessary political capital to gain greater cooperation from China in places such as Sudan.

In the absence of a better-formed and better-informed American official response to China generally, and to China-Africa relations in particular, more provocative voices fill the void in a negative and zero-sum way. Some American voices argue that the Chinese engagement in Africa is predominantly a form of crude mercantilism and political interventionism that directly threatens US interests and hence calls for confrontation, condemnation and containment.

An array of human rights advocacy groups and non-governmental organizations, for example, sustains intense pressure on the US government to take decisive, punitive measures on Darfur, including calls for forced humanitarian intervention. While the Sudanese accepted the Addis Ababa Agreement (the 'Annan Plan') of 16 November 2006 committing Khartoum to a ceasefire and three-phase expansion of a hybrid AU/UN force in Darfur, President Bashir in Sudan has obstructed its implementation. With the humanitarian situation worsening in Darfur, the American activist groups have intensified their efforts, which have included harsh criticism of China as a partner of Sudan. Others, including the authors of this paper, argue that China in Africa is a complex new reality which we only partially grasp: fast moving, multidimensional, and long-range in its various impacts. The Darfur issue, in particular, is a case in point where Chinese policy has seen subtle, incremental shifts. There is greater internal debate amongst policy elites in Beijing regarding the right approach to Khartoum on Darfur. There is also increasing recognition within foreign policy circles that direct pressures on China and its economic stakes in Sudan could escalate in North America and Europe.

No less important, Chinese views on Darfur are shaped by discussions with African states. Many leaders in sub-Saharan African states find Khartoum's actions in Darfur offensive on human rights, religious, and racial grounds. Khartoum's continued obstruction of an AU/UN force, and the inability of the international community to bring greater stability to Sudan, mean in practice that African Union peacekeeping forces, including troops from South Africa, Rwanda and Nigeria, remain under grave strain, cannot be reliably sustained and for these reasons are placed at considerable risk. China for its part is vulnerable to being called to account within Africa for enabling Khartoum's intransigence and impeding the AU's efforts.

As a result, a gradual shift in Chinese thinking is exhibited in several concrete actions taken by Beijing to exert additional pressure on Khartoum. The Chinese ambassador to the United Nations, Wang Guangya became very active, and was widely credited with gaining Sudanese acceptance for the Annan Plan in November 2006. In February 2007 there were hopes, perhaps unrealistically high, that President Hu might forcefully press President Bashir to accept the hybrid force. In public, China continued to emphasize its economic ties with Sudan and made new pledges of support, including aid in building a presidential palace. Understandably, these announcements drew international opprobrium.

In private, however, he apparently intervened personally to press President Bashir to stick to his commitments. And prior to leaving Sudan, President Hu delivered a rare public statement that outlined 'four principles' as the basis for an international approach to Darfur. The first, not unexpectedly, reaffirmed the principle of non-interference. But the fourth principle seems to contradict the first, saying: 'It is imperative to improve the situation in Darfur and living conditions of local people.' That is about as close as a Chinese leader has come publicly to supporting the emerging notion in the United Nations and the broader international community that governments have a 'responsibility to protect' their citizens from harm. Furthermore, in March 2007, Beijing announced that some economic leverage would be applied to exert additional pressure on Sudan. The Chinese National Development and Reform Commission, the country's main economic planning agency, released a public document in conjunction with the Ministry of Foreign Affairs and the Ministry of Commerce, noting that Sudan had been removed from the latest list of countries with preferred trade status.[13] According to the announcement, Beijing will no longer provide financial incentives to Chinese companies to invest in Sudan. This latest move appears to be a signal of Chinese disaffection with President Bashir's unwillingness to comply with his commitments to implement the Annan Plan.

The announcement was welcomed by the US State Department and came shortly before Chinese Assistant Minister Zhai Jun arrived in Washington to meet with Assistant Secretary of State for African Affairs Jendayi Frazer for the second round of US-China subdialogue on Africa in March 2007. The inaugural dialogue was formally launched in November 2005 under the auspices of the US-China Senior Dialogue process initiated by former Deputy Secretary of State Robert Zoellick.[14] While the first bilateral meeting on Africa focused largely on formalities, the second subdialogue in early March 2007 focused on the specific issues of debt sustainability, peacekeeping operations, Chinese companies' reputational risks in Africa, and transparency in the extractive industries. On Sudan, the Chinese side reportedly acknowledged the need for the international community to step up efforts and become more active in leveraging influence over Darfur.

Greater consensus has been achieved in the latest round of bilateral dialogue on Africa, in part because the United States is beginning to understand that China has real interests in Africa and will be engaged

---

13 Richard McGregor, 'Iran, Nigeria, Sudan off China incentive list', *Financial Times*, 2 March 2007.

14 At the official level, the United States and China in 2005 began to take some steps to think through their increasingly complex and interdependent relationship in a more constructive and strategic way. This effort, known at the 'senior leaders' dialogue', was led on the US side by the then Deputy Secretary of State, Robert Zoellick, who called for China to join the United States in becoming a 'responsible stakeholder' in the international system. Both sides agreed to hold bilateral subdialogues on key regional issues. The door was thus opened in Washington to begin thinking more seriously about an effective US strategy for engaging China on Africa.

in the continent for the foreseeable future. Hence, continuing to see China's economic, political, or diplomatic activities in Africa as a zero-sum game would be counterproductive. This emerging trend line is an encouraging sign in this early debate; the challenge would be for Washington to make a strong commitment to invest at a high diplomatic level to understand the Chinese perspective and continue to test China's intentions systematically.

Looking ahead

The current situation carries both bad news and good news. On the one hand, there will continue to be critical voices and distractions in Washington that may impede the near-term official formulation of an integrated, coherent US strategy—a strategy that might leverage areas of common US-China interest while downplaying those areas where US national interests and values are in conflict with Chinese approaches. On the other hand, the trend line for China's expanded presence in Africa—and the challenges and opportunities it presents to American interests—will demand greater and greater American attention and action. Hence critical work needs to be done to generate new, longer-range thinking and greater intellectual content to help create effective US policies to engage China productively in Africa.

Looking ahead, such strategic thinking can begin forming around some critical starting points. Firstly, any US strategy will be heavily influenced by Washington's experiences in individual African countries that are high US priorities and where China at the same time is pressing itself forward. That has certainly been true of Sudan, and will almost certainly be true of Nigeria, Angola and Zimbabwe. Secondly, any strategy will require a commitment to create a far greater understanding of evolving African opinion and approaches to China's growing presence in the world and in the region. The American response, thirdly, must reflect a far more sophisticated understanding of the complexities of Chinese motivations and decision-making vis-à-vis Africa. Fourth, there will be a need to boost awareness of potential US-China-Africa operational collaboration in areas of common interest: especially counter-terrorism, public health, peacekeeping, and infrastructure development and rehabilitation. On the other side of the equation, much more work is needed to devise strategies to press the Chinese on issues where US and Chinese perspectives clash: on democracy and human rights, business practices, transparency and accountability in the use of official wealth, and the environment. Finally, and perhaps most important, an American strategy towards Chinese engagement in Africa must more fully acknowledge and account for China's successes in negotiating its way forward with Africans in establishing new partnerships. The United States and other Western powers are neither gatekeepers nor chaperones. They are merely important players on a broadening, and more intensely competitive, playing field. How China does in Africa, for better or for worse, will ultimately depend on the nature of its relationships with African interests.

9

FRENCH PERSPECTIVES ON THE NEW SINO-AFRICAN RELATIONS

Roland Marchal

Bernard Kouchner was not elected Director-General of the World Health Organization. He didn't even make it to the shortlist [...] Professor Michel Kazatchkine was not elected President of the The Global Fund to Fight AIDS, Malaria and Tuberculosis, despite a majority vote of the Board. His candidacy was blocked by a Chinese veto. Both men have something in common: they are French citizens and benefited from the political and logistical support of the French State...[1]

Following the publication of China's Africa policy statement in January 2006, debate on the topic in the French press intensified to such an extent as to warrant sustained attention and numerous official reports from French ministries. As this chapter will show, however, the representation of China that emerges from this coverage is perhaps dictated less by Beijing's real policies in Africa than by a more complex analytical framework defined by often contradictory considerations. These include ongoing competition with the United States, the sluggishness of the French economy compared with Chinese dynamism, convergence with Beijing on issues such as the need for a multi-polar international system, the predatory character of Chinese

---

1 'Politique et mondialisation', *Le Nouvel Economiste*, 16 November 2006.

development, and the corruption that the Chinese presence feeds in Africa (Africa being, for the French press, corruptible by definition). The official discourse, by contrast, is more conventional and perhaps more realistic as well. However, it shares one common trait with that of the French media: its appreciation that China's policy in Africa does not exist *per se* but rather is a facet of China's global evolution. As a diplomat from the Ministry of Cooperation noted, 'Our vision of China is that of a global partner: there is no intention of bringing up Africa without putting it in a wider framework.'

If the goal of this chapter is to gauge French perceptions of China's emergence as a strategic actor in Africa, it must be noted from the start that this representation is not necessarily very coherent. Alternatively, one finds a veritable patchwork of realist analyses, pragmatic plans of action, and fears that are in turns publicly voiced, discreetly underplayed, or silenced. These are all elements that, in truth, originate in a series of different representations of France's role in the world in general and Africa in particular, and the instruments at its disposal at a time when the process of European integration is stumbling and American unilateralism strongly emphasizes the limits of French power in the international sphere.

This chapter starts by outlining the state of French political debates on Africa and on France's role in the world. This is followed by a brief discussion of the French vision of China and its actions in Africa and an attempt to bring out and explain the major points of contention and consensus in French perceptions of this process. The conclusion underlines several trends. To start with, France is currently having great difficulties in balancing its bilateral economic relations with China, which means that competition between the two states in Africa is a lesser concern. Secondly, an examination of the French and Chinese economic presence in Africa shows that the two countries are not clashing as competitors: France is far more present in the services sector and in market niches that have to date been of minor interest to China. It goes without saying that such a statement needs to be qualified on a sector-specific basis and has only relative validity for the time being. It is clear that in the energy sector, for instance, competition is real, though one should not discount the fact that technical complexity (for example, at the level of ultra-deep water oil exploitation) often promotes partnerships. Finally, if a compromise is achievable in the short-term it is also possible to outline scenarios of divergence between French and Chinese interests in Africa.

This chapter emphasizes three aspects that stir up or can quickly feed mutual disagreement. First, the military dimension brings up potential discord as soon as conflicting interests emerge (particularly, but not only, in the case of Chad/Sudan); the risks of proliferation, especially in the nuclear sector, are also an important source of French and international disquiet. A second problem pertains to the acceptance of common rules of the game in Africa. China voices a certain number of critiques on international aid that can find willing ears in Paris, but its absence of transparency, the way it allocates official development assistance, and its very methods arouse muted opposition, due to the extent to which they diverge from the baselines that are the product of long-standing dialogues at the heart of institutions such as the OECD. The third problem is China's willingness to play its cards on the African continent without having a medium-term vision of their effects.

France's interests in Africa

Too many observers imagine that France has a timeless interest in the African continent. Others confine their attention to a certain set of statistics related to the French presence in Africa and its role in France's external trade. In fact, France's interest in Africa cannot be limited to economic rationality or the fact of a common history alone.

It is helpful, for instance, to go back to the riots of November 2005, which essentially took place in the Parisian suburbs and not in Marseilles. On this occasion, at least two competing frameworks of analysis emerged, each one embodying different issues for the French state and society. The first chose to emphasize the colonial dimension of the events by underlining that this revolt was carried out by the subjects of French colonialism (or rather their grandchildren).[2] The other, on the contrary, was centred on citizenship and

2 Géraldine Faes and Stephen Smith, *Noir et français* (Paris: Editions Panama, 2006). Romain Bertrand, *Mémoires d'empire. La controverse autour du "fait*

reintroduced central questions about the social management of the French economic and welfare crisis. The purpose here is not to go back to these events, or to dispute the manner in which they were interpreted, but rather to remember how the debate echoed another discussion then raging among political elites about the decline of France or its international reassertiveness, despite the 'no' vote in the referendum on the European Constitution.[3] Africa, at any rate, is no longer a determinant factor in the socialization of French politicians. In fact, their interest in the continent has fundamentally decreased since 1981 for numerous reasons connected with the evolution of international politics but also the death of those generations which, for reasons of personal history, had a closer rapport with the continent; the resounding failures of a French policy that always ended up affecting French elites (diamonds from Bokassa in the case of Giscard D'Estaing, the Rwandan Genocide, the indicting of Charles Pasqua, etc.); and the increasing mutual incomprehension between French political actors and their counterparts in Africa.[4] These cursive remarks are not meant as sustained analysis but are enough to show the singularity of the former French President, Jacques Chirac, who stated the intention of reaffirming the French role in Africa as one of his key goals when he emerged from a five-year 'cohabitation' with Lionel Jospin's Socialist government in May 2002. While he kept his promise, this policy developed more as a function of international politics then of the specific reality on the continent.

When President Chirac's foreign minister, Dominique de Villepin, made his speech breaking with Washington over Iraq at the United Nations in February 2003, African delegates were the first to congratulate him. This was an apt illustration of one of the

---

colonial' (Paris: Editions du Croquant, 2006). Hugues Lagrange and Marco Oberti (eds), *Emeutes urbaines et protestations/Une singularité française* (Paris: Presses de Sciences-Po, 2006). See also www.riotsfrance.ssrc.org .

3 To size up the international perplexity vis-à-vis French political developments, see 'The art of impossible; a survey of France', *The Economist*, 28 October 2006.

4 Richard Banégas, 'Côte d'Ivoire: Patriotism, Ethnonationalism and Other African Modes of Self-writing', *African Affairs*, 105, (2006), pp. 535-52.

last international levers at the disposal of France, its capacity to get support for some its proposals from a great majority of the 53 African votes. Some might add to this the French military apparatus and an interventionist zeal that has greatly increased since 2002: more than 4,500 men in Côte d'Ivoire, almost 1,300 in Chad, several hundred in the Central African Republic as part of the military framework redefined at the time of cohabitation (1997-2002), and a pivotal role in European military operations in Africa. However, these French interventions are not considered a success. More often than not, they appear in the eyes of the nation's politicians as the cost of asserting power without the capacity to define a new doctrine: in France as much as in Africa, a sizeable segment of the elites waited impatiently for the May 2007 elections to close this chapter.

This half-hearted mutation of French political interest in Africa can be partly explained by the evolution of its economic ties with the continent.[5] In 1950, the colonial empire represented 60 per cent of French external trade, with French interests benefiting from a near-monopoly position. This situation evolved very quickly in the post colonial period on account of the exhaustion of the rentier capitalism that had essentially benefited import-export firms, agricultural and extractive industries (cocoa, cotton, minerals, petroleum) and the banking sector. While France remains an important economic part-ner for Africa at the beginning of the 21st century, the latter tends to play a shrinking role for France. France possesses a 20 per cent share of some markets in Africa but the relevance of the Franc Zone for French external trade has fallen to 1 per cent of the total, while France continues to absorb 25 per cent of exports from that region. The overall Africa share of French exports has fallen from 8.7 per cent in 1970 to 5 per cent in 2003, with Africa providing France with 4 per cent of its imports.

It would be wrong, however, to overstate this decline of Africa in France's external economic relations. Africa contributes a fourth of France's trade surplus (half of that from the Franc Zone alone). It is

---

5   This paragraph is based on Philippe Hugon, 'Permanences et ruptures de la politique économique de la France vis-à-vis de l'Afrique sub-saharienne', *Modern and Contemporary France*, 13, 1 (2005), particularly the economic data.

true that the maintenance of economic ties with the continent is still very much connected with rentier systems and political complicities, but even here one must be attentive to changes in the relationship. Oil is at the top of the list, and even more so in Nigeria than in the Francophone countries. The major French banks (Banque Nationale de Paris, Société Générale and Crédit Lyonnais) represent 70 per cent of banking sector activity in the Franc Zone. Companies such as Bouygues, Dumez, Electricité de France, Lyonnaise, Vivendi are very present in infrastructure, water supply and electricity works. This brief description illustrates why French diplomats are relatively serene when faced with current Chinese activism. A significant part of French business niches is in fact not threatened by Chinese ambitions at the present time: while the latter are enacted within the framework of a global discourse with continental ambitions for Africa, they essentially focus on no more than a dozen African states.

There is a final dimension where one can identify an important degree of convergence, even if this is not devoid of ambivalence, between France, China and African countries. For reasons relating to the downgrading of its international great power status, France welcomes reforms of the international system that put some meat into the semantics of the 'multipolar world' which the main French political parties routinely demand. One can note important affinities in this context. For instance, during the North Korean crisis in the summer of 2006 France and China were, if not in agreement, then pursuing a line of argument that was markedly different from that of Washington and its allies. Traditionally, French attention to the Third World, the rejection of brutal unilateralism and the will to bring certain demands of the developing world to the heart of Western fora form the grounds for possible additional convergence, although it is important not to overstate their depth or underplay the profound differences that remain beneath such apparent meetings of views. As the former French minister of Foreign Affairs Hubert Védrine put it, there is more agreement on what should not be than on what should exist.[6]

---

6 Hubert Védrine, 'L'émergence de la Chine vue de France', *Politique Etrangère*, Autumn 2006, available at http://www.hubertvedrine.net/index.

France and China

On 27 January 1964, France was the 'first big Western country' to recognize the People's Republic of China.[7] While bilateral relations saw slow but incremental progress, especially during the 1980s, the repression of the student movement in Tiananmen Square in 1989 opened a deep crisis between the two countries: it took five years for them to get back on track.[8] One of the legacies of this period is a recurrent debate on an end to the embargo on the sale of weaponry to China. France plays an important role in this (as Germany does also), because of the implications for its armaments industry of a possible resumption of sales. Such a decision is ostensibly to be taken by the European Union but has been highly politicized by the US perception that its allies do not implement the embargo with the same determination (especially at the beginning of George Bush's presidency, when China was perceived as a potential rival).[9]

In May 1997, China and France signed a declaration on the need for a global partnership regarding the most pressing international issues. This was strengthened by a new declaration, on the fortieth anniversary of bilateral relations, about a global strategic partnership that essentially picks up the same themes with the notable addition of human rights and the rule of law.

Paradoxically, the need for restatement underlines the difficulty of giving real meaning and substance to this strategic partnership: several French diplomats have privately argued that France is not the best partner for such dialogues and that the only credible venue should be the European Union. Yet the French want to safeguard

---

php?id_article=212

7   This claim made by the official website of the French Ministry of Foreign Affairs (http://www.diplomatie.gouv.fr/fr/pays-zones-geo_833/chine_567/index.html) is untrue unless the UK is considered as an irrelevant Western country (London recognized Beijing in 1950, long before Paris), but fits in with myth-building on French-Chinese relations. For an analysis, see Françoise Mengin, 'La politique chinoise de la France', *Critique Internationale*, 12 (July 2001).

8   For the history of relations between the two countries see the China page of the French Ministry of Foreign Affairs website: www.diplomatie.gouv.fr

9   See the China issue of *Foreign Affairs*, 84, 5 (2005).

their so-called 'foreign policy specificity' (this can be seen in French policy in other regions such as Africa and the Middle East). In addition, the points of view and policies of EU member states on any major issue of the day are frequently so distinct that Chinese officials find it difficult to identify an expression of European collective diplomacy.

The manner in which French decision-makers perceive China deserves closer scrutiny because their appreciation of its rise mirrors the perception of French decline, both economically and at the level of its international influence. Some quotes from the recent report by the Senate Commission on Economic Affairs aptly illustrate this.[10] From the viewpoint of French senators, China is in the process of becoming one of the world's biggest economies, as it was in the past.[11] China, they note, represented 30 per cent of world GDP before the Opium Wars of the 1840s, and about 1 per cent at the end of the Maoist era, but more than 4 per cent today. This enthralment with Chinese growth is signalled by constant reference to impressive figures. In Shanghai, a city with 20 million inhabitants, a building with more than 30 floors has gone up every 36 hours for the past twelve years; over the same period, 300 kilometres of urban motorways were built. Another example the senators bring up is that of certain factories which shelter and feed their workers, who put in 300 hours of work for a €100 wage. In France, the land of the 35-hour working week, these figures resonate in the national political debate. Fortunately, the report seems to say, China has some problems. It does not go into depth regarding the political context, other than to emphasize that the Chinese state is authoritarian and that its grip over the country remains uncontested. Far more interesting are the Chinese *problems* the French senators choose to highlight. They bring up the profound social inequalities (especially between the cities and the countryside), the major territorial imbalances (noting that Northern and Western China remain a China 'à l'africaine'), the voraciousness

---

10 Sénat, rapport d'information n° 307, Session ordinaire de 2005-2006.

11 The thesis is of Chinese origin and plays the role of an antidote to accusations of 'great power' ambitions: according to it, China is merely becoming what it once was.

for energy resources (one Chinese GDP percentage point requires three times more energy than the US or European equivalent), the major financial vulnerability (especially regarding the growth in bad debt), the imbalanced demographic growth on account of the single-child policy and, above all, the environmental threat posed by Chinese growth.[12]

While the report ends with some considerations on bilateral relations, the overall tone is one of anxiety: 'While China wakes up, France sleeps', an obvious reference to the 'Franco-French' debate on the decline of France.[13] The recent Chinese decision not to grant an important contract for the building of nuclear power plants to the French company Areva revived great apprehension regarding French capacity to redress the apparent structural deficit in trade relations with China (currently standing at about €12 billion). However, if the emergence of China as a global economic power worries France, then this concern is, all things being equal, far more salient in the French and European rather than the African context.[14]

To understand this, one has to return to the official analysis of the Chinese penetration of Africa highlighted above. The French Ministry of Finance notes very serenely that the strategic character of Sino-African relations is related to their growth rate, not their actual volume.[15] In 2004, for instance, China represented 6 per cent of Africa's external trade. This is far less than France or the United

---

12 This is recognized for the first time in the 2006 Chinese budget. See 'Pékin alloue un gros budget à la protection de l'environnement', *Le Monde*, 22 July 2006. US$175 billion will reportedly be spent fighting pollution in the next five years.

13 See Nicolas Baverez, *La France qui tombe: un constat clinique du déclin français* (Paris: Perrin, 2003). This has been followed by numerous other works and a vigorous debate in the French media. One can see the populism of both of the main candidates to the French presidency in May 2007 as responses to this type of discourse.

14 'European indifference towards the new energy challenges contrast with the Chinese', notes an official from the French Ministry of Defence. It must be recognized that European traumas in the energy sphere have more to do with Russian ambitions than with Chinese rivalry, as became evident throughout 2006.

15 See Ambassade de France en Chine/Mission Economique, *Lettre de Chine*, 177, June 2006.

States; yet in 1995, the Chinese share was a mere 1.5 per cent. In 2005 Africa generated 2.5 per cent of Chinese external trade, making it China's seventh largest trade partner. If compared with Russia or Singapore, this may seem modest. But the growth rate is exceptional: and·increase of 59 per cent in 2004 and 35 per cent in 2005.

There is more. In contrast with the generic continental discourse on China's African involvement, French economists note that China trades mainly with countries possessing the primary commodities China needs at the present time. Eighty-five per cent of Chinese imports come from only seven countries, six of which are almost exclusively oil exporters (in descending order: Angola, Sudan, Congo, Equatorial Guinea, Libya, Nigeria) and South Africa, which supplies China with iron ore, platinum and diamonds. In turn, these seven countries receive an estimated 45 per cent of Chinese exports to Africa. Only Egypt, Algeria and Morocco entertain a meaningful commerce with China that is not completely based on the provision of primary commodities, which among other things leads to a trade deficit of about US$1 billion a year.

From this description one can gauge that 'official' France, contrary to the French media, is not that fearful of a conquering China that would bar French products and services from African markets. To start with, Franc Zone countries, with the exception of Congo, are not much affected. While competition is fierce in some sectors (such as energy and construction), the relative specialization of current Chinese exports (textiles, electrical and electronic equipment, leather shoes) does not cast a shadow over French trade. This rivalry will doubtlessly increase, but at the present time French decision-makers seem to be betting on a slowdown of trade disagreements and a greater accommodation to Chinese competition in the medium term.

This measured pessimism stems from a series of analyses that underline certain structural weaknesses of the Chinese presence in Africa. It is noteworthy that this presence has indirect advantages such as the increase in the prices of primary commodities and perhaps even a real impact on the economic growth of the continent (5.4 per cent in 2004, the highest in eight years). Yet the Chinese concentration on primary commodities also has negative consequences for African countries. Chinese competition, for instance, has had a very negative impact on the textile sector in Southern Africa. According to some estimates, 75,000 jobs have been lost in Lesotho in 2005, and a similar number in South Africa from 2000 to 2004.

China has put in place a programme of overseas development aid that was greatly expanded during the Beijing Forum for China-African Cooperation Summit in November 2006. However, this aid is assessed in very contrasting ways. On the one hand, these aid flows constitute a significant additional source of resources for countries in great difficulties; they also tend to favour sectors frequently abandoned by Western donors and the international financial institutions, and are not subjected to political conditionality (except for the Taiwan issue). On the other hand, more than 70 per cent of it is tied aid and may not be managed in a transparent manner, with the risk that it will benefit ruling elites but not the majority of the population.

It seems obvious—as Paris found out in its direct interaction with Khartoum—that African countries do not want to lock themselves in a unilateral relation with China that is reminiscent of that which they had with their former colonial rulers. Accordingly, the creation of a competitive environment between potential donors is part of an African diplomatic *savoir-faire*, whether or not one thinks it is well harnessed and managed.

Stumbling-blocks

While France does not see China's actions in Africa as a drastic challenge to its own position, it is undeniable that there are a number of stumbling-blocks where differences of analysis and conceptions of international relations emerge. This has to do with both structuring international norms and a quite specific set of interests.

Africa is, in many respects, a continent where the military stakes are high. This is the case in terms of a market (albeit one that is smaller than the Middle East or Asia), but the recurrence of violent crises also grants it great political importance. Before the normalization of relations between China and Chad (and the severance of relations between N'djamena and Taipei) in August 2006, it took the emergence of Chadian rebellions based in Darfur for the French Ministry of Defence to worry about the proliferation of Chinese small arms. (This served the purpose of highlighting that Beijing was arming Khartoum, which was in turn arming the rebels.) Human rights organizations, for their part, have exhaustively proved that Kalashnikovs made in China have become widespread in Africa.[16] In addition to disagreements about specific crises that are discussed below, there is real anxiety about this proliferation. For a long time, China did not sell great quantities of heavy weaponry, and that which it sold was to long-time allies like Tanzania; but it has no qualms about exporting small arms, which have been used in 'poor men's wars' across Africa. In this regard, China does not subscribe to UN rules (which, to be fair, were deemed non-binding anyway).

More recently, however, Western states, and France in particular, have become concerned with Chinese exports of heavy weaponry and advanced military technology. French military circles are particularly worried about the nuclear ambitions of Angola and Algeria. They do so for not entirely altruistic reasons as France is a potential supplier of such systems and technologies. That said, French concerns about proliferation seem more robust than China's and are linked to a wider European apprehension about the manner in which China itself attains mastery of new technologies at the domestic level, without much concern for intellectual property in instances of technology transfer.[17]

It is improbable—the question is frequently raised in Sino-European meetings—that the Chinese government will be insensitive to these considerations. Yet its public diplomacy does not provide much evidence of this, all the more so as Western states are major proliferators and the biggest sellers of military hardware in Africa.

Equally important are issues linked to the new international norms on governance. It will not be necessary to evoke here the famous five principles that supposedly guide Chinese foreign policy, especially vis-à-vis African states. It has already been mentioned that China

---

16 These constitute a fourth of the total.

17 A whole range of grey literature consulted by the author points to numerous failures by French industrial entrepreneurs whose Chinese associates had a similar production plant built in another region of China before bringing about bankruptcy of the joint venture. It is unlikely that only French entrepreneurs have had such experiences.

makes ample use of ODA tools such as tied aid that the OECD has long eliminated because of their disappointing results in recipient countries. Similarly, China makes ample use of credit lines for African states on the basis of oil production, as in the case of Angola and Nigeria, an arrangement frowned upon by the IMF. These methods seem to throw African states further down the spiral of indebtedness rather than helping them escape it.[18]

Moreover, pressing questions are being posed regarding the financing of Chinese companies in Africa. Numerous experts question the behaviour of Chinese oil companies capable of mobilizing credit from public sources at interest rates much lower than those available in international capital markets for operations with doubtful profitability. While there is little hard evidence about accusations of Chinese corrupt practices (hardly a Chinese monopoly) the operating standards and code of conduct of their companies are not framed in the same way of their Western counterparts. Western companies are compelled, *volens nolens*, to align themselves with norms on account of pressure from Western NGOs and public opinion. This is not exactly the case with Chinese companies.

French parliamentary reports and the grey literature emanating from French government bodies mirror these questions and even indict the behaviour of Chinese operators in certain areas, especially in the forestry sector, which sends 60 per cent of its exports to China. The French media are far more talkative and devastating in their criticism. There are several reasons for this. Firstly, the French media are prone to hyperbole in their international coverage. The coverage of Africa and anything to do with Africa, in particular, is closer than ever to caricature. (This may be fed by the fact that official attitudes towards China are far more restrained than those reserved for some of France's allies.) Secondly, information about Chinese businesses is often collected from direct (European) competitors who do not hesitate to describe their rivals' presence in terms of 'the victory of vice over virtue', the Chinese appearing as a disruptive presence for

---

18 See the lengthy considerations about the 'Dutch disease' and the oil resource curse in Africa in the report of the parliamentary commission of foreign affairs, Commission des Affaires étrangères, *Energie et géopolique*, Rapport No. 3468, October 2006.

Western companies that were finally about to develop Africa. Thirdly, there is a reaction peculiar to the novelty of these actors. Simply because China is rocking an established order of things, its presence provokes a response. In the mid-1990s, the French press made a number of attacks against Mahathir's Malaysia, which was then getting involved in Africa. This was particularly so in South Africa where the French were also seeking a foothold in telecommunications and French companies such as Alcatel thought of themselves as the most competitive.

There is another area of disagreement with China that can potentially be linked with the two already mentioned: Chinese policies towards particular crises in the continent. The best illustrations of this are Zimbabwe and Sudan. Chinese relations with Robert Mugabe are long-standing and have always been warm. The international management of the Zimbabwe crisis has been sufficiently disastrous, especially on the British side, and the South African role sufficiently partisan to explain continuing Chinese support, even if the Zimbabwe that will emerge from the Mugabe era will have nothing in common with the prosperous country of the 1990s.

The political crisis in Sudan, the Darfur conflict and its regional repercussions, and the conditions of oil production there have placed Beijing in a negative position vis-à-vis Western public opinion. It is noteworthy that in Africa and in the Arab world, Chinese diplomacy is far less under attack over the Sudan situation. If there has been some movement in Chinese policy regarding this, it is far more on account of American pressure at the bilateral level than because of declarations by the African Union or heads of state such as the former Nigerian President Obasanjo.

French diplomats have generally gone for a very moderate approach in their disagreements with China in Africa, except when French interests are really threatened, as was the case with the Chadian crisis. Moreover, France calls for a dialogue on African crisis in the framework of the above-mentioned strategic partnership. But it will be very difficult to establish a dialogue while the framework of analysis remains defined by Chinese officials: it is hard to gauge the seriousness of the Darfur crisis if one limits one's interlocutors to Sudanese officials and their 'civil society'. In this regard, one is faced with a set of difficulties that French diplomats have already experienced with Japan over Africa: how to 'politicize' the analysis of a crisis situation and not enter into the established discourse that permits everything, including the utmost passivity.

Conclusion

The French debate about China in Africa takes place at several levels. At the level of the political and administrative elites, it is first and foremost a debate about changes in France, its real or virtual decline, its incapacity to move while others demonstrate boundless dynamism. It is also a debate about the weight of France in Europe and its European capacity to establish the political and economic relationship with China that fits the French ideal for it. The extent to which this is the source of misunderstandings at the heart of the European Union is well known: among its member states, there are several that believe that the Union does not have the vocation to become a great power like the US, interacting as such with great powers-to-be like China and India. Nonetheless, the rise of China as seen from Paris reinforces the credibility of a multipolar world and renders it possible, necessary and virtuous. France can go on labouring towards a 'great power Europe' and against a 'free market Europe' which remains a compelling vision for the United Kingdom and many of new member states.

In discussions on the African continent, Paris wants to think of itself as indispensable. It is necessary to enter a dialogue about emergencies, establish common aid policies, and go beyond Chinese reservations about the African Union and regional organizations (China much prefers bilateral discussions). But everyone agrees that everything remains to be done and that even the terms of debate are still undefined. There is therefore some disquiet, even if it is put in perspective for the present by the immediate forms of Chinese commercial presence and economic interests in Africa. Many French companies are still not threatened in their niches. They certainly are threatened in strategic sectors such as mining, petroleum and construction, but these sectors were very competitive before the rise of China in Africa. France, like other Western countries, can brandish a seal of quality and make use of a technological superiority that China currently does not possess and that corruption alone cannot always control.

Most certainly, a Sino-European or Sino-French forum will not be able to deal decisively with questions regarding the behaviour of Chinese public and private companies in Africa, the ways in which projects get to be financed by Chinese ODA, and their implications for sustainable development and for the preservation of ecosystems in Africa. The only hope at this stage is that these questions are being posed within China itself in the framework of its domestic development and that they have resulted, in an exclusively Chinese setting, in very plural debates.

SECTION 3
RELATIONS IN FOCUS

10

LIBERATING LABOUR? CONSTRUCTING
ANTI-HEGEMONY ON THE TAZARA
RAILWAY IN TANZANIA, 1965-76

Jamie Monson

In the dry month of August in 1965, a small team of Chinese railway
experts and their African guides set off on foot from the town of
Kidatu in the southern interior of Tanzania, heading southwestward
towards the Zambian border. Carrying their supplies and equipment
on their backs, this intrepid group would cover a distance of over
400 miles before returning safely to Dar es Salaam nine months
later. Their job was to scout possible routes for the construction of
a railway that would link the Zambian Copperbelt with the Indian
Ocean. As they cleared their path across the landscape they were said
to have left behind them a trail of bamboo marker poles with small
red flags fluttering in the breeze.[1]

1   R. Hall and H. Peyman, *The Great Uhuru Railway: China's Showpiece in Africa*
    (London: Gollancz, 1976), pp. 107-8; Ali Mohamed Sendaro, 'Workers'

This Chinese survey team was ridiculed in the Kenyan white settler press as an example of the ineptitude of 'communist aid' in Africa. These were not genuine surveyors with proper surveying equipment, reported the *Kenya Weekly News*, but ordinary railway technicians imported from China who (the *News* implied) had no business carrying out such an enterprise.[2] The project was deridingly called the 'bamboo railway', a phrase that simultaneously conjured up the communist threat (represented by the red flags marching into the interior) and Chinese technological backwardness (represented by the bamboo marker poles).[3]

The United States responded to China's foray into East African railway development with alarm. TAZARA (the Tanzania-Zambia Railway) was referred to as the 'great steel arm of China thrusting its way into the African interior', in a US congressional hearing; a *Wall Street Journal* article stated ominously in 1967, 'The prospect of hundreds and perhaps thousands of Red Guards descending upon an already troubled Africa is a chilling one for the West.'[4] The CIA had warned of the leftward shift of Tanzanian politics in a 1965 report that devoted several pages to the friendly relationship between Julius Nyerere and the 'Communist Nations', especially China. It was true that China was using development assistance in East Africa to achieve larger international strategic goals. And there was certainly a

---

Efficiency, Motivation and Management: The Case of the Tanzania-Zambia Railway Construction' (PhD Thesis: Department of Management, University of Dar es Salaam, 1987), p. 250; George Yu, *China's Africa Policy: A Study of Tanzania* (New York: Praeger, 1975), p. 130; Bruce Larkin, *China and Africa, 1949-1970: The Foreign Policy of the People's Republic of China* (Berkeley: University of California Press, 1971), p. 99; Interview with Mr Du Jian, Dar es Salaam, April 2000.

2   'Communist aid', *Kenya Weekly News*, 29 April 1966, p. 29.

3   Mr Waziri Juma, the railway's political coordinator, asked the delegates to a TANU party conference in 1971 to 'dispel slanders spread by imperialists that the Railway will be made of bamboo and be of low quality.' TNA C/2112/71, IS/I.317, 23 September 1971. He told delegates that construction work was of the highest quality and long durability.

4   'Red Guard line of China chugging into Africa', *Wall Street Journal*, 29 September 1967.

'thick ideological flavor' to China's public announcements of support for the proposed Tanzania-Zambia railway link.[5]

Yet the division of world politics into leftward and rightward turns was more an American than a Chinese position in the 1960s, at least in terms of African development assistance. Anxieties about scores of Chinese railway workers descending upon African villages revealed more about American fears of communism than about China's development intentions or the way they were experienced by Tanzanians during TAZARA's construction. For in the public statements about the railway that proliferated in China and Tanzania at the time, the emphasis was not so much on the clash between capitalism and communism, but on the similarities between the United States and the Soviet Union. In Chinese propaganda, it was clearly stated that China's development role in Africa would be to counter the neo-imperialist and hegemonic tendencies of the two superpowers.

China claimed at this time to belong with Africans to the 'Third World', a category that was defined racially (as non-white) and historically (as formerly colonized). The United States and the Soviet Union, on the other hand, were described as both European and imperialist. These statements resonated with the ideologies of Julius Nyerere and the TANU party, for whom citizenship in the new nation was defined in opposition to *unyonyaji* or 'exploitation'.[6] In a speech he gave in China in 1965, it was reported that Julius Nyerere distinguished Chinese assistance from other forms of foreign aid when he stated that 'China is a Third World country', and that although some other countries might use economic aid to exploit or to politically dominate Africans, 'it is not China's policy at all.'

Chinese public statements depicted the Soviets and the Americans as expansionist, profit-seeking imperialists in Africa. The Chinese described themselves in contrast as the sympathetic third world part-

---

5   He Wenping, 'Fifty Years Through Wind and Rain', Unpublished paper presented to International Conference on Blacks and Asians: Encounters through Time and Space, Boston University, April 2002.

6   The popular term for exploitation was *unyonyaji*, literally 'sucking'. James Brennan, 'Blood Enemies: Exploitation and Urban Citizenship in the Nationalist Political Thought of Tanzania, 1958-75,' *Journal of African History*, 47 (2006), pp. 389-413.

ners of African countries: the true 'all-weather friends' of Tanzania and Zambia. During TAZARA's construction, China's development principles were articulated as anti-hegemonic, and these principles were intended to be carried out through both policy and practice. The practical blueprint for anti-hegemonism lay in the application of China's eight principles of African development, introduced by Zhou Enlai during his 1963-4 visit to Africa. These development principles emphasized the importance of self-reliance, while appealing to an ideal of community and shared history between China and other Third World nations. The last two of the eight principles had particular relevance to the construction of the TAZARA railway:

7. In giving any particular technical assistance, the Chinese Government will see to it that the personnel of the recipient country fully master such techniques;
8. The experts dispatched by the Chinese Government to help in construction in the recipient countries will have the same standard of living as the experts of the recipient country. The Chinese experts are not allowed to make any special demands or enjoy any special amenities.[7]

With these principles China intentionally highlighted the differences between its own approach to foreign aid and that of other donors, in particular the United States and the Soviet Union. The TAZARA project was called the Great Freedom Railway because it was intended to free Zambia's landlocked mining economy from its historical dependence upon transportation routes through the white settler-ruled territories to the south. As an anti-hegemonic development project, the construction of TAZARA also promised another kind of freedom: a work experience that would liberate Africans by offering them an alternative to the exploitation of neo-imperialist post-independence projects.

The construction of the Freedom Railway would also be liberating for the African worker because it constituted a significant departure from the recent colonial past. Unlike colonial overseers of African

---

7   Yu, *China and Tanzania*, p. 74; Larkin, *China and Africa*, p. 106.

construction projects who were remembered by one worker as 'standing aside, hand-in-pocket, directing workers by finger-pointing', the Chinese project leaders would work side by side with their African counterparts, teaching by example.[8] Relationships between African workers and Chinese management would be characterized by cross-racial friendship and worker solidarity rather than by the exclusion of colonial racial hierarchy. Workers would be paid fairly and on time, and benefits such as health care would be made available to them in the worker base camps. The management structure would also incorporate worker participation through regularly scheduled solidarity meetings.

The construction of TAZARA was intended to be liberating in yet another way. The experience of participating in a complex technological project would free African workers (as well as the rural populations living along the railway) from their alleged ignorance and backwardness. Workers would become modernized as they acquired new skills from the Chinese technical experts who offered them education and training. Through their practice of mentoring and teaching by example, the Chinese experts would impart important values such as hard work and worker discipline to their less experienced African counterparts. The transfer of technology would bring modernity to Tanzania's economy by developing a segment of the workforce that could then be deployed in other national development projects.

And finally, the construction of TAZARA was envisioned as a liberating work experience because it was pan-African in its original intent. Not only would Chinese and African workers come together in the construction camps and lay tracks together in the trenches, but Zambians and Tanzanians would also work side by side. The work experience during TAZARA's construction was structured managerially in ways that highlighted the partnership between Tanzania and Zambia. Thus the railway project, by bringing together workers from two newly independent neighbouring countries, could exemplify

---

8 Sendaro, 'Workers' Efficiency', p. 23. A similar method of worker management and instruction is described for West Africa in Deborah Bräutigam, *Chinese Aid and African Development: Exporting Green Revolution* (London: Macmillan, 1998), pp. 149-51.

the possibilities of pan-African solidarity in regional development cooperation.

The construction of the Freedom Railway was therefore envisioned in multiple ways as a liberating project for African workers. The workers would be freed from the exploitative models of development pursued by the neo-imperialist hegemonic powers. They would be brought into modernity through the labour process as they earned wages, practiced work discipline, and mastered new technology under the supervision of their Chinese mentors. And Zambians and Tanzanians, by labouring side by side, would provide a model for post-colonial worker solidarity through this pan-African development project.

The TAZARA labour process was burdened with multiple and expansive expectations well before construction began. The project was also being closely scrutinized by a sceptical world audience that, at least in some corners, desired to witness its failure. In this challenging context, to what degree were the hopes and expectations for an alternative labour experience actually met, according to the memories and limited records available to us from the project?

For many of the young Tanzanians and Zambians who were recruited to join TAZARA's labour force, the experience of construction was in fact a liberating one. They acquired skills that ranged from the most basic fundamentals of building the permanent way to the advanced engineering technology mastered in the foundry. A select group of workers was promoted from the level of digging ditches to management positions, where they learned and practiced leadership skills. Others (about 200) were sent to China to study railway maintenance and operations, and also learned the Chinese language there. In these ways the project fulfilled China's seventh principle: the recipients of Chinese donor assistance should 'fully master' the techniques of development. Upon TAZARA's completion, Tanzanian Prime Minister Rashidi Kawawa announced that Zambian and Tanzanian workers had received 'the best kind of training' from the Chinese experts during TAZARA's construction, and that this expertise could now be applied to other development work.[9]

---

9 'Tanzania, Zambia celebrate railway completion', NCNA 24 October 1975.

At the same time, there were contradictions in the application of China's development principles in the TAZARA corridor. The emphasis on hard work and discipline that characterized both Chinese and Tanzanian development principles was frequently at odds with the need to train and educate a future workforce. Many workers complained of the gruelling pace of construction, and some left the project altogether. The way daily work was organized—on an hourly rather than a task basis—was reminiscent of work struggles in the colonial period. And the push to complete the railway ahead of schedule—in order to show the world what could be accomplished through pan-African and Third World solidarity—made the goal of skills transfer more difficult to achieve. In the end, Tanzania and Zambia asked the Chinese to leave behind a team of railway specialists to assist in TAZARA's operations.

There were also contradictions in the effort made by the Chinese to live and work side by side with their African counterparts. In the camps where workers spent most of their off-duty time, Chinese and African workers lived mostly segregated lives. The Chinese emphasized worker solidarity and brotherhood (for example in worker meetings), and the theme of friendship had become ubiquitous in Chinese development assistance. Yet while the Chinese workers referred to their Tanzanian counterparts as 'friends', they referred to themselves as 'experts.' These identities reveal the unavoidable hierarchy that existed between Chinese railway specialists and the African workforce: the Chinese technical experts were nominally friends and brothers, but in practice they were teachers and supervisors.

The African workers, on the other hand, were mostly younger men with limited schooling and experience who were recruited on the basis of their physical health; those that showed aptitude for technology and leadership were promoted but the majority remained engaged in manual labour. These hierarchies meant that for the workers there were differences in work experience as well as in the kinds of training they received. Those who were promoted gained technical skills and experienced their Chinese counterparts as friends and mentors; for those who hauled stone out of quarries and dug the ditches and culverts, the Chinese were more distant figures.

Nevertheless, these hierarchies of age and experience were experienced positively by many Tanzanian workers. Even though there were differences in age and experience between the Chinese and the African workers, and their tasks were not equivalent, they reportedly showed one another mutual respect. African workers described their relationships with the Chinese as those of juniors and elders, emphasizing the mentoring and teaching role played by the Chinese 'experts'. For many of these younger African men, building the railway is remembered as a coming of age experience, a time of moving into adulthood under the guidance of their Chinese leaders. Many recall the experience of earning a wage, learning the Chinese language and mastering railway technology as a liberating entrance into a modern, post-colonial world. In this sense, perhaps more than any other, those who built the Freedom Railway recall their work experience as a liberating one.

Hard work

From the beginning, it was clear that the construction of the TAZARA railway would involve hard physical labour. The project design was labour-intensive and tens of thousands of African workers were hired to take on jobs ranging from quarrying stone to forming the permanent way. Workers had to endure challenging conditions as they laid track through the uninhabited wilderness of the Selous Game Reserve and over the steep escarpment between Mlimba and Makambako. The idea of hard work was also an important component of Tanzanian post-independence ideology; it was repeated often in Chinese and African official communication with the workers. 'Hard work' was therefore both a material reality experienced by TAZARA's workers and a component of the ideology put forward to inspire them. It was also an integral part of the framing of the project's public image for audiences in Africa, China and the rest of the world.

The labour process was organized through twelve base camps, each of which had a resident work team and was responsible for a given section of the railway line. Chinese railway experts supervised and trained the African workers, who were divided further into sub-teams directed by Chinese field assistants. The sub-teams were each given a specific task to fulfil—some were assigned to build bridges, while others dug ditches, constructed the raised railway bed, or connected telephone lines. Each sub-team set up a temporary camp where they lived until they had completed their assigned tasks. They would then pack up their camp and move on to the next section. The sub-teams worked in even smaller gangs, sometimes as few as eight to ten people, supervised by Tanzanian foremen under the direction of a Chinese counterpart. The work gangs were spread out along the railway line during the day, some two to three miles apart. One field team could be made up of thousands of workers; at Mwale base camp in 1972, there were 64 labour gangs with about 5,500 labourers.[10]

The first phase of the construction project moved quickly, and the initial length of 110 miles of track from Dar es Salaam to Mlimba was completed within one year. Yet even this first section held challenges. Much of this track was laid within the boundaries of the Selous Game Reserve, where workers lived in isolated conditions far from village life, surrounded by wild animals. The next section of track—the notorious tunnels section that connected Mlimba with Makambako—was even more challenging and took almost the whole of the following year to finish even though it comprised only half the distance. The engineering and construction challenges of this section had seemed almost insurmountable to each of the successive teams of surveyors that had inspected the route. One third of the civil engineering works for the whole line were built here: not only 18 of the 22 tunnels but also several high bridges over steep ravines. The work required extensive road building and earthworks, and more construction sub-camps per kilometre than any other section. There were also more casualties here than in other sections, including Chinese casualties.[11] Worker injuries resulted primarily from dynamite blasting and from cave-ins. Heroic descriptions of the construction of the tunnels were published in Chinese news accounts, and this

10 Sendaro, 'Worker's Efficiency', p. 169; interview with Daniel S.M. Momello, Njombe 2002.

11 TNA file A/932/71 IS/I.317, 18 April 1971, 'Majivu ya Mafundi wa Kichina Yazikwa'.

section came to symbolize more than any other the 'hard work' of the railway workers who struggled through day and night to complete the project.

By June 1973, the construction work on the Tanzanian side had been completed—the tunnels section between Mlimba and Makambako, and most of the basic structures for the permanent way up to Kasama in Zambia. Tracklaying followed and the rails reached Kasama in December 1973. As the peak of construction work passed the overall workforce was gradually reduced, and Tanzanian workers were replaced by Zambian workers as the project moved across the border.

In practice, the Tanzanians recruited to build the TAZARA railway found the work to be challenging and exhausting. Each morning the work teams would be transported from camp out to their work sites. 'When you arrived at the work site,' recalled one worker, 'you got hold of a shovel or a spade or any work tool and worked with it under the direction of the Chinese expert.'[12] In uninhabited areas far from the reach of camps and settlements, workers were fearful of wild animals, especially lions. 'A lot of the work was dangerous and difficult,' remembers Raphael Chawala, 'we had to use our heads and be watchful.'[13] Many found the work to be so difficult, and the conditions so demanding, that they abandoned their jobs.[14] Hashim Mdemu worked at Namawala sub-camp digging culverts, a job he described as so physically strenuous that he could not continue after one year.[15] Those who stayed with the project only managed to survive the suffering they endured in these sections, according to Gilbert, through their own fortitude: 'We persevered here with the Chinese.'[16] Rogatus Nyumayo used the same term when remember-

---

12 Letter from Administrative Assistant, 17 May 1971, cited in Sendaro, 'Worker's Efficiency'.

13 Interview with Raphael Chawala, Ifakara, 20 April 2000.

14 Interviews with Rogatus Nyumayo, Mlimba, 26 July 2000; Salum Mwasenga, Mang'ula, 30 July 2000; Hashim Mdemu, Ifakara, June, 2000. Hall and Peyman, *The Great Uhuru Railway*, p. 128.

15 Interview with Hashim Mdemu, Ifakara

16 Interview with John Gilbert and Hosea Mngata, Ifakara, 20 April 2000.

ing the tunnels construction, where the work was extremely challenging, 'but we ourselves just persevered.'[17]

At the sites of large-scale projects, such as tunnel blasting and bridge construction, the Chinese installed electricity generators to allow work shifts to continue during both day and night. John Gilbert remembers working at Kisaki building bridges as part of a 24-hour crew. In the tunnels section workers put in successive eighthour shifts around the clock: 'You worked for eight hours, you then rested eight hours, then you started again,' recalled Beatus Lihawa.[18] During resting shifts the workers retreated to their temporary shelters in the worker camps. Electricity generated at the Base Camps also allowed for day and night activity. At Mang'ula Base Camp, engineers who worked in the factories and workshops often put in twenty-four hour shifts with rotating rest breaks.[19]

Work on the railway was difficult and rigorous in part because of the Chinese approach to the larger project of railway construction. The Chinese had committed themselves to building the railway using a labour-intensive rather than a capital-intensive model. With this strategy China hoped to minimize the importation of expensive capital goods and equipment, particularly from outside China.[20] The labour-intensive approach meant that there were thousands of job opportunities for Tanzanians and Zambians who had little previous education or work experience. The vast majority of those jobs required back-breaking manual labour such as digging ditches, spreading gravel and hauling heavy materials. The possibilities for transfer of technical skills were slight for many of these workers.

Strenuous working conditions were made more difficult by the determination of the Chinese authorities to finish the project well

17 Interview with Rogatus Nyumayo, Mlimba, 26 July 2000.

18 Interview with Beatus Lihawa, Mlimba, 20 July 2000; D.D.S.M. Momello, 'Final Report on Tunnels Construction', p. 9.

19 Interview with Salum Mwasenga, Mang'ula, 30 July 2000.

20 Using Tanzanian trade statistics, George Yu estimated that capital goods imports for TAZARA's construction went up from $33.6 million to over $60 million between 1970 and 1971. While basic machinery was manufactured in China, larger items such as trucks and earth-moving equipment came from Japan and Europe. Yu, *China's African Policy*, pp. 142-3.

ahead of schedule. The Chinese management was willing to push the workforce night and day to show what could be achieved—and to build African confidence—at a time when the world was watching. The Chinese signed on to work 14-hour days, and they expected the Africans to join them. Tanzanians and Zambians, however, had a mixed response to this approach to labour. While many joined in the Chinese enthusiasm for hard work, they were not always willing to endure such a strenuous timetable. Conflicts took place, for example, when African workers completed their assigned duties before the end of the work shift. The workers felt that they had finished for the day and were entitled to rest; their supervisors insisted that they take on additional work until the end of their shift. These conflicts over the definition of work and the workday were similar to those that had been experienced in colonial East Africa, and were exacerbated by language difficulties.[21]

African workers remember Chinese railway technicians in ways that reveal these contradictions and the ideals that accompanied them. The Chinese are remembered as strict supervisors who doled out harsh discipline to workers who were lazy or errant. 'They were very harsh,' remembers Chawala, 'if you were lazy or a liar or a thief, they would chase you away. They would send a report to other stations so that you couldn't work there.' Others recall that the Chinese were tough but fair: if you did your job properly, you would be paid on time without question. Those who failed to do their work, on the other hand, would be asked to leave. Stories circulated about particular supervisors who were unusually demanding: one was known as *kapitula* or 'short trousers', because he always wore safari-style shorts. When he confronted a worker who was falling down on the job, he reportedly reached into the pocket of his shorts, took out a bundle of

---

21 Sendaro, 'Workers' Efficiency', p. 187. Philip Snow, *The Star Raft: China's Encounter with Africa* (London: Weidenfeld and Nicolson, 1988), p. 173. These conflicts are similar to those described by Keletso Atkins for sugar cane workers in nineteenth century Natal in South Africa: Keletso Atkins, *The Moon is Dead, Give Us Our Money! The Cultural Origins of a Zulu Work Ethic* (Portsmouth: Heinemann, 1993), and those described by Frederick Cooper for colonial Mombasa, 'Colonizing Time: Work Rhythms and Labor Conflict in Colonial Mombasa', in Nicholas Dirks (ed.), *Colonialism and Culture* (Ann Arbor: University of Michigan Press, 1992), pp. 209-46.

shillings and handed it to the worker saying, 'Take this pay, you are now dismissed.'[22] There are also many stories of ingenious methods that African workers devised to avoid working at the Chinese level of effort. According to one local story, if a worker wanted to rest all he needed to do was to open a copy of Mao's 'little red book' and seat himself in the shade of a tree. He could sit that way for hours, and his supervisor would leave him be.

The theme of 'hard work' was proclaimed in official statements as a liberating ideal—the Chinese in particular stated that through hard work and discipline, young African workers would gain self-confidence. A similar claim was made for Tanzania and Zambia as young nations—by working hard to complete the railway ahead of schedule, they would show the world what they were capable of, and gain confidence both as individual states and as pan-African part-ners. At the same time, however, much of the hard work in practice was challenging and difficult. The struggles over the length of the work day—as well as the definition of work obligation according to time shifts rather than specific tasks—were reminiscent of struggles over work in the colonial era. Thus while 'hard work' was a liberat-ing ideal on the one hand, in practice it could be reminiscent of the impositions of labour regimes in the colonial past.

Working side by side: friends and strangers

Relations between African and Chinese participants in the construc-tion project, mirroring the larger relationship between Tanzania, Zambia and China, were described officially as embodying friend-ship, brotherhood and solidarity. This solidarity was held up by project leaders as pan-African as well as Afro-Asian; transnational as well as cross-racial. In practice, however, there were significant differences in age, experience and status between the workers. And in the construction areas, while their working conditions were largely the same, Africans and Asians were segregated within work camps and in their off-duty lives.

---

22 Interview with Salum Mwasenga, Mang'ula, 30 July 2000.

The African workers who were recruited for the project were young men, and the theme of youth and youth development was repeatedly emphasized in the way the Kiswahili term *vijana* (youths) was used to describe them in government announcements and media reports. 'These youths are working on shift basis for 24 hours,' stated TANU secretary Major Hashim Mbita in 1971, 'and many of them can now understand the Chinese language and work independently. They will be a great asset to the Tanzania and Zambia industries when the railway is completed.'[23]

Education and training were at the heart of the Chinese model of development in Africa.[24] During the recruitment of railway workers in Tanzania and Zambia, therefore, the emphasis was on good health, character and discipline rather than extensive prior education or work experience. These young recruits would be trained on the job by their Chinese counterparts, often through observation and simulation. The labour-intensive approach to TAZARA's construction meant that the majority of the workers would be engaged in strenuous manual labour in challenging environmental conditions. For this reason, physical fitness was a primary requirement for those seeking to work on the railway. Rogatus Nyumayo remembers that young men in Iringa had to submit to a physical examination, to ensure that they were fit for the demanding labour of railway work. 'They measured us up like we were soldiers,' he recalled. Those who did not measure up were left behind. Rogatus had been living in Iringa in 1971 when he responded to an announcement posted at the TANU office there. 'They took 800 people from Iringa in one day,' he remembers, 'in about five buses from Iringa town. They took us straight to camp at Mkela Base Camp, to work on the tunnels. After about three days they divided us up into work teams.'[25]

Workers were also recruited through the Tanzanian National Service or JKT (*Jeshi la Kujenga Taifa*). A group of 7,000 Tanzanian

23 TNA file C/1396/71 IS/1.317, 21 June 1971, 'TANZAM Workers Praised'.

24 See Deborah Bräutigam's work on rice projects in West Africa in *Chinese Aid and African Development* for a description of these aspects of China's development practice.

25 Interview with Rogatus Nyumayo, Mlimba, 26 July 2000.

youths were recruited from the National Service in 1970, given a two-week training programme including military drill, and then sent out to construction camps between Dar es Salaam and Mlimba.[26] Most of the recruits who responded to this national campaign were young men aged 16-25 (this was in contrast with the Chinese workers, who tended to be in their 30s and 40s), and few had much education beyond the primary level. The TAZARA project recruited these youths from the National Service, D.S.M. Momello remembers, because they were supposed to have 'discipline, dedication and energy'.[27]

Raymond Ndimbo describes being called up to work for TAZARA in July 1971 when he was newly graduated from school and working for the National Service, based at Handeni. He was taken with a group of his counterparts to work on bridge construction at Mdagaji near Mlimba, where they stayed for two months. He was worried initially about joining the TAZARA project, because he had heard rumours of the hard work and demanding conditions. 'I was losing heart,' he remembers, but in the end Raymond became committed to the project with the encouragement of his camp leader as well as his Chinese mentors.

The Chinese railway technicians who served in East Africa during TAZARA's construction, in contrast with their African counterparts, were older and more experienced railway workers who had been recruited from throughout China. Retired Chinese engineers who worked on the project recall that those who were asked to join the project included the most respected and highly qualified personnel from China's railway ministry.[28] Their ocean journey to East Africa from the southern seaport of Guangzhou took fifteen days. Over the five years of TAZARA's construction a total of some 30-40,000 Chinese railway workers would arrive at Dar es Salaam, staying only briefly at their coastal base camp before heading up country in truck

26 Sendaro, 'Workers' Efficiency', pp. 199-205; D.D.S.M. Momello, 'Final Report on Tunnels Construction, Mkela Base Camp', internal TAZARA document, 1972, p.13; *The Standard*, 19 February 1970.

27 Momello, 'Final Report'.

28 Interviews with Wang Hui Min and Li Jin Wen, Tianjin, 6 July 2007.

convoys.[29] Each work team would serve for a two-year period before returning to China; on their return journey they were reportedly allowed to travel by air.[30] Cargo loads of construction equipment including rails, cement and other goods were also unloaded onto the docks at Kurasini. As each new ship pulled into the harbour, crowds of curious onlookers gathered to greet them. The Chinese railway workers wore identical grey cotton suits and caps, and each carried a small blue suitcase balanced on his shoulder. As they disembarked from their ship, martial music blared from the ship's loudspeakers.[31]

The Chinese stated frequently during TAZARA's construction that they were committed to following development principles in Africa that were based on solidarity and friendship. In practice, Chinese railway technicians were expected to work shoulder to shoulder

---

29 It is extremely difficult to verify the actual numbers of Chinese railway workers that took part in the TAZARA project. TAZARA official archival reports are not yet open to the public in China or in Tanzania and Zambia, although some published accounts have cited closed archival records. Published estimates range from 15,000 to 50,000 for the number of overall Chinese workers; this discrepancy reflects some confusion over the actual period being considered, i.e. whether the pre-construction survey and design teams as well as the post-construction technical cooperation teams are counted. In a recent interview, retired Chinese railway expert Qin Hui stated that 50,000 Chinese workers went to East Africa during the four phases between 1965 and 1986 ('Qin Hui ... the person who dreams about the Tanzania-Zambia Railroad,' *People's Daily*, overseas edition, 25 January 2007), a figure also cited in Hu Zhichao, 'The Past, Present and Future of the Tanzania-Zambia Railroad,' *Economic Research of Railroads*, February 2000, pp. 46-7. At the peak of construction in 1972 there were 16,000 Chinese workers according to Jin Hui, while the TAZARA annual report for 1972-3 lists a high of 13,500 in July, 1972 declining to 11,500 in 1974. See also Zhang Tie San, *You Yi Zhi Lu: Huan Jian Tan Zan Tie Lu Ji Shi (The Road of Friendship: The Memoirs of the Development Assistance of the Tanzania-Zambia Railroad)* (Beijing: Zhongguo Tui Wai Jing Ji Mao Yi Chu Ban Shi, 1999) for more specific details and statistics.

30 Interview with Yang Weimin, Shanghai, July 14, 2007.

31 Interview with Lao Wan, Ifakara, July 2000; Interview with Du Jian, Dar es Salaam, April 2000; Hall and Peyman, *The Great Uhuru Railway*, p. 122; *Drum Magazine*, November 1973, from A. Smyth and A. Seftel (eds), *The Story of Julius Nyerere: Africa's Elder Statesman* (Dar es Salaam: Fountain Publishers, 1993), pp. 186-7; Larkin, *China and Africa*, p. 99; personal communication with Thomas Spear, who witnessed the unloading of Chinese ships at Kurasini harbour in the early 1970s.

with their African counterparts, demonstrating new skills and new forms of work discipline in a brotherly manner. This construction work experience was meant to be an uplifting one, both for the individual worker and for the nation, thus representing an alternative to colonial and neo-colonial African work experience.

For many of the workers on TAZARA, these ideals were fulfilled. The Chinese approach to work—especially the way they joined in on every task—did inspire the Tanzanian and Zambian workers. In response to a survey conducted in the mid-1980s, former TAZARA construction workers remembered that their Chinese supervisors had helped them the most by actually working together alongside them. 'It was a true friendship,' says John Gilbert of his relationship with Chinese technicians, 'even if you did not understand something, they explained it to you until you understood it.' Another worker stated, 'The Chinese [expert] taught us with honesty. He left you knowing that you had learned your job well.'[32]

For many, the experience of working closely with Chinese counterparts was a meaningful departure from the segregated work experiences they had during the recent colonial era. Hassan Mkanyago, a Tanzanian who was stationed at Mang'ula as camp foreman, remembers that 'this [railway construction] was a time of big changes. We could ride together in the back of a lorry, we could eat together, even have celebrations together.' He was moved by the possiblities for interracial interaction during TAZARA's construction, comparing them favourably with the behaviour of Europeans: 'I did not expect that I would find myself sitting at the same table as white person.'[33]

Over a five-year period, tens of thousands of Chinese and African workers lived together and toiled side by side along the railway line. As they camped in rudimentary shelters, dug ditches, constructed bridges and occasionally shared a meal together they had many occasions to interact. Friendship was an especially important theme in the isolated workplaces and temporary camps where the workers spent most of their time.

---

32 Interview with Rogatus Nyumayo, Mlimba, 26 July 2000.
33 Interview with Moses Hassan and Benedict Mkanyago, Mngeta, 7 July 2000.

Yet despite the ideology of brotherhood and the Chinese willingness to 'muck in' to tackle difficult tasks, life in the construction camps remained largely segregated. Here again, there were contradictions in the role played by the Chinese: at the same time that they were socialist brothers, they were also bosses. They were older than their African counterparts and far more technically experienced. And despite the best efforts of Chinese and Tanzanian leaders to cultivate an ideal of friendship, antipathy occasionally slipped through. While the workers in camp were officially known as friends, their experiences on the ground were often like that of strangers.

In these dispersed mobile work camps accommodation could be quite rustic. Once a new campsite had been cleared and graded, shelters or *bandas* and canvas tents in some cases were erected across the compound. Accommodation was constructed on one side of the camp for the Chinese, and on the other for the Tanzanians. *Bandas* were built using locally available materials; pole frames were used as supports for mud walls topped with roves woven from grasses or palm fronds. These simple dwellings offered little protection from wild animals or malaria-carrying mosquitoes; ants, termites and snakes were among the unwelcome visitors.[34] The workers also constructed canteens, latrines, bathing facilities and a medical dispensary at each camp. At the larger camps electric wires were hung overhead that allowed work activity to continue through the night.[35] In the early stages of construction there were housing shortages at some sites. At Signali, for example, the main camp accommodated only 86 of the 681 workers when construction began. Several Tanzanian workers roomed in the homes of nearby villagers.[36] This was not an option for the Chinese workers, whose relations with villagers were carefully restricted.

---

34 Interview with Hashim Mdemu, Ifakara, 2000; Interview with Jin Hui, Beijing, 5 July 2007. In my interview with Du Jian, who was an interpreter during construction, he said that some African workers brought mosquito nets with them to the camps. Interview with Du Jian, Chinese Railway Expert Team, Dar es Salaam, July 2000.

35 Interview with Du Jian, Dar es Salaam, July 2000.

36 Sendaro, 'Workers' Efficiency', p. 243.

Life in camp mirrored the segregation of the compound housing. When they were not working, the Chinese enjoyed leisure activities such as reading, smoking cigarettes, playing board games and table tennis. They also played active outdoor sports, especially volleyball. These games were occasionally shared with Tanzanian workers, but for the most part the Chinese kept to themselves. When they went walking outside the camp boundaries they always went together in a group, avoiding contact with local people. Chinese supervisors were very strict about the behaviour of their workers, even off duty. A worker who did something out of line could be sent back to Dar es Salaam, and from there to China.[37]

The African workers, in contrast, mingled more freely with the local people. In the evenings at Mang'ula workers would go out to the neighboring settlements to relax and drink home-brewed beer (alcohol was not allowed at the work camps).[38] In Mchombe village, women remember that workers from the railway often visited the beer clubs where they sold local brew. Railway workers would come after their shifts to relax and drink, and to make contact with local women. Several women remember that the workers 'found wives' at Mchombe, and some of these partnerships are still intact.[39] Life for African workers thus differed from the lives of the Chinese workers in important ways. The two groups lived in similar conditions and worked side by side. In their off-duty lives, however, there was distance between them.

Liberation through modernity

The reputation of the Chinese for demanding hard work from the railway construction teams spread widely throughout East Africa. News of the challenges of working on TAZARA had already reached

---

37 Interview with John Gilbert, Hosea Mngata and Raphael Chawala, 20 April 2000. Sunil Sahu wrote that Chinese workers engaged on the railroad construction were instructed to stay clear of politics and propaganda. Supposedly Chairman Mao assured Nyerere that 'any hint of subversion reported to him would be immediately dealt with.' Sunil Kumar Sahu, 'Sino-Tanzanian Relations', *United Asia*, 23, 2 (1971), pp. 78-80.

38 Interview with Salum Mwasenga, Mang'ula, 30 July 2000.

39 Group interview with women at Mchombe, 16 July 2000.

the ears of Raymond Ndimbo before he learned that he and other members of the national service would be sent to work on the railway. He ended up working on the tunnels section, based at Mpanga, and then stayed on to become a specialist in communications. Ndimbo credits his work experience on TAZARA's construction for the progress he has made in his life. His ability to speak Chinese was an enormous asset for him, he says, one that he feels was central to his personal progress and the well-being of his family. 'When learning a language,' he stated, 'the most important thing is to have the right intentions.' Ndimbo felt he had to know Chinese well so that he could help the Chinese experts. Yet in the end, it was their language that helped him—knowing Chinese allowed him to obtain and hold a good job, to build a house, and to educate his children. One of his sons now lives in England.

For the young men who participated in TAZARA's construction, building the railway was an experience of modernity. Most of them were from rural areas and had limited experience with technology beyond what they may have learned in primary school. For many of these young men it was their first time to be employed for a wage and to follow a structured and regimented work schedule. Workers themselves describe their experiences during construction as a process of maturation, as a coming of age. They remember joining the work-force as very young men, unmarried, many having served briefly in the National Service (most of the African workers were between the ages of 16 and 25). They recall that the experience of construction was demanding and difficult for them. At the same time, they developed skills and in many cases developed a viable trade that gave them a new position in society. The experience of building the railway, wrote D.E. Stambuli after TAZARA's completion, had lifted workers and their families out of their deteriorated condition into 'a modern civilized type of life'.[40]

Hosea Mngata described his construction experience this way: 'I was still a very young man when I started working, I had just finished school. I had a very young age [he was 26], and then I had a great de-

---

40 D.E. Stambuli, 'Staff Commentary', Appendix IX in 'Final Report on Tunnels Construction, Mkela Base Camp', D.D.S.M. Momello, 1972.

sire for work, and my Chinese brothers liked me very much.' Mngata began working first at Mang'ula, breaking up stones at the quarry in the forest. After 1973, when the Tanzanian workforce was reduced, he was one of the fortunate workers to be kept on. 'We kept working with the Chinese for a long time,' he remembered, 'almost three years, and then the Chinese left us on our own. Indeed, until today we are caring for the railway, we had grown experienced ourselves by that time.' Mngata's memory conveys the coming of age not only of himself, as he learned skills and eventually assumed responsibility after the Chinese departure, but also of the larger Tanzanian workforce.

The theme of modernity as a liberating process was common in interviews with TAZARA workers who continued to work for the railway after the Chinese departure. It is possible that workers who left the project after a year or two felt differently about the transformative possibilities of building the railway. Still, those who worked on the project were given certificates upon its completion that verified their training and work experience, and they were viewed nationally (even, perhaps, internationally) as a unique group of trained labourers. News accounts had praised the successes of 'our youth' who were building the railway. Public officials lauded the project for helping to create a cohort of young people who had learned skills and practiced discipline, and who were now ready to undertake the challenges of building the nation.

Conclusion

The TAZARA railway was called the 'Great Freedom Railway' because it was intended to liberate the economies of east-central Africa from their reliance upon transport routes through the countries under white settler regimes to the south. After the Unilateral Declaration of Independence in Southern Rhodesia in 1965, the need for such a transport alternative appeared urgent. The decision of the Chinese government to finance and supervise the construction of the Freedom Railway was in large part a response to this post-independence and Cold War political context. At the same time, China was implementing principles of development assistance in Africa that made claims to promote another kind of 'freedom', a freedom from the neo-colonial and neo-imperialist hegemony practiced by the United States and the Soviet Union. The eight principles of China's development assistance for Africa were applied to financing (in the form of long-term interest-free loans) and also to the practice of development, including relationships between Chinese and African counterparts. To the degree that they shaped the Afro-Asian experience of development during the construction of the TAZARA railway, these principles can be seen as embodying anti-hegemonic development assistance through practice.

The approach to TAZARA's construction was intended to be liberating for the African worker and for other African populations in multiple ways. The most important theme was that of working side by side in transnational, pan-African and cross-racial friendship and solidarity. In this and other ways, the TAZARA project would lift up the African youth who were recruited to join the project to new levels of skill and self-confidence, thereby bringing them and their nations into a form of modernity. This would provide a powerful contrast with their experience of the recently ended colonial period, thus resulting in a new form of liberation rather than a second colonization by neo-imperial hegemonic interests.

In practice, there were multiple contradictions within the construction work experience. The transnational, cross-racial solidarity promoted in official statements was compromised by the actual segregation of everyday life in the work teams and camps. There were struggles over the definition of work tasks and the work day, and many workers ended up leaving the project because of labour demands that must have been reminiscent of the colonial work models that the project intended to supplant. Even the vision of pan-African solidarity that had shaped the project from the beginning was only implemented in limited ways, for Tanzanian workers dominated on the eastern side of the border until 1973, when the project crossed over into Zambia and Zambian workers were hired to replace them.

The workers who participated in the construction of the TAZARA project recall their work experience as a coming of age. They were recruited as young men, just out of school or recently recruited to the National Service, and were taken into remote regions where work was hard and conditions were rustic. Some gained technical skills and learned to speak Chinese, while others engaged in more manual forms of labour. All received a certificate at the end of their work experience that documented the work they had done and the special training they had received. For most it was an initial experience with earning a wage for their labour, for a defined work day.

Working on the TAZARA project was experienced as a form of modernity for the Tanzanian workers, an entry into 'a modern, civilized kind of life', in the words of Stambuli, especially for those select few who were promoted to positions in engineering, management and communications. This cohort of workers, the *vijana* or youth, were celebrated in the press as construction proceeded across the southern interior's challenging landscapes. And the 'construction generation' of TAZARA's workers continues to be highly respected in Tanzania until today; despite a contested layoff in 1982 of 116 workers, their positions have been among the most stable and remunerative in post-colonial Tanzania. TAZARA's workers credit their participation in this post-colonial, Cold War project with helping them to build their lives. In this way, the construction of the Freedom Railway can be seen as bringing a form of liberation for labour.

11

MEDICINE AS BUSINESS: CHINESE MEDICINE IN TANZANIA

Elisabeth Hsu

To the annoyance of any anthropologist embarking on fieldwork, Chinese medicine in Tanzania was a media item when I started my research in 2001. The first Chinese medical clinic in Dar es Salaam had been set up in 1996, in Upanga, catering to the upper middle classes. In the following six years, clinics mushroomed to between 20-40 in Tanzania, with over 15 estimated to be in Dar alone, and others in Arusha, Moshi, Mbeya, Iringa, Dodoma, Mwanza, and even the remote Shinyanga. However, many clinics were short-lived and numbers declined in the following years, during which I conducted fieldwork in eight one-month periods at least once a year.

This does not mean that Chinese medicine in Tanzania has a history of only ten years. There are at least five different fields of medical care in which proponents of Chinese medicine have been involved since Tanzania's independence in 1961. I will first sketch out the first four, and, after an interlude outlining research methodology, discuss the private sector. As will become evident, the entrepreneurial set up of Chinese medical clinics has the potential to contribute in meaningful ways to primary care in Tanzania, not least because the Chinese medical doctors, in skilful ways and on multiple levels, have combined Chinese and Western medical services. However, the Tanzanian government must ensure that well-educated Chinese medical doctors set up business.

Five fields of Chinese medical care in Tanzania

Julius Nyerere, Tanzania's first president (1962-85), who was socialist in orientation, cultivated contacts with the People's Republic of China from the very start. Collaboration extended to the medical field. At one stage, the PRC despatched Chinese medical expert teams in Tanzania on a bi-annual basis, sending over two hundred biomedical doctors to government hospitals in the country's major cities. These were generally mid-career doctors, respected both for their professional expertise and for personal reliability, and chosen by their superiors; they were on two-year contracts, which they spent continuously away from spouse and child. As became evident during fieldwork in Dar es Salaam, apparently each of China's 22 provinces was 'in charge' of an African nation: Yunnan for Uganda, Shandong for Tanzania, and Jiangsu for the semi-independent Zanzibar (none for Kenya). However, by 2001, these teams had shrunk to the insignificant number of only about four (each with around ten doctors) in Tanzania. One worked in Muhimbili hospital's first-rate institutes such as the Institute for Orthopaedic Surgery, built with the aid of the Swiss, or the Institute of Microbiology, which housed a Swedish research programme on HIV/AIDS. Another worked in the city of Tabora, and two in more modest conditions on Zanzibar.[1] Most of these teams also included an acupuncturist, since Chinese medicine—and acupuncture in particular—belonged in the package

---

1 The two medical teams I visited in December 2003 included two inner medicine specialists (one in cardiovascular diseases, one in endocrinology), one anaesthetist, one radiologist, one stomatologist, one oto-rhino-laryngologist, one urinary surgeon, one gynaecologist, one head nurse, and one acupuncturist stationed at Mnasi Mmoja on Unguja. At the Abdulla Mzee Hospital on Pemba, there was an inner medicine generalist, an anaesthetist, a radiologist, an oto-rhino-laryngologist, a surgeon, a gynaecologist and an obstetrician. These medical specialists were in both places accompanied by an interpreter and a cook. They were mostly men, while each group included two women. E. Hsu, 'Zanzibar and its Chinese Communities', *Population, Space and Place* 13, 2 (2007), pp. 113-24.

of world socialism that China then exported.[2] However, by 2001 the 'acupuncturist' in Muhimbili was not a professional, being a trained biomedical clinician. He offered a greatly underutilized service and was already off duty at eight in the morning after seeing less than a handful of patients. Evidently, the socialist fervour with which acupuncture once used to be promoted had cooled down.

The Chinese doctors who lived on most vividly in the memory of the Tanzanians I spoke to were the general practitioners who had worked on the Tazara project.[3] Strictly speaking, this second group of Chinese health professionals comprised only practitioners of Western medicine, as peoples' memories in fieldwork suggested. They were fewer in number, probably not as expert in their speciality (they were employees of the Ministry of Railways and not the Ministry of Health), and they worked in Tanzania, in one or two year spells, during the construction of the railway from Dar es Salaam to Zambia between 1968 and 1975. Their main objective was to guarantee the health of the Chinese railway workers but they did not shy away from treating the locals. The encounter appears to have been mutually edifying as the Chinese doctors have also maintained vivid memories of the Tanzanians.

A third and less well-known Chinese medical impact on African health care is of a different order. It was not mediated through Chinese physicians who were sent abroad, but through the World Health Organization (WHO). The way socialist China dealt with its indigenous *materia medica* became a model for the WHO and appears to have been implemented by its traditional medicine programmes.[4] African medicinal plants have accordingly been recorded and researched according to the criteria of the Chinese *materia med-*

---

2 Alan Hutchinson, *China's African Revolution* (London: Hutchinson, 1975), p. 222; quoted by M. Zhan, 'The Worlding of Traditional Chinese Medicine: a Translocal Study of Knowledge, Identity and Cultural Politics in China and the United States', PhD thesis in Social and Cultural Anthropology, Stanford University (2002), p. 45. The teams had Western medical staff, including one acupuncturist; none consisted only of Chinese medical professionals.

3 Fieldwork in Mbeya, July 2003.

4 Ethnobotanical fieldtrip to Ghana, June 2000.

ica, sometimes under the guidance of Chinese experts personally.[5] Ethno-medically speaking, Tanzania has extremely rich tropical flora and fauna, and many plants have been shown to contain substances that are pharmacologically active and continue to be used by locals against minor ailments, mental problems and what we (more than the locals) consider serious diseases such as malaria. The Traditional Medicine Research Unit at Muhimbili Hospital was inaugurated in 1974 after early efforts from the late 1960s to endorse a policy of collecting plant materials among Regional Medical Officers, on the initiative of the Chinese, had failed.[6] By 1991, apparently, this Unit had identified over 4,000 healers and tested 3,000 herbs.[7] By 2001, the Unit had become an Institute and comprised a good dozen senior researchers including chemists, pharmacognocists, botanists, and even one medical anthropologist.[8] A psychiatrist from the London School of Tropical Medicine and Hygiene, who worked as an adviser to the Tanzanian Ministry of Health, was open-minded enough, during an informal encounter at an Oxford college, to credit traditional medicine with effectiveness in the realm of mental health;[9] and there is a general idea among anthropologists that traditional healers in Africa

---

5   In general, they are first identified by their indigenous names and by the Latin names indicating their Linnaean genus and species, which makes a reliable identification of synonyms possible. Then, their indigenous attributes are listed, including, for instance, information on their taste, such as whether they were bitter or sweet, or on their effects, whether they were cooling or heating. There then follows a list of their most common therapeutic usages, which indiscriminately draws on learned and popular indigenous and biomedical terms for any kind of ailment, symptom or disease. In some cases, a considerable effort has been made to identify the active substances in the plant, and isolate and purify them. Although traditional Western pharmacopoeias have much the same structure, it appears the WHO endorsed the Chinese model.

6   J. Iliffe, *East African Doctors* (Cambridge University Press, 1998), p. 211.

7   Ibid. As always when scientists work with locals, there were communication problems. I happened to encounter a healer who had initially collaborated with 'those from Muhimbili', as he called them, but since no results had been obtained or reported back, he felt cheated (fieldwork in Dar, March 2001).

8   On the Unit and its history, see also S. Langwick, *The Matter of Maladies: Ontologicial Politics in Postcolonial Healing in Tanzania* (forthcoming), chapter 3.

9   Personal communication, 2002.

have admirable psychological powers and are good at 'healing' their patients by framing and re-interpreting their problems. The Tanzanian intellectuals I encountered, however, valued their traditional medicines primarily for their pharmaceutical potential. This attitude is occasionally found among the odd plant scientist, but above all it reflects that of the Chinese socialist government towards traditional medicine during the Maoist period (1949-76). Perhaps the close collaboration with China reinforced its prominence in Tanzania.

If the Chinese schema of how to systematize, write and publish the indigenous *materia medica* came via the WHO to African nation-states, and in Tanzania through Chinese delegates directly, the fourth Chinese medical field is very peculiar to Tanzania. During the period of socialist orientation, not only were Chinese experts sent to Tanzania, but Tanzanian medical students also went for training to the PRC (though, notably, none were sent to learn Traditional Chinese Medicine). During the six years of their medical training (one year of learning the Chinese language and five years of medical training), they were obliged for at least one semester to attend a course on acupuncture because of the communist system of medical education based on the Maoist vision of combining Western and Chinese medicine.[10] In contrast to all other countries in the world, students enrolled in medical school were thus forced to attend courses on traditional medical knowledge, not only in the 1950s but also in the 1980s, and since every Western medical hospital must, by governmental regulation, include a traditional medicine section, these African students could not avoid also being exposed to herbal Traditional Chinese Medicine, bone setting and massage; and, on the streets, to the meditative practices of *qigong* and *taijiquan*. Some of them came back to Tanzania transformed, with an entirely different attitude to traditional medicine: it need not be backward and superstitious. In fact, I found in interviews with Chinese medicine patients in Dar that some said Chinese medicine was more 'advanced'

10 K.Taylor, *Medicine of Revolution: Chinese Medicine in Early Communist China* (London: Routledge, 2005).

CHINA RETURNS TO AFRICA

than biomedicine, an attitude which perhaps reflected the underlying sentiment that socialism is more advanced than capitalism.[11]

It may be that such an anti-imperialist attitude, combined with a certain pragmatism and belief in Chinese medicine, ignited the collaboration of the Chinese and Tanzanian Ministries of Health and in 1989 led to the institutionalizing of a long-term Traditional Chinese Medicine research programme on HIV/AIDS at Muhimbili hospital. I sporadically worked in that clinic between 2001 and 2003. A group of about thirty regular patients were seen every other day between 8 and 11 am. One Tanzanian doctor was in charge, seated behind a large table on which there were piles of patients' files, and two young Traditional Chinese Medicine post-doctoral fellows sat on either side of the table. She acted as translator and director (having studied medicine in the PRC, she was fluent in Chinese), assisted by two Tanzanian nurses. The files were all in Chinese. Note taking was basically conscientious, but varied in style, every page had handwriting of a different docotor. It appears that by 2001 the project had lost in kudos. I was not allowed to take handwritten copies of the patients' files, not because of a lack of 'informed consent' but because this was confidential 'research data'.[12] No results had yet been published in English. An earlier public statement of researchers on the programme had apparently upset the biomedical profession because any claim that a herbal remedy could change a sero-positive patient into a sero-negative one was flatly 'impossible' and therefore 'immoral' because it engendered false hopes. In the early years, renowned senior Chinese doctors had been on the project, whose understanding of Chinese medicine certainly was deeper than that of the post-docs but who, in the light of their striking findings, seem to have underestimated the sanctions they would encounter by not

11 E. Hsu, '"The medicine from China has rapid effects": Patients of Traditional Chinese Medicine in Tanzania', in E. Hsu and E. Høg (eds), *Countervailing Creativity: Patient Agency in the Globalisation of Asian Medicines, Anthropology and Medicine* 9, 3 (2002), pp. 291-314.

12 However, I did obtain permission for copying four file-based authentic prescriptions and correlating herbs that had been used for treating an AIDS patient during one month. They are now on display in the permanent exhibition 'Living and Dying' at the British Museum in London.

226

paying due tribute to statistical evidence. Suspended in its research activities, the programme nevertheless has had an impact on a practical level as on its basis the antiviral drug *Aikeji* was developed with Chinese medical ingredients only. It is now sold at a very high price in the private sector.[13]

This brings us to the fifth field of Chinese medical doctors' activities in Tanzania, which since 1996 has taken place in the private sector. Restrictions on private practice had been removed in the early 1990s,[14] after the World Bank had put pressure on the government to privatize health care.[15] The Chinese medical doctors who have migrated to Tanzania because of these altered health care policies differ in important ways from the ones mentioned above. First, they are private entrepreneurs. Second, their training in Chinese medicine varies: some are highly qualified but in the early 2000s the majority were 'learning by doing'. Third, some operated within grey zones of legality, in fields marked by rigid bureaucratic structures and 'red tapism', and this impacted on the ways in which they offered their services. The response I received after asking why they had come to Tanzania to do medicine was: 'For doing business'. I was surprised. It is no secret that medicine is business, and sometimes big business, but medical doctors are expected to emphasize the provision of services. The response reflected Deng Xiaoping's principle that it is to the advantage of the nation to do business. Ironically, Tanzania that is one of the lowest income countries was considered one of the best places worldwide for 'making money'.

Fieldwork

Here a note on methodology is warranted. Fieldwork was multi-sited and in only two cases was I allowed to live with the people I studied: with a doctor and his nuclear family in Mombasa and with a Tanzanian nurse and his extended family on Pemba. This is, methodologically, a weak point of my study, but at least I lived with families on both

---

13 Fieldwork in Mombasa, 2004-5.

14 Iliffe, *East African Doctors*, p. 218.

15 A foreign health worker, personal communication during fieldwork in Dar, March 2001.

the Chinese and Tanzanian sides. Language-wise, Chinese posed no problems as I had formally learned it over twenty years earlier, but I was an absolute beginner in Swahili. If the rapport was good with the doctor, tape recording posed no problems; each patient was given the choice to turn it off but only a few requested this.

I interviewed almost every doctor in Tanzania and Kenya of whose existence I knew, and thus can claim to have personally spoken to the majority of the Chinese doctors who were practising between 2001 and 2004. The first encounter with doctors was almost always difficult. They were migrants, sometimes had a considerable history of mobility, and were suspicious of my status and objectives. Many were from North-Eastern China; a number had been jacks of several trades. It is difficult to make generalizations, as these doctors each stand out for their individualism and their capacity for taking the initiative. One said he wished me to report in my publications that their lives had been difficult first in China and then in Tanzania. Thereafter he reminded me that my research permit was for studying 'Chinese medicine and other traditional medicines in Tanzania', and refused to speak to me any further on issues other than what he considered strictly medical ones.

In the interviews with patients I was not met with the same suspicion. Whenever possible I went to visit them in their homes, which in view of the size of the city, the condition of the roads (or rather, perhaps, 'tracks') and the non-existence of addresses was an adventure in itself. However probably due to this extra hardship—a very time-consuming one too, considering that it was for a brief 30-60 minutes interview only—almost all of them felt honoured, were welcoming and also forthcoming.[16] I interviewed 30 patients in Dar es Salaam twice (in January and July 2002), 30 in Mombasa twice (in July 2003 and January 2004) and 30 on Pemba (in December 2003). Not only did the doctors stand out for their individualism and initiative, but also their patients: apart from those on Pemba, they came from very different city wards. They had in common that they identified themselves as members of the 'middle class', but their

---

16 I had to explain to most that I was not an employee of the Chinese medical doctors, but nevertheless the answers may have been biased.

living conditions varied from what an outsider would call a 'slum dwelling' to a 'little palace'. Almost all were very positive about the services they had received, and praised the Chinese doctors for their regularity and reliability (most worked six or seven days a week, and eight or more hours a day). In some cases, they went out of their way to praise the effectiveness of Chinese medicines, although there were some who were not satisfied; the costs and relative ineffectiveness of the treatment were issues. On Pemba, one of the two tropical islands that constitute the semi-state of Zanzibar, the patient population I interviewed was different. The Pemba clinic had opened only a few months earlier; it was the first and only one, and owing to quarrels with his superior, the doctor in charge had to close it again a few months later. There, the patients were mostly rural, and my sample was strongly affected by a brief (three sessions-long) successful acupuncture treatment which enabled an incapacitated woman to walk again, and resulted in many villagers migrating to the Chinese clinic with arthritis problems.

Finally, I also interviewed translators, laboratory technicians, receptionists and shop attendants, who were either in collaboration with or were employed by the Chinese doctor. They all worked towards the business success of Chinese medical clinics. We were already so familiar with each other at that time that it was strange to sit apart for half an hour or so and conduct a formal interview, but from the translators, particularly, there emerged unexpectedly moving life stories of capable people. Several had enrolled in higher education in the PRC and later dropped out of the system in Tanzania because of health reasons, personal problems with their superiors, or stifling bureaucratic structures. In the odd case, they had learned Chinese in an attempt to become a Buddhist monk. Apparently, Taiwanese monks ran a preparatory course in South Africa which offered education and boarding free of charge for two years before selected candidates were sent to a monastery in Taiwan. One had even spent time in Taiwan, though only for a few months; his mother could not bear the separation, so he said.[17]

17 Fieldwork in Moshi, April 2002.

Legal regulation of T/CAM health provision

Having written about the Chinese doctors and their patients, the spatial layout of their clinics, their life stories, their relations with other Chinese, and their medicines,[18] I will focus here on their entrepreneurial set up after examining the legal regulation of Tanzanian traditional and complementary and alternative medicine health provision (T/CAM).

In contrast to the traditional practitioners of Indian descent, who quietly practised their medicine in the same neighbourhoods as the Chinese and were known by word of mouth only to their not exclusively Indian clientele, the Chinese advertised themselves loudly, often with big white script on red ground, drawn onto placards and walls. Various Indian healers had suffered from earlier hostility[19]—for example, several on the coast north of Dar es Salaam had fled from Zanzibar in the early 1960s—and this may explain their silence. Apparently, the immigrant Chinese had flooded the Ministry of Health and Ministry of Commerce with applications for opening their businesses as either 'clinics' or 'drug stores', which in effect were much the same. The executives in charge evidently had issued licences, *bona fide*, each for two years maximum with the option of renewal. After 2001, however, almost no licenses were reissued to Chinese medical doctors, and several were forced to return to China, among them even families who had hoped to stay in Tanzania on a long-term

---

18 Hsu, "'The medicine from China has rapid effects"; E. Hsu, 'Time inscribed in Space, and the Process of Diagnosis in African and Chinese Medical Practices' in W. James and D. Mills (eds), *The Qualities of Time: Anthropological Approaches* (Oxford: Berg, 2005), pp. 155-70; E. Hsu, 'Mobility and Connectedness: Chinese Medical Doctors in Kenya', in H. Dilger *et al.*, *Transnational Medicine, Mobile Experts: Globalization, Health and Power in and beyond Africa* (Bloomington: Indiana University Press, forthcoming); E. Hsu, 'Zanzibar and its Chinese Communities'; E. Hsu, 'Wonders of the Exotic: Chinese Formula Medicines on the East African Coast', in K. Larsen (ed.), *Knowledge, Renewal and Religion: Repositioning and Changing Ideological and Material Circumstances among the Swahili on the East African Coast* (Uppsala: Nordic Africa Institute, forthcoming).

19 D. Parkin, 'In the Nature of the Human Landscape: Provenances in the Making of Zanzibari Politics', in J. Clammer, S. Poirier, and E. Schwimmer (eds), *Figured Worlds: Ontological Obstacles in Intercultural Relations* (University of Toronto Press, 2004), pp. 113-31.

basis. A bill from the Ministry of Health was being prepared which differentiated between 'traditional medicine' (taken to include Arab and other local herbalists, *ngoma* and other local spiritual healers) and 'complementary and alternative medicine' (CAM), including reflexology, European phytotherapy, homeopathy, and also Chinese medicine. Perhaps it was the sudden influx of Chinese medical practitioners into Tanzania that triggered efforts in the highest echelons of government to regulate the non-biomedical health market in Tanzania? Whether and how the governmental regulation will be implemented remains to be seen. Not every Chinese medical doctor had to leave Tanzania in the last five years, and each of those who have stayed (and some had children in this time) had their own individual channel to secure further temporary licenses.

The new bill for regulating traditional and complementary and alternative medicines contains a paragraph that requests that traditional and biomedical drugs and practices be strictly separated.[20] It thereby directly targets the practice of 'integrated Chinese and Western medicine' (*zhongxiyi jiehe*), which provides the conceptual basis for 'Chinese formula medicines' (*zhongchengyao*) of the globalized form of 'Chinese medicine and pharmaceuticals' (*zhongyiyao*) that are currently on the global health market. However, perhaps it is precisely the combination of traditional and scientific/biomedical knowledge and practice that makes the Chinese medicine clinics competitive in the health market which, with the demise of the primary health care through central governmental structures by the WHO in the 1990s, has been commercialized on a global scale.

As argued earlier, the ambiguity of the term by which Chinese medicine is known, *dawa ya Kichina*, is an asset for attracting clientele. First, it designates 'Western medicine as practised by the Chinese', for instance, by the government-sent foreign experts. Thus, paradoxically, the entrepreneurial, often poorly trained Chinese medical doctors live off the good reputation that was created by highly qualified biomedical doctors during Tanzania's socialist orientation. Second, it can be understood to refer 'Chinese drugs', i.e. Chinese medical drugs or Western medical drugs produced in China (their packaging

20 Fieldwork in Dar, July 2004.

is the same: they come as capsules, tablets, pills, powders, creams, etc. in carton boxes, plastic containers, aluminium foil, covered mostly if not exclusively in Chinese script). Third, it can be understood to refer to 'drugs' that come from China rather than medical practice with an entirely different medical rationale, and thereby *dawa ya Kichina* fits into an existent local treatment strategy in East Africa.

Whyte has suggested that there are two strategies for solving medical problems in East Africa: either one can, symptomatically and furtively, try to solve it by consulting a herbalist, [21] who has 'medicines' (*dawa*) but often does not speak the local language,[22] and whose medicines are the more potent the further away they come from; or, if the problem does not subside, one resorts to involving the elders, and searches for underlying causes which may be found in an offence of the ancestors or an unpaid bride price, or something similar, and tend to involve extended village meetings with the elders and much publicity. In urban areas, people mostly take recourse to the former strategy and hence also to *dawa ya Kichina*.

Medicine as business in the private sector

The entrepreneurial set-up of the private Chinese medical clinics allows not only discretion but also a 'quick fix'. The clinics typically are located in areas of buzzing petty enterprise, even in the midst of a bazaar or at bus stations. Only rarely are they located in residential areas. I became particularly aware of this as I listened to my tape recordings, the loud motors of cars and lorries, bells of bicycles, shouting and advertising of goods, even arguments on the street. One could step into a Chinese clinic almost by accident, although often access to it was up a staircase (being located in the first floor was considered a safeguard against crime). One encounters first a receptionist, often a stylish young Tanzanian woman, who is in charge of registration but does not request any consultation fee (as govern-

---

21 S.R. Whyte, 'The Power of Medicines in East Africa', in S. van der Geest and S.R. Whyte (eds), *The Context of Medicines in Developing Countries* (Dordrecht: Kluwer Academic Publishers, 1988), pp. 217-33.

22 O.B. Rekdal, 'Cross-Cultural Healing in East African Ethnography', *Medical Anthropology Quarterly* 13, 4 (1999), pp. 458-82.

ment clinics do). One is seen by the doctor after less than 10-20 minutes in the waiting room (as opposed to waiting for hours). In the busiest clinics, the doctor's consultation room was often small and stuffy (and had the feel of a divination hut) and the door was shut during a consultation (privacy was assured). If a lab test is needed, the Chinese medical clinic can provide it (no need to go to another establishment). Chinese medical doctors rent out one room in their clinics to local lab technicians, who bring their own equipment and can provide the results of a test in less than half an hour. Tests on offer are for malaria parasites, stools, urine (routine, sugar, albumin), syphilis (VDRL test), typhoid (WIDAL), pregnancy, full blood pictures, haemoglobin, diabetes, and the like. Thereafter one returns to the Chinese doctor, who evidently is also competent in Western medicine, and he looks at the lab results and writes out a prescription. The shop attendant outside the consultation room, usually another agreeable woman (or the same person as the receptionist), prepares the package of medicines, wraps it up in a bag, cashes the money, and provides, if necessary, explanations in Swahili. Chinese medical clinics evidently have integrated traditional local and modern urban Tanzanian elements into their offering of combined biomedical and traditional Chinese medical services.

In contrast to the socialist government-sent medical teams that included an acupuncturist, the private Chinese medical entrepreneurs almost exclusively rely on 'Chinese formula medicines' (*zhongchengyao*). These are easy to consume, in contrast to the medicine that adherents of so-called 'classical' Chinese medicine (as common in Europe and North America) advocate, namely the Chinese 'herbs' as traditionally prepared, simmered, and decocted, in laborious daily routines. 'Chinese formula medicines' provide traditional ingredients in modern form and packaging. Needless to say the quality of these drugs varies. Just as there are brands of biomedical drugs, so there are of Chinese drugs and, in particular, formula-medicines. Furthermore, the rationale underlying the manufacture of these drugs varies. The contents of some consist of standardized ingredients of a 'classical' Chinese medical decoction, others are based on secret recipes and folk-medical knowledge, yet others contain Western medical additives, such as vitamins or steroids. In the tropics, some

233

doctors told me, it was impossible to treat patients in the valuable, precious (*zhengui*) way. Here the precious Chinese drugs (*zhongyao*) went mouldy and rotted too quickly. Therefore, doctors had to make use of formula-drugs (*zhongchengyao*).

Formula-drugs are handy for the patient but they make it difficult to treat people in a sophisticated way according to the Chinese medical rationale. They are designed to treat specific 'disorders'—a cough, a headache—and not the particular person's imbalances. Some formula-drugs are composed of standardized ancient Chinese prescriptions (*fangji*), which require the doctor to differentiate between, say, a *yin* depletion headache or a *yang* exuberance headache, and some doctors I spoke to emphasized that formula-drugs could be used in sophisticated ways. However, in general, treatment with Chinese formula drugs requires significantly less skills and knowledge on the part of the practitioner than treatment with Chinese drugs and recipes, and pulse diagnosis is so rarely practised that most people in East Africa do not know that Chinese medical doctors are supposed to rely primarily on it.

Conclusion

The entrepreneurial practitioners currently constitute by far the largest and most diverse group of Chinese medical practitioners in Tanzania. The finding that Chinese individuals on their own initiative set up clinics in Dar, other parts of Tanzania and Africa at large is part of a larger pattern. As seen above, many Chinese doctors come to do business—construction, textiles, the food industry. The North-East is the region in China that was the first to be intensively industrialized, not least during the Japanese occupation before the Second World War, and here the economic reforms have had the most visible impact on existing state-run 'work units' (*danwei*). With the restructuring of these units, many employees became redundant. They diversified in the private sector, some migrated to other parts of China, others to other parts of the world. In the early 1990s, I was told, enterprising individuals emigrated to Russia, in the late 1990s to Africa. By the late 1990s, the barriers posed by bureaucratic paperwork had been reduced to such an extent in the PRC that some felt the government encouraged them to go abroad. And do business. Since all sell Chinese goods, and on various levels ensure a flow of cash back into China (e.g. remittances, paying off daughter-mother company debts, taxes), the business Chinese medical doctors are doing in Tanzania ultimately is profitable also to the Chinese state.

12

SOLIDARITY, XENOPHOBIA AND THE REGULATION OF CHINESE BUSINESSES IN NAMIBIA

Gregor Dobler

Chinese investors and traders (as well as African governments) are facing growing resentment against China's new role in Africa. The most visible expression of anti-Chinese sentiments to date has been the debate on foreign traders in the run-up to the Zambian election of September 2006. However, Zambia is not the only African country where public opinion is slowly turning against China and Chinese. Xenophobia mingles with fears of a new imperialism and creates strong anti-Chinese resentment, while many governments keep up their China-friendly policies. This chapter examines the situation in Namibia. After an overview of the changing feelings towards Chinese involvement on a national level, it presents a case study on Oshikango, a trade boom town on the border with Angola, that shows how the growing opposition to the Chinese presence has shifted power relations within the Chinese migrant community, favouring earlier migrants who can profit from their better political connections. The last section addresses local practices involved in the regulation of Chinese shops, arguing that personal relations with customs officers and an alliance of interest between a modernist local elite and Chinese investors will emerge as crucial factors for the successes and failures of regulation.

Anti-Chinese resentment in Namibia

Cooperation between China and the ruling party in Namibia has a long history. China was an ally of the liberation movement SWAPO from the 1960s. The Chinese government invited its exiled leader Sam Nujoma to Beijing in 1964 as part of Mao's efforts to break China's international isolation. Nujoma came back with two thousand British pounds for exile work and a high esteem for his Chinese hosts.[1] During the liberation struggle, China supported SWAPO in both the armed and the diplomatic struggle, and in March 1990 was one of the first countries to establish diplomatic relations with the newly independent state.[2] After independence, friendship with China seemed a good way of counterbalancing Western neo-colonialism through South-South solidarity. Chinese investors were warmly welcomed by the Namibian government.

China has skilfully used a policy aimed at symbolically representing China as Africa's natural ally against Western imperialism. During his last visit to Beijing, Sam Nujoma was presented with a Chinese translation of his autobiography *Where Others Wavered*. This gesture was both highly personal, apt to win the sympathy of the most important politician in Namibia, and a clear political statement linking China to Namibian independence. Accordingly, Premier Wen Jiabao 'stressed that the western colonial rule is an important root cause for poverty and backwardness of Africa, which have not yet been eradicated even today', while Nujoma said 'that South-South cooperation is becoming more important against the present situations.'[3] When the Chinese Communist Party donated

---

1   Emil Appolus, 'Reminiscences of Times Gone By', *New Era*, 3 December 2004.

2   See Ian Taylor, 'China and SWAPO: The Role of the People's Republic in Namibia's Liberation and Post-independence Relations', *The South African Journal of International Affairs* 5, 1 (1997), pp. 110-22.

3   Cited after the official website of the Chinese Foreign Office: www.fmprc. gov.cn/eng/wjb/zzjg/gjlb/3049/3051/t144062.htm (14 October 2005).

US$30,000 to SWAPO in 2003, He Shijing, the Chinese Chargé d'Affaires in Namibia, even claimed that 'we both faced a common task and struggle against imperialism, but now have a similar one which is for the economic development of our countries.'[4] Through this symbolic policy, China's current government is capitalizing on the political efforts of its predecessors and claiming the heritage of international solidarity in the spirit of Bandung. These efforts, combined with effective trade diplomacy, frequent invitations to Namibian government officials even from lower levels, generous credits to finance Chinese exports to Namibia, and examples of public charity,[5] make China popular with the Namibian government. Many leading politicians see Chinese involvement as a possible means to lessen the dependence on the former colonial powers. Public opinion, however, has started to turn against China and the Chinese, and Nujoma's manifest sympathy for China is often suspected of being the outcome of corruption facilitated by the good contacts between both regimes from SWAPO's time in exile. These suspicions are not

---

4   *New Era*, 16 June 2003.

5   In July 2006, for example, members of the Chinese Chamber of Commerce and Industry donated 400 blankets for OEWONA, an organization supporting AIDS orphans and widows headed by First Lady Penexupifo Pohamba. They were received at State House by the First Lady, even though the blankets represent a value of about US$1,000—not a sum that one usually earns a reception in State House. The First Lady accordingly said that the donation 'should not be measured in quantity but in a quality of solidarity existing between the two friendly countries' and added that 'this donation demonstrates the generosity of the Chinese who have been our friends for many years.' (*New Era*, 13 July 2006.) There are not many examples of such charity, but they all share some traits with the higher-level forms of symbolic policy. Usually, the donation is public rather than substantial, and it is used by all participants to link today's presence of China in Africa to Chinese solidarity during the struggle years. The logic of public addresses of thanks virtually guarantees that the Namibian side takes up the solidarity argument, reaffirming both China's role as an important ally and the Namibian government's stance against neo-colonialism. Charity donations thus become one part of a highly skilled symbolic policy aimed at representing China as Africa's natural ally against Western imperialism.

always unfounded,[6] although in many cases Namibian government officials act in good faith.[7]

Local media coverage of Chinese interests in Namibia has been growing since around 2004. The Chinese factor is one of the most important topics in popular economic policy debates today and is increasingly present in parliamentary debates. In September 2006, Ben Ulenga, head of the main opposition party, the Congress of Democrats, introduced a parliamentary motion to debate 'malpractices in the building industry' and the alleged favouring of Chinese-owned companies for public tenders. In the National Assembly debate that followed, Monitor Action Group's MP Jurie Viljoen urged the government to stop what he perceived as the easy influx of Chinese into Namibia. He stated (quite wrongly) that over 40,000 Chinese were living in Namibia, and had no problems getting their work permits. Both Ulenga's concern about labour conditions and unfair tender procedures and Viljoen's xenophobic fears of being overpowered by an influx of Chinese were widely echoed in local and national media discussions. The two sectors most widely discussed in the local media were construction and retail trade.

---

6 For the example of a Chinese grant towards the completion of the new State House 'with no strings attached', followed by large contracts awarded to Chinese construction firms without a public tender, see Gregor Dobler, 'China in Namibia', in Henning Melber (ed.), *Cross-Examining Liberation in Namibia* (Uppsala: Nordic Africa Institute, 2007).

7 For example, in 2004 the parastatal transport company TransNamib decided to buy four diesel locomotives for US$900,000 each and thirty oil tanks from a Chinese company—much cheaper than a replacement of the old General Electrics locomotives. The purchase was backed by an interest-free loan from the Chinese government, and the locomotives were delivered in July 2004 with a one-year guarantee. In August 2005, government decided to borrow RMB250 million from the Export-Import Bank of China at an interest rate of 3 per cent to finance the purchase of 16 new locomotives. From the beginning, the locomotives were rumoured to have major flaws and to be unsafe; the question even came to parliament, where the Transport Minister, Joel Kaapanda, denied any shortcomings. The Namibian Transport and Allied Workers' Union's president claimed that not only did the four locomotives give continuous mechanical problems, but the local mechanics were not trained to service them, the circuit diagrams were written in Chinese, and no parts were available locally. This was used by NATAU to justify its demand to oust the CEO and the board of TransNamib. (*The Namibian*, 19 January 2004; 1 August 2005; 20 December 2006.)

Chinese construction companies have become serious competitors for Namibian firms.[8] As elsewhere, these entered the market by winning public tenders, some backed by soft loans or grants from the Chinese government. The Supreme Court in Windhoek (1994-97), the Police and Prison Training College (1996-97) and the Magistrate's Court in Katutura (1997-1999) were built by China Jiangsu International Namibia Ltd, established in 1994 as a subsidiary of the multinational giant China Jiangsu International Economic-Technical Cooperation Corporation. Other construction companies followed. Out of sixteen government construction tenders in the financial year 2005/6, six were awarded to Chinese companies,[9] even though, since late 2005, foreign firms cannot bid for government projects of less than N$6 million.[10]

Chinese construction companies have been winning increasing numbers of private contracts since 2000. The first step into the market has often been facilitated by government involvement, but Chinese contractors are succeeding in the private sector. Today, their market share of private building contracts is estimated at around 15 per cent.[11] Their competition has made life difficult for local firms, especially SMEs, while the formerly dominant players—all subsidiaries of South African construction giants like Group Five or Grinaker/LTA—can deal with dwindling margins more easily. According to industry sources, profit rates have gone down from between 30 and 40 per cent in the middle of the 1990s to around 10 per cent today, mostly on account of Chinese competition.[12]

---

8   See, for example, Chris Alden, 'China in Africa', *Survival* 47, 3 (2005), pp. 147-64; Harry Broadman, *Africa's Silk Road. China and India as Africa's New Economic Frontier* (Washington DC, World Bank, 2007); Emmy Bosten, 'China's Engagement in the Construction Industry of Southern Africa: the Case of Mozambique', paper for the workshop 'Asian and other Drivers of Global Change', St Petersburg, 19-21 January 2006 (at www.ids.ac.uk/asiandrivers); Judith van de Looy, 'Africa and China: A Strategic Partnership?' (Leiden: ASC Working Paper 67, 2006).

9   According to the Minister of Works and Transport, Joel Kapaanda, cited in *The Namibian*, 21 November 2006.

10   *Insight Namibia*, 20 April 2006.

11   *Insight Namibia*, 21 April 2006.

12   Ibid., confirmed by own interviews.

Their success creates considerable resentment. Many local contractors from the SME sector feel that Chinese firms cannot live on the margins they make with fair means. Chinese companies are often accused of underpaying their workers, violating labour rights and disregarding affirmative action legislation. In contrast to local players, however, no Chinese company was ever proven to violate these regulations, partly, at least, because of shrewdness in dealing with regulations rather than real compliance. For example, no Chinese construction company officially employs more than fifty workers permanently—the threshold below which companies are exempted from affirmative action reports and inspections. Such practices are not unknown to other companies in the industry, but they are much less commented upon. For Namibian or South African firms, they are rather seen as individual failures, whereas for Chinese companies they are regarded as a systematic feature.

Suspicion against Asian companies is reinforced by the biggest ever foreign investment in the manufacturing sector in Namibia. Ramatex, a large Malaysian textile company, opened a manufacturing plant under the Export Processing Zone regime in 2001. The decision to invest in Namibia was influenced by large benefits granted to the company by the Namibian government (ranging from tax exemptions and subsidized water and electricity to over N$100 million government money to prepare the site) and by the AGOA regime. Ramatex employs about 8,000 workers in Namibia, of whom 2,000 are of Asian origin. It increased jobs in Namibia's manufacturing sector by 40 per cent.[13] However, low wages, bad working conditions and a frequent disregard for labour rights have brought the company under attack from the media and the unions. One constant bone of contention has been Ramatex-government relations and the employment of Asian workers.[14] The Affirmative Action Act of 1998

---

13 Herbert Jauch, 'Africa's Clothing and Textile Industry: The Case of Ramatex in Namibia', in Herbert Jauch and Rudolf Traub-Merz (eds), *The Future of the Textile and Clothing Industry in Sub-Saharan Africa* (Bonn: Friedrich-Ebert-Stiftung, 2006), p. 215. For further information on Ramatex, see also Volker Winterfeld, 'Liberated Economy? The Case of Ramatex Textiles Namibia', in Melber (ed.), *Cross-Examining Liberation in Namibia*.

14 '...the relationship between the company and the Namibian government

prescribes that work permits for foreign nationals can only be issued if the required skills cannot be found locally, and that companies have to employ Namibian understudies—a regulation that is frequently disregarded or liberally interpreted to grant greater freedom to foreign investors. Although Ramatex is not a Chinese company, the multinational's presence has considerably damaged the hopes many Namibian used to place in Asian foreign investment and has substantiated the fears of Namibian government's lenience towards Asian investors. Even though the firm is Malaysian, the reputation of Chinese business has suffered. Many Namibians who are aware of the difference between China and Malaysia still feel that Chinese companies would be just as bad.

Thus, real experiences of Asian companies mingle with unclear suspicions towards Chinese. They are both newcomers and foreigners, and are suspect to many locals under both headings. This is most strikingly expressed in some pervasive rumours. Many Namibians, including journalists, politicians, businesspeople, and academics alike, are convinced that Chinese convicts can choose to serve their prison terms on Namibian construction sites. These rumours are obviously unfounded, but they are readily believed. Old figures of speech from colonial times come to a new prominence, 'the Chinese' replacing 'the Whites'. The (white) editor of the *Namibian Economist*, usually a champion of FDI and free market reforms, accused Chinese of coming to Namibia to increase their 'living space' and take Namibians' land away, a fear echoed by many popular voices.[15] Meanwhile, the old imperialists are no longer seen as a threat by many. Throughout the country, the opening of yet another South African owned Sho-

---

which has granted and continues to grant hundreds of work permits to unskilled and semi-skilled Asian workers who carry out tasks that could easily be performed by Namibian workers'. Press release by the National Union of Namibian Workers, 10 September 2004, as cited by Jauch, 'Africa's Clothing and Textile Industry', p. 221.

15 *Namibia Economist*, 16 May 2003. The article ends: 'The only thing we have which they can possibly be interested in is living space. And if I am correct, then expect to see many millions more over the next thirteen years.'

prite, Pick'n'Pay or Game supermarket is enthusiastically welcomed by the local population and politicians alike.[16]

In Northern Namibia, local traders routinely complain about the growing number of Chinese shops in the area and perceive them as a threat to their business. As a matter of fact, more than half of the shops existing in the area before 1990 have silently closed down during the 1990s owing to competition by South African firms. The first wave of new shops consisted mostly of Cape Malay or Indian owned firms, the second wave of branches of the large supermarket chains. Their arrival in the formerly strictly regulated market of northern Namibia was perceived by the local population as a step towards normalization, as a welcome consequence of the end of the colonial regime. Chinese migrants, however, are often seen as intruders, even by the people who buy at their shops.

In many African countries, South African firms are greeted with resentment and seen as the new colonialists, often along with Chinese migrants. Not so in Namibia. The country's history of South African colonialism has made economic domination by South Africa appear the normal state of affairs. It cannot serve as an explanation for Namibia's current economic plight, and South African companies are no longer seen as strangers. In contrast, there is no tradition of Chinese migration to Namibia and the growing presence of Chinese expatriates is a completely new phenomenon. Seventeen years after Namibia's independence, China and the Chinese are slowly emerging as the new imperial threat to the country's economic and social independence. In this process, social unrest is increasingly formulated along a new indigenous/exogenous divide. Even conflicts over labour rights are more and more conceptualized as an outcome of a cultural division, not as an issue of class or of economic domination within an increasingly neo-liberal economy.

Together with real malpractices by Chinese companies, the changing political climate has consequences for the government's policy towards China and especially towards Chinese migrants in

---

16 The latest example has been the opening of the extension of Maerua Mall in Windhoek, Namibia's largest shopping complex, in March 2006. The extension was hailed as an economic achievement and an expression of Namibia's modernity (see, for example, *New Era*, 31 March 2006).

Namibia. The threshold of N$6 million for public tenders was an important outcome of popular criticism and lobbying by the Construction Industry Federation. Public control of Chinese investors has tightened in recent years and it has become increasingly difficult for new Chinese arrivals to obtain work permits. Applications are more thoroughly examined for possible effects on the Namibian economy. It has become virtually impossible to obtain a permit to come into the country to open a shop. This has important—and not always intended—repercussions for the lives and the business of Chinese migrants in Namibia, as the case of Oshikango illustrates.[17]

Oshikango

Oshikango is a small, vibrant and rapidly growing town on the Namibian-Angolan border. Before 1990, it consisted of little more than a war-shattered border post, an open market, some local shops and a school. The area was in the middle of a war zone. Civilian movement was rigidly controlled by the South African army and police, who often clashed with SWAPO guerrilla units coming in from their Angolan bases. After 1990 Oshikango remained a sleepy outpost but started to develop into the main trade post for cross-border trade into South-Western Angola from around 1996. Its most important assets were the road and the border. The road, an excellent tar road built by the South African colonial government eager to control the area, links Oshikango to Walvis Bay, the nearest sea harbour that trucks can reach in around ten to twelve hours.

The border separates and links two economic and political systems. Even now that conditions in Angola have rapidly improved, it is much safer to invest on the Namibian side, and Oshikango is the nearest one can get to the Angolan markets without actually investing in Angola. Oshikango has thus profited from reconstruction in Angola during and after the war. The town has rapidly grown since 1996 and today, with only around 5,000 to 8,000 inhabitants, is the most vibrant trade centre in Namibia. The largest warehouses are owned by businessmen of Lebanese, Portuguese and South African

---

17 The material for this study was gathered during twelve months of fieldwork in Oshikango between June 2004 and December 2006.

Indian origin, while the second hand car trade is mostly controlled by Pakistani expatriates.[18] Most of the trade is done wholesale: Angolan traders come to Oshikango and buy large quantities of building material, furniture, electronics, textiles, food or liquor in order to resell them in Angola. Smaller quantities are sold to Angolan shop owners or peddlers who cross the border daily, or who have porters working for them to import goods for less than the taxable amount of US$50.

Before 2004, the Oshikango area was part of the communal lands administered by the regional government. There are no freehold land titles in Namibian communal areas outside established towns. Investors are granted permission to occupy the land and build on it, but they do not own the land. In an attempt both to encourage investors to build shops in Oshikango and to regulate the more or less chaotic growth of the town, Oshikango, together with four adjacent settlements with a total population of around 42,000, was proclaimed a town in 2004. The new administration of Helao Nafidi Town, as it is called today, is the most important regulating body at the local level, responsible among other things for land sales and granting construction permits.

Chinese in Oshikango

Chinese traders have been in Oshikango since 1999. The first Chinese to open shop there was a businessman who had come to Windhoek in 1993 and was already well established by the time he came to Oshikango. His considerable success and booming cross-border trade rapidly attracted others. In 2004, 22 Chinese-owned shops were in business in Oshikango. In 2006, with the opening of two large new warehouse complexes (one of them built by the pioneer Chinese in Oshikango, the other by a Taiwanese national who had opened the first China-Shop in Windhoek before independence), their number increased to over 75.

The first Chinese shops in Oshikango mainly sold textiles and shoes in large quantities. In 2004, for example, one single dealer

---

18 See Dobler, 'The way to consumption. International commodity flows and trade networks in Oshikango, Namibia' (*Africa* 78, 2008)).

sold more than 200,000 pairs of shoes into Angola. With growing competition, most shops have expanded their range: many are now selling everything from furniture to home electronics, motorcycles or plastic flowers. The bulk of the business, however, is still done in home textiles, clothing and shoes, with a few shops specializing in electronics. Most of the shops are bonded wholesale warehouses, the major form of business in Oshikango. Goods are imported from overseas for re-export without Namibian import taxes or duties. They can only be sold for export, and the bonded warehouses are (at least in theory) rigidly controlled by the customs office.

All Chinese traders import most of their merchandise directly from China. They—or trusted agents—buy large quantities directly from the manufacturer or (for smaller quantities) from wholesalers in China. The goods are packed in sealed containers and shipped to Durban or Walvis Bay. From there, they reach Oshikango by train and/or truck. If both shipping space and trucks are available, goods reach Oshikango three to four weeks after being packed in China, but owing to capacity problems, containers are often delayed for two or three months.

Even if they appear as a distinct group from the outside, the Chinese who are living in Oshikango are no homogeneous, close-knit community. They come from all over China, speak different dialects, have grown up in different climates and have different cultural backgrounds. Most of the older ones have had only rudimentary schooling and did not speak any foreign language when they came to Namibia, while many of the younger arrivals have been to college or university and have learned English or Portuguese. As to business, the different shops barely cooperate; most compete constantly and strive to keep their knowledge and connections to themselves. Business ideas are frequently copied and prices cut. With growing competition, margins have gone down from sometimes 50 per cent to around 10 per cent and less, and here as everywhere business has been most lucrative for the first comers.[19]

In recent times, however, with the growing number of Chinese living in Oshikango, social life has become more intense. Friends

---

19 For Chinese shops in Cape Verde, see Haugen and Carling in this volume.

often eat together after closing their shops. At weekends, the older people play Mahjong (often for quite high stakes) while the young watch TV, play Western computer games,[20] sing karaoke or compete at the pool tables of local bars. Slowly, the diverse Chinese population may develop into a diasporic community, but so far, the intensifying social life has not yet led to a higher level of business cooperation.

Chinese people in Oshikango—and, by extension, in Namibia— are not physically threatened by the changing political climate. However, growing resentment creates serious problems for Chinese businesspeople. The most important problem is the Ministry of Home Affairs' marked reluctance to grant further work permits for Chinese traders. In the past, prospective Chinese shop owners could get work permits rather easily. With growing public criticism and frequent allegations of corruption, Home Affairs officials have become more sceptical towards Chinese applications. Delays are frequent, and it has become very difficult to obtain a work permit to open a shop in Namibia. This, however, has not led to a decline in the number of new arrivals—it only encourages more creative ways of dealing with work permit procedures. Most new arrivals do not just come on their own. Established businesspeople act as migration brokers and work permit agents.

Until around 2004, new migrants usually came to work as assistants in established businesses, often with relatives. They earned their travel expenses by working in the shop for two or three years, getting used to life in Namibia at the same time, learning the trade, the language and preparing to set up a shop of their own. This remains an important source of new migration, but it has been partially replaced by a new, more commercialized form of chain migration: new migrants pay an established Namibian Chinese either for their work permit or for the complete preparation of their arrival. A one-year work permit can be had for around N$20,000, the organization of the whole migration process will cost up to N$100,000.

---

20 Internet use plays an important role, too, especially to keep up relations to relatives and to the home country at large. See also Loong Wong, 'Belonging and Diaspora: The Chinese and the Internet', *First Monday* 8, 4 (2003).

Established Chinese entrepreneurs in Namibia have thus found a new line of business. While in the normal import business they exploit their knowledge of and access to the cheaper Chinese producers and wholesalers to make a profit on an African clientele, they have started to exploit their knowledge of English, of Namibian administration and business culture, and their access to Namibian networks, to make a profit on incoming Chinese. The deal serves both sides: for a new arrival, it is harder to establish a business, the administration is less cooperative; there are not many towns left without a sufficient number of Chinese shops, good knowledge of the economic situation is required to judge the few remaining opportunities; and profits have gone down owing to competition. It is no longer possible to flourish on trial and error—if you are allowed into the country at all.

Getting a work permit and spending some time learning the trade are the two most important prerequisites for doing business as a Chinese in Namibia. The Chinese migration brokers organize work permits in two different ways. There are agents who have good contacts with higher Home Affairs officials and handle your application for a fee. All Chinese I talked to are convinced that a part of the usual N$20,000 goes to the Home Affairs official. One told me: 'Of course, it is bribery. That is normal. If you want to get something, you have to pay. But with all the talk about corruption now, it has become very difficult. If you don't know somebody, he will not even take your money. He's afraid. But those people, they have been friends for a long time. They know they can trust each other. So for them, it's no problem.'[21] In general, Chinese in Namibia do not regard corruption as an offence. They take it as part of the rules of business; expenses combined with a certain risk, but not subject to moral judgment.

The second easy way to obtain a work permit is connected to the Namibian discourse on development and foreign investment. Chinese shops have been heavily criticized for being unproductive and extractive. The general notion is that these shops hinder rather than help the development of the Namibian economy. In contrast, investment in the manufacturing sector would be more than welcome. As a

---

21 Male Chinese electronics trader established in Oshikango since 2003; statement of August 2006.

consequence, applications for work permits in order to open (or work in) a shop are by now routinely rejected by Home Affairs, whereas applications to work in a manufacturing plant are usually successful. Many Chinese have started to exploit that preference by setting up 'manufacturing plants' as a smokescreen for retail or wholesale trade.[22] In Oshikango, for example, one company built a blanket factory, imported a few old industrial sewing machines from China, and employed local women to sew duvets for export to Angola. All material—cloth, cotton filling, thread—is imported from China, and there is not the slightest possibility to compete with duvets imported from there. The real output of the production site is work permits for Chinese 'technicians' and supervisors who, in reality, work as assistants in Chinese shops. Other 'manufacturing plants' in Oshikango include Chinese food, photo printing, mineral water processing and furniture assembling businesses. None of these ventures is really functional. 'It is a good business,' as one younger Chinese told me. 'You import a few old machines, pay the transport—maybe that's N$50,000 per machine. Then you can easily get papers for some people, maybe even five or six per machine. That's quite good!'[23]

Attempts at stricter regulation have been turned into a new resource by established Chinese in Oshikango who have the local knowledge to creatively circumvent the new measures, and increase their competitive advantage over new arrivals. New regulations have not fulfilled the expectations of the regulators. They have only managed to make fraud slightly more difficult—and thus more lucrative for those capable of committing it. The consequences of Namibian xenophobia have increased power imbalances within the Chinese migrant 'community'. The growing public sensitivity over real or imagined preferential treatment of Chinese migrants has closed the circles of corruption and increased the value of existing contacts. Demands to link Chinese investment to sustainable development have turned the ability to position oneself in the development discourse

---

22 I have not been able to establish numbers; in Oshikango, however, certainly more than half of the traders have already applied for manufacturing licences or have made the first steps to do so.

23 Male Chinese trader, in Oshikango since 2002 as junior partner in a relative's business; statement of August 2006.

into an important resource. Just as the Chinese government is wrapping its interests in Africa in a rhetoric of solidarity, mutual gain and cooperation, Chinese traders on the local level are using the language of development to justify their presence and to gain access to the benevolence of both the public and the administration. The setting up of manufacturing shopfronts is only one example of that tendency. Whenever the occasion arises, Chinese migrants in Oshikango stress their contribution to local economic development, the amounts they have invested and the number of local people they employ.

By positioning themselves as players in local economic development, Chinese investors have become an interesting ally for a modernist elite on the local level. Like all Namibian towns, Helao Nafidi Town is governed by the Town Council, headed by the mayor and supported by the local administration, whose most important member is the town's CEO. The members of the Town Council are no experts; they were elected into their office in 2004, mostly without prior administrative experience, and are all working full-time in different professions. Their decisions are usually prepared by the CEO, who holds the real power in the town and can easily influence decisions according to his wishes. The current CEO of the town is a young man with a background in business administration and SWAPO politics. He sees his five-year term as a step towards a higher office, preferably in the capital, where his wife holds a post in the municipal administration. Many locals suspect him of corrupt practices; what is certain is that he can run the town at his whim, having no equally capable and equally powerful opponent on the local level.[24] His politics are modernist, business-friendly and, on foreign investment for example, neo-liberal. For him, the town administration's main role is to make Oshikango a better place for investors, and to promote it internationally. In his perception, what is good for business is good

---

24 There is not enough space here to elaborate on the relations between members of the Town Council and Chinese migrants, although there is no lack of material. To cite just two examples: one influential member of the Town Council sold a plot of land to a Chinese businessman for more than twenty times its official value, while another, though generally opposed to a growing Chinese influence, has a large collection of pirated film DVDs bought under the counter in a Chinese shop.

for the town—and for himself, extending his own powers with the town's revenue and increasing his chances in the future job market.

The CEO was also instrumental in bringing about a twinning agreement between Helao Nafidi Town and Nantong, an important industrial centre in eastern China with around 700,000 inhabitants.[25] The Mayor and the CEO of Helao Nafidi Town went on a ten-day trip there, a voyage that did much to improve the mayor's opinion of China and the Chinese. The twinning agreement was signed in Helao Nafidi Town on the occasion of a short visit by a Chinese delegation; to date, the agreement has not had any further consequences. However, through such feel-good measures, politicians of the Chinese government are brought to the local level in an African town, where they meet a similar discourse by local elites. On every public occasion, both the CEO and the more established Chinese investors talk of development, progress, South-South cooperation and Namibia's Millennium Development Goals.[26] Jointly, the two parties inscribe both Chinese investments and the Local Authority's actions in a transnational elite discourse on sustainable development that serves to highlight their own importance and obfuscate their own motives.

Even when backed by official state politics, the joint interest in linking Chinese investments to a development discourse does not guarantee the local elite's benevolence towards Chinese migrants. Rather, it establishes a common ground on which negotiations on concrete projects can be successful. These negotiations are saturated

---

25 The agreement seems part of a general policy by the Chinese government to further Chinese-African relations at local level and to position China as Africa's new partner for economic development. In Namibia, at least the following twinning agreements are in place: Windhoek and Shanghai, Tsumeb and Lanzhou, Mariental and Zhingzhou, Grootfontein and Kunshan, Outapi and Yinchuan; talks are on for Henties Bay and an undisclosed Chinese city, and the entire Erongo region has a twinning agreement with the city of Tiazhou.

26 A model occasion for such public discourse was the opening of Oshikango China Town, one of two new warehouse complexes built by Chinese investors, in July 2006. Dragon dancing, public speeches and a Chinese dinner for the local honourables were combined with a rather large number of public speeches. Every speaker stressed China's important role for Namibian development and the good mutual relations expressed in the new building.

with development rhetoric, but they are much more about both sides' personal aims than about development. As long as development can be kept up as a façade for business and as a moral argument against sceptics, the real economic benefits of Chinese investment to the Namibian economy can be left aside.

Chinese traders' real contribution to sustainable development in the Oshikango area to date has been small. There has been no spillover into manufacturing, no capacity-building on a local level, and almost no extension of networks to include native Namibians.[27] The labour the Chinese shop-owners employ is unskilled and rather poorly paid, and apart from a few assistants working closely with the owners, they change quite often. Growing resentment against Chinese in Namibia has not changed this for the better. It has led to closer and more ostentatious cooperation between Namibian administrators and Chinese investors rather than to a more critical discussion. In order not to lose their room to negotiate, both sides try to shield the cooperation from outside criticism by linking Chinese investments even more strongly to development—without reference to its real impact on the Namibian economy. In the area of local regulation, too, xenophobia has made differentiation more difficult and given more influence to the more powerful players.

Conclusion

When looking into African states' policies towards Chinese migrants, political scientists usually concentrate on a national discourse and on official rules set up at national level. In Namibia, as in many other African countries, the political climate is increasingly hostile towards Chinese migrant entrepreneurs. They are seen as representatives of a new imperialism and as unfair competition to local businesspeople. Calls for stronger regulation of the Chinese element are gaining prominence. To counter these voices, Chinese officials and their Namibian counterparts try to link the Chinese presence to the politics of solidarity during the struggle for independence, and to the new struggle for economic freedom and development.

---

27 For a more thorough assessment, see Dobler, 'China in Namibia'.

So far, growing popular opposition to Chinese investors has not led to any decisive policy changes. On the level of administrative practices, however, Chinese migrants encounter much stronger problems than some years ago. A closer look at business practices on a local level shows that this has not, as yet, discouraged Chinese business migration to Namibia. Instead, it has led to higher levels of fraud, a closing of circles of corruption and a shift in power relations within the Chinese community in favour of the longer established and better connected migrants.

What is conspicuously absent in Namibia is a real debate on the costs and benefits of the Chinese presence and the possibilities for its regulation. National and local attitudes towards the growing importance of China and of Chinese in Namibia are shaped by a web of personal interest, development ideologies, party politics and individual idiosyncrasies. The specific community of interest between Chinese investors and both national and local administrators in particular prevents an objective debate. Both investors and local modernist elites base justification of their dominant role on their participation in the development discourse. Inscribing the Chinese presence into that discourse lends them a broader base of power and an opportunity to regain their dominant role. For the opposition, an objective analysis of costs and benefits seems just as difficult. In popular perceptions, both migrant Chinese and the ruling elites suffer from being associated with each other. Foreign investment and a new imperialism serve as an explanation for economic difficulties, and attempts to discuss the problem in a less ideological way are often discredited as either naïve or dishonest.

Both the interests of local elites and the new xenophobic tendencies prevent a pragmatic discussion of possible ways of regulation, and the implementation of a political framework that channels Chinese investment into sectors where it could really benefit the country's economy. Namibia has probably more than enough Chinese shops; certainly enough Chinese manufacturing plants existing solely on paper. But with the growing competition, many of the established Chinese migrants are looking for new opportunities outside trading. Some talk of moving into the service sector, others think about the possibilities of setting up real manufacturing plants. If Namibia can both effectively control new shops and offer alternative investment opportunities, the country may still draw real benefit from the Chinese presence.

13

SOUTH AFRICA AND CHINA: A STRATEGIC PARTNERSHIP?

Garth Shelton

The world can truly achieve peace, stability and prosperity only if developed countries and developing countries enjoy common development.

Hu Jintao[1]

Our countries and peoples are united by a common resolve to build a better life for themselves. We are at one in the commitment to ensure that we build that better life in conditions of freedom and peace. We are committed also to contribute what we can to ensure a more equitable international political and economic order which addresses the just aspirations of the billions of people who belong to the developing countries of our common universe.

Thabo Mbeki[2]

China's relationship with South Africa is longstanding and complex, reflecting the politics of the Cold War and apartheid as well as the more contemporary activism emerging out of Beijing. The debate over

---

1 Quoted in B. Gilley,'The year China started to climb', *Far East Asian Economic Review*, 168, 8 (2005), p.33.

2 President Thabo Mbeki, 'State Banquet in Honour of President Jiang Zemin', 25 April 2000, Office of the Presidency, at *http://www.gov.za.*

diplomatic recognition of China, a legacy of the apartheid government's close ties with Taiwan that were surprisingly enough carried over into the post-1994 democratic period, has been one facet of relations. Another is the compelling growth of economic ties and, once formal diplomatic links were restored, close political co-operation between Pretoria and Beijing over a variety of international issues. This convergence of views has raised the matter of closer economic co-operation in the form of a proposed Free Trade Agreement, which has been the subject of intense discussion within South Africa in recent years. This remarkable trajectory over the last decade, culminating in a declaration of a 'strategic partnership' between China and South Africa, will be reviewed and analyzed in this chapter.

The Taiwan question and diplomatic relations

Diplomatic relations between Taiwan (the Republic of China, or ROC) and South Africa were initially established at the consular level in 1962 and upgraded to ambassadorial level in 1976. The relationship was based largely on a common interest in anti-communism and a desire to counter their common international pariah status. Following the establishment of formal relations, ROC-South African links across a range of areas grew steadily. Trade and investment showed a substantial increase, while defence contacts led to a large number of South African military personnel undertaking specialist training courses in the ROC.[3] Over 10,000 Taiwanese businesspeople migrated to South Africa to invest in factories providing a solid economic foundation for diplomatic links. Taiwan ignored international sanctions against South Africa, favouring instead increased trade and political interaction at the highest level. Despite good relations with Taipei, South Africa also sought to establish contacts with the People's Republic of China (PRC) during the 1980s. In 1989 the South African government conveyed an official message to Beijing, via Liang Zhaoli, the president of the Chinese Association of South Africa, requesting the establishment of formal diplomatic relations.[4]

---

3 See Deon Geldenhuys *et al.*, *The Taiwan Experience: Implications for South Africa* (Pretoria: University of Pretoria, 1995).

4 Qian Qichen, *Ten Episodes in China's Diplomacy* (New York: HarperCollins,

Concerned over a possible recognition switch following the 1994 elections, Taipei made a very substantial contribution (an estimated US$25 million) to the African National Congress' (ANC) election campaign. Most observers believe this contribution was crucial for the ANC victory in 1994. Moreover, with ROC investment of $1.56 billion which provided 40,000 jobs, bilateral trade totalling $1.77 billion and dozens of joint projects whether in progress or promised, Taipei was confident that diplomatic relations would continue for some time to come. The new ANC government chose to delay an immediate switch in diplomatic recognition, given the well-established relationship with Taipei and the financial support provided by the Taiwanese authorities. At the same time, in official interactions, the Chinese authorities repeatedly pointed out that China had long been a supporter of South Africa's liberation struggle, regarding the fight for justice as its own in solidarity with the people of South Africa.

In its communiqué with Beijing establishing diplomatic ties, the South African government stated that 'The government of the PRC is the sole legal government representing the whole of China', and added that Pretoria 'recognises China's position that Taiwan is an inalienable part of China.' Taipei lobbied unsuccessfully for South Africa to make use of the word 'acknowledges' rather than 'recognises' in describing the PRC's claim to represent all China, but to no avail. The status of the ROC embassy was downgraded to that of the 'Taipei Liaison Offie in the RSA [Republic of South Africa]', with branch offices maintained in Cape Town, Durban and Johannesburg. However, the new 'Office' continued to perform the same functions as before, retained the same staff and operated from the same premises. Formal diplomatic relations between China and South Africa were established on 1 January 1998, opening a new chapter in Sino-African relations and bringing South Africa in line with African diplomacy.[5]

2005), p. 204.

5 Garth Le Pere, 'Sino-African Synergy Matures', *The Star*, 6 May 1999. See also SAIIA Research Group (ed.), *South Africa and the Two Chinas Dilemma* (Johannesburg: South African Institute of International Affairs and the Foundation for Global Dialogue, 1995) and Deon Geldenhuys, 'The Politics of South Africa's China Switch', *Issues and Studies*, 33, 7 (1997), pp. 93-131.

The political framework of cooperation

In April 2000, President Jiang Zemin paid a state visit to South Africa where he signed the 'Pretoria Declaration' with his counterpart Thabo Mbeki. The 'Pretoria Declaration on the Partnership Between the People's Republic of China and the Republic of South Africa' commits both countries to a 'spirit of partnership and constructive dialogue' while uniting in the 'moral imperative for developing countries to strengthen capacity for co-operation and mutual support in the international system.'[6] The most important outcome of the agreement was the establishment of a Bi-National Commission (BNC), which would meet regularly to guide and coordinate all government-to-government relations between China and South Africa, while providing an effective forum for consultation on matters of mutual interest in bilateral and multilateral affairs.[7] In addition, the Pretoria Declaration committed China and South Africa to a 'constructive dialogue', a concerted effort to expand economic links and a joint initiative to advance peace, security and development on the African continent.[8]

Besides the Pretoria Declaration, China and South Africa signed six agreements covering police co-operation, maritime transport, prevention of the spread of deadly pathogens, animal health and quarantine, arts and culture, and avoidance of double taxation. However, the emphasis of public statements from Jiang Zemin and Thabo Mbeki at the time was on the need for both countries, along with the developing world, to work together to ensure benefits from globalization. China and South Africa confirmed a commitment to oppose the negative affects of globalization and also to oppose global dominance by a single country. President Mbeki stressed South Africa's desire to 'deepen existing relations' and to 'extend relations

---

6   Quoted in Garth Shelton, 'China's Africa Policy and South Africa: Building New Economic Partnerships', *SA Yearbook of International Affairs 2000/01* (Johannesburg: South African Institute of International Affairs, 2001), p. 389.

7   P. Wadula, 'South Africa, China Set Up Binational Body', *Business Day*, 26 April 2000.

8   See D. Monyae, 'Bridge to Beijing', *The Sowetan*, 11 December 2001.

to broader areas of co-operation'.[9] He also emphasized the need for South Africa and other developing countries to seek closer co-operation in international affairs with the objective of restructuring the global economic architecture. In response, Jiang pointed out that the constant expansion and deepening of Sino-South African relations fulfilled the 'long-term fundamental interests' of both countries, while supporting and advancing 'peace and global development'.

Jiang suggested that South Africa's status as a regional power and a key international actor elevated the importance of the Beijing-Pretoria dialogue and government-to-government co-operation. A long-term, stable, friendly co-operative relationship was thus the objective of Jiang's vision for Sino-South African relations.[10] Moreover, as Jiang intimated, 'hegemony and power politics threaten world peace and security,' which made it more important for South Africa as a leading African nation and China as a leading Asian nation to strengthen contact and collaboration. Both Pretoria and Beijing confirmed a belief that the two countries strongly complemented each other in many fields, thus providing an excellent opportunity for long-term cooperation and political interaction. Mbeki alluded to the history of Sino-African relations, suggesting that Africa's struggle against colonialism received consistent and enthusiastic support from China. Moreover, the post-independence era witnessed strong PRC involvement in African reconstruction and economic development programmes. Given China's constructive relationship with many African countries, Mbeki voiced support for South Africa's full participation in the FOCAC process, which he predicted would play a leading role in helping African countries overcome socio-economic problems.

Jiang's visit to South Africa also set the scene for Sino-South African co-operation and policy synchronization on the issue of advancing the establishment of a new international economic order. He pointed out that the accelerated pace of economic globalization benefited developed countries far more than developing, which face

9   Quoted in Zhong Fei, 'President Jiang's Visit to South Africa', *Chinafrica* 113, 20 May 2000, p. 5.

10 See S. Chetty, 'Forging Afro-Sino Ties', *The Sowetan*, 29 September 2000.

increasing risks and challenges. The continuously, ever more rapidly widening gap between rich and poor nations, along with increasing tensions and conflict between North and South, threatened economic development and sustained growth in the countries of the South. In this context, both China and South Africa found themselves on the wrong side of the 'digital divide' with declining prospects for bridging the North-South division.[11]

Both Jiang and Mbeki concluded that the Bretton Woods system, along with quickening globalization, required developing countries such as China and South Africa to work together in a joint programme to reform the existing economic architecture, aiming at a new, just and rational economic order. Developed countries were urged to shoulder more responsibilities, reduce developing world debt, fulfil aid promises and provide appropriate assistance to promote economic development in African and other developing countries. The developing countries in turn, and especially Africa within Mbeki's vision of African Renaissance, should strengthen solidarity, demand new global trade rules at the World Trade Organization (WTO) and unite in defending legitimate rights and economic interests.

The BNC was officially launched during President Mbeki's state visit to Beijing in December 2001. A range of discussions were held at ministerial and senior official level involving the ministries of foreign affairs, economics and trade, public security, judiciary, science and technology, energy and tourism.[12] The initial BNC meeting led to the establishment of four sectoral committees on foreign affairs, economy and trade, science and technology and national defence. A number of other government departments from both countries subsequently established direct channels of communication and also maintain a regular and constructive dialogue.[13] The BNC provides a solid framework for the further development and enhancement of bilateral China-South Africa relations. Moreover, the BNC agenda has been complemented and strengthened by a frequent exchange of high level

---

11 Zhong Fei, 'President Jiang's Visit to South Africa', op. cit.

12 'China-South Africa Bilateral Commission Launched', *People's Daily*, at

13 'Bi-National Commission Important for China-South Africa Co-operation', *People's Daily*, at

visits between the two countries. Mbeki's visit to Beijing focused on expanding relations to include scientific and nuclear research, while the Department of Foreign Affairs confirmed that South Africa was looking to the PRC 'both as a market and an investor.'

The foundation of China-South Africa relations is the 'Pretoria Declaration', concluded on 25 April 2002, which provides the framework for a broad strategic partnership between Pretoria and Beijing. Grounded on China's five principles of Sino-African relations—friendship, equality and sovereignty, common development and mutual benefit, consultation on international issues and co-operation in advancing a new international political and economic order—the Pretoria declaration commits both countries to carry on a partnership and constructive dialogue; advance the full spectrum of relations for mutual benefit; establish a Bi-National Commission to give full expression to the relationship; expand economic co-operation in the context of South-South co-operation; co-operate in supporting Africa's and the G-77's agenda; and advance a new global order based on justice and equality.[14]

At the close of the 2004 China-South Africa BNC meeting in Pretoria, Deputy President Jacob Zuma confirmed both country's satisfaction with regard to broadening interaction in trade, culture, education, science and technology and co-operation on international issues. The specific areas of co-operation noted by Zuma included an agreement on China's offer to provide human resource development; formal recognition of China's market economy status; an agreement on South African exports of agricultural products to China; an undertaking to begin negotiations on an FTA; a range of business-to-business agreements including chambers of commerce; a letter of intent by Sasol to go ahead with investments in China; and an agreement to co-operate in strengthening South-South co-operation in the context of WTO negotiations.[15]

---

14 'Pretoria Declaration on the Partnership Between the People's Republic of China and the Republic of South Africa', at *http://www.fmprc.gov.cn/eng*.

15 Deputy President Jacob Zuma, 'Closing Remarks on the Occasion of the China-South Africa BNC', Pretoria, 29 June 2004, at *http://www.info.gov. za/speeches/2004*.

In June 2006, President Mbeki and the Chinese Premier Wen Jiabao signed an agreement to help protect the South African textile industry from the ongoing influx of low-cost Chinese textiles. In agreeing to this, Beijing signalled its willingness to assist a fellow country of the South to soften the impact of globalization. The agreement provided a breathing space for the recovery of South Africa's textile industry, giving local manufacturers an excellent opportunity to modernize and restructure manufacturing processes. In addition to Beijing's major concession on textiles, China and South Africa signed an additional 13 agreements including co-operation in agriculture, minerals and energy, technical co-operation, investment and trade promotion, customs co-operation and nuclear non-proliferation.[16] The range of agreements concluded and the broad synthesis of international perspectives provided further impetus to the China-South Africa strategic partnership.[17]

Economic relations and a FTA?

During the early 1990s direct trade relations between China and South Africa were initiated, and within a relatively short period of time two-way trade began to increase significantly.[18] The volume of bilateral trade in 1991 was only US$14 million, but within six years it totalled over US$1.5 billion. The establishment of formal diplomatic links in 1998 provided a further boost to commercial interaction, with two-way trade levels reaching over US$2 billion in 2002. South Africa's exports to China have consisted mainly of raw materials such as nickel, manganese, zirconium, vanadium oxides, chromium ores, granite, platinum and gold. China's exports to South Africa have included mainly manufactured products, such as footwear, textiles, plastic products, electrical appliances, tableware and kitchenware.[19]

---

16 B. Webb, 'Deputy President Cautious on Trade Deals with China', *The Star*, 23 June 2006.

17 See J. Katzenellenbogen, 'China, SA Join Forces on Nuclear Technology', *Business Day*, 24 June 2006.

18 See Garth Shelton, 'China and Africa: Building an Economic Partnership', *South African Journal of International Affairs*, 8, 2 (Winter 2001), pp. 111-19.

19 Embassy of the People's Republic of China in South Africa, 'China-South

In addition to healthy growth in trade, bilateral investment has increased significantly. By 2006, Chinese companies had invested $180 million in over 80 projects involving agriculture, textiles, electronics, mining, banking, transport and communications. Initial Chinese investment plans outlined in 1997 pointed to an investment injection of over $300 million, but this has not materialized. However, given poor investment conditions in South Africa, such as high crime levels, low productivity and lack of labour flexibility, securing FDI from any source remains a major challenge. Chinese investments in South Africa include a $75 million deal with the Limpopo Province Development Corporation to establish ASA Minerals, based on chrome mining. The Chinese steel maker Jisco is also involved in a chrome investment in North West Province. Shanghai Industrial and First Auto Works have made investments in manufacturing plants, while Hisense and Shanghai Guangdian Co. are involved in South Africa's electronics market. In the telecommunications field, Huawei Technologies and ZTE Corporation are active.

South Africa, in turn, has invested over $400 million in over 200 projects in China. Key South African corporate investors in China include SABMillar, the MIH Group and Landpac. Beginning in 1994, SABMillar invested in China through a joint venture partnership with the China Resources Enterprises (CRE) Group, to establish China Resources Breweries (CRB). CRB has seen rapid growth over the last ten years, becoming the second largest brewing business in China by volume, as well as one of the most profitable beer businesses in China. SABMillar's strategy has been to enter into joint venture partnerships with local brewers in different parts of the country and thereby strengthen its position in what is expected to become the world's biggest beer market.[20] SABMillar is now present in a number of Chinese provinces including Liaoning, Sichuan and Anhui. Its most recent joint venture agreement is a 29.6 per cent stake in the Hong Kong listed Harbin Brewery, the oldest beer brand in China. SABMillar's corporate expansion strategy has positioned

---

Africa Relations', at http://www.chinese-embassy.org.za/eng/62966.html

20 *The South Africa-China Business Association (SACBA)* at *http://www.sacba. com.cn/about/about.htm.*

the company for future growth and market dominance in the lucrative Chinese market.[21]

Since 1998, MIH has worked with SARFT (State Academy for Radio, Film and Television) and CCTV (China Central Television) in establishing and maintaining an advanced television platform. MIH now provides services to 15 major clients, including CCTV, Macao Cable, Shanghai Cable and TVB Hong Kong. Through a range of JVs, supported by MIH's own innovative technologies, the company now also provides entertainment, interactive and e-commerce services to the Chinese market. From its Hong Kong Office, MIH is expanding operations in China with a view to consolidating their position in the Chinese market.[22] Since 1995, Landpac has been active in China, providing its Impact Compaction technology to numerous road-building projects. Landpac has engaged in construction initiatives across the length and breadth of China in the building of new roads, as well as the maintenance or repair of existing transport networks. Other important investment activities include Kumba's Qingdao port facility and its Hongye zinc refinery, Sasol's polymer investment near Shanghai and the potential $6 billion coal-to-fuel plants being finalized by Sasol in co-operation with the government of China. Other South African companies with varying levels of interest include Anglo American PLC, Anglo Gold, Anglo Platinum, Anglo Coal, BHP Billiton, Iscor, Goldfields, ABSA and Nedcor.

The China-South Africa relationship has clearly advanced significantly at both the political and economic levels. The momentum of two-way trade is certain to accelerate in the years ahead, given the evident complementarity of the Chinese and South African economies. Growing opportunities for investment in South Africa are expected to be attractive to Chinese enterprises, while the massive potential for investment in China cannot be ignored by South African businesses. South Africa needs to take advantage of China's rapidly

---

21 See African-Asian Society, 'SABMillar's Success in the Chinese Market', *African-Asian Society Newsletter,* October 2003. See also H.E. Ambassador Liu Guijin, 'Official Opening of SAITEX', Gallagher Estate, 30 September 2003.

22 Interview with Mr Wayne MacGregor, MIH Hong Kong, Hong Kong, 31 March 2006.

growing economy, and in this context there is enormous potential for South African investment in China. Moreover, China's entry into the WTO facilitates and encourages new foreign investment in China. At the same time, South African exports to China are increasing significantly, and there is clearly enormous potential for increased trade between the two countries. Co-operation between decision makers and business leaders in both countries continues to significantly enhance China-South Africa relations. There are many new business opportunities for South African companies in China following WTO entry. A China-South Africa Free Trade Agreement (FTA) would be of mutual benefit and would boost trade between the two countries. China is one of the most powerful and fastest growing economies with which South Africa can negotiate a mutually beneficial FTA.

In the early stages of debate on a China-South Africa FTA, three perspectives are discernable. The 'idealists' are hypnotized by the size and dynamism of the Chinese market and thus advance the long held view that instant riches can be quickly accumulated because of the sheer number of Chinese consumers. They also contend that a FTA with China would strengthen the China-South Africa strategic partnership and mobilize Beijing's support for Pretoria's ambitious global reform agenda. The 'pessimists' oppose a FTA, fearing that increased trade with China will lead to a major loss of employment in South Africa. The 'realistic optimists' see the opportunities in greater access to the China market, but caution against an impetuous and hurried FTA which will not advance, nor protect South Africa's interests. The varying perspectives of these broad groups are outlined below.[23]

In terms of economic interaction, the 'idealists' contend that a FTA will ensure greater access to the rapidly growing Chinese market. Initial quantitative analysis suggests a surge in Chinese exports to South Africa following a FTA, but thereafter significant Chinese market penetration for South African exporters within a five-year

---

23 The differing views were advanced by the various participants at the Institute for Global Dialogue/South African Institute of International Affairs, *SACU-China FTA Workshop*, Johannesburg, 28-9 September 2004.

period. The forecast is based on China's growing market demand and increasing consumer expenditure. However, growth of the Chinese market does not automatically mean that Chinese consumers will purchase South African products, as numerous other competitors are already well established in China.

The main argument in favour of a FTA advanced by the 'idealists' suggests that a FTA with China will further strengthen the political relationship between Pretoria and Beijing, thus facilitating increased foreign policy co-operation. In this context South Africa will, in exchange for signing a FTA, increasingly look to China for support in a wide range of areas, such as support for NEPAD and for the AU and the promotion of peace in Africa. Sino-South African co-operation and policy synchronization on the issue of advancing a new international economic order would be promoted by a FTA. Moreover, the gap between rich and poor nations, continuously widening ever faster, along with increasing tensions and conflict between North and South, requires increased South-South co-operation, such as FTAs and similar economic instruments. It is hoped that China and South Africa can work together in a joint programme to reform the existing economic structure with a view to establishing a new, just and rational economic order. Developing countries should thus strengthen solidarity, demand new global trade rules at the WTO and unite in defending legitimate rights and economic interests.

The 'pessimists' are critical of free trade agreements in general, and specifically criticize the South African government for a 'gungho' attitude towards FTAs.[24] Driven by an essentially mercantilist philosophy, the 'pessimists' contend that theoretical investigations with regard to the value of FTAs have produced inconclusive results.[25] Moreover, in FTAs between countries in unequal stages of development, the less developed country usually bears more of the adjustment costs.[26] Not only are there possibly damaging adjustment costs, empirical evidence suggests that direct net gains from FTAs

---

24 S. Makgetla, 'South Africa's Trade Talks', at *http://www.bday.co.za*.

25 See World Bank, *The World Bank Economic Review*, No. 12, 2 May 1998.

26 See B. Kite, 'Free Trade? Somebody Always Has to Pay', *Business Week*, 2 May 2001.

are not significant.[27] Besides the lack of clarity regarding the actual value of FTAs, the success of the South Africa-EU FTA remains in doubt.[28] FTAs which bring few benefits but high risks and new costs should thus be carefully considered.

Interest in China is driven by the belief that China is a huge untapped market. This is not entirely accurate as North American, European and Japanese companies have been in China for more than twenty years and are now well established in that market. South African businesses would have to compete with highly experienced, highly capitalized and established foreign companies in China, as well as with thousands of Chinese companies which produce similar products, or provide similar services. South Africa's main exports to China at present are iron ore, steel, manganese, chrome, tobacco, wool, granite, gold, copper, aluminium and motor vehicle parts. Perhaps with the exception of motor vehicle parts, it is unclear how these exports will benefit from a FTA. Economists have identified the following sectors as new opportunities: banking, telecommunications and insurance; in the telecommunications sector, Motorola is already the second biggest foreign investor in China. It is unclear how South African companies would be able to compete against giant corporations.

The 'pessimists' question South Africa's decision to grant China market economy status, which effectively prevents local manufacturers from proving that the Chinese government gives Chinese producers an unfair advantage. Consequently, proving dumping allegations or other unfair trading practices becomes extremely difficult, if not impossible. The granting of market economy status is contrary to the EU's as well as the WTO's opinion, and contradicts the Chinese government's own definition of its 'socialist, market economy'.[29] Moreover, the PRC's numerous direct and indirect subsidizing of production via support for basic services, housing and transport fa-

---

27 See A. Brunetti, *Credibility of Rules and Economic Growth*, World Bank, 1997.

28 See F. Ahwireng-Obeng, 'The EU-SA Free Trade Agreement', *South African Journal of International Affairs* 6, 2 (1999).

29 See Ding Zhitao, 'A Market Economy - Is China There Yet?', *Beijing Review*, 22 July 2004.

cilitates low wages and supports China's ability to compete unfairly on international markets. In addition, the pegging of China's currency to the US dollar at a rate far lower than market value, perhaps as much as 40 per cent undervalued, provides enormous advantages over producers in other countries, such as South Africa where the rand has been consistently overvalued for some time.

The 'realistic optimists' recognize that globalization offers huge opportunities for internationally competitive economies, but also poses very significant challenges for economic and political management. Given the high economic growth rates and highly competitive nature of the East Asian economies, especially that of China, this region of the world will become increasingly important to South Africa, as both a market and an investment destination. However, the ability to operate in the Chinese market should never be underestimated. Over 400,000 international enterprises are already well established in the Chinese marketplace, competing with many very efficient domestic producers and traders.[30]

Given that South Africa exports mainly raw materials to China and China exports mainly manufactured goods to South Africa, a comparative advantage in terms of the classical Ricardian model does not exist. Moreover, a failure to add value to South African exports to China constitutes a fundamentally flawed export strategy, given that in the long term South Africa will eventually run out of raw materials for export. For the realists, the key questions in any FTA are who gains, who loses, and what is the net gain or loss for the economy as a whole? A comprehensive well-informed strategy implemented by skilled negotiators, intended to provide solutions to all or most of the possible problems likely to be faced by South African businesses, offers the most favourable approach. The best option is to confront directly the impediments to accessing the Chinese market and build a FTA on mutual understanding along with a clear process to guarantee mutual benefit.

---

30 See G. Mills and G. Shelton, 'From Butterflies to Take-Off? Asia-Africa Trade and Investment Ties', in G. Mills and G. Shelton (eds), *Asia-Pacific and Africa - Realising Economic Potential* (Johannesburg: South African Institute of International Affairs, 2003).

Any negotiations with China on a possible FTA should be informed by a clear analysis of South Africa's specific economic objectives, both domestic and international, as well as the carefully calculated expected impact on increased two-way trade. Specific objectives would need to be formulated in consultation with business leaders, commercial organizations, trade unions and public interest groups. Those enterprises likely to be affected by a FTA (both negatively and positively) should be consulted and encouraged to participate in the deliberations. While there are unquestionably enormous potential benefits from a FTA with China, the costs, risks and benefits of any agreement need to be thoroughly investigated. Informed by a comprehensive investigation and scientific impact study, along with broad business and civil society support, a China-South Africa FTA would certainly be a major boost to economic growth and prosperity for both participating countries. The historic opportunity to expand trade with China should not be missed, but at the same time the process of economic engagement should be prudently and judiciously negotiated.

Conclusion: advancing a new global order

China's relations with South Africa have clearly advanced significantly at both the political and economic levels. The momentum of two-way trade is certain to accelerate in the years ahead, given the evident complementarity of the Chinese and South African economies. Growing opportunities for investment in South Africa are expected to be attractive to Chinese enterprises, while the massive potential for investment in China cannot be ignored by South African businesses. At the political level, the synchronization of foreign policy proposals and long-term objectives is expected to become a more urgent consideration. On the African continent, South Africa will increasingly look to China for support in the following areas: first, China's FOCAC process could be merged with NEPAD, thereby providing a major impetus to Africa's economic development; strong Chinese political and financial support for the programmes and objectives of the AU would also be a very welcome contribution to Africa's revival. Second, where the promotion of peace in Africa is concerned,

271

China's decision to deploy peacekeepers to Africa has been widely welcomed as a very positive contribution. Third, increased Chinese investment in South Africa would provide a major boost for local employment and assistance in accessing the Chinese market would be an enormous advantage for South African companies. Increasing Chinese tourism to South Africa holds the promise of significant job creation for South Africans (for this, a direct air link with China would be beneficial).

In the context of a partnership to advance a new global order, and the common foreign policy objectives identified and confirmed by Presidents Mbeki and Jiang in December 2001, South Africa looks to China for support in the following areas: first, restructuring the United Nations, in line with the Group of 77 and China's UN Programme for Reform (A/51/950) as well as the Declaration of the Twenty-Seventh Annual Ministerial Meeting of the G-77, which would bring strong permanent African and possibly South African representation to the UN Security Council.[31] Second, reform of the global trading system,[32] as outlined by the Group of 77 and China in Geneva on 22 August 2003, aimed at improving the access of developing countries to the markets of the developed, industrialized economies and strengthening programmes to eradicate poverty, underdevelopment and economic vulnerability in the world's less developed countries;[33] other objectives here include promoting a stable international financial system and co-operation to advance a free

---

31 See 'Preliminary Position of the Group of 77 and China on Actions Contained in the Report of the Secretary General: Renewing the United Nations - A Programme for Reform (A/51/950)', 29 October 1997, at *http:// www.g77.org/Docs/reform2.htm* See G. Chan, 'Is China a Responsible State? An Assessment from the Point of View of Its Multilateral Engagements', in J.Y.S. Cheng, *China's Challenges in the Twenty-First Century* (Hong Kong: City University of Hong Kong, 2003).

32 See Wang Xiaoye and Tao Zhenghua, 'WTO Competition Policy and its Influence in China', *Social Sciences in China*, XXV, 1 (2004), pp. 43-53.

33 See Declaration by the Group of 77 and China on the Fifth WTO Ministerial Conference, Cancún, Mexico, 10-14 September 2003, *Group of 77 & China*, Geneva, 22 August 2003. See also China (Hainan) Institute of Reform and Development, *China's Accession to the WTO and Infrastructure Reform* (Beijing: Foreign Language Press, 2002).

but fair global trading system (market access). Third, a set of issues concerning enhanced South-South cooperation in the spirit of the 1955 Bandung Conference's programme for African-Asian solidarity, and collaboration to address global injustice, discrimination and the marginalization of developing countries, as outlined in the New Africa-Asia Strategic Partnership.[34] This also relates to advancing of multilateralism through the UN and other fora to address global security issues, and co-operation on key international issues, such as the Middle East peace process, Iraq, Iran and Korea with a view to advancing global peace and stability. Finally, a number of development related objectives: advancing the regeneration of Africa (investment, financing and infrastructure), countering the worst effects of globalization,[35] addressing poverty and underdevelopment (including debt cancellation), sharing of information on economic development and sustainable development, and cooperation to reverse the imbalances of traditional North-South interaction.

Building on the solid foundation of a shared global political vision and accelerating economic interaction, China and South Africa are in the process of building a new form of South-South co-operation which could be very effective in advancing African interests and reforming the existing global political and economic order. The bonding of China and South Africa in a common goal to eliminate the iniquities of the existing outdated economic and political system of global governance provides hope and inspiration to developing countries. The evolving China-African relationship, at the multilateral level via the FOCAC process and at the bilateral level through (for example) a formally constituted Bi-National Commission, serves as a model for South-South co-operation and provides a new framework for effective participation in the North-South debate. Continued co-operation and collaboration based on the past augurs well for a continued warm friendship and a long-term strategic partnership between China and Africa.

---

34 See *Marrakesh Declaration on South-South Co-operation*, 15 January 2004, United Nations, General Assembly, A/58/683, 19 January 2004.

35 The 2006 China-South Africa textile agreement serves as a good example in this context.

14

FROM NON-INTERFERENCE TO CONSTRUCTIVE ENGAGEMENT? CHINA'S EVOLVING RELATIONS WITH SUDAN

Daniel Large[1]

The state visit of the Chinese President to Khartoum in February 2007 confirmed Sudan as China's most controversial 'all-weather friend' in Africa. A popular talking point in Khartoum before his visit had been why China's top leaders had not visited Sudan during its 'Year of Africa' in 2006. CNPC-sponsored signs in Khartoum proclaimed 'the friendship between the peoples of Sudan and China' to be 'evergreen', but after what Chinese sources described as 'frank' discussions between President Hu and the Sudanese President Bashir, indications of differences over the issue of allowing a UN-African Union peacekeeping mission into Darfur emerged. As China's Ambassador to the UN, Wang Guangya, commented shortly afterwards: 'Usually China doesn't send messages, but this time they did...It was a clear strong message that the proposal from Kofi Annan [to allow

---

1 Thanks to Chris Alden and Ricardo Soares de Oliveira and particularly to Jago Salmon and John Ryle for comments on a previous version of this chapter.

275

a UN-African Union peacekeeping mission in Darfur] is a good one and Sudan has to accept it.' While China 'never twists arms', Sudan 'got the message'.[2]

This chapter provides an overview of relations between China and Sudan. It considers how China was able to successfully enter and develop its relations with Sudan and how the basis of its success would produce unexpected challenges for Beijing. It argues that China's principle of non-interference has been progressively contradicted through the thickening of its relations with Sudan since the early 1990s; while China has been seeking to maintain this principle, it has been further stretched by Beijing's efforts to pursue a policy of more involved 'constructive' engagement. After considering the comparatively recent history of more substantive Chinese relations with Sudan, what follows outlines how relations developed after 1989 and the factors that enabled Chinese expansion within Sudan during the 1990s. It goes on to trace the Chinese role in the development of Sudan's oil export sector, a crucial contribution that established the foundation for a broader and deeper Chinese economic role in Sudan. The nature of political and economic relations after the Comprehensive Peace Agreement of January 2005 is then surveyed, before key trends in Beijing's evolving diplomacy over the ongoing conflict in Darfur and with Southern Sudan are considered.

Background

The principle of non-interference in internal politics provides an important reason for the Chinese government's ability to deal with successive governments in Khartoum after 1959, when Sudan became the fourth country to extend diplomatic recognition to China in Africa.[3] Even if this principle and China's actions in Sudan have not always been congruent,[4] China has maintained generally good

---

2   'China told Sudan to adopt UN's Darfur plan – envoy', *Bloomberg*. 7 February 2007.

3   Sudan also supported the PRC's entry into the UN (which President Abboud, for instance, advocated before the UN General Assembly in 1961).

4   This was illustrated in Beijing's political and military support for President Nimairi's suppression of the Sudan Communist Party in 1971, which

relations with independent Sudan's alternating periods of brief parliamentary and longer military government. Beijing supported the Sudanese government during the civil war that formally ended in 1972, during the war in Southern Sudan after 1983 and more recently amidst conflict in the western region of Darfur. By 1989, China already had some three decades of trade, aid, cultural, political and military links with Sudan.

While appreciating historical ties that continue to play out in the present, China's previous role in Sudan should not be overstated. As one of a number of foreign partners. Beijing was not particularly significant in Sudan's external relations or internal politics until relations developed after 1989. The notion of China as a 'new actor' in Sudan is thus also apt.[5] Although China and Sudan share a prominent symbolic historical connection in the form of 'Chinese' Gordon,[6] it could also be said that it was the lack of serious, widely embedded Chinese engagement in Sudan that contributed to enduring good relations until recently. China has moved from the margins to a more central position in Sudanese affairs, and in this process the foundations and political consequences of relations have importantly changed. The difference in relations 'before and after oil'[7] has been considerable. Relations that developed with oil mark a continuing phase of involvement that departs in important ways from the nature

contrasted to the Soviet response, and laid the foundations for a period of strong relations in the 1970s.

5 Francis M. Deng, *War of Visions: Conflict of Identities in the Sudan* (Washington, DC: The Brookings Institution, 1995), p. 383.

6 The legendary reputation of Gordon began in China where, from 1863, he led the 'Ever Victorious Army' against the Taiping rebels and was decorated by the Qing Dynasty. It was confirmed, after a career in Sudan where he became Governor General, through his death in Khartoum in 1885 at the hands of rebel Mahdist forces. The political symbolism of Gordon was ideologically most potent in the post-colonial period (beginning with Zhou Enlai's visit to Khartoum in 1964 when much was made of how Sudan had 'finally punished' Gordon), but it has persisted. The site of his death, and the tomb of the Mahdi, have been visited by different generations of Chinese and his name is regularly invoked in public encounters, often to demonstrate shared experience of colonial oppression and successful Sudanese resistance.

7 See Ali Abdalla Ali, *The Sudanese-Chinese Relations Before and After Oil* (Khartoum: Sudan Currency Printing Press, 2006).

of past links. In this light, it is the manner and means through which ties have expanded and deepened that has progressively contradicted the formally-declared principle of non-interference.

1989 and after

The Chinese government initially appeared cautious about the National Islamic Front (NIF) government that took power through a military coup on 30 June 1989. This was seen during the visit of its leader, Umar Hassan al-Bashir, to Beijing in November 1990.[8] While China expressed formal support for Sudan, relations only resumed through Iranian-funded Chinese arms supplies in 1991. Business activity was also promoted, including a Chinese trade fair in Khartoum in 1993, but until the advent of oil exports in late 1999, Sudan's trade with China was proportionally small.[9] China's 'energy cooperation' (*nengyuan hezuo*) with Sudan spearheaded an expansion of ties. In 1994 the Government of Sudan (GoS) expressed interest in Chinese involvement in oil, which led to CNPC conducting a preliminary survey.[10] A further visit to Beijing by President Bashir in September 1995 resulted in a deal providing a reduced rate Chinese loan. This was followed in December by an agreement between Exim Bank and the Bank of Sudan to finance oil development.[11] CNPC began operations in Block 6 (see map p.283) and, in conjunction with other companies, notably Petronas, subsequently expanded exploration and other work (see next section).

---

8 Bashir praised Chinese cooperative projects 'in an apparent bid to secure greater Chinese economic aid.' Hinting at the war, the new Chinese President Jiang Zemin told him: 'Without political stability and unity, it is impossible to push forward the economy.' Further, China's aid to Sudan was 'insignificant', and 'intended only to show China's sympathy.' Lillian Craig Harris, *China Considers the Middle East* (London: I.B. Tauris, 1993), p. 211.

9 In 1994, for example, China took a 6.1 per cent share of Sudan's exports and 3.2 per cent share of Sudan's total imports (Bank of Sudan Foreign Trade Statistical Digests).

10 Linda Jakobson and Zha Daojing, 'China and the Worldwide Search for Oil Security', *Asia-Pacific Review*, 13, 2 (2006), p. 66.

11 Yun Zongguo, '*Sudan shiyou kaifa xiangmu qianjing guangkuo*', ['Prospect for Sudan oil development project is broad'], *Guoji jingji hezuo* [International Economic Cooperation], 5 (1997), pp. 22-3.

China's economic expansion within Sudan during the 1990s was assisted by a related combination of armed conflict and the nature of Sudanese politics after June 1989. The hardline NIF regime promoted a revolutionary Islamist project within and outside Sudan.[12] The Islamist leader Hassan al-Turabi's support for Saddam Hussein in August 1990 resulted in a political backlash in the region and beyond, and triggered a marked reduction in international aid. The attempted assassination of the Egyptian President in June 1995 in Addis Ababa by a militant group active in Sudan and linked to Sudanese security elements further contributed to Sudan's regional isolation in the Middle East, reinforcing the NIF's need to turn elsewhere for external support. Sudan was already associated with supporting terrorism, the American State Department having designated Sudan a state sponsor of terrorism on 12 August 1993, but in 1996 it became the object of UN Security Council sanctions. US sanctions in 1997 were followed by an American missile attack on a pharmaceutical factory in Khartoum in 1998. The NIF had dire relations with the IMF, which had suspended Sudan for non-payment of arrears in 1986. Facing a crisis of state finance, the NIF adopted a policy of economic 'self-sufficiency' and had restricted options to develop the oil sector as its war against the Sudan People's Liberation Movement/Army (SPLM/A) continued amid this external pressure. President Bashir had said Sudan would follow the example of China in independent development, but his turn to China was made in a moment of necessity and was accompanied by debate within the GoS about the merits of seeking Chinese assistance (and of rapprochement with the US). What counted most was the fact that China provided a significant, politically dependable option, and 'instead of waiting' Sudan 'decided to go East'.[13] Relations developed as a genuine case of 'mutual benefit' for the Sudanese and Chinese governments, but have not been marked by any apparent thick solidarity. However, Beijing successfully managed to expand investment in Sudan amidst

---

12 See Alex de Waal and A.H. Abdel Salam, 'Islamism, State Power and *Jihad* in Sudan', in Alex de Waal (ed.), *Islamism and its Enemies in the Horn of Africa* (London: C. Hurst & Co., 2004), pp. 71-113.

13 Ali, *Sudanese-Chinese Relations*, p. 6.

internal political struggle in the NIF through its relations with President Bashir, who prevailed against his Islamist opponents in 1999, and other key interlocutors, especially Dr Awad Ahmed al-Jaz, the long-serving Energy Minister.

Sudan's internal instability, its economic potential and the circumstances of its foreign relations produced an attractive investment prospect for China. Sudan was viewed as a friendly, resource rich state with a market deemed to have high, untapped potential due, in part, to the lack of business competition.[14] Its political isolation and vast natural resources created an 'unprecedented opportunity' even if, as today, Sudan's complex politics and difficult economic conditions presented a mixture of opportunities and challenges, risks and benefits to Chinese businesses.[15] CNPC's engagement in Sudan spanned an important phase in the restructuring and global expansion of the Chinese oil sector. Sudan served as a key overseas arena for technical development, and CNPC's success in Sudan in 1999 contributed to the State Council's endorsement of CNPC's vigorous strategy of oil asset shopping.[16] Sudan assumed a position as China's leading energy investment operation in Africa and was briefly its leading African oil supplier; in 2002 Sudan contributed 9 per cent of China's oil imports, or 40 per cent of its African oil imports as a whole.[17] Sudan was also seen as the bridgehead into the regional economy and the African oil market.

Oil development: the Chinese contribution

On 30 August 1999 the first cargo of Nile Blend crude was shipped from Port Bashair, south of Port Sudan, and Northern Sudan finally became an oil exporter just over two decades after oil was discovered.

---

14 Liu Anpeng, '*Zhongguo gongren zou jin Sudan*' ['Chinese workers enter Sudan'], *Shijie Zhishi* [*World Knowledge*], 9 (2004), pp. 42-43.

15 'Tang Nailong, '*Sudan gongcheng chengbao shichang fenxi*' [A market analysis of project contracts in Sudan] *Guoji jingji hezuo* [International Economic Cooperation] 11 (1997), pp. 58-59.

16 See Jin Zhang, *Catch-up and Competitiveness in China: the Case of Large Firms in the Oil Industry* (London: RoutledgeCurzon, 2004).

17 Calculated from data in *China Commerce Yearbook, Almanac of China's Foreign Economic Relations and Trade*.

This was achieved amidst armed conflict in Sudan, through a concerted effort by different oil operators supported at all levels by the GoS. The Chinese oil engagement was part of longstanding efforts to create an oil industry in Sudan.[18] Before CNPC entered decisively during the 1990s, this had rendered oil central to politics and conflict in Sudan and had been one factor contributing to the breakdown of the 1972 peace accord. The CNPC-spearheaded phase of oil development continued but intensified the role of oil in the North-South (not to mention South-South) conflict. Like America (through Chevron) or France (through Total) before, Chinese, Malaysian and later Indian and other oil companies became 'far from disinterested observers' in Sudan's wars.[19]

China has different oil concessions in Sudan today (see map below). Its first important operation was the 40 per cent stake CNPC acquired in the Greater Nile Petroleum Operating Company (GNPOC), a consortium that signed an agreement to develop three blocks (1, 2 and 4) in Southern Sudan at the beginning of March 1997. At this point oil production was constrained by the lack of infrastructure. A concentrated effort to construct the apparatus of a functioning oil export industry followed, a period when select Chinese exports to Sudan correlate with demand from Chinese companies active in Sudan.[20] GNPOC constructed a 1,506 km buried pipeline to connect oil production with the international market through a CNPC subsidiary, the China Petroleum Engineering and

---

18 For accounts of Sudan's oil sector, see Peter Verney, 'Raising the Stakes: Oil and Conflict in Sudan' Sudan Update, (2000); Human Rights Watch, *Sudan, Oil and Human Rights* (New York: Human Rights Watch, 2003); 'Soil and Oil: Dirty Business in Sudan' (Coalition for International Justice, 2006); Luke Patey, *'A Complex Reality: The Strategic Behaviour of Multinational Oil Corporations and the New Wars in Sudan'* (DIIS Report, 2006).

19 Abel Alier, *Southern Sudan: Too Many Agreements Dishonoured* (Reading: Ithaca Press, [1990] 2003), p. 263.

20 This was illustrated, for example, between early 1997 and August 1999, when China's export statistics to Sudan reveal dramatic increases, often from low or non-existent bases, in key commodities such as cement (which increased by 2,832 per cent between 1998 and 1999, from 14 to 39,675 MT). See *China Commerce Yearbook, Almanac of China's Foreign Economic Relations and Trade* (various).

Construction Corp, which also built the US$215 million oil terminal in Port Sudan. Completed in time for the tenth anniversary of the NIF's coup on 30 June 1999, CNPC's first overseas refinery was built as a joint venture with the Ministry of Energy. It became operational in February 2000, rendering Sudan self-sufficient in oil for the first time. CNPC took a 41 per cent stake in Sudan's second major oil consortium, the Petrodar Operating Company, with Sinopec taking 6 per cent. This was to develop blocks 3 and 7 in northern Upper Nile from 2000. Oil infrastructure was developed in a similar fashion through field production facilities, airfields, all-weather roads, feeder-pipes and a pipeline to Port Sudan, which became operational in April 2006.

Oil development during this period was militarized and closely interconnected with armed conflict in Southern Sudan. Oil facilities were used for military purposes. The creation of infrastructure such as all-weather roads, which became military corridors, eroded the established seasonal pattern of conflict that had previously been characterized by dry-season government offensives. The leader of the SPLA, John Garang, announced in August 1999 that the new pipeline, oilfields and oil company workers were regarded as legitimate targets. The kidnapping of two Chinese oil workers on 13 March 2004, who were later released after ICRC mediation, and the killing of two other workers soon afterwards, briefly cast a shadow over China's involvement in Sudan. Other opposition groups also targeted oil facilities for sabotage.[21]

Exacerbating civilian suffering, oil companies became 'partners with the state in human destruction'.[22] The military strategy of the Sudan Armed Forces (SAF) against the SPLA in Western Upper Nile, for example, relied on aerial bombing raids and support for proxy militia attacks on Nuer and Dinka settlements and cattle camps. These were viewed by the GoS 'as a security risk, potential

---

21 In January 2000 the GOS was reportedly losing around US$1m in revenue every two hours from oil spilling from the bomb-damaged GNPOC pipeline. 'Sudanese Pipeline Sabotage Costs Millions', *Hart's Africa Oil and Gas*, 3, 2 (2000), p. 3.

22 Jok Madut Jok, *Sudan: Race, Religion and Violence* (Oxford: Oneworld, 2007), p. 198.

Map of oil concessions in Sudan

supporters of rebel movements, to be forcibly moved off the land that they inhabit to facilitate oil development.'[23] Militia attacks drove the inhabitants away into Southern Sudan, into government garrison towns, or to the government-controlled north of Sudan, especially Khartoum. For many Southern Sudanese, Chinese investment and activity represented direct support for the GoS and its military objectives. This view was strengthened as a result of increased oil revenues, a high percentage of which went into procuring weapons and developing an indigenous arms manufacturing capability with Chinese technical and supervisory assistance.[24]

The Chinese government continues to be closely associated with the NIF and is widely seen to have consolidated the political and military foundations of its power. Beijing's 'blind-eye'[25] support for the NIF has been a wellspring of grievances in many quarters. This stems from the marked incongruence between China's principle of non-interference and the way this played out in practice in Sudan since the mid-1990s. What China had promoted as a principle of intention did not materialize as non-interference in effect. Chinese investment and its role within Sudan contributed importantly toward a political outcome, sustaining the rule of the NIF. In this process, the NIF's transition from a revolutionary Islamist project to a more pragmatic, self-interested government was crucial and was bolstered by a substantially expanded oil revenue resource base, which enabled the GoS to escape from its financial crisis.

China–Sudan relations after the CPA

The Comprehensive Peace Agreement (CPA) of 9 January 2005 between the GoS and the SPLM/A ushered in a period of formal peace between Northern and Southern Sudan, as conflict in Darfur wors-

---

23 Georgette Gagnon and John Ryle, 'Report of an Investigation into Oil Development, Conflict and Displacement in Western Upper Nile, Sudan', (October 2001), p. 48.

24 For more detail, see 'Issue Brief: Arms, Oil, and Darfur: Evolving China-Sudan Relations', *Small Arms Survey Issue Brief* 7, 2007.

25 Mahgoub El-Tigani, 'China should revise policies on Sudan', *Sudan Tribune*, 22 April 2006.

ened. While Beijing contributed military and police personnel to the UN Mission in Sudan established to support the CPA, it mostly operated bilateral relations with Sudan.[26] Political relations between the Chinese government and Sudan's ruling National Congress Party (NCP), which had formally replaced the NIF, continued to be characterized by high-level political and corporate ties. An integral aspect of political relations has been military links, which were stepped up in 2002. The NCP has an official, though largely symbolic, cooperative agreement with the Chinese Communist Party.

Economic relations expanded after the CPA. Sudan's oil-fuelled economic boom, centred on Khartoum, saw real GDP grow by 11.8 per cent in 2006 according to the IMF. China became northern Sudan's most important trade partner and has been at the forefront of a reorientation of Sudanese trade that has seen an enhanced Asian and Middle Eastern role as Western trade and investment have dwindled under the impact of sanctions. China is the most important economic partner for Sudan by far, and operates a rare trade deficit. China dominates a strong Asian dynamic to Sudanese trade. As a general category used by the Bank of Sudan, Asia accounted for 43.6 per cent of total imports and 86 per cent of total exports in 2006. China accounted for 20.8 per cent of total imports (or US$1,679.4 million) and 75 per cent (US$4,243.9 million) of total exports.[27]

The proportion of petroleum in Sudan's exports to China has been over 98 per cent since 2000, when bilateral trade increased sharply on the back of oil production. Sudan's importance as an oil supplier to China has declined since the high water mark of 2001-2. It supplied 4.7 per cent of China's oil in 2004 (or 15.39 per cent of China's total African oil imports).[28] In 2006 Japan appeared to be the single largest customer for Sudanese crude[29], but Sudan accounted

---

26 The first deployment of 430 troops became operational in May 2006. The second group of 435 Chinese peacekeepers was dispatched to Sudan in January 2007.

27 Bank of Sudan Annual Report 2006. Other trade statistics from China and the IMF give lower figures, however.

28 Calculated from data in *China Commerce Yearbook, Almanac of China's Foreign Economic Relations and Trade.*

29 Bank of Sudan statistics put China as the top customer. However, other

for 6 per cent of China's crude imports in 2007. Oil exploration increased after the CPA, especially in Unity State and Upper Nile, and the oil sector began to generate considerable revenue. There have been negligible improvements for civilians in oil-producing regions, however, both in terms of services and of action to address concerns over the environmental impact of oil development.

Sudan has been comparatively important in Beijing's economic engagement with Africa. It was China's third largest trade partner after South Africa and Angola in 2004 and 2005, with total bilateral trade running at $2.52bn and $3.91bn respectively.[30] It was the top recipient of Chinese net non-financial overseas direct investment in Africa until the end of 2005 (22 per cent), and ranked as the ninth largest recipient ($352m) of China's total outward FDI by 2005.[31] Northern Sudan is also a growing market for Chinese exports. According to the Bank of Sudan, the share of Sudan's overall imports from China rose from 8 per cent in 2002 to 20.8 per cent in 2006. The amount of manufactured goods (particularly garments and textiles, electronic goods, vehicles and steel products) that China exports to Sudan has been increasing in recent years.[32] This reflects northern Sudan's status as a relatively more developed market for Chinese goods in Africa, including white goods produced by companies like

---

statistics, including those from the US Energy Information Administration, tell a different story. In 2006 total Chinese imports from Sudan were 4.8 MT or half or CNPC's total share (9.3 MT) in Sudan, meaning that nearly half of CNPC's share was directed elsewhere. Japan took 6.3 MT in 2006, which made it Sudan's biggest single customer. See Arthur Kroeber and G.A. Donovan, 'Sudan Oil: Where Does it Go?', *China Economic Quarterly*, 11, 2 (2007), p. 18.

30 According to MOFCOM statistics. Part of Sudan's importance can also be seen in the Chinese statistical measure of 'economic cooperation' (which takes in contracted projects, labour and 'design consultation') for which total turnover with Sudan stood at some $1.34bn in 2005. According to MOFCOM, Sudan's share of the total level of 'economic cooperation' as a percentage of China's African total stood at 17-21 per cent between 2001 and 2005.

31 In 2004 Sudan received $146.7m, or a 46 per cent share of China's overseas direct investment to Africa. See *China Statistical Yearbook 2006*, p. 759.

32 See *China Commerce Yearbook, Almanac of Foreign Economic Relations & Trade* (various).

Haier, which exhibited at Khartoum's International Trade Fair in January 2007 and competes with Japanese, Korean and Indian companies in Sudan.

Although Chinese investment has been heavily concentrated in oil and energy, Chinese business has been diversifying beyond oil. Promising post-war business opportunities for Chinese companies had been identified even before the CPA,[33] especially given the sanctions restricting Western investment. There were more than 124 officially registered Chinese companies in 2005, mostly involved in construction, oil, trade, and services.[34] The Chinese construction sector in northern Sudan has expanded through established large companies and firms established by Chinese entrepreneurs in Sudan. Transport infrastructure[35] and energy are two areas where Chinese companies have been active. The Harbin Power Plant Engineering Company completed the second phase of the el-Gaili Power Plant in 2007. Two Chinese companies are leading construction of the approximately $1.9bn Meroe dam funded by Exim and Middle East investors.[36] Agriculture is another area of growing activity and official cooperation. Chinese enterprises have worked on agricultural development cooperation projects. The increase in small businesses in Khartoum and beyond, including restaurants, shops and other service sector businesses, testifies to a more recent wave of smaller entrepreneurial Chinese business interest and connects to the emerging Chinese social presence in northern Sudan.[37] In Southern Sudan,

---

33 Jing Sangchu, *'Dan zhan hou touzi he chengbao shichang'* ['Sudan's postwar investment and contract project market'], *Guoji jingji hezuo* [International Economic Cooperation], 4 (2004), pp. 43-5.

34 Ali , *Sudanese-Chinese Relations*, p. 89.

35 Featuring construction of roads and bridges, two Chinese companies won a US$1.154 billion contract to build a 792km railway connecting Port Sudan and Khartoum in February 2007.

36 This project, with substantial investment from the Middle East and the involvement of German and French partners, has been controversial. See Ali Askouri, 'China's Investment in Sudan: Displacing Villages and Destroying Communities', in Firoze Manji and Stephen Marks (eds), *African Perspectives on China in Africa* (Fahamu, 2007). Downstream from Meroe, at the Third Cataract, there is also Chinese involvement in the Kajbar dam.

37 It is reflected in a popular street expression in Khartoum that 'under every

Chinese business outside the oil sector is relatively new and limited. Regional trade flows connecting Juba with the DRC, Uganda and Kenya have also meant other access routes for Chinese products being sold in Juba. A small number of Chinese businesses entered Juba after the CPA via Kenyan and Ugandan brokers in the form of construction joint ventures and a hotel.[38]

Going global: China and Darfur

Darfur became a far more consequential foreign policy issue for the Chinese government than Southern Sudan ever was. It has influenced wider perceptions of China within Sudan, in Africa and around the world. Although commonly reduced to material, pragmatic economic interests, Chinese diplomacy has also reflected, as Shichor has argued, 'fundamental and ideological concerns'.[39] There was undoubtedly concern about creating a high-profile precedent running at odds with the commitment to sovereignty that has formed a key pillar of its African engagement. Investment protection connected to geopolitical dynamics also played a role. The Chinese government appears to have prized political stability in Sudan and been distrustful of the objectives of proposed intervention in Darfur. Amid persistent suspicion of the US's non-humanitarian motives, there were also questions about why further sanctions were being recommended once China had 'succeeded' in Sudan.

China's political involvement has changed as part of an evolving diplomatic strategy. Beijing initially underestimated the severity of the conflict and the political risk.[40] Firm insistence on the sovereignty and territorial integrity of Sudan and consistent UN Security Council abstentions from 2004 were accompanied by high-level meetings

---

stone you will find a Chinese' (to which is also added 'and a UN worker').

38 For example, the Nile Construction Company entered into a joint venture with the Chinese company Golden Nest in October 2006 to work on construction projects and another Chinese company, COVEC, won contracts to renovate ministers' quarters and the hospital.

39 Yitzhak Shichor, 'China's Darfur Policy', *China Brief*, 7, 7 (2007).

40 Linda Jakobson, 'The Burden of "Non-interference"', *China Economic Quarterly*, 11, 2 (2007) p. 16

with the NCP and aid donations.[41] Amidst an international arms embargo, there were arms supplies alongside military cooperation and training programmes between the SAF and the PLA. Chinese companies such as Norinco were among those supplying light weapons and other military hardware used in Darfur and Chad.[42]

Chinese diplomacy became more engaged over the course of 2006. Beijing welcomed and supported the Darfur Peace Agreement of May 2006. More involved diplomacy was first evident in behind-the-scenes encounters, as when President Bashir attended the Forum on China-Africa Cooperation. Most notably, this was seen later in November 2006 when the Chinese Ambassador to the UN helped to broker a compromise deal in Addis Ababa on the 'Annan plan' calling for an expanded UN peacekeeping role in Darfur.[43] This occurred amid ongoing discussion within the Chinese government about its Sudan policy.[44] There were different pressures at work. Exposure to criticism over Darfur meant sustained scrutiny and condemnation. Chinese investment in Sudan was threatened not merely by possible new sanctions but also by conflict in which the close association between China and the key architects of the Sudanese government's brutal counter-insurgency campaign in Darfur rendered China an enemy of the main Darfurian rebel groups. Chad's switch away from

---

41 Including US$610,000 worth of humanitarian aid to Darfur pledged in August 2004 after a trip to Khartoum by the Assistant Foreign Minister, Lu Guozeng, and donations to the African Union Mission in Sudan.

42 The UN Panel of Experts established under UN Security Council Resolution 1591 suggested 'that most ammunition currently used by parties to the conflict in Darfur is manufactured either in the Sudan or in China.' Report of the Panel of Experts established pursuant to paragraph 3 of resolution 1591 (2005) concerning the Sudan (30 January 2006), para. 125, p. 37. Opheera McDoom, 'Chinese arms in Darfur: the twisted trail of weapons', *Reuters* 19 June 2006.

43 Described by the American envoy on Sudan, Andrew Natsios, as 'a vital and constructive role' in evidence to the US Senate Foreign Relations Committee 11 April 2007.

44 Policy discussions in China on appropriate action broadly divided, it appears, between those wanting to resist US pressure and those who regarded Sudan as not worth damage to China's international standing, sometimes suggesting that China had over-invested in Sudan, had poor returns, and had lost face internationally to the extent that it was regarded as a 'reckless country'.

relations with Taiwan in August 2006 presented China with a further interest in regional stability, whilst also drawing it further into conflict between Khartoum and N'djamena.

The Chinese government went to some lengths to emphasize its 'responsible' role over Darfur before and after President Hu Jintao's February 2007 state visit to Sudan. The change of diplomatic positioning and more proactive public engagement were discernible before the 'genocide Olympics' campaign led by a coalition of activist groups in the US, which aimed to make Sudan rebound on China and compel Beijing to exert influence in Sudan. By invoking the spectre of an Olympics boycott, this appears to have briefly catalyzed Beijing's response. However, President Hu's visit illustrated the combination of flexible diplomacy in addressing international concerns on the one hand and continued practical support for President Bashir and the NCP-led government of national unity on the other. China made its most critical public comments on Darfur. President Hu even proposed his own 'four-point plan' to resolve the conflict, but at the same time offered further support to President Bashir through debt cancellation, aid, economic and military cooperation. Beijing had insisted on the need for Khartoum's consent to admitting a UN force into Darfur. It abstained on Resolution 1706 (31 August 2006), which authorised a UN peacekeeping force in Darfur, for this reason, but signalled acceptance of a UN force and subsequently offered to provide troops for the UN mission. The notable change was Beijing's efforts to persuade President Bashir to accept the UN force, followed by calls to recognize China's 'constructive' contribution and its 'influence' in securing the passing of Resolution 1769 on 31 July 2007.

The widespread suggestion of a qualitative shift in Beijing's diplomatic strategy was misleading. There was certainly a more proactive approach. The visit of Assistant Foreign Minister and special envoy Zhai Jun to Darfur in April 2007 and the appointment of a new special envoy, Liu Guijin, testified to China's efforts to contribute and redress the damage to its image, as well as continuing to promote its own agenda through more active diplomatic participation and media relations. However, this was accompanied by continuity in China's opposition, for example, to sanctions. A broadly dual-track strategy appeared to operate: Beijing speaking to and wanting to be seen to align with American and EU constituencies, while affirming and renewing practical support for the NCP. Set alongside Beijing's claims of, and attempts to gain credit for, its 'responsible' actions, then, were the continuation of political and strengthening of economic relations between China and Sudan.[45] In this process, Khartoum continued its efforts to attract Chinese business (as illustrated, for example, in September 2006 when a ministerial delegation led by Dr Al-Jaz attended the 10th China International Fair for Investment and Trade in Xiamen).

The Chinese government was attempting the difficult task of reconciling 'non-interference' with the facts of its considerable involvement and economic importance in Sudan and a desire to receive credit for exerting constructive 'influence'. The nature of conflict in Darfur was also changing. Despite Beijing's new diplomacy, its close association with Khartoum rendered it vulnerable. It was increasingly likely that the rebel attack in November 2006 on Block 6 would be replicated and Chinese assets targeted as the most high-profile foreign oil operator in Sudan and one closely associated with the NCP. To face this danger, China's reliance on the Sudanese government to protect facilities increased but the nature of its diplomacy also demonstrated a willingness for flexible engagement within Sudan beyond its established relations with the North.

Towards 2011: China's evolving relations with Southern Sudan

The new Government of Southern Sudan (GOSS) established by the CPA and largely under SPLM control in Juba presented new challenges for Beijing. It had not dealt directly with the SPLM before and had been the principal backer of its wartime enemy. The SPLM's post-war China policy was to turn 'enemies into friends'[46] and it was

---

45 In the first quarter of 2007, for example, new engineering contracts for Chinese companies were signed worth $1.4bn. Wang Wei, 'Wider Cooperation and Deeper Friendship - Feeling China-Africa Pragmatic Cooperation in Sudan', *Renmin Ribao* [People's Daily] BBC, 16 July 2007.

46 Pagan Amum, SPLM General Secretary, conversation in Juba,

thus in principle open to dealing with Beijing as one of a number of potential investors. The CPA enabled contact between the Chinese government and SPLM members of Sudan's government of national unity. It also facilitated the first notable connection between the SPLM and China, a friendly visit by a high-ranking SPLM delegation to Beijing in March 2005 led by Salva Kiir Mayardit, who became President of Southern Sudan and First-Vice President of Sudan in August 2005 following the death of John Garang.

The possibility of Southern secession in 2011 contained in the CPA, and the location of the main oil fields in Southern Sudan, were amongst the factors behind the apparent growing recognition by Beijing that it would need to respond to the new political reality in Juba in a manner that departed from its past practice of strict bilateral relations with the central government.[47] Salva Kiir met President Hu Jintao in Khartoum in February 2007 and welcomed Chinese investment in Southern Sudan. Beijing subsequently offered a loan to the GOSS. In July 2007 Salva Kiir made another visit to China and was reported to have reassured the government that China's oil investments were secure.[48] A Chinese government delegation made an official visit to Juba in late August 2007. A new Chinese aid package was subsequently announced, which targeted hydro-electric projects and infrastructure construction. These developments cumulatively suggested a momentum toward the 'normalization' of political ties indicative of Beijing's need to adapt to the changing nature of politics in Sudan. However, this process has involved political elites to date and has given rise to questions about why the SPLM is engaging with Beijing. Opposition and critical popular attitudes towards China in Southern Sudan reflect the legacy of China's support for the GoS during the war. At times these are articulated in racial terms as seen, for example, in critical Southern reaction to the November

---

December 2005.

47 Peter Adwok Nyaba, 'An Appraisal of Contemporary China – Sudan Relations and its Future Trajectory in the Context of Afro-Chinese Relations', paper present to the Centre for Advanced Studies of African Societies conference on 'Afro-Chinese Relations', 23-24 November 2005.

48 The CPA itself also stipulates that oil contracts 'shall not be subject to re-negotiation'.

2006 Sino-Arab Friendship conference in Khartoum, which produced renewed complaints about China's continued preference for Northern 'Arab' Sudanese.

Conclusion

Together with the oil-fuelled prosperity of state elites, Sudan-China relations today have also involved growing disenchantment with, and resistance to, the impact of China's business in Sudan. Views accentuating the positive economic impact of China are articulated in business quarters, but there are also mounting grievances against Chinese employment and business practices, including product dumping. Such views, and other criticisms, contrast with the more positive memories of China's role in Sudan during the 1970s.

As a foreign relations issue in Africa and more generally, Sudan was a high profile case that brought into question both China's efforts to respond to the American challenge of being a 'responsible' rising power in the international arena and its own attempts under Hu Jintao to promote a more 'harmonious' international society. The Chinese government pursued a difficult balancing act of attempting to respond to different constituencies. It has publicly supported the political process of negotiations on Darfur and the African Union-UN mission, while attempting not to be seen as responding to US pressure and reassuring the government of Sudan (and the NCP in particular) of China's continuing support. Beijing was thus in the awkward position of appearing to want to be seen as a progressive force on Darfur while endeavouring to maintain a distinctive principled difference, conscious of the ramifications its diplomacy might have for its wider African engagement, as well as its own national interests.

This chapter has reviewed a rich subject on which much more remains to be researched. After 1989 China's engagement in Sudan progressed from that of a comparatively insignificant economic partner to that of key patron. China's role in Sudan's oil sector initiated a new phase of relations that approximate the crossing of boundaries ('*chuangxin kuayue*') called for by the four-character slogan under the CNPC sign on the Sudan Hotel in Khartoum. Sudan is an important and, from China's perspective, successful case of directed investment:

in 'Chinese oil investments overseas, CNPC's Sudan operation represents the single most outstanding success'.[49] China's comparative success in Sudan was driven through by a concerted state-backed effort and, like that of Malaysia and India, benefited from the unintended consequences of Western foreign policy. This success has meant a highly mixed impact in Sudan. The deepening Chinese role has inevitably entailed political outcomes as part of an involvement that has incrementally undermined from within the principle of non-interference as experienced by Sudanese. The nature of the Chinese government's relations with the NIF/NCP has also meant that non-interference has increasingly been conveyed as rhetoric cloaking the defence of China's established interests in Sudan and support for a government with a particularly violent record. Within northern Sudan, oil development contributed to a transformation within the politics of the NIF from its former revolutionary Islamist interest in social change to a more self-interested politics in which the changing extractive resource base of the government was crucial. For China, however, the principle of non-interference remained even as it continued to attempt a more engaged role in Darfur, Southern Sudan and the uncertain future of Sudan.

---

49 Jakobson and Zha, 'China and the Worldwide Search for Oil Security', p. 67.

15

CHINA IN ANGOLA: JUST A PASSION FOR OIL?

Manuel Ennes Ferreira

On account of its scale and political relevance, China's involvement in Angola ranks amongst its most visible in contemporary Africa. However, the assumption shared by most analysts in explaining Chinese motives as exclusively concerned with access to natural resources is simplistic.[1] As Chris Alden notes, 'While the drive to secure energy resources is at the heart of Beijing's renewed engagement with Africa, there is nonetheless a growing depth and complexity to relations that bears closer analysis.'[2] This widespread oversimplification also omits the economic, political and social implications of China's presence within the host state itself.

This chapter seeks to provide a multi-layered analysis of Chinese-Angolan relations and the role of China in Angola today. The first section outlines the principal characteristics of bilateral economic relations with a focus on external trade, foreign direct investment

---

1 Denis M. Tull, 'China's Engagement in Africa: Scope, Significance and Consequences', *Journal of Modern African Studies*, Vol. 44, No. 3 (2006), pp. 459-79.

2 Chris Alden, 'Leveraging the Dragon: Toward "an Africa That Can Say No"', South African Institute of International Affairs, 2005.

and the proliferation of public works made possible by the opening of Chinese credit lines. Over the past three years, this emphasis on public works has turned Angola into a veritable building site with the potential to transform the infrastructure that is indispensable for national development. While mostly concerned with a description of the Chinese presence, this section places it within the context of Angolan politics and brings out the domestic implications of what is defined as a 'perfect marriage' of convenience for Angolan elites and Chinese investors alike. The second section raises important questions regarding the long-term nature of Angolan-Chinese relations. Through examination of the likely economic, political and social developments in Angola, future challenges concerning the reception and consolidation of a Chinese presence in the country are discussed.

China's entrance into Angola

Although relations between Angola and China can be termed 'excellent' today, this was not always the case. Angola's ruling party, the Movimento Popular de Libertação de Angola (or MPLA), counted on Chinese support throughout the years of anti-colonial struggle.[3] However, by the time of independence in November 1975, and in counterpoint to the Soviet Union's strong support for the MPLA,

---

3 Mário Pinto de Andrade, the first President of the MPLA, was quoted as saying that 'our [the MPLA's] first money came not from Moscow but from China. This story has never been properly told. In one way or the other this was officially hidden because of the Sino-Soviet schism and the fact that the Soviet Union eventually became our main source of direct support. In 62-63, China, because of the dispute with the Soviets, stopped being our major supporter. It continued [to provide some aid] but not in as substantial a manner as in the beginning' (Michel Laban, *Mário Pinto de Andrade – uma Entrevista*, Lisboa: Sá da Costa, 1997), pp.162-163). In 1963 Mário Pinto de Andrade and Viriato da Cruz, the secretary-general of the MPLA and one of its major intellectual voices, abandoned their respective party positions as a result of internal tensions that culminated in the future Angolan President Agostinho Neto's takeover. Viriato da Cruz was ostracized to Beijing where he would die in 1973, his name and ideological outlook for long a taboo within the MPLA. For more on China-Angola relations, see Ian Taylor, *China and Africa: Engagement and Compromise* (London: Routledge, 2006), pp. 75-92.

Chinese assistance concentrated on two rival rebel groups, the FNLA and UNITA. On account of this, there were many harsh words from the MPLA leadership about China in the ensuing period. This did not prevent the establishment of diplomatic relations in 1983, but relations would only gain momentum at a later stage. A China-Angola Joint Economic and Trade Commission was created in October 1988. Its first meeting occurred only in December 1999, the second in May 2001, and curiously, in view of the growing bilateral economic involvement after this meeting, the third meeting would not occur until March 2007.

Bilateral visits by important state officials have become more frequent in recent years. High-level Chinese visits are now common, geared towards maintaining influence over the application of Chinese lines of credit, and the presence of Angolan members of government in Beijing has also been noted. In March 2004, when China's first credit line to Angola was opened, Manuel Vicente, the CEO of Sonangol, Angola's national oil company, went to China. This resulted in the establishment of two joint ventures between Sonangol and the China National Petroleum Corporation (CNPC), China's biggest oil company. One focused on oil and gas production in Angola, and the other on industrial, petroleum and infrastructure investment not only in Angola but also in other countries including Argentina and Venezuela.[4] In late May 2004 the Angolan Foreign Minister was invited to Beijing by his Chinese counterpart.[5] In September 2004 the President of China's Exim Bank, Yang Zilin, visited Luanda to discuss the application of the first Chinese credit line with the ministers of Finance and Petroleum, the head of Sonangol and the Governor of the National Bank of Angola. Also in 2004, following a scandal about alleged attempts to siphon off Chinese credit line funds, the Angolan Finance Minister went to Beijing to reassure the Chinese government about Angolan intentions reharding those funds.

In 2005 the Chinese Deputy Prime Minister Zeng Peiyan and the Deputy Foreign Minister came to Luanda on separate occasions.

---

4   'Angola: a bola de neve das relações com a China', *ÁfricaMonitor Intelligence*, 1, 22 June 2005.

5   'Chinese, Angolan FMs hold talks', *Xinhua*, 26 May 2004.

The commander of the Angolan Armed Forces, General Sanjar, visited Beijing in June 2005. Premier Wen Jiabao visited Angola and announced a third Chinese loan in the value of US$2 billion in June 2006. This happened shortly after the signing of a Sinopec-Sonangol partnership for the construction of a large refinery in Lobito. While the initial Chinese credit line in March 2004 had elicited from the Angolans the concession of an oil block to CNPC, the refinery deal in turn led the Chinese to extend their financial assistance to the Angolans. The Angolan Minister of Commerce and the Deputy Minister of Foreign Affairs were present in Macau in September 2006 for the Second Ministerial conference of the Forum of Economic and Commercial Cooperation between China and the Portuguese-Speaking Countries, and at the end of October the Angolan Prime Minister made a 'working visit' to Beijing that was extended so that he could represent the Angolan President at the third Forum for China-Africa Cooperation. The President's was a much-noted absence among the 42 African heads of state present on this occasion.[6]

In 2007, however, the enthusiasm of Chinese leaders about travelling to Angola appeared to wane. The Chinese Minister of Foreign Affairs, Li Zhaoxing, visited seven African countries in January. Later that month, President Hu Jintao made stopovers in eight African countries in his third major visit to the continent.[7] Angola was left out of the itinerary in both instances, something that caused concern in Luanda. (Perhaps not unrelated to this was the reactivation of the Joint Economic and Trade Commission, which had not reconvened for six years.)

The end of the civil war and Chinese financing of reconstruction

The reasons behind the sea-change in the Angolan government's policy towards China must be understood in the context of post-war reconstruction. Faced with the obstacles that Angola's main

---

6   'China aims to increase its clout in Africa; Unsaid goal: redraw world's strategic map', *New York Times*, 2 November 2006.

7   'The Chinese People's Republic of Africa: will Chinese peacekeepers soon embark on a conquest of the Black Continent?', *Kommersant*, 31 January 2007.

partners and the international financial institutions (principally the IMF) continued to pose in regard to the extension of credit, in the absence of structural reforms, the MPLA government turned to China.[8] Ironically, this is reminiscent of the way in which the MPLA had sought out Chinese support during the anti-colonial struggle when faced with the lack of assistance from Western countries.[9] China has substantial financial resources, state-owned corporations that benefit from the state's activist policies, an entrepreneurial class strongly supported by the state[10] and an overriding need for natural resources, especially petroleum.[11] Angola possesses some of these natural resources in great abundance, especially petroleum. This is, in a certain way, a perfect 'marriage of convenience'. As President Eduardo dos Santos noted: 'China needs natural resources and Angola needs to develop its economy. That is why the two countries have engaged in constructive cooperation.'[12] During Premier Wen Jiabao's visit in mid-2006, he also affirmed that bilateral relations are based on the establishment of 'mutually advantageous' partnerships with no 'political preconditions'[13] and a 'pragmatic posture' on both sides.[14]

When faced with the void left by the international community, the sense of timing on both sides was noteworthy. The first credit

8   'Silêncio da comunidade internacional ditou recurso ao empréstimo chinês', statement by the Angolan Deputy Minister of Planning, *Jornal de Angola*, 31 August 2006.

9   Manuel Ennes Ferreira, 'Realeconomie e Realpolitik nos Recursos Naturais em Angola', *Relações Internacionais*, 6 (2005), pp. 73-89.

10 Chris Alden and Martyn Davies, 'A Profile of the Operations of Chinese Multinationals in Africa', *South African Journal of International Affairs*, 13, 1 (2006), pp. 83-96.

11 Ian Taylor, 'Unpacking China's Resource Diplomacy in Africa', Center on China's Transnational Relations, Working Paper 19, Hong Kong University of Science and Technology, 2006.

12 'Angola gives Chinese PM full backing for Africa policy', statement of the Angolan President during the Chinese Prime Minister's visit to Angola, *AFP*, 20 June 2006.

13 'JES considera compreensão e diálogo chave do equilíbrio nas relações internacionais', *Voz da América*, 21 June 2006.

14 'PR defende cooperação construtiva com a China', *Jornal de Angola* , 21 June 2006.

line of US$2 billion was agreed on 2 March 2004. The conditions attached to this loan are seen by the Angolan government as advantageous despite the fact that it is an oil-backed loan, a 'benchmark according to which any future loans will be measured'.[15] Contracted by China's Exim Bank,[16] the loan is for repayment in two tranches of US$1 billion each over a period of 12 years with a grace period of five years, which in practice means 17 years, at a market-based interest rate of 1.7 per cent. The agreement makes room for the hiring of local companies for up to 60 per cent of each contract.[17] It is the responsibility of the Chinese authorities to decide which Chinese company gets allocated specific contracts in tenders open only to Chinese companies, with payment made directly by the Exim Bank. The agreement states that the minimum value for individual projects is US$10 million.[18]

In January 2005, the first tranche of the US$1 billion was made available; the second tranche was released later, with the interest rate reportedly revised downwards to 0.25 per cent.[19] Shortly after the visit of the Chinese Deputy Premier, a new interest-free loan of US$6.3 million was also announced in 2005.[20] A further oil-backed loan of US$1 billion was agreed in March 2006.[21] At this stage, according to the Angolan Deputy Minister of Finance, Severim de Morais, Chinese credit to Angola was worth US$3.2 billion, or 58 per cent of the total credit Angola had obtained after the end

15 'Crédito chinês flexibiliza bancos', interview with the Angolan Minister of Finance, 4 October 2005.

16 'Chinese financing already deployed', *Angola Peace Monitor*, Vol. 10, 7, 21 April 2004.

17 'Acordo histórico: invasão chinesa', *Semanário Angolense*, Vol. 1, 53 (March 2004), pp. 20-7.

18 'Assinados primeiros 12 acordos de financiamento com o Eximbank da China', *Notícias Lusófonas*, 16 May 2005.

19 'Angola flexes newfound muscle', *BusinessDay*, 23 March 2007.

20 'Governo chinês anuncia concessão de novo financiamento a Angola', *Angop*, 26 February 2005.

21 'China turns to Angola for bulk of oil imports', *Lloyd's List International*, 30 March 2006.

of the civil war in 2002.[22] A third major credit line of US$2 billion was announced in June 2006 when Wen Jiabao visited Luanda.[23] On this occasion, the two parties signed a Memorandum of Understanding on additional credit[24] as well as seven agreements for financing in the telecommunications and fisheries sectors.[25] An additional loan obtained outside the context of the credit lines made available by Exim Bank was brought to public attention in October 2005. According to the media, Sonangol raised a US$2 billion syndicated oil-backed loan priced at 250 basis points over Libor,[26] and meant for financing of oil production and gas projects and to repay a previous oil-backed loan. Management of this loan is led by France's Calyon Bank, which acts as banker to both Sinochem and Unipec in China[27] and as the long-term purchaser of Sonangol's oil.[28] Furthermore, a China International Fund, described as a 'private entity, based in Hong Kong, whose purpose is the financing of projects defined by the Office of National Reconstruction' in the amount of US$2.9 billion, was created in 2005.[29] In sum, the total of credit obtained by Angola from both private and public Chinese sources amounts to at least US$7 billion at the time of writing.[30]

---

22 'Angola recebe empréstimos de USD 5,5 biliões (desde 2002)', *Jornal de Angola*, 17 April 2006. See also Minister of Finance statement, 'Angola: China entrenches position in booming economy', *IRIN*, 17 April 2006.

23 'Governo aprova Acordo de Crédito do Eximbank da China', *AngoNotícias*, 28 November 2007.

24 'China concede crédito adicional de dois biliões de dólares a Angola', *Angop*, 21 June 2006.

25 'Áreas de Telecomunicações e Pescas incluídas na cooperação chinesa', *Angop*, 21 June 2006.

26 The widely used benchmark for short-term interest rates.

27 'Angola to raise another $2 billion oil-backed loan', *Energy Compass*, 14 October 2005.

28 'Angolan oil loan likely to raise transparency issues', *Financial Times*, 11 October 2005.

29 'Ministério das Finanças descarta irregularidades na utilização da linha de crédito da China', *Angop*, 18 October 2007. This includes the financing of projects such as the new international airport in Luanda, the railways, roads between provincial capitals and infrastructural works in Luanda.

30 Ibid.

Economic relations

From an economic viewpoint, there are three major areas of Chinese involvement in Angola: external trade, foreign direct investment and public works financed by Chinese credit lines.

External trade. Throughout the 1990s, Angolan exports to China ranged from US$136 million to US$600 million. Only in 2000 did they exceed US$1 billion (reaching $1.842bn) for the first time.[31] In anticipation of the closer relationship that was about to develop, Angolan oil exports already took up 20 per cent of China's African oil imports by 2002. At this stage, Angola became China's main African supplier. In 2004, Angolan oil exports to China reached US$4.7 billion, or 33 per cent of all oil imported from Africa by China and 20 per cent of China's total oil imports. This made Angola China's third most important supplier worldwide after Saudi Arabia and Iran, with 25 per cent of Angola's oil production exported there.[32] In 2005, Angolan oil represented 45.5 per cent of China's African oil imports[33] and Angola became its second most important worldwide supplier after Saudi Arabia.[34] In the first nine months of 2006, Angola became China's leading oil supplier at 500,000 bpd, supplanting Saudi Arabia. This represented 16.6 per cent of total Chinese oil imports during the first half of 2006, and about 70 per cent of all Africa-derived oil.[35] In the same period in 2007, Angola fell to the second position, but was still responsible for 14.1 per cent and 60 per cent of Chinese world and Africa imports respectively.[36]

31 Centre for Chinese Studies, 'China's Interest and Activity in Africa's Construction and Infrastructure Sectors' (South Africa: Stellenbosch University, 2007).

32 Carlota Garcia Encima, 'La Política Africana de Pekin: Oportunidad o Amenaza?', *Ari*, 27 (Madrid: Real Instituto Elcano, 2006), pp. 3-4.

33 'Africa accounts for 30 percent of China's oil imports: official', *People's Daily Online*, 19 October 2006.

34 Ibid.

35 'Saudi Arabia tops China's Sep crude imports list with 2.49mil mt', http://www.platts.com; 'Angola já é o maior parceiro da China em África', *Diário Digital*, 26 October 2007.

36 Ibid.

		2003		2004		2005		2006	
	Value	Rank Africa	Value	Rank Africa	Value	Rank Africa	Value	Rank Africa	Value	Rank Africa
Imports	1,087		2,231	1°	4,717	1°	6,578	1°	11,050	1°
% from Africa	19.6		26.7		34.8		32.9		38.8	
Exports to	61		145		190		372		894	
Total	1,148	5°	2,376	2°	4,907	2°	6,950	1°	11,944	1°

Table 1 – China-Angola External Trade (US$ millions)[37]

Although there was an increase in the value of both imports and exports in bilateral trade between 2002 and 2006, in absolute terms the difference between the two has expanded. The Chinese trade deficit has increased from US$1 billion to US$11 billion (Table 1).

From the Angolan perspective, during the 1990s imported Chinese products ran at the very low level of between US$10 and US$30 million.[38] However, as shown in Table 2, in 2005 China had become Angola's fourth largest supplier at US$372 million with a quota of 4.5 per cent, up from being its seventh trade partner the year before (Portugal was its main supplier at 20 per cent).[39] In 2006, China became the third supplier, surpassing South Africa and increasing its market share to 9.3 per cent, or US$894 million.[40] China became a

---

37 Sources: 'China´s trade with major partners in 2004', *Business Daily Update*, 23 February 2005; 'Prospecting for oil, Hu kicks off Africa tour in Morocco', *Agence France Presse*, 24 April 2006; 'Companhias chinesas em Angola criam câmara de comércio', *Diário Económico*, 21 March 2006; 'Angola: China entrenches position in booming economy', *IRIN*, 17 April 2006; 'The trouble with putting energy first', *South China Morning Post*, 16 June 2006; 'Angola and China hold Third Meeting in Beijing', *Africa Files*, 13 March 2007; 'Chinese businessman in Portugal wants to make use of Portugal's position for China-Angola trade', *MacauHub*, 19 March 2007; 'Angola em Movimento', ICEP, 32, May, Luanda, 2007; CCS, 'China's Interest and Activity in Africa's Construction and Infrastructure Sectors'; 'China encourages African imports', *Chinadaily*, 17 January 2007.

38 CCS, 'China's Interest and Activity in Africa's Construction and Infrastructure Sectors'.

39 'Angola: China climbed to fourth-largest exporter in 2004', *Lusa*, 3 June 2005.

40 'Angola importou 1,21 bilião de euros em mercadorias diversas de Portugal em 2006', *Jornal de Angola*, 5 March 2007; Banco de Portugal (2007).

	1995	1996	1997	1998	1999	2000	2001	2002	2003	2004	2005	2006
Imports	1.3	1.5	1.4	1.8	1.3	nd	nd	1.6	2.3	3.3	4.5	9.3
Exports	3.8	5.0	13.2	4.0	7.3	22.8	10.6	13.6	23.6	35.7	29.6	35,6

Table 2 – Chinese Market Shares in Angolan External Trade (%)

Source: Banco de Portugal (2003, 2006, 2007); 'Angola importou 1,21 bilião de euros em mercadorias diversas de Portugal em 2006', *Jornal de Angola,* 5 March 2007.

major destination of Angolan exports, taking a 22.8 per cent share (mostly petroleum) in 2000 and a 35.6 per cent share in 2006. It is expected that in the next few years the penetration of Chinese products in Angola will be considerably reinforced to the point of reaching the level of Portuguese imports.[41] To prevent this growth from taking place in an un-coordinated manner, the Chamber of Commerce for Chinese Companies in Angola was recently created, bringing together 26 leading Chinese firms operating in Angola.[42]

Chinese investment. Data from the Angolan National Agency of Private Investment (ANIP) from 2005 show a total of 290 foreign investment-approved projects valued at US$2.5 billion, of which 86 per cent is FDI. China is placed fourth behind Portugal, South Africa and Brazil, and ahead of the UK and the US.[43] Data on FDI outside the petroleum sector for 2006 shows a decrease (to US$650 million, with only US$163 million in industrial development). The three main investors were Portugal, South Africa and the US, the latter investing only US$23 million.[44] From this one can deduce

---

41 This is on account of both the general competitiveness of Chinese exports in the world market and the materials imported for use in the infrastructure projects made possible by Chinese credit. See 'Angola em Movimento', no. 38, November 2007, AICEP, Luanda.

42 Among others this includes the China National Machinery and Equipment Import and Export Corporation (CMEC), Jiangsu International, the China International Water & Electric Corporation, ZTE Corporation, Huawei, the Sinosteel Corporation, China Petroleum and Chemical Corporation (Sinopec), the China National Overseas Engineering Corporation (COVEC), and the China State Shipbuilding Corporation (CSSC). See *Macauhu*b, quoted in 'Companhias chinesas em Angola criam câmara de comércio', *op. cit.*

43 *ANIP Bulletin News*, Vol.3, 4, 27 January 2006.

44 'Volume de investimento no país atinge USD 650 milhões em 2006', *Angop*, 20 January 2007.

that Chinese FDI in Angola has been extremely small. Perhaps this situation may change when the US$5 billion development fund announced during the third FOCAC as a means to 'encourage Chinese companies to invest in Africa' becomes operational.[45] For now, apart from the petroleum sector, few Chinese investments can be clearly identified. There are signs of growing Chinese investment in small-scale retail trade and restaurants. Beyond this, there is also Chinese involvement in cement production and the iron and steel industry. The Chinese Jasan Corporation wants to invest an estimated US$50 million in a cement factory in the Kicombo Commune in the Province of Kwanza Sul in the second semester of 2006.[46] Chung Fong Holding has signed a 15-year management contract with the Angolan government to repair the Luanda-based iron and steel producer Siderurgia Nacional, which came to a standstill in 2000. The re-launching of production presupposes investment of US$28 million and the Chinese company has acquired a controlling stake (51 per cent).[47] In other circumstances, this could become an opportunity for some of the existing Angolan industrial operators which could conceivably furnish some of the needs of this project. However, this will not occur because of the conditions underpinning the Chinese credit line. For instance, in March 2007, Hangxiao Steel Structure signed two contracts to supply construction materials including 'the installation of the steel structures, which will be produced in the company's factory'.[48] These could eventually have been produced with the modernization and diversification of the Siderurgia Nacional company's plant. Finally, the opening of CSG Automóvel Angola, a US$30 million investment by the China Inter-

---

45 'China-Africa co-op to break "products-for-resources" doctrine', *China View*, 6 January 2007.

46 'Chineses investem USD 50 milhões em fábrica de cimento', *Jornal de Angola*, 9 January 2004.

47 'Relançamento do sector industrial à vista, investimentos não petrolíferos', *Expresso on-line*, 6 October 2005 and 'País vai reduzir importação de ferro', *Jornal de Angola*, 5 October 2005.

48 Vol. 4, 12, 'Chinese Company Signs Contracts for Two Construction Projects', *ANIP News Bulletin*, 23 March 2007.

national Fund designed to assemble Japanese Nissan cars in Luanda, is expected in late 2007.[49]

These smaller investments aside, clearly Chinese companies are keener to get involved in extractive industries. For the diamond sector, the Angolan Council of Ministers accepted a joint venture agreement between Endiama EP (the Angola state player in the diamond sector) and China International Fund Limited on 6 April 2005. It also authorized Endiama EP to participate in the creation of a Hong Kong-based company called Endiama China International Holding Limited. This company will aim to prospect, produce and market diamonds, including diamond-cutting and production of jewellery, and other legal activities in Hong Kong.[50] In September 2005, the Minister of Geology and Mines allowed the establishment of a partnership between Endiama EP, MIRACEL and Endiama-China, as well as approving its contract for prospecting of diamonds.[51]

The petroleum sector has attracted the lion's share of Chinese investment. In the aftermath of the first Chinese-Angolan agreement in March 2004, Sinopec acquired 50 per cent of Block 18, which is operated by BP, having set up the Sonangol Sinopec International (SSI) joint venture to take that stake in the block. Sinopec holds a 75 per cent stake in SSI and this investment was around US$1.5 billion. This first Chinese involvement in Angolan oil took dramatic proportions on account of the last minute sidelining of ONGC, the Indian national oil company, which had been set to take this stake.

In 2005 the Angolan government did not renew the contract for Block 3/80, which had been held since 1982 by the French company Total. Instead, in an example of Angolan *Realpolitik* in the use of oil as a diplomatic weapon, it handed this to Sinopec.[52] Later that year,

---

49 *Jornal de Angola*, 'Fábrica de carros em Luanda começa a produzir em Outubro', 10 July 2007; 'Primeiros carros fabricados no país chegam ao mercado ainda este ano', 15 October 2007; and 'Angola garante confiança ao investidor', 21 November 2007.

50 'Comissão Permanente do Conselho de Ministros reuniu sob orientação do Presidente da República', *Angonotícias*, 6 April 2005.

51 'Mining Ministry Okays Constitution of Association in Participation', *Angola Press Agency*, 12 September 2005.

52 Manuel Ennes Ferreira, 'Realeconomik e realpolitik nos recursos naturais em Angola', *Relações Internacionais* 6 (2005).

the two parties agreed on the first participation of China Sonangol International Limited, a 25 per cent share of blocks 3/05 and 3/05-A in the Angolan offshore.[53] In April 2006, the Italian company ENI won the public tender for the deepwater block 15, with Sonangol Sinopec offering US$750 million for a 20 per cent share. By May, SSI had cornered 27.5 per cent and 40 per cent of the remaining areas of Blocks 17 and 18, in the process establishing a world record for signature bonuses by putting forward US$1.1 billion for *each* concession.[54] In tandem with this decision, Sonangol reached an agreement with Sinopec to the effect that SSI would undertake to build the Lobito Refinery, a US$3 billion project with 200,000 bpd capacity long pursued by the Angolan government.[55] Somewhat surprisingly, the Angolan government announced in February 2007 that it was pursuing the Lobito Refinery project alone 'because there was no agreement with the Chinese company on the products that would be produced' once the refinery is operational.[56] The Chinese government reacted quite un-dramatically to this, explaining the end of the partnership in terms of the normal functioning of the free market.[57]

Lastly, in order to be able to act in external markets, China Sonangol International Holding (CSIH), a subsidiary of Sonangol EP, signed a 2004 Memorandum of Understanding with Energia Argentina SA (Enarsa) that was expected to result in the investment of more than US$5 billion over the next five years (this amount would

---

53 'China assume participação em dois blocos de exploração petrolífera em Angola', *Lusa* , 5 October 2005. The consortium exploiting these two blocks (which are 25 per cent owned by Angola's NOC Sonangol) also includes Japanese, Italian, Serbian and Croatian investors.

54 'Blocos proporcionam bónus de USD 2,2 biliões', *Jornal de Angola*, 23 May 2006. According to the results of this bidding round, Total will be the operator of Block 17 (40 per cent) and Petrobrás of Block 18 (30 per cent).

55 'Bónus constitui recorde mundial em Angola', *Apostolado*, 10 May 2006.

56 'Sonangol compra refinaria de Luanda', *Jornal de Angola*, 24 February 2007.

57 'Pequim desvaloriza fim de parceria entre Sonangol e Sinopec', *Jornal de Negócios*, 8 March 2007. See also 'Angola flexes newfound muscle', *Business Day*, 23 March 2007. However, it is noteworthy that later on China did not (or perhaps was advised not to) make bids for blocks 15, 17 and 18 which are expected to be picked up by Galp (Portugal), ONGC (India) and Petrobras (Brazil). This seems to point towards an Angolan strategy of diversification of foreing partners identifiable elsewhere. See, for instance, 'Analistas aplaudem nova investida da Galp em Angola', 30 November 2007

not be made available by the Sino-Angolan company alone).[58] This Argentine excursion became clearer during the visit of President Hu Jintao to Buenos Aires, during which he signed an agreement to invest US$5 billion in oil exploration through CSIH, underwriting the previous Sino-Angolan commitment 'as part of a larger US$19.7 billion Chinese package for possible investments ranging from construction to railroad expansion'.[59]

Recent developments also point to growing Chinese interest in Angola's copper reserves. In November 2004 a joint statement by the Ministries of Geology and Mines, Transports, and Energy and Water created a Technical Multisectoral Commission to study the project of exploiting the Mavoio Tetelo e Bembe copper mine in the municipality of Maquela do Zombo in Uíge Province. This measure is based on the fact that the initial studies recommended that the project would only be viable if a railway, road and electricity infrastructure were also built. The China National Electric Equipment Corporation is currently conducting these works.[60]

Public works. The financial needs for the reconstruction of Angola are immense and the Angolan government has shown considerable gratitude to China for making this available. What follows is a survey of the sectors to which the Chinese credit has been applied. The 'building site' that is Angola today now includes an estimated 30,000 Chinese workers, with 80,000 expected by 2008.[61]

In the roads sector, the China Roads and Bridges Corporation and the China International Fund are rebuilding numerous road and bridge connections. The basic sanitation sector (water supply

58 'Sonangol entra em negócio de USD 5 biliões na Argentina', *VOA*, 20 November 2004.
59 'Angola will be part of a Chinese-Argentine oil-exploration deal', *The Miami Herald*, 23 November 2004.
60 'Criada comissão para estudar projecto de exploração de mina no Uíge', *Angop*, 5 January 2005.
61 *Agora*, quoted in http://www.club-k.net, 'Revista da imprensa: sucessão de JES, bolo chinês e palancas negras', 23 June 2006. For a more detailed view on public works see the CCS, 'China's Interest and Activity in Africa's Construction and Infrastructure Sectors'.

networks, public water taps, fill pipes for water trucks, and electrical energy payment centres) is led by the China International Fund Ltd and the China Export Corporation.[62] In the area of housing and public buildings, the China International Fund and Jiangsu International play a leading role. In the railway sector, a consortium of three companies chosen by the Chinese government—the China National Machinery Import and Export Corporation (CMEC), Transtech Engineering Corporation (TEC) and Kenwo International Development Limited (KIDL)—is operating. Through a state-owned enterprise, CLIC, China collaborates with Raids-Indian in the rehabilitation of CFM-Caminho de Ferro de Moçâmedes, the railway connecting the port of Namibe to Menongue (a four-year total investment of US$1.2 billion starting in March 2006). For the main national railway, the Caminho de Ferro de Benguela (CFB), the Chinese consortium, China International Fund Limited, has a 20-month deadline to complete rehabilitation (August 2007), which does not seem possible. Finally, the Congo railway (CFC) project, initially expected in 2008, is now a priority and is being studied.

In the air transport sector, the new Luanda airport project at Bom Jesus, a €9 billion investment, will be led by Chinese companies hired directly by the Angolan government[63] and under the direct control of the Office of National Reconstruction.[64] In the agricultural sector, the supply of tools and equipment to Mecanang EP is made by the China National Machinery and Equipment Import and Export Corporation. In the health sector, several Chinese-built hospitals have already been inaugurated, including one in Luanda built by the Chinese Construction Company (COVEC).[65] In telecommunications, the Angolan Council of Ministers discussed in February 2005 the plan by the Chinese ZTE Corporation International that aims to invest US$400 million. On another occasion, the Angolan company MundoSartel (56 per cent privately owned by Angolan investors and

---

62 *ANIP Bulletin News*, Vol. 3, 17, 5 May 2006.

63 *ANIP Bulletin News*, Vol. 3, 23, 23 June 2006.

64 'Angola: novo aeroporto de Luanda', *ÁfricaMonitor Intelligence*, 114, 15 June 2006.

65 *ANIP Bulletin News*, Vol. 3, 6, 10 February 2006.

44 per cent by Telecom Namibia) and ZTE Corporation signed a US$69 million agreement to develop phone networks throughout Angola.[66] In 2006 the Angolan Council of Ministers approved contracts for the provision of equipment between Angola-Telecom, EP and a consortium of Chinese companies led by CMEC and involving Alcatel Shanghai Bell and Huawei, for a total of US$273 million.[67] Finally, in the context of the Sino-Angolan Memorandum of Understanding signed on the occasion of the additional credit line of June 2006, telecommunications and fisheries were considered priority areas. On technology for the electoral process, the Angolan government approved a contract between Angola Telecom and ZTE. In the security sector, Jiangsu International is building new installations and providing equipment for the BATOP (Brigade for Tactical-Operational Support), which is expected to be a technologically sophisticated centre covering Southern Africa and parts of Central Africa. In maritime transport, a 2005 agreement on merchant shipping was signed between Angola's Sécil Marítima and a group of Chinese companies, Pan Asian Oasis Inc.[68] In 2006, Sécil Marítima and China's Shipping Logistics, the biggest state-owned Chinese company in this sector, signed a similar agreement. The China National Machinery and Equipment Import-Export Corporation has also come to an understanding about investment in Angola, selling fishing vessels which, it is hoped, will come to employ 20,000 people directly and 100,000 indirectly.[69]

The future

Several questions remain unanswered about the future of the Sino-Angolan bilateral relationship. One concerns the consolidation of Chinese companies in the Angolan market beyond the execution of the Chinese credit line-supported public projects, themselves based

---

66 'China, Angola sign cooperation agreements', *Afro News*, 7 March 2005.

67 'Decisões económicas na agenda do Conselho de Ministros', *Angonotícias*, 3 April 2006 and *ANIP Bulletin News*, vol. 3, 21, 9 June 2006.

68 'Relançamento do sector industrial à vista: Investimentos não petrolíferos', *Expresso on-line*, 6 October 2005.

69 'Comunicado do Conselho de Ministros', *Angonotícias*, 22 February 2006.

on imported materials manufactured in China. At present the transition towards a new operating mode, away from the traditional forms of 'tied financing', does not seem to be occurring. There seems to be every intention to continue connecting Chinese loans with contracts to Chinese state-owned companies, despite the recently voiced views of the Chinese Deputy Minister of Foreign Affairs.[70] While investment opportunities in the Angolan market are considerable, there must be reasons why Chinese investors shun the prospect of substantial investment outside the extractive industries. Perceptions of risk, or perhaps high opportunity costs when compared to other markets, are factors that play a role here. This has greatly disappointed Angolan businessmen keen on joint venture arrangements as well as the Angolan authorities who regularly call for Chinese investment outside natural resources.[71] This is despite the Chinese Deputy Foreign Minister's pleas to the effect that China is 'encouraging not only its SOEs but also its private sector to invest in Angola, especially in infrastructure'[72] and his references to 'more than 10000 Chinese businessmen who have already visited Angola to get to know the market and search for local opportunities'.[73] As Sino-Angolan economic relations deepen, it is to be expected that Chinese companies seeking to seize the moment, both private and state-owned, will be active in Angola independently from the credit lines made available

---

70 'Empresas privadas chinesas de construção vão investir no país', *Jornal de Angola*, 22 July 2005.

71 According to a statement in Macau by Irene Neto, the Angolan Deputy Foreign Minister for Cooperation: 'Angola aposta na diversificação do investimento directo chinês' and 'Empresários chineses encorajados a investirem em Angola', *Angop*, 25 September 2006. See also the statement by the Angolan Deputy Minister of Commerce Manuel da Cruz Neto, 'Vice-ministro do Comércio convida empresários chineses a investir em Angola', *Angop*, 20 October 2007.

72 'Empresas privadas chinesas de construção vão investir no país', *Jornal de Angola*, 22 July 2005.

73 'China: Angola atrai milhares de potenciais investidores chineses', *Lusa on-line*, 15 March 2006, Statement by Huang Zequan, business consultant for firms wanting to invest in Africa and an academic at the University of Beijing.

CHINA RETURNS TO AFRICA

by the Chinese government.[74] This is likely to occur across several sectors of the economy. When a cooperation agreement was signed between the Chinese business group Asian Oasis Inc and the Angolan company Sécil Marítima in October 2005, the Chinese CEO, Edmond Y. Yao, declared that about fifty Hong Kong-based firms aimed to invest US$8 billion in Angolan industry, construction and iron and steel production from 2006 to 2008.[75]

This leads to a second question, the expectation by the Angolan authorities of growth and development in Angola's private sector through partnerships with Chinese companies, especially through the legal requirement to sub-contract Angolan companies in Chinese credit line-related projects. The obligatory Angolan share of 30 per cent of such contracts has not been fully respected, and numerous instances of dissatisfaction and protest have resulted. The process whereby Angolan companies are chosen for the existing partnerships is also perceived as wholly un-transparent.[76] Furthermore, the implications of the credit line-derived partnerships go beyond mere economics. The political repercussions are evident, as shown by the dispute within the current Angolan leadership for access to, and co-ordination of, the disbursement of these funds. While in many ways predating the advent of Chinese credit lines, the flames of intra-elite enmity were decidedly fanned by the prospect of access to them. Immediately after the first loan was granted in March 2004, frenzied political machinations burst into the open. With some hyperbole, the Angolan press reported fears that this might create a new 'civil war'.[77]

The problems started with the sidelining of Carlos Feijó, a long-serving top adviser to the President, and of António ('Toninho') Van

74 As the CEO of a Chinese company, stated, 'This is private investment by Chinese companies and not state-to-state investment': 'Mais USD 8 biliões para investimentos', *Jornal de Angola*, 5 October 2005.

75 Ibid. See also 'China & Hong Kong Firms Invest $8 Billion', 14 October 2005.

76 *Semanário Angolense*, 'Financiamento chinês: Lei obriga a subcontratação de empresas angolanas', *ANIP Bulletin News*, Vol. 2, 41, 179, 1-8 July 2006.

77 'Toninho versus Feijó: crónica de um duelo anunciado', *Voz da América*, 10 December 2004.

312

Dúnem, the Secretary of the Council of Ministers and one of the main negotiators of the Chinese loan, because of alleged profits they were seeking to extract from the process. Rumours surfaced that it was the Chinese secret services, the TEWU, that warned the Angolan Presidency, going as far as providing President Dos Santos with a list of twenty businesses connected with elite Angolans said to be illicitly benefiting from the newly available resources.[78] This took such proportions that by December 2004 the Angolan Finance Minister was sent to Beijing to reassure the Chinese authorities about the proper use of the credit line.[79] Subsequently, President Dos Santos created an Office for National Reconstruction (GRN), headed by General Kopelipa, the Presidency's Military Adviser.[80] This has the task of direct administration and disbursement of the Chinese loans. This robust reinforcement of the Presidency as the centre of political and economic gravity marks a permanent sidelining of the Government and the National Assembly, as evidenced in the fact that no less than four cabinet ministers must report directly to General Kopelipa.[81]

A third question concerns the sort of complaints that have been raised by the methods of Chinese companies, which are by no means unique to Angola. These include instances of cultural misunderstanding and racism,[82] the scant use made of the Angolan labour force,[83] and the disparities in Chinese pay-scales, all of which have

78 'José Pedro de Morais sossega chineses', *Semanário Angolense*, 25 December 2004. According to *Semanário Angolense*, 'Chineses disseram a verdade mas ainda guardam preciosos triunfos', the case of António Van-Dúnem 'was the most blatant one. He had ambitions to control, amongst others businesses, the Caminhos de Ferro de Luanda e de Benguela [the national railroad company]': *Semanário Angolense*, 95, 15-21 January 2005.

79 Ibid.

80 'PR tira da cartola um Gabinete de Reconstrução Nacional', *Semanário Angolense*, 85, 30 October-6 November 2004.

81 http://www.club-k.net, 23 June 2006.

82 'Inclui despedimentos anáquicos: gestão chinesa da Siderurgia Nacional acusada de racismo e outros insultos', *Semanário Angolense*, 157, 1-7 April 2006.

83 See, for instances, *Público*, 'Em Angola foi chegar e vencer', 31 January 2007. For the president of the Liga dos Jovens Empresários Angolanos, Artur Almeida, 'The rules of Chinese investment (that is, the Chinese loans)

contributed to a certain malaise in Angolan perceptions of China.[84] In the medium term, this could acquire very problematic dimensions if it is not handled properly. While Chinese assistance may have been welcomed by the elite and the population alike in the initial post-civil war stages, this was not the case some four years afterwards. The political benefits and economic gains reaped by the elite currently are not matched in the lives of average Angolans, and this may lead to an increase of tensions between the latter and Chinese expatriates. In this context, rumours about the Angolan government's intentions to settle a very large number of Chinese citizens in the Central Plateau, Angola's richest agricultural region, could be a dangerous time-bomb,[85] because this region is politically very sensitive, with traditional heavy support for the defeated UNITA rebels and a historic sense of marginalization by Luanda. In addition, there are issues pertaining to land access that have recently created serious friction between local people and essentially speculative and politically connected new landowners. The trauma of the civil war and the lack of local grassroots organization may be interpreted by some as showing popular complacency or even tolerance towards such settler projects. But there is no guarantee, should such ambitious ideas come to pass, that the current popular passiveness vis-à-vis the Chinese will continue.

A fourth question concerns the economic and political impact of Chinese construction of public works. Beyond the positive economic externalities which these projects encompass, there is an important political issue associated with them: the holding of presidential and legislative elections. At this stage, it is clear that the government and the ruling MPLA are betting on the rehabilitation of Angola's infrastructure as a key element in their electoral strategy. However, expec-

---

should be revised to include more Angolan workers in the projects.' See also Centre for Chinese Studies, 'China's Interest and Activity in Africa's Construction and Infrastructure Sectors'.

84 See http://desabafosangolanos.blogspot.com, 'Angolanos escravizados: chineses reconstroem e ditam as regras', 24 July 2006.

85 This may well be a strategic goal for China, as evidenced in recent discussions at the National People's Conference of March 2007 of a law 'On Assisted Employment'. Its goal would be the reinforcement of China's presence around the world through institutional support for Chinese citizens wanting to work abroad.

tations about meeting deadlines have not been met, and the resulting disappointment has been made clear by the Angolan authorities on numerous occasions.[86] Many important works will not be completed any time soon, as is especially evident in the case of railways. The case of Hangxiao Steel Structure which, having won a March 2007 US$3.3 billion contract from the China International Fund, declared itself incapable of fulfilling outstanding commitments and is under investigation by the Shanghai Stock Exchange, is one of the most serious setbacks in the timing of Angola's reconstruction. It has also raised considerable suspicions over how the financing is managed, to the extent that the government had to publicly confront rumours of supposed malfeasance.[87] The delay in starting certain infrastructure projects and significant delays in finishing others may explain why elections have been repeatedly postponed. Does the resulting discontent explain the cancellation of Sinopec's involvement in the Lobito refinery[88] or the cancellation of a protocol between Endiama EP, China International Fund and the Future Pensions Fund?[89] Is the investigation into Hangxiao Steel Structure, regarding the sale of products and service provision in house building for Angola—an operation mediated by the China International Fund—[90] connected with President Hu Jintao's avoidance of Angola during his 2007 visit to Africa?

---

86 'Roberto de Almeida defende qualidade nas obras de reconstrução', *Angop*, 15 July 2007; *VOA*, 'Chineses podem ser afastado do CFB', 13 September 2007

87 'Atraso em projecto chinês coloca negócio milionário em Angola em risco', *Lusa*, 8 August 2007; 'Angolan loan casts light on ties with China', *Financial Times*, 19 October 2007; 'Siphoned off funds may be starving Chinese construction projects', *Southscan*, 19 October 2007; 'Ministério das Finanças descarta irregularidades na utilização da linha de crédito da China', *Angop*, 18 October 2007.

88 The semi-official version for the termination of this project refers to the incompatibility between Chinese intentions of having the refinery produce for its internal market and the Angolan intention to use it to service other markets.

89 'Conselho de Ministros', *Angop*, 2 March 2007.

90 'China: suspeitas de corrupção em negócio milionário com Angola', *Diário Digital/Lusa*, 26 March 2007.

The final question concerns the role that Chinese authorities believe Angola can fulfil, especially as it is currently very clear what role Angola expects China to perform vis-à-vis its own interests. Is China in Angola following a 'strictly business' approach? If this were so it would amount to a modest objective given the ambitious role that China wants to play in the international sphere. In view of the multifaceted potential of Angola in Africa, an ally like Angola can prove to be of unquestionable usefulness. If this were so, what would the consequences be for Angola, not only for the elite, but in terms of domestic politics? The same should be asked of repercussions at the regional level.

Conclusion

The momentum behind China's success in Angola is partly explained by a 'happy conjuncture' of mutual interests, but the preeminent factor is certainly the great sense of timing on both sides in what amounts to a 'perfect marriage'—for the time being. This also provides further illustration of the Angolan government's seemingly perennial capacity to play off different external interests to suit its own purposes.[91]

The Angolan civil war ended in February 2002 with the death of the rebel leader Jonas Savimbi, not so long after the end of the first FOCAC Summit in October 2000. Angola's pressing need for physical reconstruction, especially in infrastructure, found the right source of financing in the Chinese. In turn, this was made available as a bargaining chip to allow China secure energy supply and equity oil production. The Chinese *modus operandi* fitted perfectly with Angola's needs at a time when the Angolan government seemed unable either to attract non-oil investment into the country or to ensure the holding of a international donors' conference. It also resolved its longstanding difficulty in accessing international financing without political conditionalities. In particular, the Chinese involvement allowed Angola to bypass the IMF. While the relationship between Angola and the Fund has always been notoriously difficult (Angola never went through an IMF reform programme and negotiations

---

91 See Ferreira, 'Realeconomik e realpolitik nos recursos naturais em Angola', *Relações Internacionais* 6 (2005).

have broken down countless times in the recent past), China's provision of an alternative source of funding was well-timed to allow Angola to disengage. The lack of Chinese conditionality is one of the reasons why, despite the fact that current oil prices and the exponential increase in Angolan oil production allow the government some additional breathing space, Chinese assistance and its 'no moral harassment' underpinnings continue to play a pivotal role.

In this way, economic objectives (rebuilding the Angolan economy) and political objectives (holding elections only after the effects of reconstruction start being felt) seem like a 'perfect marriage of convenience'. Moreover, and no less important, this strategy permits power holders to argue that the civil war, and not poor governance by the MPLA, was mainly to blame for the chaotic state in which the country has found itself since independence. Lastly, the implications of the Chinese loans are visible well beyond the realm of economics. The internal political struggle remains intense, reflecting among other things the fight for appropriation of rents emanating from the joint ventures allowed by the Chinese loans.

16

MIXED FATES OF A POPULAR MINORITY: CHINESE MIGRANTS IN CAPE VERDE

Jørgen Carling and Heidi Østbø Haugen

Over the past decade Chinese immigrants have become the most visible immigrant group in Cape Verde. While Chinese immigration to other parts of Africa is met with considerable scepticism and even violent riots, the Chinese in Cape Verde are generally a popular minority. In a 2005 survey of Cape Verdeans 85 per cent responded that immigrants from Asia (essentially the Chinese) contribute positively to the development of the country. Fewer people, 74 per cent, saw European immigrants as contributing to development. At the bottom of the list were immigrants from mainland Africa; only 38 per cent of the survey respondents thought the Africans contributed to Cape Verde's development.[1] China was among the first countries to open an embassy after Cape Verde's independence in 1975. It was a close ally during the years of single-party rule, and remained a principal source of development assistance after the introduction of multi-party democracy in 1991.

---

1 Afrobarometer, 'The Quality of Democracy and Governance in Cape Verde: Summary of Results 2005' (Praia: Afro-Sondagem, 2005), p. 54.

During the 1990s, when the liberal-democratic Movimento para Democracia (MpD) was in power, China funded and executed several high-profile projects in Cape Verde, including the construction of a new parliament building, a national library and a giant statue of the liberation hero Amílcar Cabral, with an unmistakable Chinese design.

Chinese migrants were virtually non-existent in Cape Verde under Portuguese colonialism. Once in a while Chinese sailors passed through, since the islands were an important bunkering and maintenance stop for fishing boats and other ships in the Atlantic. A small number of Chinese embassy officials have been present in Cape Verde since the embassy opened, and Chinese have stayed temporarily on the islands in connection with development projects. It was not until the large influx of Chinese small-scale retailers in the late 1990s, however, that the Chinese became a sizeable minority. The Chinese population now stands at several hundred people. This is obviously minute in the context of the Chinese diaspora, but it is sufficiently large to have had a momentous impact on the society and economy of Cape Verde.

Cape Verde will remain a relatively unimportant partner for China in the drive for energy and raw materials from Africa, since the archipelago has no petroleum or mineral resources. Furthermore, the domestic market counts less than half a million people and is of little interest as a market for Chinese exports. Nevertheless, China's Foreign Minister Li Zhaoxing began his January 2006 African tour in Cape Verde's capital Praia. During this visit, he announced an offer of an interest-free loan to upgrade one of Cape Verde's hospitals, the latest addition to the series of Chinese aid initiatives in the country.

This chapter gives an overview of Chinese-Cape Verdean relations, with an emphasis on recent entrepreneurial migration to the archipelago. We then return to the results of the 2005 survey, and discuss why the Chinese immigrants are viewed much more favourably in Cape Verde than in many other African countries.

Chinese small-scale entrepreneurs in Cape Verde

The first Chinese shop opened in Cape Verde in 1995. Within a few years, Chinese entrepreneurs set up shops on all of the nine inhabited islands. The analysis below is based on fieldwork in Cape Verde in 2002, 2003 and 2006 among Chinese shop owners, Cape Verdean workers and customers in Chinese shops, and Cape Verdean government officials. The fieldwork was concentrated to Cape Verde's second largest city, São Vicente. Recorded interviews were carried out in Mandarin Chinese and Cape Verdean Creole Portuguese.[2]

With a couple of exceptions, all Chinese-run shops in Cape Verde offer the same range of goods and cater to the same customer groups. The shops are not specialized, but sell clothes, shoes, household consumer goods, cosmetics, toys and nick-nacks, mostly imported directly from the wholesale markets in Yiwu in Zhejiang Province, China by the shop owners. Typically, the goods have to be sold at more than three times their price in China in order to recover transport and operating costs. The Chinese goods are nevertheless significantly cheaper than what was available in Cape Verde before the Chinese arrived.

When the first Chinese shop opened in Cape Verde in the mid-1990s, the country offered a rare combination of political stability, security, high price levels and relatively high local purchasing power. The lack of existing Chinese businesses on the islands constituted an opportunity for making better profits than in more mature markets. As one Chinese woman put it, 'In Europe there have been Chinese running businesses for sixty years, so it's hard to manage.' In São Vicente the first Chinese shop was established in 1997. Two years later there were six shops. Since then the number of Chinese shops has doubled every two to three years, and surpassed 50 in 2006. While the first shops were spaced out across the city centre, new shops have filled the gaps so that certain streets are now completely dominated by the Chinese (Figure 1).

The growth in the number of shops is intimately connected with the growth in the number of Chinese residents. Chinese shops have multiplied in two ways: new owners have entered the market and established shop owners have expanded their businesses and

2   H. Haugen and J. Carling, 'On the Edge of the Chinese Diaspora: The Surge of Baihuo Business in an African City', *Ethnic and Racial Studies* 28, 4 (2005), pp. 639-62.

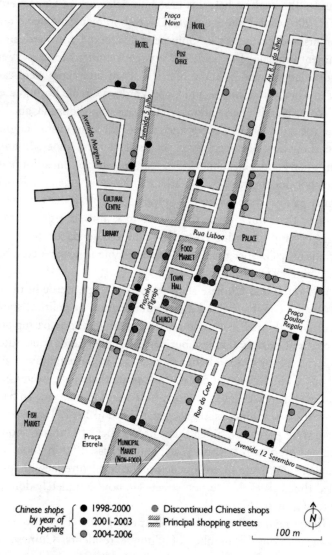

Chinese shops by year of opening
● 1998-2000
● 2001-2003
● 2004-2006
● Discontinued Chinese shops
▨▨ Principal shopping streets

100 m

Figure 1. Chinese shops in São Vicente

opened more shops. Having several outlets increases the turnover of goods. Shop owners therefore have an interest in increasing the number of shops under their control, either through direct ownership or by lending goods to new establishments and sharing the profit. New owners usually have a relationship with incumbents, as relatives, former employees, or both. Cape Verdean employees are usually not entrusted with handling cash in the shops. Increasing the number of outlets therefore requires more people to be brought over from China. The new Chinese immigrants generally come to Cape Verde at the invitation of migrants who have already established themselves in the country and can produce the necessary documents for visa applications.

The early Chinese migrants to Cape Verde came from different parts of China, including Shanghai and Beijing. After a few years, however, people from Zhejiang province came to dominate through rapidly expanding chain migration. The majority of the Chinese in Cape Verde now come from the region of Wenzhou in the southern part of Zhejiang province, a region with a long history of emigration, especially to Europe.[3]

The competition in the market for general merchandise has become fierce as a result of the large number of shops. Profit levels have dropped sharply, and the success and failure of individual shop owners depends largely on when they arrived with respect to the wave of Chinese immigration. The gradual Chinese domination of a market niche, and subsequent market saturation, are not a phenomenon unique to Cape Verde, but can be observed in different parts of the Chinese diaspora. The widespread pattern of growth by copying existing enterprises creates a rigid and isolated industry that is ill prepared when the number of suppliers grows out of proportion to the demand, and profits are pushed to critical levels. A typology of responses to this situation can be outlined based on the recent history of Chinese migration to Europe (Table 1).

---

3 F.N. Pieke, 'Introduction', in Gregor Benton and Frank N. Pieke (eds), *The Chinese in Europe* (London: Macmillan, 1998), pp. 1-17; Li Minghuan, '"To Get Rich Quickly in Europe!" - Reflections on Migration Motivation in Wenzhou', in F.N. Pieke and H. Mallee (eds), *Internal and International Migration. Chinese Perspectives* (Richmond: Curzon, 1999), pp. 181-98; M. Thunø, 'Moving Stones from China to Europe: The Dynamics of Emigration from Zhejiang to Europe', in Pieke and Mallee (eds), *Internal and International Migration*, pp. 159-80.

	Same business	Same location	Existing concept	Required resources	Examples
Geographical expansion	Yes	No	Yes	Accessible regions with unsaturated markets	Textile trade from Russia through Eastern Europe (1980s–1990s)
Price wars	Yes	Yes	(Yes)	Price-cutting potential, docile labour power	Restaurants in Denmark and the Netherlands (1970s–1980s)
Sectoral expansion	No	(Yes)	Yes	Information, capital, skills, networks	From restaurants to shops in the Czech Republic and Spain (1990s)
Innovation	Yes	Yes	No	Information, capital, skills, networks	Restaurants in the Netherlands, Denmark and Norway (1980s–1990s)

Table 1. A typology of responses to market saturation

Source: H. Haugen and J. Carling, 'On the Edge of the Chinese Diaspora: The Surge of Baihuo Business in an African City', *Ethnic and Racial Studies* Vol. 28, No. 4 (2005), pp. 639-62.

Among Chinese immigrants in Cape Verde, *geographical expansion* has so far been the most important reaction to the increased competition. Shops spread from the capital Praia to São Vicente and other islands. The opportunities for spatial expansion were originally considerable. Cape Verde consists of nine populated islands, some with several population centres where the demand for cheap consumer goods is large enough to sustain at least one Chinese shop, with little competition from other businesses. Today, Chinese shops modelled on the original ones are established in all Cape Verdean population centres, and the potential for geographical expansion within the country is exhausted.

Some shop owners have responded to market saturation in Cape Verde by searching for opportunities for geographical expansion in mainland Africa, notably the major Portuguese-speaking countries, Angola and Mozambique. Those who have realized their plans to move keep their shops in Cape Verde as security while establishing themselves on the mainland, letting Chinese employees and relatives run these businesses. Once the shops in mainland Africa prove profitable, the Chinese migrants shut down or sell some of their shops in Cape Verde. However, lack of information and connections in other African countries, as well as the capital tied up in the shops in Cape Verde, serves as a barrier against moving on to the mainland.

Engaging in price wars is the second way in which Chinese shop owners in Cape Verde have responded to falling sales. Consequently, the net profit on sales has fallen markedly. Some shops do not display prices out of fear of being undercut by competitors, and only tell customers the price upon request. Cape Verdeans have become more conscious of the quality of what they buy, and many importers have reduced their profits by selling higher quality goods without raising prices. The decrease in profits makes the situation especially difficult for newly established shops, which share the profit of their sales with importers. The original price cuts were possible because the early shops maintained very high profit margins. The potential for cutting prices is now almost exhausted, however, as is the potential for generating income by exploiting a docile labour force more intensely.

The third response to market saturation is *expansion into other business sectors*. In many other countries, Chinese have moved from one niche to another, with catering, trade in consumer goods, and traditional Chinese medicine being the most important sectors.[4] In Cape Verde, by contrast, the Chinese entrepreneurs have faithfully kept to trade in consumer goods. Sectoral expansion is inhibited at the individual level by the need for capital or for business-specific information, skills or networks. The migration chains to Cape Verde have so far been confined to one line of business, with skills and information being passed on through apprenticeships and family networks. The consumption patterns in Cape Verde may also make it difficult to run Chinese restaurants and clinics. One successful attempt at expansion into another sector, however, has been the opening of a garage in Praia where Chinese mechanics repair cars at higher speed and lower prices than the market standard.

Finally, one may respond to market saturation by implementing *innovative changes* to get an edge over co-ethnic competitors. Within small-scale retail, there are apparently still areas where prices are surprisingly high and there is a potential for Chinese expansion. An example is canned and dry food, which is often more expensive in Cape Verde than in Western Europe. The Chinese explain their absence from the food sector on the basis of their limited knowledge of lo-

---

4   M. Moore and C. Tubilewicz, 'Chinese Migrants in the Czech Republic. Perfect Strangers', *Asian Survey*, 41 (2001), pp. 611-28; G. Nieto, 'The Chinese in Spain', *International Migration*, 41 (2003), pp. 215-37.

cal tastes, lack of necessary connections for importing foodstuffs and shortage of capital.

Paradoxically, the fierce competition from other Chinese shops serves as a disincentive for both sectoral expansion and innovation. Successful initiatives are quickly copied, profit margins are driven down, and the benefits of innovation are shared between several Chinese shops. In the case of failure, however, the pioneer bears the loss alone. Other obstacles include the lack of local social networks and disapproving attitudes from other Chinese towards attempts at innovation.

Chinese entrepreneurs have so far established themselves in Cape Verde independently of the Chinese state. The migrants emphasize that they came to Cape Verde on their own initiative and by their own means, and that the only time they need to be in contact with the embassy is in connection with paperwork such as renewal of travel documents. As one Chinese shop owner put it: 'Frankly, we don't have great need for the embassy's help. [...] Their development aid is completely separate from the Chinese people who live and do business here. It's just government relationship.' On one occasion in 2003, Cape Verdean authorities requested the Chinese embassy to assist in improving the compliance of Chinese shop owners with Cape Verdean labour laws. This initiative was welcomed by many shop owners who had found it hard to understand local legislation. In Praia, the Chinese embassy also provides an institutional setting for social interaction among the Chinese on festive days. Despite the lack of any direct connection with the Chinese state, many Cape Verdeans—including high-ranking officials in the area of commerce—wrongly assume that the Cape Verdean government gives Chinese traders preferential treatment in return for Chinese development aid.

Entry into higher-value sectors

While the Chinese engagement in small-scale retail in Cape Verde was initiated and developed independently of official relations between the two countries, government institutions have played a more active role in connection with attempted Chinese entry into higher-value sectors in Cape Verde. This is not a question of small-scale shopkeepers advancing, but of well-established Chinese entrepreneurs entering the market at higher levels. In this process, the Chinese government plays different roles.

First, projects funded by the Chinese government can be used as a stepping-stone for entering the Cape Verdean market. When the Chinese fund development projects, they often bring Chinese companies and professionals to do the work. For instance, a Chinese construction company recently came to Cape Verde to carry out a construction project in the Chinese embassy compound. According to two Chinese employees, the company's intention was to use this opportunity to assess the potential of the regular Cape Verdean construction market. The company is present in several other African countries, and has a large pool of Chinese professionals to bring to Cape Verde when and if its business expands. While working in the embassy, the company filed an application for a local license necessary to work on projects that were not funded by the Chinese government. The initial plans were to enter the construction and real estate business with a view to expanding into other areas with time. The property market in Cape Verde is already attracting considerable attention from Italian, Portuguese and other foreign investors.

Second, Chinese investment in development projects can leverage support from the Cape Verdean government for commercial ventures. So far, money for development projects in Cape Verde has come from the Chinese government rather than the private sector. This is about to change if the plans of David Chow, Cape Verde's Honorary Consul in Macau, are realized. Chow intends to invest US $100 million in Cape Verde over the next two years, possibly extending to as much as US $300 million over a ten-year period.[5] The scale of investment is unprecedented in a country where the average net foreign direct investment per year was only US$18.5 million in 2000-4.[6] David Chow's immediate plans include building a luxury casino on the islet of Santa Maria off the shorefront of the capital

---

5   CCITPCV, *Sector do Turismo em Cabo Verde, breve panorâmica* Lisbon: Câmara de Comércio, Indústria e Turismo Portugal Cabo Verde (CCITPCV, 2006).

6   World Bank, *World Development Indicators* (Washington, DC: World Bank, 2006), p. 298.

Praia, and to build hotels. In return for the rights to use the land, Chow has promised to construct social housing and clean up beaches in Cape Verde. Such deals whereby Chinese entrepreneurs pay for Cape Verdean resources in favours rather than in fixed amounts of money obscure the real value of the contracts.

Third, Chinese authorities may facilitate investment through high-level political dialogue. This may be required for Chinese companies to enter into sectors with heavy state regulation. A case in point is the Cape Verdean telecommunications market, where Cabo Verde Telecom, a subsidiary of Portugal Telecom, until recently held a monopoly for both the mobile and landline networks. A week after Cape Verdean Prime Minister Jose Maria Neves met with the mayor of Shanghai in August 2004, rumours spread that Shanghai Telecom was to receive the licence to offer mobile, internet and cable TV services in Cape Verde. These reports were later publicly denounced by the Cape Verdean Ministry of Information and Transport and the new telecommunications licence ended up being given to an American company.

It is too early to evaluate the economic and political consequences of Chinese investment in higher-value sectors in Cape Verde. However, it seems clear that the influence of Chinese investments in such areas may become as forceful as the impact of Chinese entrepreneurs on the small-scale retail market.

Why are Cape Verdeans so positive towards Chinese immigrants?

People in Cape Verde hold a strikingly positive view on immigration from China. The reasons can be found both in the positive change brought about by the Chinese small-scale entrepreneurs and in the absence of negative consequences of Chinese immigration for the majority of the population. We will now account for the characteristics of Cape Verde that we believe underlie the positive attitudes and explain some of the contrast with other parts of Africa.

Local purchasing power has increased. The most important reason behind the popularity of the Chinese is probably the fact that their presence has exerted a downward pressure on consumer prices in

Cape Verde. Before Chinese shops opened in large numbers, prices for clothes and durable household items in Cape Verde were often at European levels or above. With a GDP per capita at one sixth of the average OECD level, the high prices severely restrained people's ability to purchase basic consumer goods. Chinese and Cape Verdeans alike commonly assert that the living standard of poor Cape Verdeans improved with the entry of the Chinese. One shop owner had heard that 'before the Chinese came, very few people wore shoes. At least now they have shoes.' Locals confirm this, saying that the arrival of the Chinese has meant that children in Cape Verde no longer need to go barefoot to school. Another, equally emotive example frequently referred to by Cape Verdeans is that now all parents can afford to buy Christmas presents for their children.

In the past, Cape Verdeans often relied on gifts and parcels from emigrant relatives for obtaining clothes and household items. Today, with lower prices and a wider selection in the local market, emigrants on holiday increasingly bring cash to their relatives and let them buy what they want. Furthermore, emigrants are shopping in the Chinese shops and bringing the goods back with them to Europe or the United States.

It is worth noting that in a situation with parallel development aid and small-scale trade from China, the latter appears to have been more important for the Cape Verdeans' positive view of the Chinese. Attitudes towards the Chinese are no more positive in the capital Praia, which has received the bulk of Chinese development aid, than in other parts of the country.[7] In fact, the development aid has been a cause of suspicion against Chinese entrepreneurs. One of the most common misgivings expressed by Cape Verdeans during our fieldwork was that Chinese shop owners were exempted from paying import duties as a counter-favour for Chinese development aid. The accusation is unfounded, as there are no special tax arrangements for Chinese shop owners in Cape Verde.

Chinese imports have little impact on local production. Chinese undercutting of local industries has been a source of discontent in

---

7 Afrobarometer, 'The Quality of Democracy and Governance in Cape Verde', p. 54.

several African countries with a significant manufacturing sector, such as Morocco, South Africa and Lesotho. Local industry in these countries faces tighter competition caused by the increasing supply of cheap Chinese goods. The lifting of EU and United States import barriers against Chinese goods has further contributed to this by depriving African manufacturers of the competitive edge they previously possessed.[8]

The local manufacturing sector in Cape Verde is very small, and much of it is export-oriented and not affected by imports from China. There is, in other words, very little domestically oriented production that is driven out of business by competition from China. One exception is clothes repair, which is less in demand because people can now afford to buy new clothes from the Chinese instead of having old ones repaired.

The relatively high standard of living in Cape Verde has primarily been financed by income in the form of migrant remittances, overseas development aid, and export earnings from services. The Cape Verdean diaspora now outnumbers the resident population, and many families have emigrant members who send them money.[9] Despite the relatively high standard of living in Cape Verde, the level of aid per capita has been the world's highest in some years. In 2004, the most recent available data, Cape Verde ranked third with an inflow of more than US$280 per person.[10] The dependence on transfers from abroad ensures that people enjoy the benefits from the drop in retail prices caused by cheap imports from China, while not experiencing deterioration in income due to the increase in supply of Chinese goods.

While there is no significant manufacturing sector that suffers from the increase in Chinese supply, there is also no raw material sector that benefits from the increase in demand from China. Cape Verde is therefore not among the African countries that benefit from

8 J-C Servant, 'La Chine à l'assaut du marché africain', *Le Monde Diplomatique*, May 2005, pp. 6-7.

9 J.Carling, 'Emigration, Return and Development in Cape Verde: The Impact of Closing Borders', *Population, Space and Place* 10, 2 (2004), pp. 113-132.

10 UNDP, *Human Development Report 2005* (Washington, DC: United Nations Development Program, 2006) p. 281.

the price rise caused by China's increasing demand for natural resources.

No substantial Cape Verdean job losses from Chinese shops. The entry of Chinese retailers has transformed the local small-scale retail market in Cape Verde. However, the incomes of most Cape Verdeans remain unaffected by this change. This can be explained by the structure of the retail market before the arrival of the Chinese. The market was roughly divided into two segments. At the top end of the market, there were the so-called *boutiques,* many of which were run by relatively wealthy women who did not depend on the income from their shops, but were motivated by the prospect of frequent travel to purchase goods. Their shops were often confined to a space of less than ten square metres, and they kept a selection of clothes, shoes and accessories bought mainly in Brazil or Southern Europe. Typically, they had a very low turnover and high profit margins. Many *boutiques* have suffered competition as a result of the increasingly fashionable stock of the Chinese shops.

At the other end of the market in São Vicente, there was the municipal market, dominated by mainland Africans. These vendors either travelled abroad to buy goods, or bought wholesale from traders travelling regularly to Portugal or Senegal. The clothes imported from such places were often produced in Southeast Asia, but had become anything but cheap by the time they reached Cape Verde. The establishment of Chinese shops has resulted in a transformation of business at the municipal market. Many of the stalls have now closed, and those that are still in business specialize increasingly in goods other than clothes.

Neither the *boutique* owners nor the mainland African traders are groups average Cape Verdeans strongly identify or sympathize with. The number of Cape Verdeans employed in *boutiques* and by mainland Africans is small, and the employment losses are outweighed by the new employment opportunities in Chinese shops.

Limited corruption problems in Cape Verde. In countries where corruption is a widespread problem, resentment may arise against an immigrant group that is seen to exacerbate this problem. A recent example is the Solomon Islands, where rioters attacked Chinese business owners partly as a result of frustration with politicians who exploited the China-Taiwan rivalry for their personal gains.[11] While the ultimate target were politicians known to be corrupt for years, Chinese business owners was an easy group to go after.

In Cape Verde, by contrast, corruption is a problem that is perceived to be relatively limited. In the 2005 survey referred to earlier, only between 5-8 per cent of Cape Verdeans were concerned corruption among parliament or cabinet members, civil servants, and members of the police force.[12] Most of the Chinese we interviewed during our fieldwork said that they found corruption to be less of a problem in Cape Verde than in China. Many cited the lack of corruption as a trait that made Cape Verde an attractive country to run a business in, and saw greater corruption problems in other African countries as an obstacle to moving.

Although corruption is not a problem that causes Cape Verdeans to perceive Chinese immigrants negatively today, there are some indications that it is a problem on the rise. Some officials who deal with Chinese have started asking for personal favours, and a culture of corruption is underpinned when requests for bribes are met. The consequences of crackdowns on corrupt practices may reach beyond those directly involved. A few years ago Cape Verdean residence permits, which enabled Chinese immigrants to apply for Schengen visas from Cape Verde, could be acquired quite easily. However, some Chinese began to bribe local officials to speed up the processing of their permits. The Cape Verdean government reacted to this practice, and it has since become more difficult for all Chinese to obtain residence permits and visas to Europe. The potential for corruption may also increase as the economic interaction between Cape Verde and China becomes deeper and more complex. Practices such as offering development aid in return for rights to pursue commercial interests make transactions less transparent and unethical practices harder to disclose.

11 R. Callick, 'Corruption the catalyst behind Pacific pattern', *The Australian*, 25 April 2006.

12 Afrobarometer, 'The Quality of Democracy and Governance in Cape Verde', p. 11.

Chinese immigration is not perceived as a threat to national identity.
Visible and culturally distinct immigrant groups are often seen as
a threat to national identity and social harmony. In Cape Verde,
however, the presence of Chinese immigrants is not perceived as
threatening in this way. The centuries of mixture, Creolization and
outbound migration from Cape Verde are key to understanding how
a distinct cultural and racial group may be readily accepted as part of
Cape Verdean society. Virtually all Cape Verdeans are descendants
of both mainland Africans and Europeans, and their national identity has been created out of this mixture. Migration from Cape Verde
has resulted in a widely dispersed diaspora, and the country's position
at an Atlantic crossroads has ensured a steady flow of new impulses.
Cape Verdeans have come to perceive themselves as open towards
cultural difference and experienced in interacting with foreigners.[13]
Many of the Chinese we interviewed expressed appreciation of this
cultural openness, and contrasted it with the discrimination they
feared they would have faced in Europe.

In one way, however, the Chinese presence may pose a challenge
to the national identity of Cape Verdeans. Many people in Cape
Verde perceive their country as poor, and understand their personal
and collective poverty as place-bound.[14] Searching for opportunities
elsewhere is often seen as the only way to wealth. The arrival of a
considerable number of Chinese who search for, and in some cases
attain, wealth in Cape Verde challenges this common world-view.
Some Cape Verdeans consider the (perceived) success of the Chinese
as a cause for suspicion, and conclude that the only explanation must
be that the Chinese do not play by the rules or are granted favours
such as tax exemptions for political reasons. Such logic may be used
to justify property crimes against the Chinese, from shoplifting to
armed robbery, which are serious and increasing problems.

---

13 L. Åkesson, 'Making a Life. Meanings of Migration in Cape Verde',
Unpublished PhD thesis (Department of Social Anthropology, Göteborg
University, 2004).
14 J. Carling, 'Migration in the Age of Involuntary Immobility: Theoretical
Reflections and Cape Verdean Experiences', *Journal of Ethnic and Migration
Studies* 28, 1 (2002), pp. 5-42.

The Chinese are not reinforcing internal conflicts. During the past couple of years, there has been an increase in Western media reports of China undermining efforts to promote human rights and good governance in Africa by selling arms to regimes known to turn them against their own citizens or extending diplomatic support to assist repressive regimes to keep in power. Unlike many African countries, Cape Verde has faced no wars, neither during decolonization nor later. The country is marked by relative political and social stability, and Cape Verdeans have faith in their political system. After the 2001 elections, only 5 per cent of the population thought that the elections had not been 'free and just'.[15] The Chinese presence does not add to the repression of any population segment in Cape Verde. The fact that the Chinese presence is not reinforcing internal conflicts in Cape Verde helps ensure that the Chinese immigrants are not negatively viewed.

Sources of resentment

Despite the largely positive attitudes towards the Chinese, their settlement in Cape Verde has not proceeded without resentment. While Cape Verdeans expressed gratitude for the lowering of consumer goods prices brought about by the Chinese, they often also commented on the low quality of the Chinese goods. Discussions between Chinese shop owners and customers who wanted to return broken products occurred frequently during our fieldwork. The increased competition among the Chinese traders has partly affected quality as well as price, and in general, the quality of the goods is now higher than when the first Chinese shops opened. However, upmarket goods from China are difficult to sell because of the poor reputation of Chinese merchandise. Disappointment with the goods purchased from Chinese stores continues to be a source of conflict between Cape Verdeans and the Chinese.

Another source of tension between the Cape Verdeans and the Chinese is the employee-employer relationship. Most Chinese shops have two to five local employees who assist customers, watch out for

---

15 Afrobarometer, 'The Quality of Democracy and Governance in Cape Verde', p. 7.

shoplifters and do other work in the shops. While unemployment in Cape Verde is high, the Chinese shop owners said they had difficulties finding employees they could trust. Some shop owners introduced strict control measures to catch employees stealing. Others assumed that all employees would start stealing after some time and kept a high turnover, firing employees after a couple of months, before they acquired any protection under the country's labour laws. Yet others invested in their relationships with the employees to build loyalty and retain good workers. The relationship between shop owners and employees continued to be a source of tension, however, with each side complaining about being cheated and let down by the other. Both the Chinese and the Cape Verdeans attributed such tension partly to cultural differences. It remains to be seen how the relationships between Chinese employers and Cape Verdean employees will play out when the Chinese are moving into other business areas but small-scale retail.

Conclusion: *The future of Chinese-Cape Verdean relations*

While the days when small-scale Chinese retailers could make good money in Cape Verde have passed, the number of Chinese small-scale entrepreneurs has kept growing. Barriers to exit are high. Entering new markets requires knowledge and contacts that many entrepreneurs do not have access to. Shutting down the existing business carries high costs as unsold goods are expensive to export to a third country and are hard to sell wholesale locally. Those entrepreneurs who have higher education from China worry that their skills will already be outdated and useless in modern China. Those without an education fear their opportunities for making a profit will be even slimmer in China, where they are now out of touch with the market. While a few chose to go to Cape Verde mostly to get the experience of living abroad for a while, many came because they were not doing very well in China, either at school or in their jobs.

The lucky retailers came when profit levels were still generous, and some moved on while it was still easy to sell off their goods to colleagues. The unlucky late entrants have to make do at least until their sunk costs are recovered. It remains to be seen whether some of them will introduce innovations in the ways they run their businesses or move into new business niches. So far the opposite has happened—Chinese who tried starting restaurants or bars have shut them down and opened shops instead.

While the entry and proliferation of Chinese entrepreneurs in Cape Verde took place without encouragement or much intervention from the state on either side, a second generation of Chinese entrepreneurs has started entering Cape Verde, and these, backed by political connections and more capital, are attempting to enter higher value markets such as property, natural resources and communications. This involves tighter cooperation between Cape Verdean and Chinese political and commercial players, and lead to greater intertwinement of fields such as commerce and development aid.

China's pronounced ambitions to move into higher value markets in Africa are paralleled by Cape Verdean expectations that China will be a strategic partner in turning Cape Verde into a commercial and service hub in West Africa.[16] The consequences of the second wave of Chinese business investment, and how this will affect the way ordinary Cape Verdeans regard the Chinese, are not yet known. It is evident, however, that the impact of Chinese investments on the small island economy of Cape Verde is potentially extensive. While taking a principled stance for or against Chinese investment is a meaningless exercise, it is pertinent for Cape Verde to carefully weigh advantages and costs related to concrete cooperation projects.

The case of Cape Verde is in many ways a Chinese success story in Africa. The principal losers so far seem to be the Cape Verdean *boutique* owners, the mainland African traders, the women who used to make a living on clothes repairs, and indeed some of the Chinese traders themselves. The late entrants often ended up struggling to recoup their investments and felt stuck in a market with dim prospects. For the majority of Cape Verdeans, however, and for the image of the Chinese in Cape Verde, the encounter has been overwhelmingly positive. As we have shown in this paper, this outcome has much to do with specific factors in Cape Verde. The Cape Verdean case

---

16 Embassy of the PRC, 'Chinese foreign minister kicks off African Tour', Press Release, 12 January 2006.

illustrates how the variety in local markets and social and political contexts across the continent precludes sweeping conclusions about the impact of China's growing presence in Africa.

SECTION 4
LOOKING FORWARD

17

TEN CAVEATS AND ONE SUNRISE
IN OUR CONTEMPLATION
OF CHINA AND AFRICA

Stephen Chan

This brief chapter is an *aide-mémoire* and not an academic work. It
is not strewn with data and footnotes and makes no pretence to be
scholarly. There is already a surfeit of poor and tentative scholarship
on this issue—which this book seeks to ameliorate and correct—and
its other chapters will make plain the latest data. The present *aide-
mémoire* stems from my completely accidental involvement as a sort
of participant-observer in the very recent diplomatic jostling among
Africa, the USA and China. I had no previous sustained track record
in published research on China and Africa. My usefulness to various
parties lay entirely in the exotica of my being an Africanist who was
also Chinese. I should also add that I am an Afrophile, so my usefulness is predisposed. However, exoticism is precisely the hallmark of
so much published work on China and Africa, especially in the USA,

as Africanists who are not Sinologists and Sinologists who are not Africanists, and political scientists who are neither, stray as amateurs into fields other than their own. I do not claim immunity from any of this. My Chineseness is diasporic and, in the wake of the Tiananmen Square slaughter, I maintained a boycott against visiting China, despite several invitations, for well over a decade and a half. I am not literate in Chinese and I speak only a rudimentary Cantonese. I admit a large gap in my credentials. Nevertheless, it seems to me that there are at least ten very common misperceptions or misjudgements on China and Africa, and I have taken the liberty of suggesting what these are.

(i) On a global scale

The preoccupation with China's expanding economic profile in Africa should not be seen as an isolated and disconnected phenomenon. China is expanding rapidly around the world. It has become one of the world's largest economies, has one of the world's fastest growths in GNP, and is bringing on tap new generations of technologically and electronically skilled personnel. Economic links with Africa could scarcely begin to absorb the restless economic energy emanating from China and, indeed, Africa accounts for only 3 per cent of total annual Chinese world trade. There is growing Chinese foreign direct investment in Africa, and a growing aid profile. However, this growth notwithstanding, the real issue at stake in terms of Western, and especially US, concern is to do with oil flows from Africa to China. These flows clearly service the burgeoning industrial capacity of China and, in due course, this will become even more of a competitive factor in Western manufacturing and trade strategies. This is not, however, the key concern. This concern is indeed future-based. It is not that the US requires African oil now, it doesn't. But it sees a future of US growth in energy demand, and the possibility that African oil will have been 'sewn up' by long-term African commitments to the Chinese—for which the Chinese are now paying in terms of grants and lines of liquidity. The US is concerned about one product and about that product's future market. With that single product out of the equation, there would be no fuss about China and

Africa. There is no 'scramble'. There is a chess-game beginning about a single commodity's future. In other respects, the Chinese global strategy sees far greater importance in expanded trade and other economic links with Europe than with Africa.

(ii) Disparities within Africa

Often there are generalized analyses of China and 'Africa'—as if there were relations between two countries, instead of between one and 53; and as if there were only one official characteristic demarcating the relationships. But taking an even slightly closer look at the 3 per cent of Chinese global trade that Africa enjoys, one sees that 20 per cent of that 3 per cent is with South Africa alone. If the South African and Nigerian shares of that trade are combined, the rest of Africa becomes a group of much smaller and even marginal players. There is also an important typology of Chinese actors to be drawn. There are directly official Chinese actors: the Chinese variant of the multinational corporation, with strong Party influences and, sometimes, direction and backing; individual Chinese entrepreneurs, who may (or may not) benefit from a Chinese government incentive scheme, but who take private risks in setting up shop (often literally) in Africa; and the usual bunch of adventurers, chancers and con-men who flood in with any growth of official economic investment. There are also generations of the more individual or 'private' Chinese, including those who chose to stay behind, for example as restaurateurs and herbalists, after projects like the TAZARA Railway. It is true that the Chinese construction methodology is to keep Chinese workers in their own labour and social groups, within their own accommodation, and working to Chinese practices of speed and health and safety; but it is not true that all go home afterwards.

The Chinese diaspora is a peculiar one that requires some sociological investigation; and it differs from country to country. Having said that, it is very often the newer 'privateers' and entrepreneurs who create racial tensions most. Under-briefed and under-educated about Africa, assiduous in Chinese work habits and risk-taking—sometimes blatantly exploitative—Chinese make demands of African workers that can be illegal and demeaning. Moreover, on the 'high street', when these same private businesses undercut longer-established lo-cal ones, often by importing Chinese manufactures that are cheaper than those locally-made, resentment among both workers and com-petitors grows. The profile of this resentment, and whether it can be corrected, differs again from country to country. There is therefore a need for far greater economic and sociological nuance in discussing the 'Chinese' in Africa. Finally, even in the matter of oil, there are differences in the Chinese profile. The Chinese, for instance, simply are not much good at offshore technology; their expertise is in land-based exploration and exploitation. For extensive offshore work the Chinese need to form partnerships with Western companies. This may indicate greater scope for future cooperation over oil than im-mediately meets the eye.

(iii) The vulnerable international base

It is not as if the Chinese government has an endless well of financial inducements to give to Africa. The international Chinese profile has several component parts and these have great interdependence—with various components under pressure or facing dissatisfaction. Put suc-cinctly, the Chinese would have no capacity for international gener-osity, no matter what the long-term benefits, if in the short term the extremely favourable balance of trade China enjoys with the US in particular was to cease, or became reversed. International pressures towards de/revaluation of the Chinese currency, trade walls erected by Europe—even the need to invest significant sums in North Korea to keep the 'hermit kingdom' stable and compliant with international norms—all constitute pressure on the short-term largesse which has typified the Chinese approach towards Africa.

(iv) The vulnerable national base

For all the Chinese rhetoric of seeking to assist in African devel-opment, development in China itself is immensely uneven, and the domestic basis for Chinese prosperity is in fact politically volatile. Chinese leaders go out of their way to 'manage' the domestic situa-tion into an overall national stability—but this requires much effort, and much hope that an astoundingly Western and Walt Rostow-style 'trickle-down' effect will occur quickly enough for dissatisfactions with uneven development to subside. The sheer dishonesties and brutalities of land-grabs, embezzlement and corruption, favouritism, and related vendettas come through clearly even in the coded language and politesse of the People's Assembly—the polite parliament which is voicing genuine concerns and grievances. In addition, the huge Chinese savings rate—which allows money to become available for both national and international purposes—depends upon domestic stability, faith in a financial future, and a sense of growth. One sudden surge of panic withdrawal of savings from banks would transform Chinese financial capacity dramatically; and one even temporary surge in inflation could dent saver confidence. But the economy is manifestly ebbing and flowing from and towards overheating—the booming stock market, for instance, is both a blessing and a curse, as savings are sunk and sometimes lost, and 'returns' are sometimes predicated against creative accounting procedures. The Chinese will have to put a lot more regulation into their financial sector: this might reduce cheating and overheating, but might also reduce confidence.

(v) Expansion prospects in Africa

When it comes to the question of oil from Africa, the Chinese in fact face the same future problem as the US. If all the proven oil field production is biased towards the Chinese market, leaving no future spare capacity for the US, that means there is no future spare capacity for the Chinese. This is where the Chinese have stolen a march upon Western interests. They see themselves as competing, not with other states, but with international oil companies. They can directly and immediately, therefore, link public aid packages to commercial resource exploitation—and they are able to do so on a speculative basis. The Chinese, to use unlovely jargon, are prepared to pay (and lose) upfront for 'foothold' and, particularly, for 'upstream acreage'—basically, betting investment against oil deposits not yet fully prospected and proven.

(vi) Methodology

None of this is necessarily random. It is coordinated to an extent that Western oil companies cannot match. Moreover, it is not necessarily accomplished by simple crude pursuit of gain. There is talk of an emerging 'Shanghai School'—an alternative to thought and methodology in the 'Washington Consensus'. To an extent, this is hot air, a fanciful Chinese conceit of achieving a model with the same influence as, for example, the 'Chicago School' of economics. Yet, the nascent 'School' has already attracted disciples and imitators. Indian investment, with Mittal Steel as a lead partner, has used the 'Chinese' methodology of aggressive bidding and promises of significant infrastructural investment in Nigeria. Watch out for the Malaysians and, beyond Asia, the Russians. In effect, the 'Shanghai School' is a very simple combination of methods that, together, may be seen as a methodology: high-level state-to-state political friendship, conditionality-free lines of finance and liquidity, highly visible aid and infrastructure projects, and a planning foundation for partner-states. Like a fixed-rate mortgage, the Chinese may be factored into planning as a non-volatile trading partner. But it works both ways: the Africans, in Western fears, are locked into China for many years to come; but the Chinese are locked into Africa. So the key omission in the 'Shanghai' model is how to deal with African instability and resultant disruptions in supply. Working on a state-to-state basis, for instance, would not make the Chinese any more immune to rebel activities in the Niger Delta than Shell.

(vii) The advantages and disadvantages of history

This is where the vaunted Chinese political-historical linkage to Africa has both strengths and weaknesses. There is implicit in the Chinese model, whether termed 'Shanghai' or not, two key supportive elements of solidarity. Firstly, the Chinese are not the West, with its history of imperialism and neo-imperialism in both politico-economic domination and exploitation and in terms of imposing political norms such as democracy; secondly, since Bandung, the Chinese have always identified themselves in a very public, philosophical and political, ideological and almost theorized manner (e.g. the so-called Chinese 'Three World Theory') as being for Africa and being a developing country not unlike those in Africa. The linkages run deep. Sudan, for instance, was the fourth African state to recognize the People's Republic of China, and the Chinese have never forgotten this diplomatic debt from their own days of isolation and pariah-statehood. Before liberation, I remember sitting down to eat with officers from Robert Mugabe's guerrilla forces, all of us using chopsticks. They had received their training from Chinese sources, and Mugabe has never forgotten the debt he owes China. Some of his own high-level supporters even say the chaos caused by the farm invasions is simply that moment of transition that Mao sought to accomplish with the Cultural Revolution. But these linkages are fraught with their own destabilizations. They risk becoming prisoners to history. While, for instance, the Chinese parade the doctrine of 'non-interference' over Sudan, the African Union is itself turning towards the new and alternative doctrine of 'non-indifference'—and there is deep concern in Africa, under the surface, about both Sudan and Zimbabwe. It almost seems as if Washington has suddenly woken up, surprised about the extent and depth of political connectedness between China and Africa; but Beijing has barely begun to have its bad dream about the lack of dynamism in its historically-crafted connections.

(viii) High political weight

But, insofar as the Chinese remain concerned to play out a model based on the Shanghai School, historical political friendship, and non-interference, they are going for it with a vengeance and, being very good at high-level symbolic political acts, they have thrown their state leaders into the continent. President Hu Jintao has visited Africa five times since 1999. Premier Wen Jiabao has visited three times. This is a direct courtship unmatched by US presidents, even by British prime ministers. And, insofar as the Chinese have something to learn from the West, the end of 2006 Sino-African summit in Beijing was a direct steal from the Francophone-African jamborees in Paris. Red carpets and flatteries really do seem to work.

(ix) But naiveties are in play

Having said that, Chinese diplomacy and manoeuvres can be astoundingly naïve. They are established on a state-to-state basis, and

345

centred on the old Bandung and Non-Aligned doctrine of non-interference, and the Chinese do not seem to know how to react when the government of a state might be about to change. The reaction of the Chinese ambassador to Zambia, during the 2006 Zambian elections, when Michael Sata launched an opposition manifesto hostile to China and seemed momentarily poised to win, was hasty panic and intervention—warning about consequences should Sata both win and enact his anti-Chinese policy. Similarly, the official doctrine of non-interference has become as much dogma as doctrine—so that the slow emergence of an African Union doctrine of 'non-indifference' to the internal tragedies of member states has caught the Chinese by surprise. The Chinese would find it embarrassing to be seen as supportive of Khartoum if the African Union were to be visibly non-supportive. The Chinese postures seem also to be based at least in part on research, both in the state academies and in Politburo research arms, that can be astoundingly limited and based on worn assumptions. There is very little actual fieldwork, and 'evidence' can be no more than interviews with African officials. Often embassy personnel based in Africa cannot speak either English or French very well, and very seldom do any speak any of the African languages; so they exclude themselves, as it were, from the back-gossip of even official occasions, still more from that of unofficial events where, in any case, Chinese diplomats are conspicuous by their absence. What goes into Chinese risk analysis when it comes to Africa can only be generalized and one-dimensional.

(x) New and old combinations

Nevertheless, old doctrines and new needs are propelling the Chinese involvement in Africa. How the new and old combine differs from African state to state. Western governments concerned about the pace of Chinese activities should be mindful that there are huge insecurities and contradictions in the Chinese profile—and huge risks predicated on continuing stability and liquidities being available within China and as a result of Chinese trade with the West. It is not a house of cards; the Chinese don't play cards anyway; they play

Mahjong—gambling blocks. It is like a house made out of gambling blocks.

xi) But the Africans are laughing nicely

Africans are not naïve and should not be patronized with concerns that they are being taken for a ride. Like Hugo Chavez in Venezuela, they are rejoicing at last in having options and having suitors. For the Africans it is not as dangerous as trying to play the US off against the Soviets in the old days. But the Chinese provide not only an alternative to the West but also leverage to use in continued dealings with the West. Being courted might be the prelude to being taken seriously and, in a long string of African capitals, this is the true sunrise that the Chinese bring.

18

AFRICA WITHOUT EUROPEANS

Chris Alden

To talk about the relationship between Asia, a land of venerated civilizations, and Africa, the continent that gave birth to mankind itself,
is to embark on a terrain fraught with unsubstantiated superlatives
and systemic misrepresentation, which challenges some of our most
cherished perceptions of Africa's international relations. First, we
have to admit that a focus on 'Asian relations with Africa' that omits
the Indian subcontinent necessarily understates the most significant
and sustained interaction between Asia and Africa, which transcends
all the periods of contact. Since the migration of merchants, settlers and slave traders from the Indian land mass began in earnest
in the 10th century, the steady growth and exchange of relations has
served to bind the two regions together. In all the serious indicators
of cultural penetration—whether language, religion or cuisine—the
impact of Indian civilization can be read in the daily lives of ordinary
Africans. The cultures of the Far East have had no equivalent imprint upon African society, nor Africa upon them. Secondly, in order
to understand the ties between Africa and Asia, and in particular
Africa's ties with an emerging China, we need to resurrect and reori-
ent our thinking about the past if we are to come to terms with the
meaning and impact that this relationship may hold for the future.

It is the very nature of 'otherness' in the experience of Chinese contact with Africa ('two unlikely regions' in Philip Snow's memorable phrase)—the fact that it stands outside the pattern of international relations and historical memory—which forms one of the key features of this relationship to this day.[1] This notion of 'difference' allows us, as Mark Duffield has said in his work, to see in these relations on the periphery, or boundaries as he prefers to call it, something deeply significant about the broader shape of international relations in the contemporary period.[2]

Africa-Asia relations in the era of colonialism and the Cold War

Of course it bears mentioning that before the advent of European colonialism in Africa, there is considerable evidence and historical record of Asian contacts and presence on the continent. Alongside the traders and slavers from Arabia, Persia and the Indian subcontinent were peoples from the Indonesian archipelago who came to settle on the island of Madagascar. Ibn Battuta, under the orders of the Moroccan Sultan, commenced a lengthy expedition in 1325 across the Islamic world that took him along the trading routes to East Africa, India, Southeast Asia and China. Zheng He (Cheng Ho), the eunuch admiral sent by the Ming dynasty to explore the outer reaches of the known world, visited these same shores in the early 15th century. Indeed, when Vasco de Gama arrived on the Malabar Coast seventy years later he was 'immediately challenged by two Spanish-speaking Muslims from Tunis' who demanded to know why the Portuguese had come to India. 'We have come in search of Christians and spices,' was his astonished reply.[3] A map from that period depicting the eastern and southern reaches of the continent, presented as a gift to South Africa in the 1990s, underscores this

---

1   Philip Snow, *The Star Raft: China's Encounter with Africa* (Syracuse, NY: Cornell University Press, 1988), p. xvi.

2   See Mark Duffield, *Global Governance and the New Wars: The Merging of Development and Security* (London: Zed Books, 2001).

3   Glenn James, *Renascent Empire? The House of Braganza and the Quest for Stability in Portuguese Monsoon Asia, ca. 1640-1683* (Amsterdam University Press, 2000), p. 59.

clear message—that unlike the Europeans, the Chinese respected the Africans, traded with them and made no effort to proselytize, colonize or enslave the population.

The era of European colonialism began a process by which Asian-African relations were primarily mediated and understood through Western institutions and experiences. In this way, much like their Chinese counterparts when faced by the dominance of 'alien' influences such as the Mongols and the Manchus, the actors came to be 'indigenized' by nationalist historians. For instance, the administrative headquarters of the Portuguese and Dutch colonial empires—which had territorial enclaves in Southern and Eastern Africa—were in Goa and Batavia respectively. The Portuguese presence in East Africa, owing to time and distance from the metropole, was mostly sustained by economic and military ties to the Viceroy in Goa from 1530 to 1752.[4] Goan society itself was, according to historians, dominated by a Hindu Brahmin caste, while incoming Portuguese made common cause in pursuit of profits with Indian or Indonesian merchants, who flew the flag of the *Estado da India*.[5] Jan van Riebeeck, founder of the 'refreshment station' on the Cape of Good Hope in 1652 that marked the start of European settlement, had been transferred from his posting at the Dutch East India Company's office in Nagasaki, where he had held office for seven years, to the African wilderness.[6] Like Portuguese East Africa, the economic logic borne of distance meant that the Cape station was run by Batavia from its inception to 1732. Until the 19th century, thousands of slaves from the Dutch territories in Malaysia, Indonesia and the Indian Ocean region were brought to the Cape as craftsman and house servants, making up a large proportion of the colony's population.[7] A Sufi

---

4   Malyn Newitt, *A History of Mozambique* (Bloomington: Indiana University Press, 1995), pp. 106-25.

5   James, *Renascent Empire*, p. 142; Newitt, *A History of Mozambique*, p. 108.

6   Masako Osada, *Sanctions and Honorary Whites: Diplomatic Policies and Economic Realities in Relations between Japan and South Africa* (Westport: CT: Green, 2002), pp. 27-8.

7   Robert C.-H. Shall, 'Islam in Southern Africa, 1672-1998', in Nehemia Levtzion and Randall Pouwels (eds), *The History of Islam in Africa* (Oxford: James Currey, 2000), p. 330.

saint and political leader, Sheik Yussuf, was exiled to the Cape in 1693 from Sulawesi and his burial mausoleum (or *kamarat*), along with that of his followers, remains an international site of pilgrimage.[8] Reflecting this predominance, Afrikaans emerged as a language of slaves, *'kombuis taal'* ('kitchen Dutch'), and it was no accident that the first document written in Afrikaans was the Koran.

The high noon of European colonialism, coinciding with the end of slavery in British and French territories, brought with it a new influx of Indian labourers to Southern and Eastern Africa. It was the struggle for political rights in the Union of South Africa, played out as a bureaucratic tussle between Britain's India Office and Colonial Office, which brought a Gujarati lawyer, Mohandas Gandhi, and his peculiar campaign of civil disobedience to prominence.[9] Few realized at the time that Gandhi's twenty-one years in Africa honing his campaigning technique would eventually be used to topple the British Raj and ultimately inspire nationalists in Asia and Africa. As the 19th century came to a close, a sprinkling of Chinese labourers and traders were brought to South Africa, Madagascar and French West Africa, paving the way for future generations after colonialism's demise.

Africa's age of nationalism is a product of co-operation between the leaders of the two regions and gave shape to the independent South. India's role in supporting African decolonization in the newly established United Nations was crucial to engineering the institution's shift away from the shibboleths of European empire to the post-colonial era. Of equal, if generally underrated significance was the impact of the Afro-Asian Solidarity Conference at Bandung in 1955, which not only situated the emerging states in relation to the bipolar conflict but gave them a common outlook on key features of the international system such as sovereignty, intervention and the pursuit of multilateralism. These exercised, and continue to exercise, considerable influence over the shape of the modern African state system and the conduct of foreign policy.

---

8 Shall, 'Islam in Southern Africa, 1672-1998', p. 328.

9 See Richard Huttenback, *Gandhi in South Africa* (Ithaca, NY: Cornell University Press, 1971); G.B. Pyrah, *Imperial Policy and South Africa, 1902-1910* (Westport, CT: Greenwood, 1976).

However, the advent of independence in Africa, far from loosening the European hold over our understanding of Africa-Asia relations, in fact merely shifted its focus to the ideological prism of Cold War. And though consciousness of a shared set of concerns and experiences did emerge through Bandung and was sustained (in an admittedly fractious way) through initiatives like the Non-Aligned Movement, too often this sense of solidarity was lost in the course of Cold War rhetoric and posturing by African and Asian leaders. So while the ideational dimensions of decolonization had taken hold, the contours of interest-based relations between Africa had only begun to take shape among one of the three leading Asian states, Japan. Japanese foreign policy towards the African continent was essentially forged during this period and represents an attempt to shake off the narrow strictures of Cold War politics placed upon Tokyo. Resource diplomacy provided the first substantive, interest-based rationale for deeper engagement with Africa, and in Tokyo's increasingly complex approach to the continent, which expanded to include development and humanitarian assistance as well as trade policy, we begin to see the outline of the first truly Asia-Africa relationship unencumbered by external forces. Throughout this period, however, India's Africa policy remained subject to its autarkic economic practices, which limited the country's capacity for trade and investment, as well as being complicated by its relationship with the hundreds of thousands of immigrants from its shores. These 'people of Indian origin', who were designated 'ambassadors of India' by Indira Gandhi, occupied a particularly vulnerable status in the political and economic life of some African societies that erupted into controversy and, in the case of Uganda, their wholesale expulsion. As for China, locked into a revolutionary phase that disavowed capitalism, it pursued an ideological foreign policy towards Africa that owed as much to the Sino-Soviet dispute as to its ongoing diplomatic contest with Taiwan.

A Chinese scramble for Africa?

The end of the Cold War and, since the mid-1990s, the emergence of China (and more recently India) as a significant economic and political force in Africa has instigated a transformation in the continent's traditional international relations orientation. While the ideological period did see some instances of genuine African embrace of the Soviet Union, manifested in Mozambique, Angola and Ethiopia in particular, the vast majority of African states retained preponderant economic and political ties with the West. One result of the growing Chinese engagement in the continent is the emergence of debate in Africa, echoed if not fuelled in Western circles, about whether China is a new imperialist power on the continent. Those who suggest that it is focus on three dimensions of the relationship, one primarily economic in nature, a second political and a third related to (depending on one's view) either misperceptions and xenophobia or deeper social challenges posed by China's growing presence in Africa.

In South Africa, Nigeria, Botswana, Mozambique and other states, African voices from primarily local business and trade unions are raising the alarm about the dire impact that Chinese imports and businesses are having in their areas of concern. Indeed, within the most important diplomatic and trade relationship, China and South Africa, this concern has caused rethinking about embarking on Free Trade Agreements with China. Reflecting this new wariness, Adebayo Adedeji, the former head of the Economic Commission for Africa, has noted that the trade links with Asian economies, where Africa supplies primary commodities and Asia supplies manufactured goods, merely replicate the structural inequities found with traditional Western trading partners. He says:

The traditional scenario that obtained in our trade with the developed world, whereby our country supplies the former with commodities and imports from there manufactured products including capital goods, is being reproduced, deliberately or not, in our intra-third world trade. I feel such a situation is completely unacceptable to us.[10]

A second array of concerns surrounds the 'no political strings' approach which has accompanied—or indeed been instrumental in—China's breaking into African markets. The norms and values articulated as part of the NEPAD agenda and incorporated in the

---

10 Cited in Jagdish Hiremath, 'Indian Foreign Policy in Africa: Current Status and the Future', in N. Vohra and K Mathews (eds), *Africa, India and South-South Co-operation* (New Delhi: Har-Anand, 1997).

African Union's founding constitution, which support accountability, human rights and democratic practice, are crucially dependent on Africans—in partnership with Western states, NGOs and co-operating MNCs—for implementation through a range of incentives. The 'Beijing Consensus' challenges this formula and may embolden states, even those not recognized as pariahs, to opt out of the complexities that these norms and values introduce to their economic and political programmes.

The last concern, murmured more than directly articulated, is that the growing physical presence of Chinese in Africa is merely a prelude to widespread immigration. Essentially this is a contemporary version of the 'yellow peril' phobia, and is based on a fear that Chinese numbers, industriousness and ingenuity will swamp Africa. The Sudanese government, for example, despite its close ties to Beijing, has expressed concern about the failure of thousands of Chinese labourers to renew their work permits, and has jointly set up with the Chinese embassy a bureau devoted to handling this problem. The spread of Chinese retail trading posts across many parts of Africa, especially notable in rural towns where there had not been any retail outlets for a generation and certainly no Chinese presence, is another area of marked concern.

While each of these concerns has compelling aspects, the suggestion that what is happening is a form of emergent Chinese imperialism towards Africa is wrong on a number of counts. Specifically, such an approach ignores or misconstrues China's approach to the continent in three important ways, relating to ideology, territorial sovereignty and mercantilist trade relations.

Ideology. In contrast to European imperialism, there is no overriding 'civilizing mission' driving China's approach to Africa. One could accuse Beijing of paternalism through the mutual benefit/self-interest framework of relations but there, unlike the revolutionary period in the 1960s, no effort has been made (or intended) to 'convert the Africans' to any ideology or rehabilitate their way of life. What one sees in relations between China and Africa is more reminiscent of the 'tributary state system' which, through the use of 'soft power', caused kingdoms to emulate Chinese civilization. But no effort has been expended to force themselves on Africa and, indeed, the Chinese government has demonstrated that it can quite happily work with any political and social environment it finds itself in. Moreover, the absence of ideology has served to facilitate the entry of Chinese businesses into the fabric of prevailing economic structures formed and shaped by the West, in a way that, unlike militant Islam in other parts of the continent, does not necessitate a direct challenge to the established order of things.

Territorial sovereignty. In another difference from the classic imperialist period, there is no move by China to claim territories and peoples beyond its historical arena of action. The defence of ethnic Chinese, recalling one of the classic impulses for imperialist intervention, was indeed a matter for Chinese foreign policy during the anti-Chinese riots in Indonesia and perhaps, at the level of just a murmuring, with the recent killing of nine Chinese oil workers in Ethiopia in 2007. But it has yet to do more than motivate diplomatic notes and, despite some concerns about crimes against Chinese citizens found in the Chinese press, there is no suggestion that it would ever go further than that. It should be noted however that on questions of sovereignty, the recognition battle with Taiwan and an essentialist notion of citizenship do come into play and do provoke a response on the part of Beijing. Having said that, there is no reason to think that, even in the dire case of military conflict between China and Taiwan, African states with close ties to Taipei would experience anything beyond diplomatic and possibly economic snubs from China.

Mercantilist trade relations. Exclusive control of markets, a hallmark of classic late imperialism (and one which proved to be a constant source of problems for the metropole in each empire), plays no part in Chinese trade policy.[11] China's competitive advantage in labour costs is, of course, a key feature of its ability to undercut manufacturing in other markets, and its adherence to the liberal trading regime embodied in the WTO is a sure sign of its acceptance of this

---

11 See D.K. Fieldhouse, *Economics and Empire, 1880-1914* (London: Macmillan, 1984).

key global economic framework. The desire to promote Free Trade Agreements, binding the Chinese economy more closely to South Africa through privileged trade arrangements, is about as near as it comes to control of markets (and would be a gross exaggeration of the meaning of an FTA); but, of course, such an agreement would still conform to WTO principles.

At the same time, there are elements of China's conduct which do echo Africa's experience with Western imperialism. If one looks back at the West's actions in Africa, and indeed its actions towards China and Japan, up to the mid-19th century, these did not conform to the period of late imperialism which we more commonly associate with imperialism generally. In China, for example, between the late 16th century and 1839, Western countries and companies were involved in carving out spheres of influence with small territorial enclaves to facilitate trade, some modest recognition of special status and rights of access being negotiated with Beijing, sometimes under duress, often not. Missionaries were seen by all parties in this period, Western merchants and Asian governments alike, as a dangerous nuisance. With African international politics it was much the same until the 19th century events culminating in 1884 Berlin Conference. Western trade enclaves, close ties with African counterparts, respect for indigenous political system and formal diplomatic relations grew alongside slavery, resource exploitation and the uprooting of indigenous peoples. The territorial impulse came later, in the wake of changing dynamics within Europe itself that ushered in new powers on the world stage and hence a virulent form of competitive nationalism that transformed the search for resources and new markets into a dangerous extension of European political rivalries.

Thus, if we are looking to understand the possibility of Chinese imperialism, perhaps it is this trajectory and transformation away from seeking and maintaining spheres of influence based essentially on trade to the need to capture markets from rivals by gaining territorial control that is the most important signifier in future relations. Pessimists would point to the Chinese government's post-FOCAC 2006 commitment to establish special economic enclaves in five African countries, where Chinese businesses are to enjoy privileged treatment as well as preferential access to Chinese capital and African markets. Furthermore, an examination of the European colonial period offers another comparative dimension that is suggestive of China's contemporary involvement in Africa. The use of 35,000 Indian labourers by British firms to build the transport infrastructure of its colonies in East Africa, famously in the case of the railway from coastal Kenya to the Ugandan interior in the 1890s, was the start of longstanding Indian settlement in the region. This historical pattern of migration, with former contract labourers staying on to take up commercial ventures, open retail shops and encourage further immigration, seems to be replicated in the growing Chinese presence in Africa today.

However, as mentioned above, in the absence of an ideological impulse coming out of China and without 'salvation merchants', there can be no pressure group at home to inspire the need for use of power in the name of higher good—one of the overriding arguments for territorial control, developed from David Livingstone's memorable rallying cry of 'commerce, civilization and Christianity'.

Rising Sun, Wheel of Dharma and Red Dragon: an Africa without Europeans

More than anything, it is the rise of China that has introduced new dimensions into relations between the two regions and is itself indicative of a fundamental change in the pattern of international relations. Linking the foreign policies of all of the major Asian powers—Japan, India and China—is an explicit commitment to multilateralism as well as an insatiable drive for resources to fuel the industrialization that has sustained their rapid economic growth. The quiet diplomacy of Japan can be contrasted with the exuberance with which China has proclaimed its interests and the flourishing presence of Indian trade and settlement on the continent. For all three, Africa represents a place where their global ambitions can be given expression at the same time as their economic needs are being fulfilled.

Africans, as agents of their own destiny to an extent not seen before, are increasingly deciding the shape that relations with Asian states will take rather than allowing these to be experienced and understood through Western eyes. Are they set to abandon the transformative projects like NEPAD, founded as they are on Western norms and values, in pursuit of Chinese ties? Relations with China certainly provide an attractive alternative to African governments weary of Western interference and conditionalities. The wholesale adoption of such a position would spell an end to the universalistic ambitions contained within the post-Cold War project of challenging the prerogatives of sovereignty through recourse to humanitarianism.

And finally, it can be argued that the most significant outcome of the African-Asian relationship is the beginning of an 'Africa without Europe' as a cardinal point of reference for the continent's international relations. With the age of imperialism well and truly gone, a new set of relations can take hold and a 'brave new world' is emerging in which Europe and the United States are merely bystanders. This impotence is felt perhaps most acutely by Western NGOs, in some ways the contemporary version of imperialism's salvation merchants, for whom the loss of influence over African lives is deeply troubling.

Will the newly acquired economic prowess of Asia and its accompanying political dimensions result in a kind of proxy conflict in Africa, echoing the European conflicts of the 19th and 20th centuries? There are signs that this could be the case, for example the stiff competition between Japanese, Chinese and Indian companies for commercial rights to oil in Sudan and Angola. Does this indeed mean that Western interests, whether commercial or normative, are in the decline in Africa? Possibly, but the selective engagement of the United States and the residual presence of European interests will remain a feature of external relations for African states. Nevertheless, the much vaunted 'Pacific Century' is at last upon us and it is in Africa, the once-forgotten continent, that the dynamics of Asia's rise may be seen most clearly.

19

FITTING CHINA IN

Christopher Clapham

China's irruption onto the African scene has been the most dramatic and important factor in the external relations of the continent—perhaps in the development of Africa as a whole—since the end of the Cold War. The speed and scale of the increase, especially in trade relations between African states and the PRC, is by any standards astonishing. Economic relationships that appeared to be set in stone, and notably those between Africa and the former colonizing states now grouped in the European Union, are being transformed before our eyes. Unlike the Soviet Union's engagement with Africa during the Cold War, moreover, China's involvement shows every sign of being a lasting one, and is indeed likely to be extended and entrenched in the years ahead. Whereas the USSR attempted to build relationships with Africa as one element in a strategic contest that it was ultimately unable to sustain, China is doing so as an integral part of the expansion of its own economy, and of its insertion as a major player into the global economic order.

In sounding a note of caution as to the likely impact of China's role in Africa, I therefore certainly do not wish to downplay either its scale or its likely permanence. I assume, rather, that it will both broaden and deepen, displacing in the process many of the ties that have been established especially with Western states since the colonial era and before. In fitting China into the broader picture of Africa's development and its relations with the wider world, however, I hope that it will be helpful to indicate some of the constraints which have historically affected Africa's external engagement, continue to do so in the present, and are likely to prove extremely resistant to change. Seen in this light, China's appearance, however dramatic, fits into patterns that have been long established, and that Africans have historically absorbed and adapted. There is, I believe, every prospect that China will conform to those patterns, rather than transforming them.

The intractability of African governmentalities

For a start, Africa's states and societies have historically proved extremely intractable to grand projects of social and economic transformation—far more so, indeed, than have Asian states and societies such as the PRC itself. This intractability, and the problems of governance associated with it, ultimately derive, as Jeffrey Herbst reminds us, from the enduring features of the continent's demography. With a population sparsely and very unevenly spread over an extremely large land area, it has been difficult to control not only in terms of simple physical communications, daunting though those have been, but still more importantly in terms of the attitudes, assumptions and forms of social organization—governmentalities, to appropriate Foucault's useful term—that Africans have developed over a very long period as an eminently rational response to the situations in which they have found themselves. Established territorial states have historically been extremely difficult to maintain, and institutionalized forms of social organization appropriate (not least in China) to the management of densely settled populations have given way to expedients in which personal pre-eminence, genealogical (or pseudo-genealogical) relationships, and various forms of spiritual authority have instead played major roles. Africa is, in short, an extremely difficult space to organize and manage, and these difficulties, which have deeply affected both the colonial project and the articulation of modern forms of statehood by Africans themselves, will likewise form an enduring backdrop to the Chinese presence—all the more exasperating, in all likelihood, because they run so sharply counter to equally embedded but markedly contrasting Chinese attitudes and trajectories.

Patterns of extraversion

To these essentially indigenous factors must then be added the peculiar, and often intensely damaging, nature of Africa's forcible incorporation into the global economy and structure of government. This has characteristically taken the form of incursions by external forces, guided by a premise of inequality and indeed superiority to the African populations whom they sought to exploit. Even though China's arrival is in no way remotely equivalent to the role of the slave traders or colonialists who characterized previous episodes in Africa's encounter with the wider world, neither can it be fitted, except in the most facile rhetorical terms, into the ideal of equality in which politicians both Chinese and African have recently sought to clothe it. Despite the claim that both China and Africa are part of the 'developing world', this is a deeply unequal relationship. South Africa apart, there is no African economy that can even begin to engage with China in the way that China is engaging with Africa; and the size of South Africa's economy—by far the largest and most developed in the continent—is trivial by comparison with that of the East Asian leviathan. While China has developed with astonishing speed into Africa's third-largest trading partner, and may well, if current trends continue even for a few more years, reach the number one position, Africa accounts for no more than some 3 per cent of China's total overseas trade. Although other indices of comparative strength are more difficult to measure, there is no point at which they can plausibly be reckoned to run in Africa's favour.

Africans, nonetheless, have long-established mechanisms for coping with their accustomed position on the downside of relationships of inequality, and have historically adapted with considerable skill to each new manifestation of them. One such mechanism, identified by Jean-François Bayart as 'extraversion',[1] is the appropriation by African elites of resources provided by external actors in order

1 Jean-François Bayart, *The State in Africa: The Politics of the Belly* (London: Longman, 1993).

to consolidate their own authority. One very important reason why China's involvement in Africa has been so widely welcomed and readily accommodated has been that it fits so neatly into the familiar patterns of rentier statehood and politics with which Africa's rulers have been accustomed to maintain themselves. After a brief period following the end of the Cold War, when the political terms of trade between Africa and the newly hegemonic states of the West turned so sharply to the latter's advantage that African bargaining power was drastically reduced, China has provided a counterweight to the governance agendas promoted by the 'Washington consensus'. When Zhou Enlai, in his 1964 visit, proclaimed Africa to be a continent 'ripe for revolution', he presented China correspondingly as a challenge to Africa's place in the existing global order. In the current era, on the other hand, far from providing any new model for Africa's involvement in the global economy and political system, China's role has been precisely to reinforce the old one.

One corollary of this is that if—as we can confidently assume—China becomes permanently engaged as a major player in Africa, it will need to go through the same learning processes that other outside powers have been through in the past, and is likely to come up with similar responses to similar predicaments. In particular, both Chinese companies and the Chinese state itself will need to grapple with ways to protect their own political and economic investments, within the uncertain and potentially rapidly changing environment that Africa provides.

One element that is likely to be modified in this process of adaptation is the insistence on the ideology of unfettered state 'sovereignty', with which China has made very welcome common cause with its African partners, in striking contrast to the 'conditionalities' insisted on by its Western competitors. This is not to deny that China's commitment to sovereignty has a genuine resonance in that country's own historical (and even very recent) experience: it is far more than a mere tactical response to the need to gain favours in Africa. It is worth remembering, even so, that 'sovereignty' was a doctrine developed by the states of western Europe, in response to their own distinctive predicaments, but came to be eroded by those states, in their relationships not only with Africa but with one another, once it had ceased to serve its purpose. China, certainly, is unlikely to experience the conditions that led to the decay in the idea of sovereignty in Europe, but this is nonetheless a paradoxical doctrine for a very large and powerful state to adopt in its dealings with very small and weak ones, and it is not difficult to envisage the circumstances in which it may fade.

In Africa, support for the doctrine of sovereignty by external patrons has served—as it did for both Western states and the Soviet Union during the Cold War—to promote a particular response to the ongoing problem of maintaining 'political stability'. It translates in practice into an attempt to protect investment within an African state by providing almost unconditional support for that state's existing political order, and indeed in many cases for the individual ruler who currently controls it. For so long as that ruler is able both to remain in power, and to project effective control over the parts of the national territory in which the patron is particularly interested, it generally works very well, subject only to the danger that the client ruler may seek to throw off the yoke of an overbearing patron and look for an alternative one.

Over time, however, the deficiencies of this strategy became increasingly apparent to the patrons who initially adopted it during the Cold War, and are likely to become equally evident to the latest comer on the African scene. One problem is that it locks the patron into support for a client ruler who may become extremely unpopular with his own people, and whose demise then triggers a reversal in external alliances. A much more basic difficulty, however, is the decreasing viability of a formal doctrine of sovereignty in coping with situations in which the state's actual level of control over its own territory and population is progressively eroded. A classic indicator of this is the counter-productive impact of external arms supplies, which have characteristically been one of the most important mechanisms through which an external patron enabled a client government to maintain control. The central problem of 'stability' in Africa has been the weakness not of physical control (the possession by the state of the weapons needed to secure compliance) but rather of social control (the capacity to create the forms of authority needed to secure voluntary obedience). When, as readily happens in

365

fractured African states, control over weapons escapes the grasp of the formal state structures which they were originally intended to support, these weapons rapidly become an extremely dangerous element in the *destabilization* of the very territories that they were supposed to stabilize. Given China's recent emergence as a major source of arms supply to Africa, it cannot be long before the PRC comes to appreciate the threat that such arms present to the vastly more important priority of maintaining stable access to mineral supplies and other resources. The threat is all the greater in that—given the vast size of the Africa continent, and the distance of many sources of production (as in the Democratic Republic of Congo) from ports of transhipment to China—stability of supply entails not just point defence of specific installations, but the control of long and vulnerable lines of communication.

The sovereignty doctrine fails, in short, when it translates into support for a state structure that is itself incapable of ensuring control over the resources needed by its external backer. In the short (and maybe medium) term, actors such as mining companies, which need to maintain the conditions under which they can extract minerals, are obliged to do deals with local actors ('traditional' authorities, disruptive local protesters, even criminal gangs), simply because these actors, and not the state, effectively manage the local political terrain. Western oil companies operating in the Niger Delta provide a case in point. Chinese oil companies coming to terms with the same predicament are unlikely to be any different. Were they to seek instead to increase the coercive capacity of the state, in the belief that this could then 'secure' their own installations and lines of communication, they would very rapidly discover their mistake.

In the longer term, no external power with long-term economic interests in Africa, especially in vulnerable enterprises such as mineral extraction, can escape the issue of 'governance', because this is the essential precondition for maintaining stable economic relationships. If this issue cannot be handled, as European powers first sought to do, by the direct imposition of external colonialism, then it has to be handled instead through other mechanisms, such as the establishment of an effective legal order, and forms of accountability that link state power to the welfare of local populations. Although the 'Beijing consensus' provides a doctrine suited to the needs of an incoming operator on the African scene, seeking to build a continental presence through linkages with particular regimes that have specific reasons for welcoming its arrival, established economic actors such as China is likely to become will have every reason to turn to its 'Washington' equivalent.

An inherently limited engagement

China's capacity to develop long-term relationships in Africa also faces constraints that derive from the problems of inserting itself into a set of structures that are already deeply established and extend well beyond the limited range of Chinese interests and involvement. Essentially, what China and other Asian states (including India and other east and Southeast Asian states such as South Korea and Malaysia) are seeking to do is to insert themselves into an existing bilateral relationship between Africa and the West, converting it into a triangular one. This does not however involve any change in Africa's role within either system as a supplier of raw materials. China's dramatic arrival in Africa has not led to any change in the composition of African exports; it has led only to the diversion of those exports away from Western economies, and towards eastern Asia.[2] Indeed, the extraordinary efficiency and low cost of Chinese industrial production is already deeply undermining African attempts to break out of the historic dependence on primary production, a challenge that especially affects the high-cost, unionized and often undercapitalized industries of its principal African competitor, South Africa.

In striking contrast to the role that the PRC at least aspired to play during the Maoist era, there is absolutely no 'project of transformation' for Africa involved in China's extremely successful project of transforming its own economy, by inserting it into a particular niche in the global division of labour. The rhetoric of solidarity apart, Africa today is in no way what China was in 1949, nor is there any remotely plausible agenda for Africa in the future to become what China in now. Such feelings of solidarity as China is currently able

---

2   As Andrea Goldstein and Nicolas Pinaud in this volume clearly demonstrate.

to draw on in Africa—and these appear to be heavily oriented towards governing elites for whom China's presence provides tangible benefits—are unlikely to be able to survive for long in the face of the structural divergence in the interests of the two parties.

At this point, the narrowness of China's engagement in Africa is likely to prove damaging. At one level, certainly, the fact that China seeks to impose no ideological agenda of its own on Africa—in contrast to ideological concomitants of Western capitalism—means that it poses less of a 'threat' than its often overbearing Western counterparts. But 'ideology', no matter how great the arrogance with which external powers seek to promote it, is not merely an alien imposition on unwilling Africans. It also strikes a local resonance, and serves to build moral linkages that extend beyond mere economic interests. For Africans who have been subjected to sometimes appallingly brutal domestic regimes, the demand for 'human rights' strikes a deep and legitimate chord. Equally, no matter how great the difficulties of instituting multi-party democracies in many parts of Africa, there is a significant part of the continent in which considerably more accountable regimes have been installed since the end of the Cold War, and despite the enduring problems of converting new political forms into economic welfare, these still represent a very substantial improvement for local populations on military dictatorship or single-party rule. In cutting itself off from changes in African governance over the past two decades, China runs the risk of presenting itself merely as an interloper bent on short-term economic gain.

Nor is there any spiritual dimension to the Chinese presence, even in the form once presented by Maoist Marxism. It must strike any observer of the African scene that this is a deeply, indeed intensely spiritual continent, in which the rival agendas of Christianity and Islam, along with extensive indigenous systems of belief, are best understood not merely as some new kind of religious Cold War, but as an extremely important part of ongoing attempts to make sense of human life under rapidly changing and often deeply troubling circumstances. China does not engage Africa in the way that both radical Islam and numerous and competing forms of Christianity create linkages with the Arab and Western worlds.

No matter how exploitative the African experience of Western colonialism may have been, it created linkages that have proved enduring because—despite Western indifference or even hostility—they have come to be valued by Africans themselves. Given the chance (which European immigration policies increasingly deny them), Africans readily gravitate to those states which once colonized them: Congolese to Belgium, Senegalese to France, Eritreans to Italy, Ghanaians and Nigerians to Britain. The United States and indeed the Scandinavian countries provide a ready magnet for Africans of all descriptions. Regardless of the prospects of an 'Africa without Europeans', a Europe (let alone an America, with its still deeper and more wounding relationship with Africa created by slavery rather than colonialism) without Africans is now simply inconceivable. China remains entirely outside this pattern of relationships, and—given the deep ambivalences and continuing problems that it embodies—would certainly wish to remain so. But their absence nonetheless casts it as only a partial participant in Africa's engagement with the wider world.

None of this analysis, to repeat, is intended to downplay the striking changes that China's recent engagement with Africa have brought especially to the continent's economies, or to cast doubt on the likelihood that the new relationships between Africa and the world's most dynamic industrializing power will continue and even deepen. It does however very strongly indicate that China is likely to adapt to and modify the African experience, but is highly unlikely to change it fundamentally.

CONCLUSION
'ALL OVER AFRICA'

Daniel Large

'China', it appears, is now 'all over Africa'.[1] It might alternatively be said that this has recently become more apparent to the wider, now-watching world. It is not hard to see why there has been a scramble to engage the latest phase of Chinese engagement in Africa.[2] As the chapters in this volume show, the subject is compelling not only in the African context, where the growing Chinese footprint appears set on making a lasting impact, but also in terms of Africa as a regional dimension of China's rise in world affairs.

The expanding Chinese presence and role in the continent is at the forefront of a broader Asian involvement that, as Alden considers here, has implications for Africa's politics and established relations with external powers. Focus on China in Africa has tended to upstage the involvement of India, Japan and other actors, together with the

---

1 'We [Chinese] are all over Africa now.' Chinese government official quoted in 'China in Africa: just business', *New York Times*, 10 August 2004. Bob Geldof remarked: 'They [Americans] know the Chinese are all over Africa, they are there building the roads, the conference centres and the stadia.' Patrick Wintour, 'We've got the script, now let's make the film', *The Guardian*, 12 March 2005.

2 In light of the widespread, sustained interest catalysed by FOCAC 3, it remains notable that as recently as the 'Year of Africa' in 2005 featuring the G8 Gleneagles Summit, China was not considered seriously as a force in Africa amidst the huge mobilization of different groups under the slogan 'make poverty history'. Tony Blair's Commission for Africa may have included a senior Chinese Africa specialist, but it's report essentially overlooked China and India.

continuing engagement of the more 'traditional' external powers under more competitive political and economic circumstances.[3] In light of this, one question that this book raises is how Africa's growing relations with China are framed. It also demonstrates the importance of disaggregating two general terms that refer to historically rich, diverse and complex entities. Given that growing Chinese relations with Africa are constitutive of and intertwined in globalizing forces, situating China-Africa relations within a global framework offers a more dynamic, multi-layered perspective. It additionally provides one route toward transcending the tendency to represent 'China' and 'Africa' as neatly demarcated spheres, the recourse to overly state-centric analysis or artificial, binary assessments of positive or negative impact.

An emerging research area

Research on African and Chinese politics and foreign relations has in the main proceeded without serious overlap and cross-fertilization until relatively recently. Africa has not featured as a mainstream subject in research on Chinese foreign relations, instead tending to be subsumed as part of China's relations with the Third World. In a similar way, and given that China's post-colonial engagement in Africa was in practice less involved than its official rhetoric suggested, China has hitherto not been deemed sufficiently important in the study of African politics and foreign relations to merit dedicated, sustained research. There has also been little in the way of serious or sustained exchanges between research communities in Africa, China or beyond. As Li Anshan has noted, 'African studies in China have been more or less a mystery to Africanists in other parts of the world.'[4]

This volume presents a contribution to an emerging area of research. It provides a snapshot of a dynamic moment in China-Africa relations. The subject has enjoyed unusual prominence since being

---

3   It wasn't too long ago that North and South Korea were also 'all over Africa'; Aidan Foster-Carter, 'Seoul cleans up in Africa', *Asia Times* 6 September 2006.

4   Li Anshan, 'African Studies in China in the Twentieth Century: A Historiographical Survey', *African Studies Review*, **48**, 1 (2005), p. 59.

catalysed by FOCAC 3, with regular media headlines concerning fresh, ground-breaking Chinese deals in different parts of Africa. In many instances, these have yet to be properly followed up on, evoking episodes in China's post-colonial relations with Africa when headline Chinese statements tended to be accepted at face value.[5] However, despite its current salience, the subject remains under-researched. While there are examples to the contrary featured here, indepth research on the empirical detail of China-Africa relations has thus far been comparatively limited. The salience of energy politics and governance concerns is understandable but has rendered other notable aspects in China's increasingly multifaceted role throughout the continent neglected or marginalized (including informal trade flows, the creation of new trading elites amidst thickening transnational economic linkages, the transmission of ideas, questions of gender, race and power, or African roles and presence in China). Linked to this is the relative paucity of Chinese and African perspectives, with the exception of South Africa where the subject has been experienced and considered for some time. It is to be hoped that beyond the first waves of interest, research will develop to become more empirically grounded and theoretically informed.

Between Chinese 'exceptionalism' and Western convergence in Africa

The consolidation of China's newly attained position in Africa presents challenges that are at once the ordinary stuff of preserving these interests but also, and more profoundly, negotiating and reassessing its position within the international system. The Chinese government's distinctive mode of conducting its relations with the continent, which might be broadly labeled Chinese 'exceptionalism', is founded in an historically-informed framework and reinforced by official contemporary rhetoric emphasising equality, mutual benefit,

---

5   Hutchison, for example, noted that 'far from having revolution pure and simple as its driving force, China's African policy was pragmatic, some-what cautious and depended for success, like all other nations' foreign policies, on good timing and on good luck.' Alan Hutchison, *China's Africa Revolution* (London: Hutchinson, 1975), p. 106. As a welcome corrective, see *Africa-Asia Confidential* for detailed news and analysis.

sovereignty and non-interference. Chinese diplomacy has operated on a different basis from the more overtly hierarchical power relations of established external powers. It has been mostly successful to date, even to the point where external reactions have problematically suggested that China is somehow immune to the prevailing forces of political and economic gravity in Africa.

This volume illustrates the striking diversity of emerging Chinese activities and interests ranging from Southern Africa to former Lusophone Africa, east Africa or the Horn, and across strategically important cases like South Africa, Angola or Sudan to less prominent but nonetheless revealing cases such as Tanzania, Namibia or Cape Verde. Investment protection amidst burgeoning economic activities has become more important to the Chinese government and companies. In places the expansion and consolidation of Chinese interests appears to entail a logic of deepening political involvement. China's approach has been more than sufficient to confer legitimacy and enable flourishing relations with many African states. However, this has been subject to increasing strain by the growing complexity of ties. One consequence of China's sheer visibility and the fanfare accompanying its ascendancy in Africa is that Beijing faces the challenge of managing the high expectations it has generated and continuing to deliver in Africa, while continuing to achieve development in China. In responding to grievances concerning business practices, environmental impact, increased security threats and demands for protection by Chinese nationals in Africa, the central Chinese government is attempting to direct a diverse array of Chinese actors, over which its ability to exercise control appears to be not as great as widely assumed.[6]

Current relations amount to an emergent phase marked by an evolving set of issues. Greater involvement has already brought unanticipated challenges as different Chinese interests have been exposed to the vagaries of politics in different parts of Africa. Chinese actors are becoming more established in Africa through experience and the progressive deepening of links. This process whereby a range of Chi-

---

6   Bates Gill and James Reilly, 'The Tenuous Hold of China Inc. in Africa', *The Washington Quarterly*, 30, 3 (2007), pp. 37-52.

nese interests become a more normal part of Africa's socio-economic and political life is one likely to erode the popular reputation for exceptionalism China has enjoyed from below. Nonetheless, with China's newly prominent role in Africa rejuvenating debate about development against a backdrop of future geopolitical uncertainty, the importance of maximizing African benefits beyond elites remains a pertinent concern. At the same time as bringing positive dimensions and holding undoubted potential, China's re-engagement also renews enduring questions of power, the constraints on development and Africa's unfavourable, structurally subordinated position in the world economy.

The claim that China's ties with Africa are distinct and substantively different from those of the West is thus more significant than it first appears because it connects with the core of China's identity and nature of its relations with the continent. China today presents mixed images to Africa: it remains a developing country that has also achieved impressive development, and one whose very success is transforming its economy through reform and opening has entailed a process whereby its relations with the rest of the world trajectories China's uncertain status. Today many African states consider linking their economic and political direction to a Chinese future precisely because of its demonstrable accomplishments and the presumed economic path that it is proceeding along. However, the Chinese government's insistence on its exceptional condition – that it will remain a benevolent partner for Africa in a 'win-win' strategic partnership despite the unavoidable hard facts about the nature of its deepening commodity-based trading relationship – places a significant burden on China's foreign policy to ensure that it is conducted in a manner that retains this moral high ground against the backdrop of its evolving commercial and other attendant interests on the continent. Will Beijing be drawn to replicate Western practices, perhaps under the impact of disciplinary constraints as Clapham seems to suggest, or will it endeavour to retain its 'friendship between most unequal equals'[7]

---

7   As Nyerere once described China-Tanzania relations. Quoted in George T. Yu, *China and Tanzania: A Study in Cooperative Interaction* (Berkeley: Center for Chinese Studies, University of California, 1970), p. 97.

with African states irrespective of the cost? In this, how far will Western efforts aimed at socializing China as a 'responsible' power in Africa proceed and in what ways will China influence currently prevailing standards? More than any other process, the incremental revision or even the abandonment of exceptionalism will signal the desire to converge with other foreign actors in Africa and, concurrently, the end of the last vestige of Mao's ideological project.